Making Histories

Also by CCCS and published by Hutchinson

Resistance through Rituals
On Ideology
Women Take Issue
Working Class Culture
Culture, Média, Language
Unpopular Education

Making Histories

Studies in history-writing
and politics

Centre for Contemporary Cultural Studies

Edited by   Richard Johnson
            Gregor McLennan
            Bill Schwarz
            David Sutton

Hutchinson

London Melbourne Sydney Auckland Johannesburg
in association with
the Centre for Contemporary Cultural Studies
University of Birmingham

Hutchinson & Co. (Publishers) Ltd

An imprint of the Hutchinson Publishing Group

17–21 Conway Street, London W1P 6JD

Hutchinson Group (Australia) Pty Ltd
30–32 Cremorne Street, Richmond South, Victoria 3121
PO Box 151, Broadway, New South Wales 2007

Hutchinson Group (NZ) Ltd
32–34 View Road, PO Box 40–086, Glenfield, Auckland 10

Hutchinson Group (SA) (Pty) Ltd
PO Box 337, Bergvlei 2012, South Africa

First published 1982

© Centre for Contemporary Cultural Studies,
   University of Birmingham 1982

Set in Press Roman

Printed in Great Britain by The Anchor Press Ltd
and bound by Wm Brendon & Son Ltd
both of Tiptree, Essex

British Library Cataloguing in Publication Data

Making histories.
   1. Historiography
   I. University of Birmingham. *Centre for
   Contemporary Cultural Studies*
   907'.2   D13

ISBN 0 09 145210 4   cased
     0 09 145211 2   paper

Contents

Acknowledgements

The authors and publisher are grateful to the following for their kind permission to reproduce illustrations used in this book:

Shell UK Ltd: pp. 278, 279, 283, 286; Mary Evans Picture Library: p. 302; National Portrait Gallery: p. 302.

Preface

+ elton - Tory

History and politics are fundamentally connected. Historians themselves have
frequently made the links between the two explicit. The great liberal historians of
the nineteenth century made no secret of the direct political intentions of their
work. Similarly, the predominantly conservative strain of much professional history
in this century has a long political pedigree. Indeed, a key moment in the formation
of a professionalized history - the foundation of the Historical Association in
1906 - was motivated by the desire to produce a specific version of the national
past as part of the struggle for national and imperial survival. Later, the main form
of political history which emerged in the 1920s and 1930s was suffused with a
rhetoric of 'Englishness'. At worst, this involved an almost mystical reverence for
the English people, for 'their' political system and constitutional heritage, sharply
distinguishing them from those of other nations who could only manage their
affairs by periodically annihilating their historic traditions. Some of these assumptions still persist, especially (until very recently perhaps) in school histories. However, the onset of the Cold War and the unsuccessful bid by its theoreticians to
defend free scholarship from 'ideologies' shifted the whole complexion of the
study of history. Historical conservatism, under its often unacknowledged political
impulses, now claimed a monopoly on scientific and 'objective' inquiry, criticizing
other historians as selective or biased. This venture in turn, however, has been
unable to sustain itself as ideology *and* adequately engage in critical, lively historical
argument. As a result, we appear to be in a period, once more, when the political
credentials of historical practice are more openly recognized. This we take to be the
starting-point for our book.

Postmodernity

    The analysis of the conservative traditions of historical scholarship deserves a
volume to itself. As we imply later, the connections which have been built up
between conservative conceptions of the national past and contemporary popular
cultures are of great political importance and should not be ignored. In this book,
however, we attempt something different. We investigate the conditions in which
the history–politics relation has been developed in histories critical of the dominant traditions. For example, explicit links between politics and history have been
made in the liberal and radical histories of the Hammonds and R. H. Tawney; in the
work of the Communist Party Historians' Group in the 1940s and 1950s; and in
feminist history-writing today. Many of the early practitioners would not have
identified themselves primarily as historians, and certainly not as professionals.

Rather they arrived at a study of history as intellectuals involved in political conflicts. The writing of history *became* an important dimension of their political practice. Sometimes the politics of the histories needs little explanation. For instance in E. P. Thompson's *The Making of the English Working Class* or in Sheila Rowbotham's *Hidden from History* the predominant purpose is clear enough – to recover past struggles in order to create a politics for the present. On other occasions the links between politics and histories need fuller explanation and reconstruction, especially when we are more distanced from the political moment itself. In such cases it is necessary to be aware not only of the conjuncture of political events, but also of the dominant historical traditions which are challenged. For example it is by no means obvious to readers today that the new form of social history pioneered by the Hammonds and exemplifed in *The Town Labourer* crystallized in the struggles for social reconstruction at the close of the First World War. 'Making histories' for the Hammonds was a practice intertwined with their politics. It was a complex moment of distancing themselves from immediate political struggles, of engaging with competing positions in the broader ideological field, and of developing a theoretical intervention in order to justify and clarify their politics. We take the case of the Hammonds as posing in a particularly clear way the complexities and ambiguities of the relation between politics and history-writing.

In this context the cumbersome term 'historiography' is useful in order to refer to the study of history as an intellectual practice, distinct from the 'movement of history' itself. Making this distinction prompts a number of questions, some of them decidedly historical. How is this practice of historiography constituted? What theoretical or philosophical protocols are necessary for its development? How does the relation between historiography and theory get *produced* in specific conditions (in WEA classes, in political parties, in universities, in community projects)? What are the political consequences of adopting one approach rather than another? These questions have created a great deal of heat among socialists in the last few years. Those who have put most emphasis on the theoretical frameworks have been accused of intellectual elitism and theoreticism by others who insist on historical perspective. The latter, for their part, have been the butt of charges of 'historicism' and 'empiricism', that is, of neglecting the role which generalization and conceptual consistency assumes in historical analysis. This argument about the most appropriate way to handle the relations between theory and history has become focused around Thompson's critique of the philosophy of Althusser in *The Poverty of Theory*.

Our own book is written in the belief that the choices exemplified by the opposition between Althusser and Thompson are too stark and unproductive. The relation between theory and history is intrinsically uneven and difficult to finalize. Indeed the very distinction is ultimately hard to sustain. In countless cases historical analysis feeds off, then modifies, theoretical elucidation. We do not believe that the 'moment of theory' of the last decade has been barren for historical research, despite the torsions engendered by its relentless epistemological anxieties.

The idea that theory must be fully applied or interventionist commands the assent of many socialist and feminist researchers and teachers today. This sense of empirical engagement is above all due to the sharp social and political crisis, world-wide, but especially in Britain under the Thatcher regime. A critical and radical historiography has properly been directed by these imperatives. But it is important to be realistic about the political impact of history-writing. Historical research and publication is necessarily slow. Its typical finished products – the book, the essay, the rejoinder – are the results of a painstaking process. Its audience, as it is constituted at the moment, is relatively small. There does exist a danger of *over*-politicizing the intentions and effects of historical study. We say this even though we are convinced that historiography is an important moment in political practice, in that it can deliver a full analysis of *concrete* situations.

But the concreteness of historical work can sometimes be deceptive and contrived. It can rightly be used to counter the abstractness of the sociologist or philosopher. At the same time a faith in the relevance of history can invite the belief that it is closer to real struggles, to the real people – that the study of history spontaneously generates its own democratic politics. We reject the latter supposition on the grounds that there is nothing *inherently* concrete about historiography: it can be good or bad, empirical or abstract. To be effective, historical analysis has to be *made* concrete and we believe, paradoxically, that this requires abstraction and theory. The empirical density and political relevance of the historian's materials can't in themselves guarantee adequate historical interpretation. In this sense there can be a fetishism of the empirical as well as of theory, both of which empty historical analysis of its political purchase.

Furthermore it is sometimes forgotten that historical works which we now take for granted were theoretically pioneering in an earlier period. This may be especially important to keep in mind when we approach studies in which the theoretical premises are embedded within the histories, rather than explicitly stated. However, some of the most influential histories have revealed distinct conceptual absences as well as undoubted strengths. For instance, the Communist Party's *Democracy and the Labour Movement*, Thompson's *Making of the English Working Class*, and the initial products of History Workshop have been of formative importance for socialist history-writing today. Yet however innovatory they have been, these earlier interventions cannot be assumed to provide ready-made models for contemporary practice. New theoretical and political issues have forced us to rethink old problems, sometimes very dramatically.

But to think of historiography in terms of theory alone tends to narrow the scope of the discussion to problems facing (traditionally formed) intellectuals writing histories. Associated with this are all the now-familiar criticisms of the monopolization of 'history' by academics, the divorce from an active political constituency, and the overwhelmingly masculinist identification of the issues. All these points hit home. It *is* the case that as a consequence of the expansion of higher education many of the radical and marxist histories are produced in the image of the dominant historiography. This is especially striking in patterns of consumption, in which the stylish and expensive monograph reaches a very restricted audience. It is also true that many former gains have been eroded, most of all the crucial educative sites which once existed in the labour and democratic movement. On the other hand, this cannot be separated from the structural effects of the recomposition of the educational system which displaced older forms. Nor was the academicization of history ever quite complete or unchallenged. The development of feminism, of oral history, and the resurrection of 'people's history' in a radical idiom all combined to scuttle the complacency of much academic history.

One major response to this challenge has been to rethink the very terms of 'history' itself. Ironically, perhaps, this rethinking has been accompanied by some (highly theoretical) developments in historiography and philosophy which pointed in a similar direction. Although it would be too optimistic to speak of a convergence between these two trends, an overlap of concerns has occurred. Two aspects of this general question about the scope of history are taken up in this book. The first is the insistence that historiography is concerned not with the past, but with the relation between past and present. A central determinant in this relation, and in its transformation, is political practice. Second, we indicate the significance of popular conceptions of history. Here we raise questions about popular memories, and the social constructions of the relation between past and present which intervene in daily life. These representations of the past and present are as much the provenance of 'history' as is the conventional textbook or monograph. For us, the dimension supplied by popular conceptions of history illustrates how cultural studies converge with historiography. In fact a larger 'Gramscian' task emerges here: to link the politics of history-writing to the sense of history active within contemporary cultural and political movements.

Although no typical history book, this volume has been a long time in the making. The idea for it originated in 1977. Some of us involved in historical work felt compelled to get to grips with the accumulating body of theoretical analysis which was directly focusing on historical practice. This influence was, roughly, 'structuralist marxism. At their most inflated these theories – for example, of Althusser or Hindess and Hirst – appeared to lead to the disintegration of historiography; in their more concrete and conceptually engaged forms, they provoked questions which we found could not be ducked. At the same time, the work of Edward Thompson – rather like that of Raymond Williams for cultural studies – impressed itself from the first upon historical concerns at the Centre for Contemporary Cultural Studies. To say that the elements of admiration and critique have always been thoroughly interwoven in our appreciation of Thompson's work is an indication of the strength of the tradition of critical dialogue which he himself represents so forcefully. Indeed, the shadow of Thompson's achievement falls over many parts of this collection.

The sympathetic reader will see that we have not provided (nor intended) a fully unified text. These studies are interlinked, but they also display a *variety* of concerns and also different degrees of work in progress. Some essays complete a sequence of study; others, especially in Part Three, point to future work. This reflects the fact that the project has shifted considerably over the years and that many of our early working assumptions have undergone profound alteration.

Chapter 1 introduces our general interest in 'social-democratic' politics and history through an account of the Hammonds. The second chapter is a sustained interpretation of the marxist history characteristic of the Communist Party Historians' Group of the 1950s, whose members have since achieved considerable international and academic recognition. One of those associated with the group, E. P. Thompson, is the subject of the third chapter. Here the theoretical and political dimensions of Chapter 2 are extended and focused upon a single *oeuvre*.

Part Two is devoted to the relation between history and theory within marxism generally. These chapters are explicitly theoretical in focus, and may prove to be the least accessible. In the case of Chapter 4 the material assessed may be unfamiliar to historians, and is less directly 'historical' in impact. Chapter 5 is an extended attempt to elaborate the methodological protocols for historical inquiry yielded by Marx's own most useful texts and formulations. Together, these chapters work through some of the theoretical and philosophical positions which gave initial impetus to our project. In key ways, they continue to inform the critical perspectives which lie behind the opening chapters. Despite their general character these philosophical and methodological assumptions play, we argue, a decisive role in more narrowly empirical and historical debates. History, in this sense, is necessarily 'philosophical'.

The third part of the book presents three discussions of newer forms of political history-writing, marking a partial break with the concerns of Part One. While there are a number of common threads, in Part Three questions of historical representation simultaneously take a more 'popular' turn, and one which raises a new set of methodological issues. In Chapter 6, the nature of oral history is examined, raising parallel questions about subjectivity and about alternative forms of evidence and historical understanding. Chapter 7 deploys ideas from French and German debates to analyse the public construction of the national past in the forms of 'National Heritage' and 'community'. In the final chapter a feminist assessment is given of the histories of the suffragette movement, concentrating particularly on modes of memoir and autobiography. The couplet 'public/private', and the problem of evaluating historical consciousness, are central to this assessment.

Each chapter, then, is self-contained, but forms part of a common stock of interests, objectives and readings. Though the membership of the group has changed over the years, we have been fortunate to be able to explore these problems collectively. The editors represent the rump of the group, who started out on the project and ensured its completion. Many others have been involved at the various stages of discussion, research and publication. We would especially like to thank all the contributors to the book, as well as past members of the history group: Andy Green, Andrew Lowe, Ray Mason, Patrick Scanlon, Tom Wengraf and in particular Janet Batsleer, Rebecca O'Rourke and Mary Langan. Thanks also to Claire L'Enfant of Hutchinson, to Rajinder Bhogal and Mary Ballard for help in typing, and to John Field for reading the bulk of the book at draft stage.

Part One

Historians and 'the people'

1 Radical liberalism, Fabianism and social history*

David Sutton

As we noted in the Preface, marxism is not the only philosophy which unites politics and history-writing. In England, for example, one dominant historical strand has been conservative and nationalist. It is not the long march of labour which is celebrated, but moments of national unity under the leadership of heroes and (more rarely) heroines. It is a history of kings and queens, national saviours, great statesmen, leaders in peace or in war. Sometimes ordinary citizens are granted an appearance, duly heroic and unified. Variants on these themes, suited to the contemporary occasion, are a staple of many popular historiographical genres.

This dominant historical conservatism, whose contemporary versions are examined later in this book, have been challenged by alternative traditions. Though often influenced by marxism, these alternative traditions have not necessarily been marxist or socialist in character. They have often been connected with a radical liberal, social-democratic or 'social-reforming' politics. It is arguable that this has been the commonest political anchorage, in Britain, of a social historiography. Certainly, in an important recent essay, Raphael Samuel has demonstrated the force of these non-marxist traditions on marxist historiography. 'People's history', he argues, had its precursors in 'radical and democratic rather than socialist' history-writing. Until the 1950s, 'Marxist history in Britain may be said to have existed as a tributary of a very much broader stream.'[1] † Before looking, therefore, at a specifically marxist historiography in the work of the Communist Party Historians' Group, it is important to grasp the character of this social–historical mainstream.

This poses major problems of selection. It is not possible to cover the whole field, past and present. There is a huge range of practitioners and texts even for the early period, that is from the 1880s to the inter-war period: the early economic historians from Rogers to Unwin, the cluster of distinctively 'social' histories (the Webbs, the Hammonds, Tawney and then Cole) and an extremely interesting group of feminist historians, pioneers, in retrospect, of modern feminist writing.[2] And there are liberal/social-democratic historiographies today as well, notably in one strand in labour history (constitutionalist and 'Whiggish') and, more immediately, in recent reassessments of the history of liberalism and the Liberal Party itself.

* Thanks are due to the History Group, John Field and John Mason who made comments on this chapter.
† Superior figures refer to the Notes and references on pages 325–72.

The solution adopted here is to focus on one period (mainly pre-First World War) and, within that, on one or two exemplary cases. The most creative historiographical connections of this time were undoubtedly with a radical liberal politics and, its close relation, a Fabianism. The work of John and Barbara Hammond exemplifies these connections perfectly, wedding a vital and innovative social history to radical liberal agitations. For the early twentieth-century politics of class their work is of great interest. An important sub-theme of this essay, however, is the relation between a gender-based politics and history-writing. Early feminist histories interest me for two main reasons: first, because they show the need for a different but related analysis of the position of women in an intellectual politics; second, because they provide a parallel but different case of the Liberal and Fabian connections, since, as I shall show, much early feminist history was written within a 'Fabian' framework.

My treatment of these themes is organized in the following way. I start with some points of theoretical clarification concerning the problem of 'political intellectuals'. I then look at the Hammonds as part of a radical liberal cultural group, the main lines of whose political activity and thinking is sketched. I analyse their historical practice within this context, as an example of the history–politics link. The parallel case of 'pioneer' feminist history is then discussed, and its link to Fabianism. Finally, I look at some of the ways in which the Hammonds' work was taken up, espoused or opposed, by later writers and social movements. I stress particularly those elements which now seem innovative in their work, especially their consistent empathy with the culture and aspirations of 'the common people'.

Political intellectuals

Peter Clarke's *Liberals and Social Democrats* (1978) is an exemplary placing of the liberal intellectuals of this phase - including the Hammonds - in their historical setting. Clarke is guarded, however, about the more particular determinations on liberal ideas. Assured of the force and significance of these, he focuses on their content in an approach characteristic of the history of ideas. To do more, he argues, risks reductions:

As to what is believed, there will doubtless be *some* link between a person's social position and his [sic] intellectual bearings, but the problem is to specify what connections are helpful as explanations.

The connections which marxists stress, Clarke argues, are of an unhelpful kind. They present the liberal intellectuals who pressed for reform as organizers of a new 'ideological manipulation'.

All that has happened, according to historians who take this view, is that an

ideological necessity to reorganise the state has led to the manipulation of its
potential for social control in a different way, *through* social reform. Such reform,
then, has been essentially conservative even though radicals pressed for it at
the time.

Against this view of the liberals' creed as 'a bourgeois socialism', 'ideologically
constricted to reformist methods by their class interests', Clarke asserts the
authenticity of their radicalism. Was not their social reform a more effective
'strategy of political change' than 'the revolutionist position'?[3]

Despite the lack of clarity of its terms ('ideological necessity', 'ideological
manipulation', etc.), the critique is effective enough if directed at the more
mechanical versions of 'social control'. With Freeden (*The New Liberalism*, 1978),
he convincingly shows that philosophical liberalism had an internal logic that was
not reducible to class interests. But his argument has the character of much anti-
marxist polemic: it hits out robustly at a 'marxism' crudified for the purpose.
He fails to pose the question in its most interesting modern forms, faces us with
absurd choices (taking ideas seriously or reducing them to 'interests') and ends up
giving little serious consideration to the problem of theorizing the relations between
political ideologies, intellectual groups and social classes.

Actually, Clarke's choices are quite artificial. It is possible to combine a concern with ideas and their authors with an interest in the social consequences that
flow from their propagation and with their social roots. Nor do these questions
have to be explored only with the abstractness of general formulae. One major
theme in Gramsci's *Prison Notebooks*, for instance, is the working through of
precisely this set of problems on the grounds, mainly, of Italian history. The
question of 'intellectuals' has loomed large in recent marxist writing too; indeed,
it has been a rather obsessive concern. Two examples are especially interesting here.

Raymond Williams, referring to the Bloomsbury fraction, has usefully considered the relation between a group's self-definition and its objective position in
a given social formation. While political parties, trade unions, and other large
organizations leave behind manifestos and statements of aim and intent, small
informal groupings are more resistant to definition and characterization. To describe this less explicit form of unity, Williams employs the term 'cultural group'.[4]
Class position and institutional setting will give to the group's culture a distinctive
character, but the method of examining 'cultural groups' requires a close re-creation
of their ideas and the precise milieu from which they grew. Similarly, in examining
the social groups who agitated for state education in the 1830s in Britain, Richard
Johnson argues against simple models of 'social control'. The aim of exercising
'moral and intellectual leadership' is a 'product of the subjective awareness of the
"lived culture" of the middle class'.[5] Their will to intervene culturally is a product
of their lived relation to the material circumstances of their own social position.
Such groups articulate a middle-class 'ideal'. Methodologically, an approach of this
kind involves the detailed construction of a collective biography, focusing on 'the
way of life' of sections of the professional middle class. This should include, we

might add, the analysis of middle-class notions of personal relations, of the family and of other social relations, not reducible to class, including the particular social networks and nodes of organization through which influence is sought.

In what follows I treat the Hammonds according to the method of collective biography. Dwelling on the determinations of their middle-class culture, however, does not preclude asking questions about the ideological tendency and the political effects of their efforts at intellectual leadership. Political intellectuals like the Hammonds were, in the first decade of the twentieth century, instrumental in driving a social reformist wedge into a Liberal Party, which, in the nineteenth century, had been given more to 'Retrenchment' than 'Reform'. They recognized that liberalism had to take on board social reforms for fear of being swamped by the emergent Labour Party and the threat of working-class legislation. In their role as journalists (and here we are referring mainly to John Hammond) they retained many of the attitudes characteristic of the nineteenth-century liberal press. They were fearful that the mechanisms of educating responsible public opinion were breaking down[6] but their self-ascribed role as 'educators' and intellectual pace-setters remained unstinted. It is important that the culture and politics of intellectuals are not completely severed from their class position. So much has been written in recent years about the intellectual origins and philosophical convolutions of liberalism that the connections between class formations and ideologies tend to be forgotten. The historical period which stimulated the Hammonds' history has been aptly characterized as one of *The Challenge of Labour*[7] and demonstrates the centrality of class divisions. It is in the context of this cultural and political background that the Hammonds' histories are examined.

The culture of the historians: a radical liberal cultural group

The intellectual culture in which both John and Barbara Hammond were formed was Oxford Liberalism. Before the Hammonds attended Oxford University, the Liberal Russell Club (1850) had provided a forum for discussion. From this Oxford base individuals took different routes. Some moved closer to the Fabians, others like Belloc, Simon, Hirst, and John Hammond, began to restate Liberal principles in a new collectivist manner. Cambridge produced few prominent Liberals, the major exception being Charles Masterman. It was through common writing projects, journalism and groups like the Rainbow Circle[8] (founded in 1893) that a close-knit grouping of what became known as 'new liberals' within the Liberal Party was formed. It is this relatively small grouping who are commonly held responsible for the founding ideologies of the welfare state and of navigating a path through 'authoritarian Fabian dogmas and emotional, irresponsible toryism'.[9] Their organizing role as intellectuals is considered by Emy as 'one of the best examples of the role of intellectuals in politics'.[10]

John Hammond, born in 1872, was the son of a thoroughgoing Gladstonian vicar. He was educated at Bradford Grammar School, studied at St John's College, Oxford, and graduated with a second in Greats in 1895. At Oxford he worked closely with those who were to become prominent Liberal intellectuals – Phillimore, F. W. Hirst and J. A. Simon. Further influences on him were his teacher Gilbert Murray and the Fabian Sidney Ball. Although impressed with Ball, Hammond's activities and thinking were contained within a liberalism revitalized by the participation of such figures as Hilaire Belloc. But both Clarke and Tawney agree that Ball's Fabian influence transformed his liberalism by turning his interest to the 'social question' and collectivist solutions.[11] In 1894 Hammond was working closely with Hirst, was secretary of the Oxford Union and was assisting the running of the Palmerston Club. In 1896 Hirst joined with Hammond, Phillimore, Belloc and Simon to write *Essays in Liberalism by Six Oxford Men* (1897). Its dedication to John Morley placed the text within Gladstonian *laissez-faire* but it is noteworthy that Hammond's article on education was regarded as the most collectivist, bearing the hallmarks of the influence of T. H. Green.[12] His university collaborations encouraged him to seek out opportunities in journalism. He worked briefly for the *Liberal Mercury*, was unsuccessful in his approaches to the *Manchester Guardian*, and accepted editorship of the refurbished journal, *The Speaker*.

Barbara Hammond, born in 1873, was daughter of the Rev. E. H. Bradby, one-time headmaster of Haileybury. She studied at Corpus Christi College, Oxford, and was taught by the radical L. T. Hobhouse. At university and through her family's activities Barbara was involved with the settlement movement. Beside other middle-class families, like the Nevinsons and Boyles, the Bradbys lived in London's East End, seeking to foster 'closer contact' between social classes. Canon Barnett's settlement, at Toynbee Hall, provided many middle-class intellectuals with a route into social work and often into government. George Lansbury, in his memoirs, was as cynical about these efforts as many subsequent historians:

The most important result of the mixing policy of the Barnetts, has been the filling up of the bureaucracy of government, and administration with men and women who went to the East End full of enthusiasm and zeal for the welfare of the masses, and discovered the advancement of their own interests and the interests of the poor were best served by leaving East London to stew in its own juice while they became members of parliament, cabinet ministers, civil servants. . . .[13]

When John and Barbara married in 1901 they were both enthused with the 'social question'. Barbara might have settled for an academic career as Fellow of Lady Margaret Hall but was seemingly troubled by what Beatrice Webb called a middle-class 'conscience of sin'. Moreover an interest in defending the interests of the Boers in South Africa gave the pair common motivations. John had been a prominent force in the League of Liberals Against Aggression and Militarism between 1899 and 1900 and shifted *The Speaker* towards an ardent pro-Boer position. In 1900 Hammond, Hirst, and Murray wrote *Liberalism and Empire*, which was directly influenced by John Hobson. Hobhouse's *Democracy and Reaction* (1904), arguably the most significant statement of new liberalism at this time, made no bones about the way in which the Boer War split the Liberal Party. He argued that a period of reaction held sway from 1886 to the signing of the Peace of Vereeniging in 1902. *Democracy and Reaction* had begun as a series of articles commissioned by Hammond for *The Speaker*. After Oxford, Hobhouse had joined the *Manchester Guardian* and his co-operation with Hammond was just one of a series of relationships between radical liberals which blossomed while party Liberals disputed amongst themselves and Fabians shifted away from progressives over the issue of imperialism.[14] The Rainbow Circle, which in its beginnings had promised so much, was one victim of the rupture. The Fabians' promiscuous modes of operation, their courting of undemocratic company, and the Webbs' support of the 1902 Education Act, furthered the differences, and all combined to make previous alliances impossible. Nevertheless a common preoccupation, of both Fabians and radical liberals, continued – the 'social problem'. Hammond's *Speaker* regularly ran articles on subjects like municipal trading, a subject close to Fabian hearts, but would vilify the political methods of the Fabians in the same breath.[15]

Under Hammond's guidance *The Speaker* shifted in five years from expounding Gladstonian foreign policy to a 'progressive approach to domestic policy'.[16] This claim is borne out mainly by the publication of sixteen articles between 22 October 1904 and March 1905. The series became a book entitled *Towards a Social Policy*. The articles ranged from a major concern with the land question, to unemployment schemes, housing, trade union law and liberal finance for social reform. Certainly these ideas prefigured Liberal policies after 1906, especially as the campaigning issues that figured in the Liberals' propaganda for the 1906 election were the traditional chestnuts of temperance, Chinese labour and education.[17]

In 1905 Hobhouse, now political editor of *The Tribune*, employed John Hammond as a leader writer for three evenings while he continued to edit *The Speaker*.[18] The move to *The Tribune* coincided with the first appearance of Barbara's tubercular ailments. By moving to the fresh air of Hampstead Heath the Hammonds enjoyed the closer proximity of fellow intellectuals – Brailsford, Nevinson, Vaughan Nash, Ramsay MacDonald, Hobhouse, Wallas, and after 1914, Hobson.[19] After *The Tribune* Hammond worked on the solidly Liberal *Daily News* alongside Masterman. At the point when Hammond resigned the editorship of *The Speaker*, Hirst succeeded in persuading the Rowntrees to finance the flagging paper. *The Nation* was the result, under the editorship of Massingham. From its appearance in March 1907 it marked the zenith of the self-confidence and coherence of this group. It brought together Cambridge and Oxford Liberals. The *Nation* Lunch, a weekly seminar, provided enthusiastic discussions perhaps equalled only in Beatrice Webb's drawing room. The most regular attenders – Massingham, Hammond, Hirst, Hobhouse, Hobson, Masterman, Brailsford and the Reverend Morrison – formed a self-conscious and mutually supportive group of would-be opinion-makers. They were encouraged in their optimism by a new Liberal Government which they considered to be the harbinger of social reform. Interestingly, the only major source of real disagreement was the continuing Liberal intransigence to the mounting campaign of the suffragettes. Masterman, for one, never prioritized the question, and appears to have felt justified in this because Labour women like Margaret Bondfield thought the Vote important only as a symbol. Brailsford and Nevinson, on the other hand, were militant suffragette supporters and felt strongly enough to resign from the *Daily News* in 1909. Slowly but surely, however, *The Nation*, with the backing of Hobhouse and of both the Hammonds, developed support for the 'adult suffragist' demand and supported the People's Suffrage Federation (1909). The argument they used against limited women's suffrage was that votes for propertied women would strengthen the representation of property; '. . . we are anxious that women should take a direct part in the life of the community. But we are not prepared to pay the price of a shifting in the class balance of power.'[20]

It is impossible to understand the Hammonds and their later historical work without being aware of the cross-fertilization of ideas which this group of intellectuals facilitated. Increasingly the piecemeal day-to-day life in journalism frustrated Hammond, and John became involved with Wallas, Hobhouse and Hobson in more ambitious writing projects. Indeed, by the evidence of the Hammonds' frontispiece dedications it was those same individuals who found the time and means to develop a deeper theoretical perspective, who had most influence on their historical writing. Wallas complained of the fatigue of combining journalism with 'concentrated thinking'.[21] Hobson contributed a series to *The Nation* under the title of 'Open questions late in 1907', but had gradually been withdrawing from journalism. Hammond himself, partly due to bad health, also began to turn away from day-to-day journalistic activity. A salaried job as Secretary of the Civil Service Commission, to which he was appointed in August 1907, encouraged him to devote more time to historical work. It was at this stage that the Hammonds' historical partnership began to flourish. Theirs was a partnership seemingly more affectionate than the Webbs' instrumental dedication to 'the public', but it invites comparison. Mary Agnes Hamilton described the synthesis of the two hands this way: 'Hers, the exact research; his, the artist's presentation'.[22]

The class and the politics of the historians

The appearance of socialist and labour militancy in the late 1880s with the 'new unions' of the unskilled brought new forms of violence into the British political scene. But the years 1906–14 were much more immediately formative for engaged intellectuals who wrote history. Radical liberal optimism about the welfare reforms of the 1906 Liberal Government dissipated as its course was interrupted by a combination of grave political crises. Dangerfield's *The Strange Death of Liberal England* (1935) has been taken to task for its emotive language and factual errors, but it nevertheless captured the atmosphere of a society undergoing a complex of struggles. Under these pressures the language of the Webbs, the Hammonds and Tawney are not dissimilar from his.

The political upheavals of the period, it has been argued, transformed Tawney, a

Christian, into a 'socialist'.[23] His private *Commonplace Book*, written between
1912 and 1914, reads as a jumbled search for moral guidance in a world falling apart.
'Modern society is sick through the absence of a moral idea.' What is most noticeable
in Tawney at this moment is his criticism of the failings of middle-class reformers
and their inability to appreciate the needs of the class they administered to. Of the
Fabians he wrote, 'They tidy the room, but they open no windows on the soul'.[24]
Meanwhile the Webbs themselves were busy with their new foundling, *The New
Statesman*, in which they launched a series of essays in 1913 called 'What is
socialism?'. But even for the Webbs the crisis increasingly became unmanageable.
Beatrice, writing on the verge of war, was near desperation point.

Meanwhile, Europe has flared up. All the great powers may be at war in a few days,
perhaps in a few hours. A hideous business. Ulsterites, Suffragettes, Guild Socialists
and Rebels of all sorts and degrees may be swept out of mind and sight in National
Defence and National Subsistence.[25]

For radicals like the Hammonds it was the War that was to break the camel's back
of the liberal conscience. It came as the last and most catastrophic challenge to
liberal values, following hard upon militant sections of the working class turning to
industrial syndicalism, and the violent protests of the suffragette women. The
coincidence with the rebellion in Ulster further taxed liberalism's historical nerves.

As to their class position and its effects on their politics it is profitable to
consider Hobsbawm's analysis of the Fabians. His interpretation of the Fabians as
a *nouvelle couche sociale* can be applied to the radical liberal intellectuals.[26]
Hobsbawm argues that the Fabians' socialism was in part a search for a secure
position in society. A highly bureaucratized, efficient society would welcome the
public expert. In the same way it is demonstrable that the tax changes advocated
in *The Nation* were intended to benefit the middle groupings. Asquith's 1907
budget was received with complaints from Labour's representatives.

The free breakfast table had again been relegated to the dim and distant future . . .
in order that the man with £2,000 a year might be relieved of a contribution which
would in each case have provided the old age pensions upon the scale they were
asking for them. This budget was a mere pandering to the city clerk and the small
gentry, who thought themselves superior persons and took their politics from
the *Daily Mail*.[27]

The Nation, though, celebrated the 'brilliant budget'. Noting the possibility of
financing a pension scheme it went on to stress Asquith's financial relief for the middle
classes: 'He has chosen to give the smallest income taxpayers the first place, and no
one can deny that as a class they stood in need of relief. The Government owes
something to the laborious middle classes, and today they have a substantial boon
on hand.'[28] This concern with the lot of their own social grouping is less often
emphasized than the radical populism embodied in Lloyd George's 1909 budget,

which was blocked by the Lords. The slogan 'the people versus the aristocracy' represented a radical populism which sought to invoke 'the masses versus the classes', the community over 'sectional' class interests, and the people versus the vested interests. As Freeden argues, the new liberals increasingly sought a politics of social reform which had a sufficient ethical and generalizing appeal to stand above class conflicts. 'The slogan "masses versus the classes" implied the rejection both of a sectional middle class party and of a sectional working class party, the ideal of an organisation of all progressive forces in the country, able by persuasion and by numbers to pursue a national policy.'[29] The problem was whether generalizing, ethical appeals could be stronger than the effects of class differences within the people.

In the *Eighteenth Brumaire*, Marx noted how 'democrats' who invoked the people against privilege were equally ready to sidestep the question of specific class struggles. Moreover Marx made useful observations about radical democrats and their reliance on, and relation to, the *petit-bourgeois* strata. He is clear that *petit-bourgeois* intellectuals do not have any necessary close personal relation to the middle groups since the relation is one of political and ideological representation, not a reflection of economic class interest. As Marx wrote, '. . . the democrat because he represents the petty bourgeoisie, that is a transition class, in which the interests of two classes are simultaneously blunted, imagines himself elevated above class antagonism generally'.[30]

Only one must not form the narrow-minded notion that the petty bourgeoisie, on principle, wishes to enforce an egoistic class interest. Rather, it believes that the *special* conditions of its emancipation are the *general* conditions within the frame of which alone modern society can be saved and the class struggle avoided. Just as little must one imagine that the democratic representatives are indeed all shopkeepers or enthusiastic champions of shopkeepers. According to their education and their individual position they may be as far apart as heaven from earth. What makes them representatives of the petty bourgeoisie is the fact that in their minds they do not get beyond the limits which the latter do not get beyond in life, that they are consequently driven (theoretically) to the same problems and solutions to which material interest and social position drive the latter practically. This is, in general, the relationship between the *political* and *literary representatives* of a class and the class they represent.[31]

Of course, there is no direct equivalence between Marx's nineteenth-century 'bourgeois democrats' and early twentieth-century radical liberal intellectuals. But what the quote demonstrates is that the latter's heralding of tax concessions for middle-class groupings cannot simply be seen as a personal celebration of economic relief for their own social stratum. Rather the relation between radical liberal intellectuals and their professional middle-class social grouping was one of ideological representation and political invocation. Radical liberalism was one form of politics offered to the middle class both as a means of universalizing particular interests and providing a form of leadership to the nation as a whole. The degree to which middle-class groups would carry the task of ideological and cultural leadership *within* the people was central to the radical liberal strategy. In what was still a limited franchise the middle classes made up a large proportion of the electorate, and, as has been argued, radical liberalism was a 'rationalist politics' which depended upon the active understanding and action of intelligent, educated voters.[32] Hobhouse, in *Democracy and Reaction*, argued that the shift into 'intellectual Reaction' and Conservatism was symbolized by the decaying public spirit in the 'great middle class' which had once been the 'backbone of Liberalism'.[33] The transition from the steady 'fundamental honesty of John Bull' to the unthinking man-in-the-street led Hobhouse to be apprehensive about the future role of the middle classes. 'Suburban villadom is a political and social portent the meaning of which has never yet been fully analysed.'[34] Masterman, in *The Condition of England*, took up this analysis and set about the suburban middle classes with such critical vehemence that he had to temper his remarks in the preface to the second edition.[35] What these texts convey is a contradictory attitude to the middle classes. On the one hand Masterman characterized the 'suburbans' as an insular, sedentary stratum obsessed with status and the 'struggle to attain'. Absorbed in, 'aimless activities; "random and meaningless sociabilities" which neither hearten, stimulate, nor inspire,'[36] the lower middle classes' insecure status had turned into a fear and loathing of the proletariat and hostility to social reform. On the other hand Masterman considered that with the 'suburbans' rested 'the healthiest and most hopeful promise for the future of modern England'. He added,

it would seem that it is from the suburban and professional people we must more and more demand a supply of men and women of capacity and energy adequate for the work of the world . . . they yet offer a storehouse of accumulated physical health and clean simplicity of living.

In education, in party politics, in municipal government, in the churches and chapels he considered the suburbans to be model 'servants of the state'.[37]

The radical populism of Lloyd George and the radical liberals aimed to mobilize the people against a privileged class. But its revamping of the nineteenth-century slogan 'the masses versus the classes' signified that the privileged enemy was the aristocracy and not the capitalist class. By invoking the 'people versus the aristocracy' the liberals were calculating that working people would still see their main enemy as the aristocratic landed interest. They hoped that the threat of Labour Party class legislation could be contained by the Liberals appropriating its fundamental concern for welfare, and integrating it into the 'old analysis' of early nineteenth-century radicalism.[38] Masterman's political journalism concentrated on the possibility that the threat of class politics might disrupt the liberals' espoused social politics. Writing in 1908, he summed up the task for the Liberal Government in words which bore the seeds of optimism, but which also questioned the practicability of the task ahead.

It appears specially anxious to promote legislation which will obviously benefit one section of the community without exacting compensating anger in any other; a class of legislation, indeed, which all the world has been seeking for a considerable number of centuries.

Will the Liberal party continue to hold within its embrace all these diverse elements? Can it retain, for example, its few men of wealth, without losing those adherents who demand direct taxation of that wealth in the interests of social reform? Can it continue to bridge over that wide chasm of interest which exists today between the lower middle class and the working class . . . which is causing in that middle class a violent revolt today at the pampering of the working man and a vague fear of an advancing social revolution?[39]

Radical liberal commentators recognized the existence of class antagonism but thought that social reform through state institutions could ameliorate the struggle. Their preoccupation with the *petit bourgeoisie* – as a non-classed stratum – represented their aspirations for doing away with all classes. For Marx the 'peculiar character of social democracy' was that it was a 'transformation of society in a democratic way . . . within the bounds of the petit-bourgeoisie'. Their strategy closely followed Marx's description.

The peculiar character of Social Democracy is epitomised in the fact that democratic-republican institutions are demanded as a means, not of doing away with two extremes, capital and wage labour, but of weakening their antagonism and transforming it into a harmony.[40]

It is useful at this point to pause in the argument and note some key features of the radical liberal 'cultural group'. They came, like most English intellectual groupings including Williams's Bloomsbury set, from 'a professional and highly educated section of the English upper class'. They were contemptuous of their own class, which led to their 'negative identification', to use Williams's term, with the lower classes. Their critique of their own class was first and foremost an ethical one and their mutual identity as a 'group of friends' centred on an ethos of 'social conscience' and 'concern for the underdog'. Present in this grouping as in Bloomsbury were the effects of the 'specific contradiction between the presence of highly intellectual and intelligent women' and their larger 'exclusion from male institutions'. Yet this distance from their own class was not accompanied by a 'positive' identification with the culture or institutions or active political potential of working-class people. Rather they took a social stance, typical of intellectuals within the professional strata, that was outside or 'beyond' the antagonisms of the major social classes. Their project was to render these antagonisms harmonious, or by just measures of social reform, to remove them entirely.

Theoretical developments

We can see many of these themes concerning the intellectual's social position and stance worked out in their theoretical elaborations. While Masterman wrote in the middle-class journals with his engaged sense of political expediency, others, as we have noted, turned from day to day politics and journalism to formulate the theoretical revisions which underlay this strategy. Hobson's work is crucial in this respect, and was to be very influential on John Hammond's writing. Hobson's thinking drew upon a unique combination of a revised 'political economy' and an understanding of society as a biological 'organism'.[41] Hobson is probably most famous for his study of *Imperialism* (1902) which influenced Lenin. His economics were unorthodox but there seems little evidence to suggest that he was convinced by marxist economics.[42]

In Hobson's main texts (*The Social Problem* (1901), *The Industrial System* (1909), *The Crisis of Liberalism* (1909)), one can see the evolution of a theoretical rationale for the political economy and the politics of the new liberalism. As with Hobhouse the theory developed as a revision of nineteenth-century Liberal political economy. Society seen as a biological organism was at the base of Hobson's theory. Thus the 'body politic' was understood almost literally as a functioning organism.

In a body which is in health and functions economically, every cell contributes to the life of the organism according to its powers. It also gives the true significance to political rights. Each limb, each cell has a 'right' to its due supply of blood. It has a 'right' to complain if it does not get it and it does complain. It is this right and habit of complaint that we must look for what in social politics corresponds to the franchise.[43]

In political-economic terms society could only function fairly if each individual was rewarded according to his/her contribution; any unearned property could be appropriated through taxation to be used for funding welfare reforms. Hobson continued,

. . . a clear grasp of society as an economic organisation completely explodes the notion of property as an inherent individual right for it shows that no individual can make or appropriate anything of value without the direct continuous assistance of society. So the idea of society as a political organism insists that the general will and wisdom of society, as embodied in the State, shall determine the best social use of all the social property taken by taxation, without admitting any inherent right of interference on the part of the taxpayer.[44]

In his more academic *The Industrial System*, Hobson aimed to clarify criteria for calculating the correct distribution of incomes. He sought to give a 'true out-line picture of the industrial system of the present day as a single organic whole, continuously engaged in converting raw materials into commodities and appor-tioning them by a continuous series of payments as incomes to the owners of the factors of production in the different processes'. The social reformer's idea was to separate out an 'unproductive surplus' in the form of an 'unearned increment'

which then could be employed in the 'development of public services'.[45] Hobson's
theory of the rights of distribution is not to be confused with Marx's labour theory
of value and Hobson objected to '. . . the refusal of socialists to recognise the actual
industrial services rendered by savings and the direction of industry and the
validity of some interest and profit in payment for these services . . .'.[46] In fact, of
course, fastening on to the 'economic rent' (unearned increment) derived from
land had long been a liberal preoccupation, and remains so to this day.[47] It had
been particularly stimulated by the 'single taxer' Henry George who has been
mistakenly regarded as a socialist.[48] However Hobson went further than the single
taxers when he recognized that, '. . . in this country at any rate, most large and
evidently unearned incomes are not derived directly from the monopoly of land
but from other economic advantages'.[49] This flexibility in Hobson's thinking, his
ability to apply the same logic to capital as well as land, places him as the most
advanced of the radical liberal thinkers and marks the subtle transition between
liberalism and social democracy. Such a transition is also evident in the
evolution of the Hammonds' history-writing.

Political implications

What were the political implications of these theories? Which social strata are
favoured, implicitly or explicitly, and why?

The theoretical writing of Hobson and Hobhouse prioritized the political role
of the middle and professional classes. They are productive and thus the rewards
of their labour are not part of any unearned increment. Consequently they stand
as part of the 'people' in the struggle against privilege and vested landed interest.
State taxation on privilege would redress the unfairness of the distribution of
rewards. Economically, then, each part of productive society would receive its
just rewards and function harmoniously in relation to all its parts. Taxation of
privilege would provide the finances for social reform and remove what was considered a just threat 'from below'. The unfair excesses of the competitive system
would be eliminated. Economic interests balanced, society would function
according to the 'general will'. So much depended upon the support of the professional and middle classes, because before 1918 they still formed a substantial
part of the electorate. Placating their economic fears was only part of the strategy;
their more important function was to exercise political and ideological leadership
over subordinate classes. With such a limited franchise, winning middle-class
'educated public opinion' for progressive social reform became the radicals' most
pressing problem. But of major historical consequence was the fact that the
strategy of attempting to amalgamate and transcend class divisions had significant
effects on the evolution of the parliamentary and executive functions of the
Labour Party. *The Nation* was convinced that, 'No pure workman's party can go
very far. Middle-class brains and training are indispensable to it'.[50] This quote
should ring bells for anyone interested in the Labour Party and its 'socialism'. At
the very moment the vast majority of the working class was enfranchised,[51] the

1918 Labour Party constitution (drafted by Sidney Webb) made it possible for individuals to take out membership, thereby broadening the party to include workers 'by hand and brain'. In this way the Webbs accommodated the 'professional bourgeoisie' within the ranks of socialism.[52] Ramsay MacDonald, whose pre-war writings were indistinguishable from radical liberalism, provided no resistance to the permeation of the Labour Party by radical liberal and Fabian intellectuals.[53] By the 1920s, therefore, it is appropriate to talk about a specifically 'Labour socialism', with definitely opposed aims and objectives to those of 'revolutionary marxism'.[54]

The Hammonds' histories

The Hammonds' histories cannot be seen in isolation from their politics – indeed their historical writing represented a contribution to, and an intervention in, the politics of their time. How do these histories fit into the cultural and political milieu we have described and with the strategic moral intentions of the radical liberal group?

The Hammonds' histories can be divided into the following rudimentary categories: institutional histories, biographies, and those innovative histories which addressed working-class culture. The trilogy made up of *The Village Labourer* (1911), *The Town Labourer* (1917), and *The Skilled Labourer* (1919), comprises their densest histories and is the foremost example of the third category. Subsequent biographies apart, it appears that their writing after the trilogy was less to do with research and more with histories having a longer chronological sweep and involving a more popular elaboration of the previous work.

The Hammonds were prolific biographers. One of their main modes of writing history was through the history of an individual: for instance, James Fox, James Stansfeld, Shaftesbury, Gladstone and C. P. Scott. As Gilbert Murray remarked, 'In each of these biographies the man selected represented a cause, but a cause expressed through a personality.'[55] The Hammonds' heroes stand for progressive causes. They are altruistic, and as members of the progressive middle classes, their lives say much about the source of inspiration for social change. Their subjects were case studies in reforming zeal. For instance, John Hammond's late and lengthy *Gladstone and the Irish Nation* (1938) highlights his view of the 'Grand Old Man' as the embodiment of an ideal, as well as saying much about the 'Irish Problem' which so plagued the Liberal conscience before 1922. While noting that Gladstone was never a social reformer, he is compared favourably with Shaftesbury and Chamberlain in their attitude to the poor. 'Gladstone became the greatest popular leader of his age, though he never mastered or seriously studied great social problems on which their comfort largely depended, because he offered the working classes something that satisfied their self-respect.'[56] Constitutional resolution of conflict was a strong theme in *James Stansfeld: A Victorian Champion of Sex Equality* (1932). Supporters of female equality and women's suffrage, one of the Hammonds' aims in the biography was to highlight Stansfeld's patient and painstaking arguments for repeal of the Contagious Diseases Act alongside the better known part played by Josephine Butler.[57]

The play of the 'institutional' and the 'cultural'

The first major product of the Hammond partnership was *The Village Labourer*. The research was almost wholly done by Barbara who spent three days a week in either the British Museum or the Public Records Office, while John wrote it up. In June 1911 Longmans decided the manuscript was too long and Barbara devised a scheme of splitting the book into two parts. *The Village Labourer* appeared in 1911, *The Town Labourer*, owing to the interruption of the War, in 1917.[58] The first took on special political significance. For example it was referred to approvingly in the introduction to the enormous Rural and Urban reports of Lloyd George's Land Enquiry Committee published in October 1913 and April 1914. Although this report ended up as little more than an 'academic exercise', it can be seen as a further working up of the ideas in *Towards a Social Policy*.[59]

All three books of the trilogy exhibit the same structure. *The Village Labourer* is organized around a basic dichotomy: the interests and the 'mind of the enclosing class' as against the attitudes of the commoners. The 'agricultural community' of the eighteenth century, they argue, was a hierarchical system – a 'social mobility' existing between firmly graded groups.[60] The major advantage that individuals enjoyed in the village life of the eighteenth century was independence. The system of enclosure produced a more polarized society through a more or less complete destruction of three classes: 'the small farmer, the cottager and the squatter'.[61] It is through the procedures and the reactions to the enclosing of land that the authors describe the dichotomy. The two sides are constructed in their institutional forms as embodying different 'ideals'. The landed class, in 'dictatorial fashion', and with the ideological support of political economy, systematically dismantled the traditional rights and holdings of the commoners. The procedures of the enclosing class are shown to be only formally accessible to the poor; petitions were written and ignored. The reader is left with the decided impression that the political machinery of parliament and the economic interests of the landlord class were at one in a 'dictatorship'. The consequence was that, 'The rich and poor were thus growing further and further apart, and there was nobody in the English village to interpret these two worlds to each other'.[62]

The major innovation of this historiography was the sympathetic representation of the interests and way of life of the poor. The importance of this is clear only if we stress the dominance, in this period as later, of histories which were both 'top downward' in perspective and largely institutional in focus. The Hammonds were true precursors of the social history of the 1950s and 1960s and indeed exercised a profound influence on some of its major practitioners, especially for example Edward Thompson and George Rudé. Their concern with 'consciousness' beyond the imprint of the institutional setting marks an achievement, in this respect, in advance of the Webbs'.[63] However, even though the evidence of anger and despair is persuasively and persistently documented, there is always a political sub-text in the historiography which attempts to secure the resolution of class interests. Exceptional individuals stand in as personifications of class harmony. Alfred Young is recruited as a reforming critic, Charles Fox and Samuel Whitbread are praised for their advocacy of the alternative policy of a minimum wage.[64] In spite of their purposeful reconstruction of the various 'Defences of the poor', it is ultimately with members of another class that the poor must find their salvation.

The Town Labourer appeared in 1917. The Preface blamed the delay in publication to the War but added that it had given opportunity to relate the work to '. . . problems that are beginning to engage the attention of the nation as the war draws, however slowly, to its end'. The horror of war coloured John's whole characterization of the early nineteenth century.

The more closely any period of history is studied, the more clearly does it appear that the mistakes and troubles of any age are due to a false spirit, an unhappy fashion in thought or emotion, a tendency in the human mind to be overwhelmed by the phenomena of the time, and to accept those phenomena as the guide to the conduct and judgement, instead of dealing and criticising them by a reasoned standard of its own. Men came to think that it is their business to explain, rather than to control the forces of the hour.[65]

Different periods, then, can come to be guided by a reckless and mismanaged 'false spirit'. The First World War had been the result of such a reactionary spirit, while the Industrial Revolution had been governed by a 'complacent pessimism' which had allowed the formation of the 'two nations'.

Both texts, then, have a similar structure. In The Town Labourer a 'rich' class of 'manufacturers' emerge out of yeomen and aristocratic stock and have their mirror opposites in the propertyless poor. The emergence of a bourgeois class is accompanied by the 'new discipline' of political economy, with its ideology serving the function of stripping the labourer of his/her wherewithal. Of the 'new regime' of factory and town life they wrote:

No economist of the day, in estimating the gains and losses of factory employment, ever allowed for the strain and violence that a man suffered in his feelings when he passed from a life in which he could smoke or eat, or dig or sleep as he pleased, to one in which somebody turned the key on him, and for fourteen hours he had not even the right to whistle.[66]

Not forgetting their faith in 'Englishmen who could break through the prejudices of their class',[67] and with the two sides assembled, the Hammonds make combat. They describe the attack on the trade unions through the Combination Laws, and the struggles for their repeal.[68] In opposition to the manipulations of the rich they build up a picture of the 'Defence of the poor' (chapters 12 and 13): the formation of an 'artisan civilization', the collective and mutual self-help institutions such as the trade unions, the friendly societies and the co-ops. All too often in the Hammonds' writing the two classes confront each other independently and almost on equal terms. However, there is a carefully nuanced description of the role of Methodism, which goes some way to filling an otherwise rather unidimensional attention to ideologies.

The teaching of Methodism was unfavourable to working class movements; its leaders were hostile and its ideas increasingly hostile; but by the life and energy and awakening that it brought to this oppressed society it must, in spite of itself, have made many men better citizens, and some even better rebels.[69]

Finally in Chapter 14 – the 'Mind of the poor' – there are formulations that E. P. Thompson developed in the early 1960s. The Industrial Revolution produced 'two different systems of morals'. Only the 'experience' of working-class life enabled the transformation of an 'inchoate and illiterate' class of the 1760s into the conscious movement of Chartism; 'the alienation of the working classes, [was] due not to the positive influence of ideas or enthusiasms, but to the effect of experience on ways of thinking and looking at life.'[70] To argue that the working class, through *their* experience, were the authors of their own actions, was an unprecedented position to adopt, and one of the first histories 'from below'. It recognized creative initiatives by ordinary people, independently of the purview of goodly social reformers and management from above. Yet the implications of these radical insights were contained within the limits of the Hammonds' own politics. The people spoke for themselves but the active answers and solutions came from state-sponsored reforms that really were capable of expressing and absorbing working-class needs. In the end, then, working-class movements were robbed of a social dynamic or creativity of their own; at best they were an object for reformers and an object lesson for the responsible sections of the governing groups. If this is considered a harsh characterization of the limits of their politics, there is no doubt that other historians who followed took direct inspiration from these formative statements, and drew conclusions which already nestled in their writings.

The Skilled Labourer (1919) was the longest and densest of the trilogy. The introduction repeated a familiar characterization of the early nineteenth century as one of 'civil war'. But its structure differed, with chapters giving specific analyses of different workers and trades. The theme of portraying the 'working men's point of view' remains a priority. Thus in studying the miners of Tyne and Wear they used a mass of local papers and pamphlets to record the 'effects of the workers to secure by combination some share in the profits of the industry, and some degree of independence and assurance'.[71] The book's concluding comments succinctly summed up their perspective on the development of industrial capitalism, which resembles much of the social criticism of the 'culture and society' tradition.[72] In addition, they quote approvingly from Engels's *Condition of the English Working Class*, and were influenced by his approach. The state acting as a 'police system' affords the overpowering 'organization of capital' and denies the interests of the poor to education and the right to organize for higher wages. Such normative assumptions meet with the Hobsonian concern with equitable distribution and consumption and the reformed maintenance of the social system:

> ... we should argue that the power of [these] men to turn the help they got from the capital to the best account, would be impaired if they were stinted of food or leisure, and if their natural faculties of mind and body were left underdeveloped. ... This was the unconscious instinct behind the revolt of the workers in all industries against the new tyranny.[73]

As Clarke concludes in his study, theirs was not a revolutionary critique of capitalism at all but a 'condemnation of *unregulated* capitalism'.[74]

Pioneer feminist historians: women as part of the people?[75]

As we noted above, the feminist history of this period is relevant to our themes in in two main ways. First, feminist historians and social investigators (categories often in practice indistinguishable) most commonly worked within a radical liberal or Fabian framework, and provide us with another illustration, therefore, of the contemporary link between history and politics and of its limitations. Second, the feminism of these writers, most obvious in the fact that as politically active women they choose to study the problems of women's position, requires a separate emphasis. This is especially so since the Hammonds cannot be regarded as 'feminist' in this sense, despite their biography of the social reformer James Stansfeld. The way they sought to find evidence which would allow victims of the Contagious Diseases Act to speak for themselves is of interest to feminists, but there is no explicit challenge in their work to a male-dominated history.[76]

There are several reasons for seeing the later Victorian and Edwardian period as transitional in terms of women's structural position in society and for explaining their growing consciousness of that position. Here it is only possible to mention the struggle that middle-class women fought throughout the nineteenth century to enter the 'professions'. By the end of the century the number of lower-middle-class jobs opening up for women increased. Literary representations show a shift from 'self-sacrifice to self-awareness'.[77] Patricia Stubbs has argued that in the period 1880–1920, though mainstream novels continued to place women within the confines of a 'private domestic world', there was an identifiable 'evolution' and a 'remaking of women's image in fiction'.[78] A central factor in this transition was the escalation of the struggle for women's suffrage. Self-awareness began to gain active expression in the struggle for participation in the public sphere. Schreiner's notion of 'parasitism' provided a powerful frame for characterizing the way middle-class women perceived their predicament.[79] Conventional nineteenth-century prescriptions of women's role as nanny, wife, governess, or hostess, all of the 'private sphere' of the home – the 'Madonna role' – were extended into the public sphere.[80] Statistical disputes continue over the number of women working outside the home in this period.[81] From the late nineteenth century with the additional work brought about by the feminization of teaching and clerical work, more and more women were living two roles: at home and at work. As teachers and as professionals they were expected to transfer their humanizing and harmon- izing family influence outside the home.[82] Women's existence outside the home was, of course, governed by their class position. For instance, by 1902 elemen- tary education was considered just provision for all. But opportunities for working-class girls were severely curtailed by the call of domestic chores. The noisy and makeshift working-class home was not an appropriate environment for their education. As one commentator put it, she will 'often be attempting to solve diffi- cult mathematical problems while giving a hand in the washing of the baby'.[83] Education beyond an elementary age or the desire to work in the new offices were seen as distracting girls away from their domestic and maternal training and duties. We do not know enough yet about how working-class girls and women negotiated and experienced a desire to 'better themselves' before so many were subjected to the compounded discourses of class and motherhood.

But in the case of middle-class women rich sources are more readily available which help us understand women's reconnaissance of public life. Beatrice Webb and Mrs Humphrey Ward both signed the 1889 petition against women's suffrage and yet, ironically, were two of the most active women in public life. Beatrice changed her mind about women's suffrage, of course, but not before she had sorted through many confusions and contradictions. Her early autobiographical memoirs portray her attempting to negotiate her desire to undertake public work and the expectations of would-be suitors, Joseph Chamberlain and later Sidney Webb.[84] Mrs Humphrey Ward never relented over the issue of women's suffrage – indeed she was a prime activist in the Anti-Suffrage League. Her public life was a living paradox. Only much later the contradictions of working with anti-suffrage men became clear.[85]

Beatrice Webb and the group around the Fabians provided the organizational framework for the emergence of feminist history – the Fabian Women's group and the London School of Economics. It is important to see women intellectuals both in the context of their class position and in relation to their politics. It is necessary to consider how this group thought its politics within the available languages of the time – within radical liberalism and, especially significant here, social Darwinism. Space prevents any systematic description of these different philosophies and politics. What is most interesting about this period is the constant philosophical reworking of terms like 'socialism' and 'liberalism'. In terms of the concrete situation we would do better to analyse the interrelations between these philo- sophies and politics rather than to think that 'Fabianism', for instance, is identifiable as a coherent entity in itself. Rather than take the labels at face value it is more appropriate to draw out the main aspects of these competing 'ideologies of social reform' and see how different politics converge, interact and separate out in particular situations.

My aim here is to lay out some of the defining elements of Fabianism,[86] to assess how the aspirations of 'women intellectuals' fitted with this model, and to examine how far new developments in feminist history grew out of the social location of these women. First, the Fabians (particularly Sidney Webb) formulated a gradualist conception of socialism. In 1894 Webb lectured to the Fabian Society: 'For all these years we have held on our course, turning neither to insurrectionism on the one hand, nor to utopianism on the other'.[87] Second, the bearers of this brand of socialism were middle-class 'experts'. These experts would occupy key state institutions in order to engineer and 'permeate' socialism through local government boards, the educational apparatus, trade boards and so on. Third, it was hoped that these apparatuses would provide the institutional means for introducing social reforms ameliorating the plight of the so-called 'submerged fifth' of the nation. Those who could not care for themselves would be catered for by the provision of a 'national minimum' living standard. Fourth, it abandoned the equation of socialism with working-class struggle. It replaced the class discourse of socialism with a 'nationalist' discourse. Citizenship replaced class. In terms of political action this nullified the independence and vitality of working-class demands. A change in consciousness was not a necessary prerequisite for social change. Their elitist programme assumed that political subjects were malleable, and could be constructed from above. In Sidney Webb's seminal *Twentieth Century Politics* he spoke of the electorate in this way: 'They are not thinking of Liberalism or Conservatism or Socialism. What is on their minds is a burning feeling of shame at the "failure of England".'[88]

How far did the Fabian women fit into this scenario? And what were the divergencies? In 1908 the women's suffrage issue forced the Fabian women to organize their own group. They saw first that women did not have the constitutional rights which were the precondition of 'social citizenship'. Second, they met to discuss and clarify the 'intimate relation between the two most vital movements of the time, Socialism and Women's Emancipation'. Third, there is evidence that these women readily took on the mantle of expertise. They identified themselves as experts of the social problem. There is a recognizable shift, in middle-class women's perceptions of themselves, from the private Madonna role to a more public identity concerned to resolve the 'social problem'. Women of the calibre of Mary Macarthur and Margaret Bondfield, to name just two, readily took up the challenge of occupying new state apparatuses to ameliorate the social problems of particular classes of women.[89] Ultimately these conceptions belonged within a statist framework highlighting women's place within national efficiency. On most counts, therefore, women active in the public sphere fitted Fabian categories. However, this is perhaps to look at their achievement too negatively. For there is good reason to suggest that their own situation as women, and their choosing to study women, enabled a number of breakthroughs in terms of their politics. In other words, while they fit closely the class and politics of Fabian and radical liberals, it was the experiential level of the 'cultural' which, again, drew out new perspectives.

One of the consequences of 'going out' to study women as wives and mothers was to make them question how middle-class experience differed from that of their working-class subjects. B. L. Hutchins and A. Harrison in *A History of Factory Legislation* (1911) were very critical of previous assumptions of middle-class women – the 'Lady Bountiful' image. 'The mistake some of them have made is in transferring their own grievance to a class whose troubles are little known and less understood by them.'[90] This became apparent with the material collected by the Fabian women and published by Maud Pember Reeves as *Round About a Pound a Week* (1913). As Sally Alexander argues in a new introduction, the compilation of working wives' budgets in Lambeth meant that insights were gained into 'daily life' which would have otherwise been hidden from the vision of middle-class philanthropy.[91] Their conclusion that working-class mothers were not incompetent and that their 'improvidence' was due to the lack of suitable housing and domestic equipment was based upon analysis of the structural conditions of their predicament and the immediate experience of the women they went to see. *Married Women's Work*, edited by Clementina Black, also sought to destroy another myth about 'motherhood': 'the general opinion . . . especially, perhaps among persons of the middle class, that the working for money of married women is to be deplored'. Their research sought to break the commonplace equation between 'working mother' and 'maternal negligence'. From their results, they found no determining relation between infant mortality and the fact that women went out to work.[92]

As has been pointed out by modern-day feminists the Fabian solution (influenced by eugenical ideology) of a 'state endowment of motherhood' was wrapped up in the notion that mothers were a 'special category' to be given differential treatment by the state. If the basic 'sexual division of labour' was not challenged, however, what these women did was to go and see – to try and relate to the gruelling predicament of working-class motherhood. The Women's Cooperative Guild was active among such women attempting to give women collective support and some dignity.

The stress on *experience* – of listening to working-class women's predicament – is noteworthy. As with the Hammonds, where there is an emphasis upon 'culture' and 'way of life' there is also a moment of rupture between an institutional solution from above, and the desires, aspirations and experiences of the women involved. To let women speak of their own lives shifted the emphasis away from somebody else solving their problem – state officials, reforming intellectuals – and began to put the solution in the hands of the people themselves. Even if both Fabianism and radical liberalism tended to place the ultimate solutions with the state, they opened up questions of consciousness and of women speaking for themselves, thereby anticipating the concerns of modern-day socialist feminism.

A further aim of the Fabian Women's Group was to conduct an 'Enquiry concerning the economic position of women'. This brought them into the heartland of the 'economic historians'.

With all deference to Rogers, Ashley, Toynbee and Hasbach and Cunningham, the economic history from the point of view of the workers, to say nothing of women workers, has yet to be unearthed, and there is no research so important to the socialist movement on its intellectual side.

After a stint of day-schools and lectures given by women, Mabel Atkinson developed the group's arguments and conclusions in *The Economic Foundations of the Women's Movement*. The arguments made in the pamphlet rely on Schreiner's inspiration and prefigure Alice Clark's work.

The group built its argument around 'The two sections of the women's movement' – middle- and working-class women. Middle-class women were said to be rebelling against 'parasitism' in which their only real activity had been 'helping mamma' and 'visiting the poor'. 'They remained within the family group occupied in the futilities of an extraordinarily conventional social intercourse. Dusting, arranging of flowers, and paying calls were the important duties of their existence.'[93] This section of the movement proposed three ways to overcome 'sex exclusiveness'. First, they would revolt 'against their exclusion from human activity'. Second, they would strive 'to earn a livelihood'. Third, they would seek a 'share in government'. Though displaying an increasing 'sex consciousness', they argued that working-class women were inspired more by the issue of 'labour revolt'. Parasitism for them was not an immediate problem, but they added 'one of the possible dangers of the future is the working-class women in their right and natural desire to be protected against that exploitation which the first development of machinery brought with it, should allow themselves to drift, without observing it, into parasitism, which was the lot of middle-class women'.[94] The emphasis on class differences within the women's movement clearly reflects the historical conjuncture and has been stressed by later socialist feminist historians like Rowbotham and Ramelson. This leads to a somewhat telling contradictory position as regards the unity of women. On the other hand the Fabian women noted the growth of 'sex consciousness amongst working women' and a resulting tendency for the convergence of aims in securing economic independence from men. On the other hand there is something of a double standard offered to women in a different class position. Middle-class women were to be freed from parasitism and gain a place in the public sphere. For working-class women, although not, as we have seen, completely unaware of the possibly debilitating effects of 'protection', the Fabian Group recommended the 'State Endowment of Motherhood'.

Alice Clark's *The Working Life of Women in the Seventeenth Century* (1919) was a major intellectual contribution which took up these preoccupations. Her opening comments startle in their modernity.

Hitherto the historians have paid little attention to the circumstances of women's lives, for women have been regarded as a static factor in social developments, a factor which, remaining itself essentially the same, might be expected to exercise a constant and unvarying influence on Society.[95]

Her aim, to specify historically women's 'economic' position in production, took up the claim that the pre-industrial family, and not the individual, constituted the productive unit. While sticking close to her particular study of women's position in different class situations in the seventeenth century, she did allow herself a few 'conjectures' and comparisons. Thus she argued, 'In modern life the majority of Englishwomen devote the greater part of their lives to domestic occupations, while men are freed from domestic occupations of any sort, being generally engaged in industrial or professional pursuits'. By contrast, in the seventeenth century, 'men were much more occupied with domestic affairs than they are now. Men in all classes gave time and care to the education of their children, and the young unmarried men who generally occupied positions as apprentices and servants were partly employed over domestic work'.[96] Clark insists upon considering women's productive activity in new terms, since 'other writers on industrial evolution have considered it only from the man's point of view'. To do this she situated a history of women's productive activity within three different evolving models – domestic industry, family industry and capitalistic industry or industrialism.[97] Her historical comparisons enabled her to challenge the 'eternal feminine' and essentialist or universalistic explanations of woman and her place. Her successive models allowed her to begin to deny a universal categorization of woman as non-productive and to argue that capitalism compounded that image. She also looked for another explanation. 'These far reaching changes coincided with the triumph of capitalist organisation but they may not have been a necessary consequence of that triumph. They may have arisen from some deep-lying cause, some tendency in human evolution which was merely hastened by economic cataclysm'.[98] Clark, in 1919, also puzzled how the long *durée* of patriarchy combined with the development of capitalism.[99]

Like the Fabians, Clark saw the function of the state as one of patriarchal control. But the state could also be used to redress the balance between the sexes.

... we may even ask ourselves whether the instability, superficiality and spiritual poverty of modern life, do not spring from the organization of a State which regards the purposes of life solely from the male standpoint, and we may permit ourselves to hope that when this mechanism has been effectively replaced by the organisation of the whole, which is both male and female, humanity will receive a renewal of strength that will enable them to grapple effectively with the blind force of Capitalism; – that force which, while producing wealth beyond the dreams of avarice, has hitherto robbed us of so large a part of the joy of creation.[100]

Beatrice Webb also held this optimistic view of the state. State provision for children and the extension of the system of maternity benefit, 'entirely apart from wages', could, if linked with social policy as a whole, be 'in the interests alike of maximum productivity and race preservation – a system of "National Minimum", in which there should be no sex inequality'.[101] As we argue in 'The public face of feminism' (Chapter 8 of this volume), access to parliamentary representation and social citizenship in this period was the first and necessary moment for the progress of the women's movement. However, the politics of Fabianism and liberalism placed so much shrift with the potential operations of the benevolent state that it severely underestimated the degree to which the state could continue in its patriarchal and reinforcing function. There was an uncritical acceptance of the sexual division of labour. There was no clear awareness that 'equal but different' could easily be, in effect, 'unequal but different'. As Jane Lewis writes of inter-war feminism, 'The promotion of maternal welfare and in particular the reduction of maternal mortality was also important, because it was as much in the interests of the race as the mother'.[102] Often feminists of the period continued to put national or class considerations before the position of women themselves. From the viewpoint of modern-day feminism there is now much sharper debate on the disadvantages of seeing women as a 'special category' either in need of protection, or requiring differential treatment from the state in terms of benefits.[103] Although much of this pioneer feminist history-writing remained within Fabian protocols it nevertheless opened up new areas for feminist histories. It made the study of women a priority, it invoked women's experience, and it brought to the women's movement's contemporary struggle a historical imagination.

Receptions

The subsequent history of the Hammonds' influence would require a separate essay. The later development of feminist history, within and outside Fabianism, would require a separate book. But, in the Hammonds' case at least it is possible to sketch some of the main sites of their influence and the many and varied receptions of their work. Just as the War divided feminists so it splintered the Liberals. The so-called new liberals scattered in different directions. Some stayed with the forlorn Asquith, a few with Lloyd George; others stayed in the 'progressive' clubs or turned to Labour. John Hammond, for example, had reluctantly persuaded himself that he must fight for the right of Belgian self-determination. He threw himself into post-war 'reconstruction' and was involved in discussing War reparations and conciliation in 1918. After the War Hammond does not seem to have been so wrapped up in his own journalism with the problem of Liberal–Labour Party relations as were others like Masterman and Massingham. The War rekindled the old Liberal shibboleth of the rights of small nations and in 1921 he wrote about Ireland in the image of the responsible, non-imperialist liberal. He argued that the Irish Nationalists had made the mistake of becoming embroiled in the exigencies of British party politics and especially in the calculations of Lloyd George. Sinn Fein by contrast 'looked not to Parliament but to Ireland'. They represented 'all the forces which have been gathering in Irish life for twenty years'. Especially praised was the work of the Gaelic League which embodied the 'country's spiritual independence' and was the Irish equivalent to the Workers' Education Association (WEA).

The WEA was to become a central preoccupation for Hammond. Its merit, he argued, was that it had broken from a Smilesian patronage of the working classes.

[It] is in some respects, the most interesting movement in our modern life; it is led by men with the gift of leadership, like Temple, Greenwood, Mansbridge and Tawney; it is blessed by the trade unions, patted softly on the back by the Board of Education and helped, not too generously, by the Universities out of their inadequate resources.[104]

John Hammond's celebration of the WEA fits well with his class and politics. Tawney, who spent a lifetime with the WEA, saw in Hammond's histories the attempt, 'to bridge the gulf between history and common life'.[105] From the 1890s there had been an explosion in various 'socialist' educational groups and politics. There were, as Brian Simon has argued, 'two trends in the movement for adult education' in the period.[106] These two trends were in ever-increasing conflict with each other. On the one hand there was in the 1900s a revival of the initiatives of University Extension, Oxford University and the Church, and later the Board of Education sought closer links between the working class and the universities. Socialist groups, particularly the Social Democratic Federation and Socialist Labour Party committed to marxism, were beginning to disavow middle-class leadership and make their education more directly organic to their working-class constituency. The two educational strands had similarities in that they both took working-class education as their starting-point, but they were guided by different policies. The WEA, for instance, was expressly 'non-political'. 'It is neither capitalist, nor proletarian, Liberal nor Conservative, individualist or Fabian.' Moreover its ethos was the old tradition of bringing a humanizing education to the working classes. 'The worker who in his scant moments of leisure wishes to glean fragments of information about the stars in the heavens, or the fossils in the rocks, or the fish in the sea, must draw upon funds of knowledge and enquiry accumulated by the labour of students trained in universities.'[107] This version of education *for* the working class was spectacularly rejected in the 1909 Ruskin College strike. Students there determined upon reading marxist 'classics', rejected Oxford University's efforts to incorporate more closely the college and went on strike when Hird, the sympathetic Principal, was dismissed. Out of the strike came the resolve for independently run working-class education. The Plebs League (1909) and *Plebs Magazine* were the results. The Central Labour College was set up in 1909-10 and the National Council of Labour Colleges in 1921.[108] The Hammonds themselves seem to have been largely unaffected by these developments. Indeed, for John Hammond liberal education meant education of all 'classes for leisure', training the 'baseness of the raw mass of untrained minds'. Of 'the ideal of democracy, we should say that it attempts so to educate its citizens as to give them independent qualities of intelligence and temper'.[109] This split reproduced within popular adult education an increasing divergence in political aims. Nevertheless it must be remembered that marxist developments had some historical prefigurations in nineteenth-century and early-twentieth-century adult education. As Macintyre notes,

Such agencies helped to fix the distinctive character of late nineteenth century adult education with its earnest and generally uncritical tone and progressive assumptions; but it would be wrong to regard them on such grounds as simple projects of the bourgeoisie or instruments of social control.[110]

It was in this milieu that works like the Hammonds' histories were read probably in very large numbers. Take, for instance, the largely Hammond-inspired *English Rural History* by Geo. Guest. 'The purposes of this little book are to introduce the people of the countryside to the history of rural life, and to create in the minds of the workers a desire to understand more fully the past and the present.' That understanding the author hoped would serve as a framework for building upon the new-found 'spirit and outlook of the workers' during the War and lead towards the 'recreation of rural society on a basis of political and economic democracy'.[111]

In style and in its consideration for the 'general reader', the Hammonds' histories sought to connect with popular needs and aspirations. More than likely it was Tawney who, in reviewing *The Town Labourer*, thought it touched upon the 'one still unsurmounted difficulty – the mind of the working class'. The years 1760–1832 were worthy of study because 'To understand what the working class went through in those years is to have the master key to its unspoken philosophy today'.[112] Such sentiments were bound to excite accusations of political bias. An early review of *The Village Labourer* argued that the 'passionate indictment against English landowners' is 'marred by exaggeration and disregard of proportion. They have written, not a history, but a political pamphlet'.[113] Increasingly the Hammonds' work was criticized by 'professional' historians. An early indication of what became known as the 'optimist' interpretation of the Industrial Revolution appeared in a leading article in *The Times Literary Supplement* which questioned the Hammonds' image of the plight of the working class in the early nineteenth century. 'Happily this view of economic history, though still taught for political purposes, is being gradually dispelled . . . .' Moreover the author noted a less severe indictment in the pages of the *Rise of Modern Industry*.[114] Indeed, the Hammonds' later popularizations of their earlier texts are littered with temporizing equivocations of their previous stridency. They gave much ground over the attacks by economic historians.[115] Thus in response to economists seeking to prove that the working classes did improve their economic position, the Hammonds conceded, 'Let us take it that so far as statistics can measure material improvement there was improvement'.[116] Again in *The Bleak Age*, while noting the inadequacy of remaining in the 'sphere of strictly economic conditions', they considered the 'statisticians' 'probably more or less correct'.[117] From the other side, the economist Clapham welcomed the Hammonds' concession and the possible avoidance of an 'arithmetical wrangle'. In return he argued, 'I agree most profoundly with his opinion that statistics of material well-being can never measure a people's happiness'.[118] Therefore the first round of debates between pessimists and optimists ended in conciliation. As for the Hammonds themselves their major historical output was over, and it remained for others to take up their cudgels. It is difficult to say quite why the Hammonds did not reply more rigorously. Both sides tended to retire content that they were arguing with different criteria. But also part of the answer must lie in the fact that after the First World War the political tasks that had informed their history had largely been fulfilled. As for many radical liberals, it was the issue of war and pacificism which spurred their pens to protest; at the outbreak of the Second World War John Hammond returned to journalism with the *Manchester Guardian*.

A second round of arguments from economic historians directed against the Hammonds came to fruition in the activities of the Mont Pelerin Society and F. A. Hayek.[119] The seminar produced a collection of essays, *Capitalism and the Historians*. The book represented a call to professional economic historians to counter the 'one supreme myth' which resided in public opinion. That myth 'more than any other has served to discredit the economic system to which we owe our present day civilisation and to the examination of which the present volume is devoted. It is the legend of the deterioration of the position of the working classes in consequence of the rise of capitalism . . .'.[120] This call to reverse academic opinion had a later successor in the almost propagandist collection compiled by the Institute of Economic Affairs – *The Long Debate on Poverty* (1972). The intro- duction explained that, 'the volume as a whole forms a corrective to the imbalance still widespread in historical teaching that modern poverty has its roots in the advent of industrialisation'.[121] In the meantime, though, a third round of the battle between the optimists and pessimists had taken place in the pages of the *Economic History Review* – a series of unflinching arguments which became almost institu- tionalized as the 'standard of living debate'. This debate, itself, concerns us here only in so far as the name of the Hammonds was consistently called upon on behalf of the so-called pessimists. E. P. Thompson's *The Making of the English Working Class* was quick to take sides with the classical 'catastrophic' view in the 'academic battlefield'.[122] Thompson was not uncritical of the Hammonds and noted that their 'Fabian persuasion' led them to play up the ameliorative role of the state and the Whig opposition, and consequently to research with an a priori assumption that there existed no 'bona fide insurrectionary scheme'.[123] Such important criticisms apart, as Raphael Samuel has noted, Thompson's work 'may arguably be seen as a vast elaboration of their (the Hammonds') original insights'.[124] The influence of the Hammonds is not only identifiable in the *Making*. Thompson's essays on 'The moral economy of the English crowd' and 'Time, work discipline and industrial capitalism' have clear prefigurations in the Hammonds.[125] But perhaps most important, Thompson took up their stress on culture, on conscious- ness, and on the struggle of the working class actively to create their own institu- tions. If our analysis of the Hammonds' problematic is correct they left a contradictory legacy for socialist history-writing. The contradiction lies in terms of what we have described as the play of the institutional and the cultural. The first refers to the propensity of liberal middle-class intellectuals to reform on behalf of popular aspirations; the second refers to the independent initiatives of the people. Once divested of their Fabian persuasion the Hammonds could be directly accommodated as historians of the popular tradition.

A significantly different re-evaluation of the Hammonds came from Hobsbawm in his introduction to *Captain Swing*. Hobsbawm's and Rudé's analysis again starts from a subject covered in *The Village Labourer* – the 1830 rebellion by farm labourers. Hobsbawm argues that the Hammonds' work was seminal because of their 'empathy' with the plight of the poor and their commitment to research on their behalf. However, although historians are still dependent upon similar historical sources, their 'liberal-radical' history is considered severely foreshortened, leaving further questions to be asked of extant sources. Such questions, he argues, are notably about the economic theory of development, social structure, collective behaviour and especially 'the interaction between the social-economic base and the ideology of various strata'.[126] The attention to changes in the economy enables Hobsbawm to situate the motives of the rebellious farm labourers in the context of a logic of the economic transformation of social relations in the countryside. 'What happened was . . . that a rural society which was in some sense traditional, hierarchical, paternalist, and in many respects resistant to the full logic of the market, was transformed under the impetus of the extraordinary boom (and the subsequent though temporary recession) into one which the cash nexus prevailed, at least between farmer and labourer.'[127] The contextualization of the farm labourers' resistance to the transgression of customary rights owing to the determination of the logic of the economy introduces what might be called classical marxist theoretical questions which the Hammonds themselves never really asked. Moreover, the attempt to place the consciousness of the labouring poor more precisely within a theory of capitalist development connects with ongoing 'arguments within English Marxism'. Perry Anderson's recent criticism of E. P. Thompson's tendency to use the criterion of consciousness as the touchstone of class identity at the expense of questions about 'the objective determinants of the formation of the English working class', would apply straightforwardly to the Hammonds' history.[128] For instance, Maurice Dobb, using categories from Marx's *Capital*, argued that the uneven development of the capitalist mode of production made it impossible to identify a fully formed working class before the last quarter of the nineteenth century.[129]

A legacy for social democracy

What, then, of the political aspects of the Hammonds' legacy? As we have seen, both radical liberal and Fabian-influenced historiography undoubtedly invoked the people in resistance and struggle. This was why, later, the Communist Party historians found much to defend and extend in the Hammonds' tradition. Similarly, modern-day socialist feminist historians have their pioneering forebears in feminist historians of the early twentieth century, who began to study women in their own right and highlighted the active experience and consciousness of their subjects. But what is critical in this early 'people's history' is the way in which popular aspirations were appropriated, fashioned and resolved through the politics that informed the writing. Radical liberal and Fabian politics contained, in nascent form, almost all the elements of a developing British social democracy. Central to the perspective was the emphasis on the ameliorative role of the state and of liberal intellectuals' ability to translate and resolve popular demands from above.

2 'The people' in history: the Communist Party Historians' Group, 1946-56*

Bill Schwarz

The decision by the historians in the British Communist Party to organize them-selves as a group in 1946 will probably appear as an excessively parochial and antiquarian subject for a chapter in a book written in 1981, when political problems of the day are so pressing. But I want to argue, first, that the historio-graphy which emerged from this venture decisively reworked our notion of the past (so much so that for many today it now appears conventionally mainstream) and, second, that an integral dimension to the work of the Historians' Group was a securely founded conception of the politics of intellectual work. Furthermore what is most immediately striking is how many of today's leading historians were intellectually formed in the milieu of British Communism from the late 1930s to the early 1950s. Christopher Hill, Victor Kiernan, Rodney Hilton, Eric Hobsbawm, George Thomson, Royden Harrison, Raphael Samuel, Edward Thompson, Dorothy Thompson, Leslie Morton, George Rudé – it is a formidable array. 'These were the people', writes Hobsbawm,

> who would make their way . . . through what memory recalls mainly as the dank, cold and slightly foggy morning streets of Clerkenwell to Marx House or to the upper room of the Garibaldi Restaurant, Laystall Street, armed with cyclo-styled agendas, sheets of 'theses' or summary arguments, for the debates of the moment.[1]

The Group, it appears, had its own touch of romantic ardour. Fascism had been defeated, a radical and popular movement generated in the War symbolized the aspirations and potential for social reconstruction, and to these young Communists history *mattered*. Why it was that so many outstanding intellectuals were attracted both to the Communist Party and to the study of history is itself an intriguing question which I can only touch on here. But for anyone curious about the formation of history as a component in the national intellectual culture the role of the Communist Party in the 1940s must play a crucial part in any analysis.

The decision to organize the Historians' Group developed from the need to discuss a new edition of A. L. Morton's *A People's History of England*, first pub-lished in 1938 by the Left Book Club. As Raphael Samuel has perceptively commented this was a text which marked the closing of a tradition of popular,

* Thanks are due to the other editors of this volume and to Michael Green, Stuart Hall and Rodney Hilton for comments on drafts.

political and non-academic history-writing, explicitly agitational and synthesizing in its objectives.[2] Within the Communist Party such histories had typically relied on the skills of activist-intellectuals closely drawn into the day to day organizational (especially journalistic) work of the Party. Few of the authors were educated at university and fewer still received much formal training in history. (Morton was a rare exception having spent two years at Cambridge studying history.) From the middle or late 1930s this genre of historiography gave way to the work of professional historians, although not till much later did this become predominantly university-based: involvement in schooling and, most of all, in adult education was characteristic. Indeed it could be argued that adult education was *the* medium through which the Group's histories were organized.

In part, this greater professionalization may be an instance of the protracted disintegration and diversification of the nineteenth-century intellectual aristocracy and the expansion of a new professional lower middle class, a change in class composition associated with the long formative period of monopoly capitalism. In a discussion of the Bloomsbury Group, Raymond Williams has drawn attention to the modernization and liberalization of the English intelligentsia at the time of the First World War and the 1920s, arguing also that there occurred at the end of the nineteenth century 'a comprehensive development and reform of the professional and cultural life of bourgeois England'. The emergence of the historians, for the most part as paid, professional intellectuals, should be situated within this context. An implicit argument which runs through this essay, however, is that it was not only their numbers which expanded, but also the function of such intellectuals.[3]

One aspect of this transformation, especially after the winning of universal constitutional rights in 1918 and 1928 and the consequent restructuring of the political field, was the new forms in which political issues were articulated to theoretical ideologies. Changing constructions around the concept of 'the people' are of the first importance. Such concepts were often closely tied to the problem of 'culture' or 'popular culture'. In the 1930s the ideologies most highly charged in this respect were grouped around the themes of literary criticism. In the post-war world the growing and influential discipline of sociology was perhaps the most important. In this chapter I want to trace how external political determinations registered inside the historiography itself. For example, the very title of Morton's book marks with precision the continuing, constitutive concerns of the Communist Party historians of the 1940s and 1950s. A central element in their project focused on the relation of 'nation' to 'people'. Through an excavation of the historiography it may prove possible to pinpoint the extent to which the Historians' Group effected a major, qualitative contribution to the concept of the 'national-popular', although it needs to be spelt out from the start that this is only a single theme which runs through some of the histories.

No extensive assessment of the Historians' Group is attempted here: even to treat it as a single entity may appear quite suspect when more work has been done on the sections which composed the Group (such as the four period sections, or those of the professional historians and the teachers); I hardly touch on the relation between the historians and the Party as such (liaison with the Cultural Committee, the Party press, the industrial organizations, the Peace Movement, and the whole problem of democratic centralism); nor is there space for detailed treatment of those activities which the Group inspired (the long struggle to organize local history groups, the celebration of significant anniversaries – such as the Albert Hall pageant to commemorate 1848, heroically performing a dramatized version of *The Communist Manifesto*); nor do I examine the ambitious schemes which (by 1956) failed to materialize (the books which never got written, the attempts to intervene in the production of school histories, the plan to set up a Labour and Socialist History Society). My account is weighted towards an intellectual history and to the histories written by the professional historians. What interested me most was the developing concern with 'the battle of ideas' (or 'the B of I' in the jargon of the day) and how this was linked to the question of the production of historical knowledge. This of course cannot be resolved without investigating the range of material and institutional forms which constituted the dominant apparatuses of historical scholarship, and the specific barriers these imposed which constrained the possibilities for connecting with popular ideologies in this period. My account, in sum, may appear rather fragmented. First, I examine the critical influence of Maurice Dobb; second, I sketch some of the salient political and cultural conditions of the formation and early years of the Historians' Group; then I look at some aspects of the historiography; and last at the problem of nation and people.

The history of the Communist Party itself has not yet been produced for this period, so caution is called for. Equally significant, although perhaps less immediately obvious, an approach such as the one adopted here can persistently threaten to short-circuit the complex passage which links the politics of historiography to political practice, for as we maintain throughout this book, the nexus history–theory–politics is always constructed by multiple, complex and potentially conflicting strands. Inevitably I concentrate here more on the politics of the histories than the history of the politics.[4]

Maurice Dobb

Eric Hobsbawm states that at the time the Group was formed 'There was no tradition of Marxist history in Britain'.[5] Although this judgement may be much too sharply drawn the point which follows is not, namely that the historians set out to fashion a distinctive body of marxist historiography which was intended both to connect with a popular politics and to engage with the academic establishment itself. The first paradigmatic text came from Dobb in the same year the Historians' Group was founded: according to Hobsbawm 'The major historical work which was to influence us crucially was Maurice Dobb's *Studies in the Development of Capitalism*', who claimed it 'formulated our main and central problem'.[6] It is with Dobb that one must start. His social background was impeccably respectable, conservative and lower middle class, a trajectory disturbed only by his rather swift radicalization between school and university at the very moment of the Armistice.

He studied economics, had a brief spell at the LSE, in 1924 returned to Cambridge for the remainder of his life, associating with Keynes and Piero Sraffa, and eventually rose to a prominent position as an academic economist. He joined the Communist Party in 1921, first visited the Soviet Union in 1925, and although employed full time by Cambridge University seems to have directed most of his energies to the Council of Labour Colleges, the Plebs League, and for a short stint, to the editorship of *Plebs*. What, for the 1920s, is unique about this career and makes him something of a precursor is not that a middle-class university student should become a Communist (although that was exceptional enough) but rather that he should subsequently have taken up employment in the higher reaches of the educational system.[7]

Dobb's contribution to contemporary marxist historiography in Britain and elsewhere is profound, but his relation to the discipline of history is ambivalent.[8] From his decision to switch from history to economics in his first days at university – which he recalled as a political choice – his intellectual formation was essentially within economics, not history. This is not to deny his determination to stretch as far as possible the boundaries of his subject in a direction both historical and 'applied' (the latter, for example, in his lecture courses on wages, welfare etc.). But this primary commitment to economics did tend to separate him from the younger generation of historians. In the 1950s he followed interests in the economics of the Eastern bloc (particularly towards the end of the decade in problems of pricing policy) which diverged quite drastically from the typical concerns of the Historians' Group as a whole. Thus any judgement has to assess the balance of the particular theoretical input derived from his training in economics, and his work on history.

Logic and history

With the publication of the *Studies* in 1946 and *Soviet Economic Development since 1917* in 1948 Dobb's historical writing reached a peak which coincided with the early years of the Historians' Group. Both these works had long been in gestation: the former first saw light as *Capitalist Enterprise and Social Progress* (1925) and the latter as *Russian Economic Development since the Revolution* (1928). The first of these was also his first published work. It was divided clearly between two sections, 'Logic' and 'History'. Looking back, this appears an appropriate start, indicating the persistence of the unusually self-conscious theoretical purpose in all his histories. This explicit concern with 'logic', until the past few years, perhaps, has been uncharacteristic in most marxist historiography in Britain. His immersion in the study of economics involved a prolonged and explicit wrestle with theoretical issues, for far more openly than in history dissensions within economics revolved around differences between various conceptual systems. Crudely, Dobb's broad methodological conclusions could be summarized as three premises: the need for theoretical abstraction; the need to distinguish between determinate (or adequate) and indeterminate (inadequate) abstraction; and the primacy of explanation. Dobb was no philosopher and the conceptual power of his theoretical discourse – especially in its more pragmatic moments – may well seem slight in comparison to those theorists discussed later in this book.[9] What is decisive however, and what makes him seem peculiarly contemporary, is the measure to which he aimed to develop these problems within the field of historiography.

On Dobb's initial premise there is not a great deal to say, as all his work was grounded in a knowledge and appreciation of theoretical economics. Against a naive empiricism he was quite straightforward – 'facts never speak for themselves'.[10] His most abstract book, *Political Economy and Capitalism* (1937) included investigation of some of the theoretical issues which were to reappear in more concrete form in the *Studies*. He noted that for all explanatory work 'a certain level of abstraction is required',[11] and went to some lengths to demonstrate that Marx's critique of classical political economy did not involve a rejection of abstraction. Nor could it be maintained – given Marx's extensive theoretical analysis of the extraction of surplus labour – that the problem of exploitation was essentially ethical, immune to what he called 'rigorous scientific definition'.[12] Dobb's concern with abstraction was linked precisely to the question of structure. To grasp the internal specificities of a particular economic form (a mode of production) he insisted on abstraction – the clarification of a specific field of interconnected concepts – as a necessary precondition for thinking economic relations in their historical complexity. His reading of Marx, especially of *Capital*, was one that was primarily conceptual in its inspiration.

Distinguishing 'good' from 'bad' abstraction is obviously more complicated. As examples of the former it is important to note he included not only Marx's mature theory but also classical political economy itself, both of which he contrasted to vulgar 'modern trends'. All worthwhile theory, he argued, depends on internal logical consistency (and here Dobb seems to have had in mind the equational or mathematical properties of an economic model). Beyond that, determinate abstractions may be constructed by excluding certain variable features, as most clearly demonstrated by Marx in *Capital*. Alternatively 'one may base one's abstraction, not on any evidence of fact as to what features in a situation are essential and what are inessential, but simply on the formal procedure of combining the properties common to a heterogeneous assortment of situations and building abstraction out of analogy'.[13] Against the formation of this second approach, Dobb's is centrally an empirical procedure. Not only does it rely upon initially determining – from 'evidence of fact' – what is more important, but more than anything 'The ultimate criterion must be the requirements of practice: the type of practical question which one requires to answer, the purpose of the inquiry to hand'.[14] The 'ultimate criterion' cannot, therefore, be constant but itself must be shaped by the object of study. The categories change as the object changes, and powerful abstractions are precisely those most open to concretion and *historical* explanation. The key issue in this schema is 'how far one's knowledge is able to *reach*'.[15]

Laying out the conceptual bones of the Dobbian position in this way may confirm for some his pragmatism and empiricism, and for others (not caring for the emphasis on abstraction or 'rigorous scientific categories' in historical explanation) his rationalism. Either way there is no doubting that the drive of the argument is directed towards the moment of explanation, and this is the major theoretical justification embodied in the *Studies*. (In the Preface he scorned a procedure which relegated empirical work to 'verifying' the theoretical categories.) In the opening chapters Dobb juggled with a complex set of connected problems. Overarching all of them is the tension between the 'nihilistic standpoint' of historians whose 'attitude seems to spring from an emphasis upon the variety and complexity of historical events, so great as to reject any of those general categories which form the texture of most theories of historical interpretation', and the functional, anti-historical consequence of hypostatizing conceptual structures which tend 'towards interpreting new situations in categories of thought which were products of past situations and towards super-historical "universal truths", fashioned out of what are deemed to be immutable traits of human nature or certain invariable sorts of economic or social "necessity".'[16] The conjunction of 'theory' and 'history', of the relation between abstraction of general structures and the kaleidoscopic, contingent movements of 'history' forms the very basis of the *Studies*. The conceptual strength of the book – which would need much more extensive, substantive illustration than I can give here – derives from the care with which determinate problems at lower levels of abstraction are thought through in the structured progression from abstract to concrete. Analytically, this is what the book is about. It is made most explicit in its negative counterpoint: 'Economic theory, at least since Jevons and the Austrians, has increasingly been cast in terms of properties that are common to any type of exchange society, and the central economic laws have been formulated at this level of abstraction'. For Dobb, the decisive point is to grasp analytically relations at lower levels, relations which will always be in the process of transformation. For questions of 'economic *development*' he perceived the need to depart from 'in general' categories, 'to shift the focus of economic enquiry from a study of exchange societies in general to a study of the physiology and growth of a specifically capitalist economy'.[17]

Dobb and the historians

To discuss Dobb in this way, highlighting those abstract and formal aspects of his work which he frames most frequently as negative protocols, is paradoxical given his continual stress on substantive criteria for assessment. It might also result in quite an unjust appraisal in that his most positive contribution to historiography may ultimately lie more in his interpretation of the formation of capitalism than in the construction of *general* theoretical or methodological maxims. But this approach has been made necessary on two counts. It is important to be aware of the fact that the 1970s revival of theoretical issues within marxism, in so far as it touched on historiography, pointed to questions which had received pioneering, if provisional, treatment from Dobb at the very moment of the creation and crystallization of an indigenous marxist historiography.

Second, Dobb is now getting pulled and pushed in every direction. E. P. Thompson in *The Poverty of Theory* claims that Dobb, Thompson himself and all the marxist historians discussed in this chapter form a single theoretical tradition on the grounds that they were or are all committed to marxism as an open, empirical method of historical investigation. Certainly Dobb and Thompson share at least that much, but it is slender evidence for announcing a theoretical tradition. Indeed, Dobb's rejection of apriorism and rationalism, but consequent refusal thereby to ditch all formal or epistemological matters is radically removed from the position outlined in *The Poverty of Theory* (see Chapter 3), just as Dobb's insistence on the centrality of abstraction to marxist history, as exemplified in Marx's own critique of political economy in *Capital*, is at odds with Thompson's dismissal of the mature Marx. Whereas Thompson sees the Marx of *Capital* locked into an idealist, self-propagating maze of categories, divorced from real social relations, Dobb is at pains to demonstrate how abstraction from historically concrete circuits of capital is an integral and necessary moment in marxist historical inquiry in order even to reach the concrete as the ensemble of 'many determinations'.

These are more than local qualifications. They signal distinct problematics which, if any sense is to be made of marxist historiography in Britain since the War, need to be identified in their specificity. Simon Clarke has recognized this need for specification and argues against Thompson on this point. But by inflating difference to such heady, exaggerated proportions, Clarke contends that because of the 'fatal flaw' of Dobb's reductionism, absolutely no connection can be countenanced between Dobb and Thompson, Hobsbawm, Hilton and Hill. Even on empirical grounds this is nonsense, since it suppresses a whole web of shared acknowledgements and debts.[18] It also ignores the extent to which Dobb opened up and pioneered a historiography to which all the Communist Party historians owed a substantial debt, even if real conceptual differences (and refinements) were to emerge in the course of the 1940s and 1950s.

There is no need for the purposes of this article to get caught up in the vortex of detail and complexity of the debates on the transition from feudalism to capitalism which followed the publication of *Studies in the Development of Capitalism.*[19] However some brief comments are necessary. The first round of the debate was opened in 1950 by Paul Sweezy in the North American journal *Science and Society.* It was international in scope and marked a vital moment in establishing a creative marxist historiography. The very terms of the discussion were steeped in theoretical insight, ranging from commentaries on the logical structure of the categories in *Capital* to breathtaking surveys of the feudal economy. It is difficult to gauge with precision exactly what impact this made on the British historians as a whole. We know that Christopher Hill and Rodney Hilton intervened: Hilton to dispose of Pirenne (on whom Sweezy heavily relied for his attack on Dobb) and to emphasize the struggle over surplus labour as a factor 'internal' to the decline of feudalism, and Hill to address the problem of the ruling class in fifteenth- and sixteenth-century England, the period of absolutism. Yet it is sometimes forgotten that the debate itself was substantially the product of the work of the British marxists: in the pages of *Science and Society* the only contributors apart from Dobb, Hill and Hilton were Sweezy himself and Takahashi.

Although the debates in *Science and Society* are justly celebrated, a better idea of the milieu from which the *Studies* emerged can be gauged from the earlier debates between the British Communist historians on the nature of the English Revolution. The British historians showed little enthusiasm for developing a general theory of transition. Rather, they endeavoured to analyse the particular variants of absolutism – the nationally specific state formations in the era of late feudalism. Thus the questions posed by Hill in his contribution to *Science and Society* were: 'What was the *ruling* class of this period? How are we to characterize the state?'. And he went on to note that 'these specific problems were debated in some detail by the English Marxist historians in 1940 and again in 1946–7'.[20] Christopher Hill was himself the central figure in this respect. His chosen field of study was the seventeenth century. In 1935 he spent a long period studying in the Soviet Union (where, given Russian social conditions, the historiography of absolutism was perhaps the most advanced in the world and certainly the most politically charged) in close association with E. A. Kosminsky.[21] It was the publication of his *The English Revolution* in 1940 which provoked 'PF' (who, it appears, was Jürgen Kuczynski) to attack wholesale the claim that the 1640s in England witnessed a social revolution commensurate with the great French or Russian Revolutions. The gist of Kuczynski's critique was that the breakthrough to capitalism had been achieved in the early sixteenth century, with the clear implication that the 1640s should be understood as a counter-revolution. After a good deal of discussion this controversy was dropped early in 1941, and only taken up again much later, in 1948, when the collective History Group's article on 'State and revolution in Tudor and Stuart England' restated the Hill position.[22] This was a crucial debate for the Communist historians, more so perhaps than the *Science and Society* response to *Studies in the Development of Capitalism*. These points may strengthen the suspicion that the distinctive tenor of the British marxism was more fully historical than Sweezy's general perspective.

Sweezy's dominant concern was to establish theoretically the laws of motion of feudalism and capitalism and to think their logical, as much as their historical, conditions of transformation. Takahashi's objective was to demonstrate that this had a legitimate warrant in Dobb (and in Marx). The characteristic focus within the British historiography was on the English social formation and the question of absolutism. This too followed closely from Dobb. But in general the latter concern showed far less preoccupation with those logical issues proposed by Dobb. Emphatically, this is not to assert that marxist historical writing in Britain was 'untheoretical' after Dobb. (Although when in the History Group there were complaints about the poor theoretical showing of the historians and it was perceived that 'basic discussion on historical materialism was badly needed', it was Dobb they turned to.[23]) It is the case, however, that the problem of 'logic' in the explicit Dobbian sense ultimately tended to become much more impacted, sub-merged and concealed – indeed, historicized – within the histories themselves.

The lines of continuity linking Dobb to the other British historians can't be dissolved retrospectively, in the light of subsequent inroads made into economism. In the opening chapter of the *Studies* Dobb noted that many of the questions which were to be raised by his investigation could not be satisfactorily answered 'unless the existing frontier between what is fashionable to label as "economic factors" and as "social factors" is abolished'.[24] Much ink has been spilt in proving that this was inadequately achieved by Dobb and that he was consistently pulled towards economism. By and large this is right, although in itself it doesn't tell us very much. Robert Brenner offers the most judicious assessment when he argues that Dobb neither ignored political and cultural relations nor thought them simple reflections of an economic base, but did in the end counterpose the economic to the political and cultural.[25] This difficulty registers in the very heart of Dobb's inquiry, for the strength of his economic explanation is offset by much too thin a presentation of the seventeenth-century Revolution. This failure was compounded by his indecisive reading of the period in England from the collapse of commutation in the fifteenth century to the Revolution of 1640. To a large degree this was an effect of Dobb's (and Sweezy's) incomplete abolition of that frontier.[26] At critical moments in the debate 'mode of production' categories established at a high level of abstraction in order to determine abstract laws of motion were conflated with the historically concrete determinations of a social formation. In effect, the problem of how to assess when a society becomes 'capit-alist', and what criteria should be employed, was left unresolved.

But we need to be reminded of Hobsbawm's observation that it was Dobb who developed the 'main and central' issues for the Historians' Group. Primarily the *Studies* was appropriated by the British Communists for its imaginative account of the economic conditions of the long transition to modern capitalism in England, the period of primitive accumulation. At the heart of this account was the attempt to think the long duration of transition as a history generated by *struggle*. Dobb's conceptualization of mode of production took for its foundation the analysis of the extraction of surplus labour; the key internal determination of the transition – its prime mover – was pinpointed as the struggle to impose 'over-exploitation' and, as an inseparable dimension of this process, resistance and protest. In these formulations he focused, as I have argued, on the conceptual structure of produc-tive relations, on the internally defining properties (or structures) of different modes of extraction of surplus which condition struggle.

It is evident that Dobb's emphasis on structure was conceptual, primarily a means to *think* historical issues. He didn't reify structures such that they became 'things' in history itself, precluding human agency. Indeed in all his work, struggle was the key which unlocked problems of transition and transformation. However, it also needs to be realized that although this methodological standpoint tended to view struggle, in its various forms, as itself a determinant and a producer of a new complex of (economic) relations, in its unintended effects the accumulation of past struggles was also seen by Dobb as producing new sets of social relations; and these in turn circumscribed the possibilities for future forms of struggle and agency. Thus the extent to which specific actions break up old relations and produce new ones can only be answered historically, as for example in analysing the dramatically differentiated outcomes of the seventeenth-century crisis in East and West Europe. This difficult question of 'structural' ways of thinking struggle is dealt with in greater detail in Chapter 5. All I want to do here is to suggest that the problem was one which Dobb began to explore in his historiography, and although the results were rather uneven, the attempt centrally to theorize struggle as a factor in the transition to capitalism provides a further reason for distinguishing Dobb's work from a simple economism. If it was economistic, it was a complex, struggle-directed 'limit-case' economism, concentrating on economic relations in their combination, which provided the basis for histories analytically more sophisticated than the evolutionary, narrative sweeps through centuries of history which had characterized the more ambitious marxist historical writing before the 1940s.

The most fruitful point of contact between Dobb and the English historians was this stress on the struggle of the common people who were forcibly separated from their customary means of production by the expanding regime of capital. Or it may be more true to say that this was the overriding *potential* of Dobb's contribution, for pivotal theoretical questions raised by Dobb were never fully followed up. Hill's first interpretation of the seventeenth-century Revolution (in which – to caricature – capitalism burst through a decaying feudal order and classes acted out their ordained roles) was explicitly recast in the light of *Studies in the Development of Capitalism.*[27] The historians' reading of Dobb (and indeed of *Capital*) concentrated on the historical explanation of primitive accumulation in England. In turn, the history of the revolutionary and democratic struggles of the subordinate classes, of 'the people', also came to be rethought.

Culture and 'the people'

This short survey of Dobb's theoretical innovations indicates some of the primary conceptual conditions which underpinned the transformation in marxist historiography at the end of the 1940s. What I haven't touched on is the altered conception of the *role* of theory within historical materialism. In general in this period the histories became more substantially founded analytically, engaging with other historical interpretations rather than providing an alternative narrative account premised on 'the materialist conception of history'. Although discussion has focused on Dobb the impulse for these changes was clearly not due to him alone. The very process of professionalization itself, the distancing of the production of histories from immediate and daily political practice, the drawing inwards to talk and meet amongst themselves as historians – all of these factors would need to be considered. But attention to theory as logic (in a contemporary sense) can be misleading. It would be wrong to suppose that the major aim of the Historians' Group was to develop an internally, theoretically self-sufficient marxist historiography. (However it would be interesting to know more about the epistemological grounds on which a specifically marxist history was defended: the anti-conservative initiative in this respect was won by E. H. Carr in 1961 with his *What is History?*.) On the contrary, its primary purpose was directed much more to the anglicization of the marxist tradition, demonstrating its compatibility with a native idiom of critical social theory.[28]

This radical tradition was conceived as the theoretical framework for a popular political strategy and as a resource for the creation of a politics appropriate to nationally specific conditions. The intention was to reactivate a national-popular consciousness and in this the Group cultivated a profound sense of *Englishness*, which called for a major reassessment of English cultural and political history from the seventeenth century and before. In part, to generate a new popular sense of history *was* the theory. Far from theoretical closure this depended on appropriating for marxism the indigenous radical liberal historiography (and explains the overture to Tawney at the end of the 1940s). On this, writing in the 1950s, Hobsbawm was explicit: 'Marxists . . . believe that their method alone enables us to provide a successor to the old "Liberal-Radical" view of British history which will be adequate in science and scholarship, while giving the citizens of this country a coherent picture of our national development and answering their questions'.[29] One direct (and deliberate) result of this was *Past and Present*, emerging in 1952 straight from the orbit of the Communist Historians' Group with Hobsbawm, Dobb, Hill and Hilton all included on its first editorial board. But in no sense did the journal serve as a tactical front for the Communists. Its policy was to publish the best historical material and in so doing, implicitly, to effect that historiographical alliance with – and, ideally, supersede – the non-marxist radical histories. (None the less, as the editorial to the fourth issue illustrated, the journal was greeted with 'whispered imputations of sectarianism and tendentious bias'.) This intellectual strategy indicates not only a belief in the conceptual viability (and superiority) of a marxist theory of history, but also its potential for competing with non-marxist histories on professional and scholarly criteria. The intention was to match the bourgeois historians on their own ground of historical scholarship.[30] For this purpose, the 'correct' position could no longer serve as a sufficient guarantee.

This perspective on theory – anglicization and the popularization of a new sense of history – had its political conditions both in the politics of the 1930s and the first half of the forties, and more specifically within the Communist Party itself. The origins of the predominant intellectual concerns of the Historians' Group can be located in the Popular Front strategy and the radical movement of the War. The first years of the Group coincided with the onset of the Cold War and, in 1951, the acceptance by the Communist Party of a new programme, distinctly national in orientation, *The British Road to Socialism*. The combination of these events instilled in the historiography a peculiar conception of 'the people'. The programme embodied in *The British Road to Socialism* dropped the Party's commitment to soviet power (i.e. soviets or workers' councils as an alternative to parliament), bound the Party to a strategy by which Britain would reach socialism 'by her own road', and outlined the parliamentary route to socialism based on a 'broad popular alliance' in place of the soviet scenario of dual power. It declared that 'the people of Britain can transform capitalist democracy into a real People's Democracy, transforming Parliament, the product of Britain's historic struggle for democracy, into the democratic will of the vast majority of her people'.[31] The people; the historic struggle for democracy; the nation, – these are the elements which combined in the various strains of CP populism of the period.

Populisms

The origins of communist populism can be identified in the turn against the so-called Third Period ('class against class') of the Communist International at its Seventh Congress in 1935.[32] In the struggle against fascism the strategy of the Popular Front was inaugurated which first and foremost depended on the defence of constitutional liberties. Two further political themes were raised. First, the conception of 'progressive forces' was broadened to include 'the people' rather than *simply* the proletariat. Second, under pressures from the Italian Communist Party (in particular its leader Palmiro Togliatti) a notion of 'new democracy' was elaborated in which the immediate objective in the fight against fascism was neither to establish a dictatorship of the proletariat nor to restore bourgeois democracy in its pre-existing form, but to create an expanded democratic regime. (Hobsbawm, interviewing Giorgio Napolitano in the 1970s, gently chided him with the reminder that: 'The theory of a democracy of a new type, as you call it, was not solely and strictly an Italian perspective. The English Communist Party discussed this problem too, at the Seventh Congress'.[33] The British Party, although formally committed to a soviet route until 1951, broadly followed the perspectives opened in 1935 by the inauguration of the Popular Fronts.

One further point needs the greatest emphasis. The political switch in the objectives of the international communist movement produced new political conditions which carried the potential for reconstituting marxist historiography on new terms. This is clarified most succinctly by a statement by Dimitrov, in many ways the architect of the Popular Fronts. He declared

The fascists are rummaging through the entire history of every nation so as to be able to pose as the heirs and continuators of all that was exalted and heroic in the past.

And he went on to criticize those Communists

who do nothing *to link up the present struggle with the people's revolutionary traditions and past.*[34]

James Klugmann, just before he died, explained what this meant for Communists in Britain:

We became the inheritors of the Peasants' Revolt, of the left of the English revolution, of the pre-Chartist movement, of the women's suffrage movement from the 1790s to today. It set us in the right framework, *it linked us with the past* and gave us a more correct course for the future.[35]

According to this overall conception the production of historical knowledge is itself, necessarily, a practice constituted in and by ideology, not in the simple sense of the partisan commitments of the author (or not only in this sense) but rather because of the complex means by which histories can connect with, and reconstruct, the terrain of popular culture by redefining its history. (See Chapter 6 on popular memories.) The struggle which fixes this ideological-cultural field is staked on a democratic or reactionary articulation of the elements of 'people' and 'nation'. Thus Dimitrov's analysis depended on the recognition that fascist movements effectively had activated a popular authoritarian 'memory' or history, drawing from and reorganizing nationalistic sentiment. The unambiguous conclusion to be drawn from this insight was the political urgency of 're-discovering' (or re-creating) the democratic traditions of the national-popular.

Science

Politically, the Popular Fronts of the 1930s were built on anti-fascism and, in Britain, the desperate struggle against appeasement. Theoretically, however, the dominant way of thinking socialism in Britain was cast in a paradigm imported from the natural sciences.[36] The force of this paradigm was immense, and was destined to shadow the historians through the 1950s, only being resolved, with any finality, in a new conjuncture of political conditions after 1956. The marxism of the Second and Third Internationals had long been associated with science, cohering around a defence of reason, atheism and the development of the forces of production, which was accentuated in the 1930s to combat the mystical 'unreason' of fascism.[37] But peculiarly in Britain from the end of the 1920s this was licensed by the intellectual hegemony of a dazzling mix of Communists and socialists who were steeped in the values of Cambridge High Science: J. D. Bernal, J. B. S. Haldane, Lancelot Hogben, Hyman Levy, Joseph Needham. Many of the leading 'intellectual' positions (in the narrow sense) within the Communist Party were held by the natural scientists – so when the *Modern Quarterly* was founded in 1938 as the Party's theoretical journal more than half of its editorial board were scientists. As a *general tendency*, when translated into political practice, this sort of marxism could severely circumscribe the active role and agency of the people themselves. It could result in a programme of technocratic, state collectivism in which the planned economy was to be secured through the competences of scientific experts.[38] 'Science' was to be rescued from its abuses – from the 'perversion of scientific discovery to ignoble and injurious ends' as it was expressed in the Introduction to the opening issue of the *Modern Quarterly* – and recruited for socialism. Thus socialism was construed as the fulfilment of science, as the ultimate, rational control of nature by humankind. Not only did this underestimate the ideological structuring of scientific knowledge but its logic marginalized the self-emancipation of the popular masses. Socialism would be organized through the apparatuses of the rational state, as a 'passive' revolution. Clearly, this does not provide a particularly fertile terrain from which to recover popular, democratic traditions.

Even if the ultimate effects of this rendering of marxism tended to weaken the popular constitution of socialist politics, this is not to deny that it touched deep on a popular chord. One of the most fascinating aspects of British marxism in the 1930s is the conjunction of the Cambridge High Science paradigm of the trained intellectuals with the resilient popular traditions of science, materialism and secularism of the rank and file autodidacts, which have been charted so sensitively by Macintyre.[39] A veneration of knowledge as 'science', in the mode of Victorian positivism, was popular in the socialist movement long after it had waned with dominant intellectuals. Marxism in Britain was rooted in this popular materialist tradition and this must go some way in explaining the dominance of the Cambridge scientists in so completely defining marxist theory in the 1930s.

As formulated by Bernal this abrasively scientific marxism did have its own interpretation of history (and the scientists were themselves prolific and imaginative historians), which was primarily drawn from the later writings of Engels:

History has been the record of human intentions, of human actions, and of events which were more often than not very different from the ends consciously aimed at. It was the field of action of forces that could only be dimly guessed at, and were far too easily identified with superior beings whose playthings were men. As we come to see more in history than this, as we begin to understand something of these forces and the laws they must obey, the events of history will become the results of conscious planning and achievement. With the discovery of the science of society, as Engels said, the true history of mankind begins.[40]

From history could be learned the laws of social systems which in turn would guide the reasoned, planned society of the future. There is much here integral to any conception of socialism; but in the following years, the inflections and tone became substantially modified.

The British road to socialism

If the Popular Front can ever be said to have emerged in Britain, it was during the War, which itself[41] built on the mounting resolve of a broad, popular movement against fascism in which 'people' and 'nation' fused in a peculiarly intense, mobilizing combination. If the Seventh Congress of the Comintern outlined the strategic direction of a popular Communist politics it was the experience of the War itself which actually gave it substance; without doubt this was the experience which proved most common and formative for the new generation of Communist historians (most of whom joined the Party after the 1935 reversal in policy). The determinations which gave such coherence to this national-popular movement are only slowly beginning to be unravelled; what has proved most difficult to explain was its speedy decline by 1947-8. The external (parliamentary, diplomatic) conditions of this decline have been acknowledged in most histories. The *national*-popular was sunk by the severities of the Cold War, smashed under the impact of Natoization, Marshallization and Britain's turn westwards for the special relationship with the USA. And the *popular* reflexes, the deepest resources of the movement, were broken (destined for Ealing Studios) under the structural weights of a reactivated Fabianized collectivism and the dissipation of energies channelled into an excessively parliamentary arena of struggle. E. P. Thompson was later to recall the nature of the 1945 Labour Government by arguing that: 'The socialist meanings of each reform were surrendered . . . (and) as each surrender took place, the socialist movement weakened in morale and direction, and the protagonists of capitalism gained in brashness and aggression'.[42]

This immediate post-war conjuncture precipitated a major crisis inside the Communist Party.[43] The constraints imposed by the Cold War hit hard and fast. Pressures increased for intellectual conformity, as can be judged from the dislocating effects of the theoretical controversies: on Lysenko internationally and on Caudwell within the British Party (1950-1). The Yugoslav crisis from 1948 cut right into the heart of the international communist movement, a conflict which initiated further calls for a higher pitch of Party loyalty. Outside the Party members encountered sustained pressures from the Right which were to develop by the end of the forties into a peculiarly English distillation of McCarthyism.[44] This crisis did not immediately disrupt the internal intellectual configuration of the Party. According to Werskey 'the scientific Left was still, in 1945, in its ascendancy'.[45] But neither the unambivalent faith in science (after its destructive potential had been demonstrated in all its horror by the 'Bomb') nor that in technocratic planning (after the shared collective memory of 'pulling through' during the War, offset by the Labour experiments in a state collectivism which so thoroughly excluded popular controls) were as uncontested as in the 1930s. (And the anti-socialist, anti-science, anti-totalitarian novels of Koestler and Orwell certainly did their work.) Within the Party as a whole the models for the British road to socialism were taken as the East European democracies. 'The idea of a British road to socialism became incorporated into a family of People's Democracies which embraced the existing states in East Europe and future socialist Britain.'[46]

It is arguable how far this conception of the popular drew from elements which underpinned the scientistic view characterized as 'Bernalism', and how far it was an attempt, in politically inimical conditions in which the Left had been contained, to recover, reappropriate and politicize the popular aspirations of the 1940s for the coming decade.[47] To what extent, if at all, there may have been those inspired by positions of political 'revisionism' opposed both to sovietism and to the Party's commitment to an Eastern European model of People's Democracy (a model which, in any event, could carry various connotations), I don't know. There is some evidence – unfortunately in hindsight – that critics of the official line in the Caudwell controversy may have seen themselves as 'proto-revisionists'.[48] These are important political questions which this chapter makes no attempt to answer. But what can be said is this: the defining intellectual concerns of the Historians' Group appear to have been, decisively, theorizations of the national-popular political culture generated in the War. Whether these concerns were considered 'revisionist' or not by the historians, there was no *pressing* reason why these intellectual matters couldn't coexist with the programme of *The British Road to Socialism*. Both the Party and its Historians' Group held the commitment to people, nation and the historic struggle for democracy.

Cultural radicalism

Thus the Communist Party Historians' Group represented a particular *intellectual* tendency, producing a distinctive notion of 'the people'; it aimed to recover in theory (historiography) the high points of the popular politics of the 1940s; and this resulted in an alternative conception to that of the scientists, but one which nevertheless remained open to differing political readings. *Implicit* within this project – in theorizing both class *and* people – was a non-economistic or non-reductionist marxism. I have sketched some of the general and theoretical influences on the historiography: the missing element in this outline is the source for a specifically cultural analysis.

In all their articles throughout the 1940s the historians (although Dobb less so) stressed as a formal premise their opposition to an economic reductionism, which was understood as a mindless vulgarization of marxism. This is clear also from the emphasis on 'the battle of ideas'. One initial factor which seems to have been of some importance was literary theory and literary criticism. Perry Anderson has commented on the nationally peculiar location of social and cultural critique concentrated in literary criticism, drawing attention particularly to F. R. Leavis and the *Scrutiny* tradition.[49] In this displacement of cultural critique into literature the Communist Party did not greatly differ: one need only think of the caricatures of the Communist poets and literary figures of the 1930s to see at least some truth in this. There is evidence that the historians followed the debates within literature and literary criticism almost as closely, or as closely, as in history;[50] some studied English literature at university and only came to history through politics; Hobsbawm, on applying to Cambridge, was torn between choosing Downing College because of Leavis, or Trinity because of Dobb; in the 1930s Morton was as much engaged in literary themes as historical (he later claimed that it was *The Waste Land* which 'seized the imagination of my generation') and contributed to Eliot's *Criterion*; and the deepest intellectual controversy in the Party in the postwar years, significantly, focused on Caudwell and aesthetics. But I think it can be argued that there began in the 1940s a realignment within intellectual marxism from the dominance of a scientific or literary discourse to one which was historiographical, and furthermore that this also challenged the dominance of the literary paradigm for the study of *culture*. With the political transition in the Communist Party from 1935 to 1951, and the new 'professional' attention to theoretical engagement and scholarship, this shift can be understood as part of a specific conjuncture of events from which developed the defining concerns of the marxist historiography of the 1950s – and in some degree, of today, for there is a direct lineage from the Communist Historians' Group to the cultural histories of the 1960s and 1970s.

In the debates on the formation of capitalism, the developing attention to cultural issues is clearly marked. The particular interests of the individual historians took on new and various aspects leading in any number of directions. One is especially relevant for it is an indication of a programmatic, explicit and intentional adherence to 'culture'. In 1951 Dobb published an essay on 'The role of the economic factor in historical materialism'[51] which conceptually and in temperament was rather distant from the complex economism of the *Studies*. It is a text which, in abstract, *posed the problem* of the relative autonomy of the cultural. Alongside this, in the following year his friend, coworker and Party member Rodney Hilton published 'Capitalism – what's in a name?' in the first number of *Past and Present* and this too, at least implicitly, invited a reassessment of the reductions lodged inside the Dobbian account of the formation and development of capitalism. None of the condensed and fleeting formulations in themselves are now very remarkable. But Hilton's confident aside that 'Since men make their own history' it is vital for historians to grasp 'the political and social consciousness of the various classes'[52] in fact pointed to – as completely uncontentious – a whole dimension of history about which Dobb had been all but silent. This concern with cultural problems no doubt had diverse sources (and it's difficult to think that Christopher Hill was not one of them); it also had a much longer history among the historians than is apparent from the publication of these two articles. One critical index is that at the end of 1949, inspired most of all by the sixteenth- and seventeenth-century-period group, a conference was organized by the historians on 'The role of ideas in class struggle'; one of its objectives was to discuss the question 'How is the ideology of a ruling class imposed upon the masses and what are the stages which lead to its ultimate rejection and overthrow by them?'[53] Furthermore, a number of highly influential cultural histories had been published early in the 1940s.[54] Whatever the exact nature of the submerged history which these publications indicate it would seem that in the closing years of the 1940s and the very early 1950s the Communist historians established – *within historiography* – a novel commitment to investigate culture in a way which was all but absent from the Party histories of the 1930s, from Dobb's *Studies*, and (with some exceptions) from the most impressive academic historiography of the day, the flourishing body of economic histories.

It would seem reasonable to assume that in the prolonged and uneven transmission of cultural concerns from a marxism characteristically literary to one historical, traces of the former paradigm would coexist and be reproduced in the latter. Indeed the power of the literary discourse, as *the* definer of culture, by and large was inescapable for cultural theorists of the 1940s. The process of formation of an embryonic cultural historiography took place throughout the 1950s (and later), and although it may still be right to see the 1963 publication of *The Making of the English Working Class* as the definitive 'arrival' of a cultural history, this should not obliterate the fact that it marks not only the opening of new territory but also in some respects a culmination of a previous set of historical investigations. Here I want to touch on the question of how, in the very origins of this process, the forming of a specifically cultural history may have worked through the terrain defined by literary theory. What follows, especially the section on *Scrutiny*, needs to be situated with some care. My concern is with the conditions of the protracted emergence of cultural histories. In the immediate conjuncture of the post-war years, and into the 1950s, it is undeniable that the spirit of economic history was strongest among the Communist historians. For many of the historians *Scrutiny* and the debates about aesthetics would have been marginal at most. My interest in this part of the chapter lies in looking first at the development of cultural histories and second at the possible *resources* which existed for the production of marxist cultural histories. Only within these narrow parameters is the following argument pertinent.

To what degree marxist aesthetics and criticism were influential, I'm not sure, although we can suppose some connections. Caudwell had a compelling impact from the time he started writing (recently reconfirmed by Thompson); Alick West in *Crisis and Criticism* (1937) explored the theoretical relations between romanticism and marxism, a resonant preoccupation of the later historiography; and in *The Novel and the People* (1937) Ralph Fox touched on matters of literary and popular cultures which, again, were to be raised later in the histories. Together with those who wrote for *Left Review* (1934-8), these were pioneering marxists in cultural theory in Britain who set about undermining – and who were in *the process* of breaking from – the entrenched preconceptions of a mechanical marxism.[55] (When in *Culture and Society* Raymond Williams examined the subject of marxism and culture it was to Caudwell, Fox and West that he automatically turned.) The legacy of these theorists has been debated with some frequency in recent years and I can't deal with the arguments and counter-arguments here. But without undercutting the immediate value of this body of work, it does not seem that, in sum, it depended upon a method of inquiry which could claim any deep sense of history. This may sound contentious. Anyone can point to the historical organization of some of the major themes developed in literary theory of the 1930s – most especially, the rise and imminent disintegration of bourgeois culture. But I think Mulhern is right to suggest that this is a classic case of a history exclusively preoccupied with the problem of origins, and hardly at all with an *explanatory*, constitutive historical analysis of specific cultural formations.[56] Typically the grandiose, synthesizing attempts to unite theoretically marxism and aesthetics collapsed under the weight of their own ambitions, requiring today the skills of an archaeologist to uncover and assess the broken fragments.

Alongside this, the existence of *Scrutiny* itself – the decisive intervention in cultural theory in the 1930s – must not be ignored, especially in its attempts to become 'party' in the broad, Gramscian sense. In so far as this inaugurated a historical sociology of popular and high cultures its very programme amounted to an entire rethinking of English cultural history from the seventeenth century. In some respects *Scrutiny*'s conception of history paralleled that of the marxists of the 1930s, predicated on a teleology leading to cultural collapse. It makes little difference to the power it exerted that this history was entirely unsubstantiated and quite mythical in its make-up. It too was directed against a mechanical materialism; and some of its developing conclusions – the stress on values, on experience – were to complement those which later emerged in some marxist cultural analysis. But perhaps more than anything the wild and provocative premises of *Scrutiny* history must surely have provided a challenge to the very politics of a marxist historiography – especially as, in outline, the respective narrative trajectories shadowed each other so closely. The exact weight of *Scrutiny*'s presence has to be carefully measured for current assessment of the impact of Leavis is tending to be elevated and exaggerated out of all proportion. (Alick West's 1937 analysis of criticism, for instance, devoted chapters to Eliot, Read and Richards, but not a word to Leavis.)

What can be noted from the outset is the similar social position and concerns of the Scrutineers and those Communists who were to form the Historians' Group. Both were composed of newly professionalized intellectuals. Both groups were threatened, and appalled, by the depth of the economic crisis. Members of both groups lived the protracted disintegration of liberalism as an intellectual system. In the first instance they existed as derided figures on the margins of national academic life. (Only much later were both groups to be integrated into the highest echelons of universities with all the pomp of their professorships.)[57] In their different and contrasting ways the intellectuals in each grouping felt an urgent *mission* to safeguard the very future of civilization which so visibly seemed to be under immediate threat of disintegration in the 1930s.

Direct contact between the Communists and *Scrutiny* was not great, but none the less of interest. Morton and Hill both contributed. Morton's conclusion was clear: '*Scrutiny* is too valuable a weapon against the Philistines to be left permanently in the position of the two heroes who "wept like anything to see such quantities of sand"'.[58] Hill's *English Revolution* was reviewed by L. C. Knights. In addition there developed *Scrutiny*'s continual shadow-boxing with marxism which broke into the open in Leavis's 'Under which king, Bezonian?' in which Dobb and Morton got irritably cuffed; and a much more respectful analysis of 'History and the marxian method' by Herbert Butterfield in which Dobb was partially vindicated. A final bout between Hill and Leavis took place in 1947 in the pages of *Politics and Letters* where Leavis found the article he was defending 'so obviously reasonable' that by this time he must have been convinced of Hill's intellectual perversity. From these exchanges it could be supposed that the historians, as a Group, would have had quite close knowledge of *Scrutiny*. Moreover, its programme derived from a cultural critique so dramatic it drove its enemies in academic life to apoplexy. Even if not followed in detail it seems impossible that the historians remained untouched by the stimulus, reactionary and radical, engineered by *Scrutiny*.

In her 'anthropological' study of popular culture *Fiction and the Reading Public* (1932) Q. D. Leavis asserted with her usual forthright conviction that the first principle of a theory of 'cultural history' lay in the conception of the original unity of culture and civilization, a unity quintessentially expressed in early-seventeenth-century England. (Represented by Shakespeare's relation to a living popular culture, and to be contrasted to, say, Dickens who in the early *Scrutiny* position was rejected precisely because of his submersion in a newly massified, commercialized popular culture.) Under the impact of industrialization and science the vitality of the organic community had splintered and cultural decline followed. F. R. Leavis declared in the first issue: 'the tradition of literary culture is dead, or nearly so. . . . It was Science that killed it . . . by being the engine of social changes that have virtually broken continuity'.[59] Critical standards had been debased because of class prejudice (upper-class traditionalism, lower-class philistinism) such that the very transmission of culture was endangered. As Mulhern poses the question which faced *Scrutiny*: 'How, given the definitive abolition of the "organic community" were its constitutive values, now dispersed and weakened, to be reconstructed and made potent in the contemporary world?'[60] The solution lay in the recovery of Arnold's disinterested intellectuals, resolving the issue of class; the construction of a moral community to preserve the higher cultural tradition for the race, in which the function of culture was to civilize the masses; and the re-creation of moral values through literary experience, transcending the wretchedness of twentieth-century mass culture.

Even this synoptic view can convey some of the judgements of the minority culture position. There was no place here, in its pure form, for marxism. Any social theory posing determinancy of productive relations 'means a complete disregard for – or rather, a hostility towards – the function represented by *Scrutiny*'. The corollary was that 'class of the kind that can justify talk about "class culture" has long been extinct'.[61] Yet in other respects *Scrutiny* could not be dismissed by the marxists of the period. Most of all, Leavis's relentless attack on mechanical materialism and his insistence that it could provide no conception of 'values' was echoed by developments in the rethinking of intellectual marxism in Britain from the late 1930s. (And it is interesting to speculate whether the belief of Knights that Hill's *English Revolution* was unable to explain the poetry of Marvell may not have prompted Hill to write his 'Society and Andrew Marvell'.) In addition Herbert Butterfield's lengthy commentary on marxist historiography was surprising in its judicious sympathy. He began by rejecting the view that marxism was 'crude economic determinism'. He then listed the virtues of a marxist method – its suspicion of biographical and unilineal histories; its contribution to 'social history' in which the totality is grasped at the 'structural' level of 'the interrelations between the various departments of life'; its posing of the social rather than the individual;

and its claim to a general notion of historical process, to be ascertained empirically rather than deductively. Looking forward to the possibility that marxism might rejuvenate the study of history, his only quarrel was when marxism ceased to be regarded as an approach to historical study and became instead 'a verdict on the whole course of history'.[62] There was really very little here to which the marxist historians could have objected.

But more than this, some of the later cultural histories written by the marxists came to parallel in their most intense concerns the cultural themes of *Scrutiny*. One need only think of the centrality of values and experience, and the later distrust of scientism; the commitment to the discovery of a national culture;[63] the return to the seventeenth century in search of an organic, popular culture in contrast to the modern divide between civilization/capitalism and a 'whole' culture (compare here the 'rough jottings' for a proposed programme of seventeenth-century studies in F. R. Leavis's *Education and the University* (1943) to Hill's subsequent output: the themes are identical); the obsession with the precariousness of cultural continuity; the question of what aspects of the dominant culture could be claimed as valuable (this was explicitly raised by Morton in his contribution – what could be 'retained' in socialism – but was a common theme); and the incessant returning to and privileging of the literary imagination as an alternative to mechanicism. Undoubtedly the historians vehemently scorned this precious, civilizing, minority culture of the Scrutineers, its deep-seated elitism and anti-democratic stance, and abhorred its total disregard for the creativities of the common people. But this does nothing to dislodge the general point, for a dominant set of themes in the marxist historiography came to mirror the *Scrutiny* endeavour, partially inverting its elitism in order to develop a celebration of the culture of the people. In this version the great literary intellectuals assumed their status primarily *because of* their relationship to a popular culture. One deep dilemma resulted. The *Scrutiny* resolution to the crisis of modern civilization was to sustain its moral community of disinterested critics preserving traditional values through the study of literature. For the marxists, in refusing this idealism and elitism, the solution lay in learning from the people, in regenerating the national culture from the creative strengths of the people and their culture: it was to be found in a democratic national-popular consciousness. The paradox, as the Communists knew only too well, was that in the Britain of the 1950s such a popular culture hardly existed. A strident, but not untypical, testament to this paradox can be found in E. P. Thompson's talk on 'William Morris and the moral issues of today' at a conference organized by the Communists on the theme of 'The American threat to British culture' – which by its tone illuminates some unexpected convergences with the bleak *Scrutiny* outlook:

In place of the great proletarian values revealed in class-solidarity and militancy, we now have, even among sections of our own working class movement, the values of private living growing-up – the private fears and neuroses, the self interest and timid individualism fostered by pulp magazines and Hollywood films.[64]

As Thompson was to ask, in 1960: 'What had become, in 1955, of the socialist generation of the 1934-45 decade?'[65] A good proportion of 'the people', in the 1950s, did not overcome the effects of Cold War and Conservatism. Many had little desire to know their past - only to escape from it, into 'affluence' and 'apathy'.

A last word needs to be said on *Scrutiny* and the socialism of the forties for a more direct bid to appropriate the cultural radicalism of *Scrutiny* for the left was attempted. This materialized in *Politics and Letters* (1947-8) closely associated with Raymond Williams, who by this date had already left the Communist Party. Although he is cautious today about the term 'left Leavisism' he nevertheless maintains that 'The readership we hoped would extend from people still in the Communist Party to those who were in the orbit of Leavis'. Its formation was in 'reaction against both the Party press and *Scrutiny*', a 'revisionism' from outside the CP altogether. This trajectory was clearly stated from the first number of the journal. In an article on 'Soviet literary controversy' Williams attacked the doctrinal orthodoxy of the *Modern Quarterly* and its editor John Lewis for neglecting the whole issue of human values. The attack on *Scrutiny* could be discerned in Williams's stress on politics as much as letters, but all the same was rather muted. As he commented in retrospect, he and his coeditors believed they could win 'simply by literary argument, by cultural discourse. That was the influence of Leavis, but the idea was shared by many others'.[66] This gives some idea of the overpowering presence of Leavis for socialist and marxist cultural analysis in this period. The collapse of *Politics and Letters* after such a short period may also suggest that the appropriation of the predominant *Scrutiny* problematic within a left political context necessitated, in some way, the move *out* of literary criticism.

And - to overcome the anti-historical and ideological displacement perpetrated by *Scrutiny* - a move into historiography? There is certainly a logic to this, recognized by Williams in his treatment of Leavis in *Culture and Society*. Criticizing a confining, literary focus he declared that cultural analysis must attend 'to the experience that is otherwise recorded: in institutions, manners, customs, family memories'.[67] This nexus of problems could serve as an initial guide to some of the later preoccupations of the historians. It may also highlight the shared concerns of Williams's 'discovery' of the *Culture and Society* tradition (which, as *The Long Revolution* made explicit, carried its own democratic politics) and the historians' 'discovery' of a democratic national-popular will, the two projects originating in the same conjuncture, weaving in and out, sometimes overlapping (at one point Williams was invited to work with the CP historians) and sometimes colliding (as in Thompson's review of *The Long Revolution*, or Kiernan's of *Culture and Society*).[68] What first occurs in the 1950s is the initial *translation* of these cultural categories into a historiographical paradigm. None of this generation of historians, today, refers much to either Leavis or *Scrutiny*. The Leavis spirit was exorcized with some (but not, I think, absolute) finality. Hill was unequivocal: 'You can't have it both ways. Either you go into politics or you stay out. You can't create a Literary Critics Party to defend "traditional values".'[69]

The people in history

The historians in the Communist Party were of course consciously *political* intellectuals. Reading what the well-established academic figures of today were writing in the Party publications thirty or forty years ago – alongside their weighty, fully researched academic monographs, like Hilton's *Economic Development of Some Leicestershire Estates in the 14th and 15th Centuries* or Hill's *Economic Problems of the Church* – can sometimes shake up contemporary preconceptions. The tone was embattled and the invective harsh. Hill's uncompromising line on Marvell was symptomatic – the subordination of self to political purpose. Theirs was a collective project to *repossess* the past in order to make the future: *our* history was the history of the English common people. Gramsci's perspective on the role of (traditionally formed) intellectuals in the construction of the national-popular will is appropriate here; so too his belief that a communist party 'must be and cannot but be the proclaimer and organizer of an intellectual and moral reform, which also means creating the terrain for a subsequent development of the national-popular collective will towards the realisation of a superior, total form of modern civilization'.[70]

Peering back through the murky tunnel of the Cold War, what immediately appears so striking is the extent to which the *whole* field of historiography was formed in an explicitly political dimension. Only in the 1950s, when the conflation between ideology and politics won through, was the mainstream of historiography so effectively emptied of all explicit politics. In 1946, in a perfectly orthodox study, A. L. Rowse could write: 'The study of history leads straight to an informed, and responsible, concern with politics. This book shows why: politics is the continuation of history in our time, it is history being made under our eyes'.[71] One impulse behind such notions, and perhaps it was the most forceful, was the definition of nationhood (of Englishness) which had arisen in the War in contrast to the alien influences of 'totalitarianism'. Precedents of course existed, most of all in the historiography of Lewis Namier, which coupled a veneration of all things English with a poisonous xenophobia. One of the most forceful interventions in this respect was Herbert Butterfield's virulently anti-Communist *The Englishman and His History* (1944). There was no attempt here to duck the connection between politics and historiography. The stress persistently falls on the essential continuity of the 'Englishman' with his past – or the 'alliance' between past and present as Butterfield preferred to call it – which is contrasted to fascism; to the French (whose predilection for revolution 'destroys' the organic relation to the past); and to the Russians and Communists, 'For they count on a Millennium that will liquidate and wind up for ever the historical process as they themselves have formulated it.'[72] In this version the so-called Whig or liberal interpretation of history made no bones about its enemies.

The initiation of the Communists' project occurred at a moment of defeat when the hopes of the War radicalism were dashed and the political forces which had done so much to shape the assumptions of the Historians' Group were eclipsed. In part, this explains the displacement into the distinctly non-popular, hostile academic environment. The steady pressure from the Right, and the beginnings of the long post-war economic boom, resulted in the political objectives of the Group being *driven back* into the distant history of the common people, for from the vantage point of today (and this perspective needs to be kept in mind) the historians' lack of sustained historical analysis of their contemporary political conditions seems astonishing. It looks as if there was a critical failure of nerve to confront and explain the nature of the contraction of the radical popular movement of 1947-8[73] – the containment of which preconditioned the hegemonic Conservatism of the next decade – and the consequent recomposition of popular politics on a social democratic axis. Nor did the economic features of advanced capitalism (which *also* had been part of Dobb's investigation in the *Studies* and elsewhere) find any response from the historians (as historians). In its place there developed the reflex to turn to the deeply established romantic critiques of industrial capitalism – adopting, perhaps, the line of least resistance within the repertoire of English social criticism. Their hopes of winning over and superseding the traditions of radical liberal historiography gave way to the necessary defence of the Hammonds, or Tawney, against the dominant consensus of conservative historiography, and against conscious attempts to discredit or counter the radical histories (most blatantly represented by Hayek's *Capitalism and the Historians*). The task now rested on 'The importance and prospects of winning *allies* in the present position of attack on progressive as well as Marxist history'.[74] Furthermore the desire to popularize a communist historiography and pitch it against the 'deep sediment of values and judgements'[75] produced by school history was checked even before the end of the 1940s. As Hobsbawm later recalled the most concerted attempt in this direction had no great success: four volumes 'were designed for the public of trade union and adult education readers, which did not take them up, and for a public of students which did not exist'.[76] In these conditions the commitment to re-create or reactivate the English traditions of popular radicalism carried its costs which registered deep within the historiography itself.

The central personality of the Group and instigator of its collective project appears to have been the enigmatic figure of Dona Torr, a founder member of the Communist Party. It is difficult to find out much about her except for the over-riding fact that she was universally admired by the younger historians who gathered round her. It is rare to find a single text coming out of this milieu from the middle 1940s without some note of appreciation for her. She was involved in Party education; in 1935 she translated Dimitrov's letters from prison; she also translated the extremely influential *Selected Correspondence* of Marx and Engels (1934) as well as the first volume of *Capital* (1938), *The Origin of the Family* (1940) and Marx's writings on China (1951). In 1940 she edited two small volumes containing selections from Marx, Engels, Lenin and Stalin on *Marxism, Nationality and War*.[77] Much of her scholarship was dedicated to history and she planned to produce a vast survey of the life of Tom Mann 'and his times'. Her death in 1956 brought this to a close: the first volume was completed by A. L. Morton and

Christopher Hill, and a subsequent fragment edited and written up by E. P. Thompson. (It seems as if these three were closest of all to Torr.) In 1954 a collection of essays produced by the Communist historians, *Democracy and the Labour Movement* (edited by Saville, Hill, Dobb and George Thomson), was 'presented' to Dona Torr. Fittingly, in the Preface the editors agreed that 'She has taught us historical *passion*' and shown how 'History was the sweat, blood, tears and triumphs of the common people, our people'.[78]

It was in Torr's work that the distancing from scientism (*and* from Dobb's connecting of logic to history) was first formulated within the historiography. This did not preclude a belief in marxism as the science of history, but rather than reaching out to the proto-positivism of Engels's later investigations of historical laws, the distinctive inflection was on history as *creative process*, 'the record of man's creative struggle for freedom'.[79] History was attributed a definite subject (man), a direction (human fulfilment on the basis of real democracy) and a 'motor', the struggle between classes in which the working class 'bears the responsibility for the advance of human civilization'.[80] Contrary to the paradigm of the natural scientists this foregrounded the self-emancipation of the people. Lenin was read as one who grasped that 'the *historical initiative* of the masses is what Marx prizes above everything else'.[81] A similar perspective was adopted by Gordon Childe in *History* (1947), by Hill in his article on 'Marxism and history' (1948) and echoed by Morton in a later piece entitled 'Socialist humanism'.[82] The common theme was the rejection of a positivistic interpretation built on a model of general abstract laws in favour of a more open, humanist understanding in which history was 'not subject to any external laws imposed from without'.[83] The emphasis swung away from impersonal economic forces to 'getting back to real men and women'. The problem was not identified as the neglect of economics. On the contrary historians 'have become so obsessed with economic forces, so enmeshed in a web of detail, so weighed down by dry-as-dust documents, that they fail to see the real men and women whose lives made up history'. Both Gordon Childe and Hill defended the scientific study of history while Hill conceded that it must also be 'poetic'. His argument balanced on the belief that although scientific history had become arid and determinist in the hands of (unspecified) academics, it did not follow that it should be abandoned by marxists. The problem, it appears, was how to humanize the study of history while still accepting its determinate and objective basis. But the *drive* of the argument was the stress on humanism for, as Hill concluded, 'The history of mankind is the history of the growth in freedom of moral judgement'.[84]

From Hill's subsequent work it can be seen how the study of history and politics on rational grounds may precondition 'growth in moral judgement' by overcoming a cyclical understanding of history and by indicating the possibility for men and women to free themselves from the domination of the past. After all this is one reason for viewing a crucial dimension of the scientific revolution of the seventeenth century as 'progressive'. But this is quite different to thinking history *as* 'the growth in freedom in moral judgement'. The latter conception is underpinned by what is quite technically a historicism in which the people/history combine to speak with one voice. It has a familiar ring: the people are democratic and progressive, and history is leading to their liberation. 'History' is at once both the practice (in the sense of the people making history) and the theory of the popular. To take it to its extreme, the people need only hear their own history to be persuaded of the truth of socialism. This is a caricature. But it does seem that in the very logic of the rejection of scientistic and mechanical marxism this sort of perspective could inform one of the poles of an alternative conceptualization, inverting scientism into moralism. No single text, nor the work of any one historian, can be taken to exemplify such an inversion in a complete form – although it has been argued, especially by Anderson, that Thompson's writings immediately after 1956 collapsed into moralism.[85] But on the other hand it is right to note the persistent tendencies which pulled in this direction; and not just in abstract formulations on the nature of history, but more particularly in conceptualizing 'the people'.

The Norman Yoke

If Dona Torr was the predominant presence in the Historians' Group, the central text was Christopher Hill's 'Norman Yoke' which opened *Democracy and the Labour Movement*, a volume intended both as a tribute to Torr and as a 'shop-window' (in Hobsbawm's phrase) to the work of the Group. Hill's primary object was the politics of historical knowledge or 'history as politics'. The theory of the Norman Yoke, in its popular aspects, was a theory of lost rights which looked back to an age before the Norman Conquest when Saxon England was democratic. So far as it was taken up by the common people it contained 'a rudimentary class theory of politics', both secular and popular, in which the ruling class was perceived as an alien implantation and 'The nation is the people'. During the rise of capitalism the Norman Yoke theory became established as a 'continuous popular patriotic tradition' reproducing 'popular memories of lost rights'. However it was never an undifferentiated tradition but rather a site of sharply conflicting interpretations of the Conquest which all carried immediate political consequences. According to Hill this popular tradition was organized into four distinct political ideologies. First, the royalist reading in which the 'Conquest by the pious Normans had had a valuable disciplinary effect upon the dissolute Anglo-Saxons', a reading which disappeared with the Restoration; second, the 'bourgeois' interpretation which looked to 1066 as the moment of the imposition of a legal system based on property. While both the propertied and the revolutionaries (Levellers and Diggers) in the seventeenth century could assert Englishness – ('Men fought for the liberties of *England*, for the birthrights of *Englishmen*') – conflict between these groups focused on opposing conceptualizations of the law. Levellers and Diggers (representing the third and fourth variants) were advancing 'from historical mythology to political philosophy' in which they dropped the search for historical precedents in order to justify their politics and their definition of 'the people'. Paradoxically those who believed in the *continuity* of Saxon tradition were the revolutionaries in the seventeenth century. Thus for the Levellers 'The law became the enemy, the symbol of Normanism, instead of being the surviving pledge of Anglo-Saxon freedom'. For Hill this Leveller mentality was an embodiment of a 'bourgeois-democratic' ideology. These democratic versions disappeared from view at the end of the seventeenth century and were to remain hidden until the radical revival of the second half of the eighteenth century when the aristocracy and unreformed parliament were identified as political targets. Thomas Spence looked to the jury system and to the parish (the unit of self-government) as democratic survivals from a past age which needed to be strengthened. In *Common Sense* Tom Paine declared: 'A French bastard landing with an armed banditti and establishing himself King of England, against the consent of the natives, is, in plain terms, a very paltry, rascally original'.

But with the disintegration of rural society and 'the working class . . . slowly working out its own ideology' the theory of the Norman Yoke fast lost its purchase. One crucial ingredient in this collapse was the completion of the shift from mythology to historiography (and the birth of a new, rational intellectual paradigm). 'Serious historical analysis was necessary before the working class could become conscious of itself *as a class*'. With the consolidation of capitalism the Norman Yoke was *subsumed* by a theory of capitalism which was forward-looking and specifically anti-capitalist. This was marxism, the science of history, which incorporated 'Burke's sense of history with Paine's sense of justice'. In William Morris 'we have a Marxist imagination re-interpreting the age-old dream expressed in the idea of "Anglo-Saxon liberties"'. Hill concluded: 'Marxism has subsumed what is valuable in the Norman Yoke theory – its recognition of the class basis of politics, its deep sense of the *Englishness* of the common people, of the proud continuity of their lives, institutions and struggles with those of their forefathers, its insistence that a propertied ruling class is from the nature of its position fundamentally alien to the interests of the mass of the people'. The working class must stand as a defender of the nation. In the closing sentence, however, the confident assessment of marxism as the science of history, transcending a bourgeois and ideological conception, is qualified: 'But even a scientific programme can be sterile if it is not infused with an imaginative spirit like that which saw the enemy as "The French bastard and his banditti" '.[86]

This is a remarkable essay, not least because it formulated a series of historical issues which became of decisive significance in subsequent historiography. The essay is structured by its analysis of the struggles between absolutism and popular sovereignty, a defining theme of the marxist historiography. It highlights with force and subtlety the forms of radical popular traditions conterminous with the long duration of primitive accumulation. It takes into account the historically opposing conceptions of law and justice, and notes how these changing categories were perceived in terms of custom. And it touches on the rationality of popular cultures, the themes of lost rights and millenarianism, popular memories and the language of the subordinate classes, and last but not least, the identification of the ideology of the free-born Englishman. All these themes were to reappear in later cultural histories.

It is also remarkable for the force of its moral critique in which marxism is all but reconstituted *as* an English tradition, inheriting the cause of plebeian resistance, drawing from Burke, from Paine's sense of justice and reaching a kind of crystallization in Morris. It is a far cry from the marxism of Dobb. But none the less this critique was still informed by a hard notion of science. The theory of the Norman Yoke, even in its democratic variants, was for Hill a bourgeois democratic ideology which – to adopt a rather different terminology – provided an imaginary solution to the real contradictions thrown up by the process of dispossession: marxist science could uncover and check the falsity of ideology. Indeed Hill again raised the question of the relation between a scientific and an ethical interpretation of history, aiming to counterbalance the two. But this balance is never quite achieved. At the very moment of asserting the falsity of theories of the Norman Yoke Hill backtracks, worried by the implications of an arid scientific programme, and returns again to recover the spirit which opposed the bastard and his banditti. No *resolution* was in fact produced. One further problem is linked to this. Hill described the tenacious democratic popular tradition which burst forth in the 1640s and again in the late eighteenth and early nineteenth centuries: his analysis closed with the formation of the English working class and the beginnings of industrial capitalism. But if socialism (and marxism) were seen as the inheritors of previous popular struggles in the way that Hill maintained, where, in 1954, was the popular socialist movement? This is not glibly to suggest that Hill should have written a further essay on the modern socialist movement; only that by illuminating the revolutionary *continuity* of the popular tradition, the difficulties imposed by its very *discontinuities* should at least have been posed. This silence was not particular to Hill: borrowing from Hill in a different context, it almost amounts to a 'stop in the mind' in the Communist historians of the period, an inability adequately to think through and overcome in the historiography the breaks and ruptures which punctuated the passage from plebeian radicalism to the modern labour movement. This had its political conditions, both in the inhibitions generated by the Communist Party undergoing a spasm of contraction and closure, and also, paradoxically, in the very reaction and 'discontinuity' of the early 1950s when the prospects for a popular socialist movement were fast receding. Theoretically, also, the balance between continuity and rupture may raise decisive questions which lie right at the heart of the very concept of the national-popular. These polarities – continuity/discontinuity, science/ethics – call for further investigation.

The people

If a single common theme can be detected which bound the histories together it was the desire to demonstrate that the Communist Party was the inheritor of a long tradition of English popular radicalism.[87] The first public lectures planned by the Historians' Group on 'British Communists' were to cover Thomas More, the Levellers and Diggers, Owen and the Chartists, Tom Mann, and the Communist

Party itself – although when in 1948 this was subsequently rearranged, the Peasants' Revolt of 1381 was added, Morris was to be included in the Tom Mann lecture, and the final session on the CP was dropped. This is a record which was remarkably consistent throughout the 1950s. It can be followed in the historians' contributions to the Party journals, as well as in the four-volume 'History in the Making' series (especially in Hill and Edmund Dell's *The Good Old Cause*) which sought to reassert the dynamic of history in 'the people'. It was a resilient, insurrectional 'people' which emerged from this Communist historiography – in sharp contrast to Cole and Postgate's more orderly *Common People* – whose history began (variously) in the Peasants' Revolt or in the social revolution of the 1640s. Hilton and Fagan reappropriated the Revolt of 1381 in order to 'present to the British people one part of their own tradition of struggle for popular liberties'.[88] In 1949 the *Modern Quarterly* published a series of articles celebrating the tercentenary of the abolition of the monarchy, and in 'The English Revolution and the state' Christopher Hill – with an eye to contemporary Labour politics – stressed what was to become his persistent theme: the radical force of the Revolution had been compromised and its *completion* lay ahead as the task for the future. His insistence on the very fact of revolution in the seventeenth century, comparable to the great French or Russian Revolutions, caused considerable controversy. And it is important to be clear that continuity, as conceptualized by the Communist historians, implied no necessary slide into gradualism or constitutionalism. Hill later recalled what impact his reading of the seventeenth century had on the Party: 'I think that the celebration of 1640 – and especially of 1649 – did something for the Party in giving it confidence in a non-gradualist tradition to an extent that it is difficult for the younger generation perhaps to realise'.[89] Central to this conception was the belief in the necessity for the completion or expansion of democracy, for the working class to win over the majority of the population, and 'to advance in the battle of ideas, to seize the enemy's weapons and turn them against him'.[90] Even theoretical accounts of liberty, such as Hilton's pamphlet written in 1950, were irresistibly historicized, paying as much attention to Milton, Winstanley or Morris as to contemporary issues. This is illustrated most succinctly in the historiography by Morton and Tate's discussion of the British labour movement in which Chartism was connected back to 1381 and forward to *The British Road to Socialism* with breathless speed in a few condensed pages.

Many of these ideas were first formulated in the duplicated *Our History* bulletin which was started in 1953 (superseding the local history bulletin) and continued until 1956, when it assumed its present form. An embryonic version of Hill's 'English revolution and the brotherhood of man', for example, appeared in early 1954 and was later to be published in *Puritanism and Revolution*. But the biggest boost seems to have come from the conference on 'The history of capitalism in Britain' held at Netherwood in July 1954 and which appears to have been a decisive moment in formulating some of the characteristic concerns of the Group. It's perhaps at this point that the populist rendering of Dobb was settled – cashing that potential which derived from his account of primitive accumulation. The tone was set in the early stages of the organization of the conference when George Rudé criticized a draft outline for 'not giving enough attention to *People*'.[91] The defining, central and much admired paper was delivered by Morton on 'The role of the common people in the history of British capitalism'. Little survives from this conference – certainly not the prestigious volume which was once projected. However some sense can be gained from Lionel Munby's 'People or mob' and Morton's 'Sedgemoor' which were later circulated in the *Our History* bulletin (February 1955), and later still, supplemented by some of Rudé's work on the eighteenth century, as contributions to the slightly grander *Our History* devoted to 'The common people 1688–1800'.[92] But this is all that was ever published.

However the classic location of these themes – the common people and democratic advance – was Dona Torr's unfinished *Tom Mann and His Times*. This is partly a biography of Mann, partly a history of 'his times' – with Morris playing a large part – but more than anything the historical object is quite simply democracy itself. Precisely paralleling the dominant themes of 'The Norman Yoke' the book investigated 'the long history of the bourgeois revolution in England' in order to argue that the English working class must 'win the battle of democracy'.[93] The historical logic of this argument is clear. First is posed the existence of the popular tradition: 'Our story of the struggle for freedom begins with the great Rebellion led by Wat Tyler' when 'Englishmen became conscious of their common nationhood'. It is then stated that 'the English revolutionary tradition' is one which is unbroken for it 'extends from John Ball to Tom Mann'. It has two great high points. The first was the seventeenth century when popular beliefs in lost rights became transformed into a rational appraisal of future political prospects. Thus: 'The English Revolution saw the beginning of modern democratic politics. It is the first great turning point in the history of democratic political thought'. But the force of the argument rests on the conviction that 'The lifetime of Tom Mann saw the second'.[94] The historic significance of this second period derives from the formation and development of the socialist movement: 'Only the newfangled men of Tom Mann's epoch, by seeing capitalism as a historic process with a beginning and an end, its ideas as equally the product of history, only such men could restore to the democratic movement some of the old ideas of community without rejecting what was best in the bourgeois conception of individual freedom'.[95] And for this reason, at last, the working class has 'made good *its* claim to be called "the people"'.[96]

In a sense this takes up what was left unsaid in 'The Norman Yoke' by moving the analysis on from the history of plebeian radicalism. But it is a curiously abstract account of democratic development which mingles with the finely constructed biography of Tom Mann. True to the theoretical premises developed by Torr and Hill in the 1940s, history is definitely on the side of 'the people' and 'the people' are progressive. From this it would appear as if it is the very condition of capitalism, in itself, which provides the working class with a necessary democratic politics, such that the interests of working people will in time become identified with the nation as a whole. This sort of populism, common enough in the 1950s, has been seen as less and less tenable in the intervening years. As I suggest later, a critical issue in thinking beyond this conception of the popular has rested on understanding the necessarily *indeterminate* relations between class and politics. The varieties of political forces constituted by class can be thought as contingent on a specific complex of struggles, such that a working-class politics can take any number of forms, democratic or anti-democratic. This is a fundamental point. But the issue is side-stepped by Torr. Most of her history focuses on the 1880s when indeed a vigorous and confident socialist movement was in ascendance. Even then, however, by adopting a biographical mode she resolved this major problem through the contrivance of personification. Why Tom Mann? Because *his* achievements, his struggles (of the skilled, white, male engineer) expressed the struggles of the whole people, the pinnacle of *their* achievements. His story tells that of the class and the people.

This short survey needs to be much more nuanced. It could be demonstrated with the greatest ease that the historians were quite aware of a reactionary organization of 'the people'. It was, after all, just such a prospect which had compelled many of them to become Communists. But the general point still holds. The epochal popular tradition was recovered as the radical English idiom. It was conceived as still being carried, nurtured and reproduced in the best elements of working-class leadership (just as it had been with Tom Mann[97]) until that moment when, once again, it would burst alight in the combustion of popular forces. This notion pivoted on the idea of a 'lost' culture (as in Thompson's later contention that the radicalism of the early nineteenth century 'was, perhaps, the most distinguished popular culture England has ever known'[98]). This, again, unexpectedly converges with *Scrutiny*. However, the critical difference lay not only in the politics of this 'lost' popular culture but also in the fact that for the Communists it could be *retrieved* and remade. On the one hand the logic of this conception raised immensely interesting questions about cultural history. On the other hand, however, it tended to turn attention severely away from contemporary cultures precisely because the reorganized structures of popular culture in the twentieth century – condensed around suspicions of Americanization (Hollywood and pulp fiction) – appeared as a barrier and impediment to this retrieval. The heroic culture of the past was seen as struggling against the contemporary cultural forms of the working class, the past against the present.

Even if my argument on this score has been too compacted, and even though tighter and more extensive textual analysis would be needed to prove the point, it none the less seems that *in the historiography* there is little or no evidence that the historians' theorization of 'the people' was actually adequate either for a contemporary politics or for a historically informed explanation of their own conjuncture. It may be for this reason that there developed an increasing fascination for the utopian strands of political thought.

Utopias

Throughout this period there appeared to be no insurmountable conflict in the minds of the historians between a scientific approach to history and one which drew more self-consciously from utopian or literary (romantic) currents, carrying a much tougher ethical edge. The scientific rationalism, with its divergent sources and in all its complexity, to which the Historians' Group was attracted has been thoroughly recorded by Raphael Samuel and there is no need for repetition.[99] The shortest summary will do. The long and uneven break from a scientistic historiography was only achieved, up until the mid forties, by retaining a firm belief in the scientific study of history. Partly this can be explained by the historians' commitment to counter the academic dilettantism of the metropolitan intellectual culture; partly because marxism was pretty much unthinkable unless it provided a reasoned and logical understanding of history. But perhaps more than anything marxism – as the science of history – was explicitly pitched against irrationalism and obscurantism, and most particularly against Catholicism. It's difficult to comprehend the intensity of feeling on this, the anathema which pervaded the marxism of the period, such that at the end of the forties the Group agreed that of all the key problems in historiography 'The Pope as the champion of reaction in the 19th century and 20th century' ranked as the fourth most pressing.[100] Hill, especially, wrote biting attacks on Catholic-influenced historiography. In his own field of work Catholicism represented the full force of reaction, while in the 1930s it was not only complicit with fascism but proved a refuge for reactionary intellectuals in England – by the 1940s Communists could turn the tables and proclaim support for the national culture while castigating those subservient to the foreign power of Rome. Hill was always at pains to declare the progressive aspects of the seventeenth-century scientific revolution, and so politically urgent was this that at times it tipped him back into a crude utilitarianism.[101] This confirms perhaps that it was precisely the unevenness of the break with scientism which was most crucial in these years.

From early on the recovery of utopian thought was a decisive determination in the movement away from mechanical materialism and in the celebration of a radical popular culture. The pioneer, again, was Morton. His book *The English Utopia* (1952) comprised a study of the development of utopian thought in England from the fourteenth century to his own day. The first chapter opened with the words: 'In the beginning Utopia is an image of desire'.[102] By unravelling the changing forms of that 'desire' Morton endeavoured to shed new light on the people's history of England. His starting point, characteristically, was with the 'folk utopia' of the common people which preceded the utopias of poets, prophets and philosophers. The poetic legend of Cokaygne was the product of popular mythology, popular festivals, popular revolt – of the 'world turned upside down'. It was a legend which anticipated the fundamentals of modern socialism:

Socialism, if it is to be anything but an academic fabrication of blueprints, must take its rise from the desires and hopes of the people. It is from this that it derives its life, its actuality and its assurance of final victory. The classless society is Cokaygne made practical by scientific knowledge.

Here the popular appropriation of science *completed* and made possible the realization of the ancient utopian sensibility. (This, it needs to be remembered, was in direct contrast to the *Scrutiny* conception which isolated 'Science' as the original cause of cultural decline.) In the Middle Ages 'The conquest of nature was only then beginning, and so the final triumph of man over nature could only be expressed magically and symbolically'.[103] Variations of this early folk utopia were examined in chapters on the seventeenth-century Revolution and counter-revolution; 'Reason in despair' (Swift) and 'In revolt' (Blake); the utopian socialists and Morris – the latter regarded as the first great English marxist and the only utopian thinker who equalled Thomas More; and finally the collapse of the tradition in the anti-utopias of Wells and his followers, displaced by the ability of the men and women to imagine a scientific ordering of the social world. But, like Hill's assessment of the Norman Yoke, an ambiguity emerges in the conclusion, for Morton saw the need for science to be 'enriched' by the reflexes of utopianism:

Human knowledge, human activity, science in the service of the people not of the monopolists and war-makers, are leading to a world which, while it will not correspond to the desires of More, of Bacon, of Morris, or of the unknown poets who dreamed of the land of Cokaygne, will have been enriched by all of them and by the many others who have made their contribution to that undefinable but ever-living and growing reality which I have called the English Utopia.[104]

History, and the conception of socialism, appear again as 'poetic'.

This was a persistent theme, a sub-text to the collective historical project, although one which was never pursued theoretically. It seemed sufficient merely to state the case. 'Poetry' in the abstract served as the foil to scientism. In the concrete it was invariably thought as extending the marxist perspective to include romanticism, following closely the cultural legacy of English social criticism in its conflict with utilitarianism. In his essay on Wordsworth, Victor Kiernan insisted not only that Marx was a poet and Wordsworth a political analyst but that 'Marxism also has much to learn, that it has not yet learned, from poetry'.[105] His interpretation shared much with Hill on the Norman Yoke and Torr on Tom Mann. It was only the historic formation of a working class and an indigenous socialist movement which provided the conditions for overcoming the 'stony isolation' of the intellectual from the common people. Quoting the *Prelude* – 'My heart was all/Given to the People' – Kiernan documented Wordsworth's difficulties in effecting this bridge, and mounted an extremely convincing argument to show that those whom Wordsworth called 'the people' in fact excluded the vast majority of the new working class. But what is most interesting is that the weight of the essay stressed the *continuing* obstacles in transcending the divide between 'intellectuals' and 'people' – which, as I indicate in a moment, registers with some subtlety the debates and confusion inside the Historians' Group at this time.

But the towering influence was that of Morris – who effected the junction between romanticism and marxism, crossed the river of fire in order to dedicate his life to socialism, and recuperated, continued and enriched the English revolutionary tradition of Winstanley and Paine. For the Communist historians of the forties and fifties Morris was the political proof of the strategic viability of their project. He showed what could be done. To the question "Marx?" came the answer 'Morris!'

Morris had been one of the most conspicuous elements in 'the battle of ideas' from the 1930s when in 1934 Page Arnot published his short vindication on the centenary of Morris's birth reclaiming him for Communism against bourgeois detractors. This ideological struggle intensified at the end of the 1940s when Attlee began a concerted attempt to win Morris for the Labour Party. The Communists were incensed by this campaign. Infuriated rumblings continued in Party publications for years after (not to mention the altercation between Attlee and Gallacher in the Commons). It is apparent that all the historians (Morton, Hill, Torr, Allen Merson, Lionel Munby, Thompson, Hilton, Hobsbawm) held the deeply felt conviction that Morris essentially constituted a vital part of *'our'* history. (Thompson angrily pounced on those – with Attlee in the forefront – 'who *use* Morris's name for their own purposes.')[106] Morris was also the obvious place to look for guidance on the question of marxism and culture. When in 1952 the National Cultural Committee of the Communist Party organized a conference on 'Britain's cultural heritage' the historians 'agreed that the contributions made by the Group should deal with:- (a) The contribution of British archaeologists and historians – ie British historiography – to Britain's cultural heritage (b) The British political tradition – some emphasis on the gains won especially in bourgeois radical fights which now the working class is fighting to keep (c) Story of the fight for working class culture – bringing in here some of the material obstacles involved. Cde E Thompson be asked to contribute on Wm Morris'.[107]

Thompson receives separate treatment in this volume so here I can be brief. In what must have been one of his first articles in a Party journal his 'Comments on a people's culture' invoked Morris in the celebration of the new democracies of Bulgaria and Yugoslavia, contrasting the resilience of their popular cultures to the metropolitan culture of England, which was represented, as for all the marxists of this period, by Connolly and *Horizon*, cemented by an English McCarthyism.[108] Many of these themes are quite consistent with Thompson's present interventions. They were taken up again, with much greater seriousness, in *William Morris: Romantic to Revolutionary* in a context which fully engaged with the basic issues of the historians' project. Crucially, the relationship between romanticism and marxism was taken as something which needed to be elaborated. Morris was presented as someone with romanticism bred in his very bones but who (like Kiernan's Wordsworth) had 'no hope – except that hope in the power of the working class which (in 1850) Morris had yet to learn'. In crossing the river of fire and 'taking a step which broke through the narrowing charmed circle of defeatism of bourgeois culture',[109] his romantic dreams could be realized and the breach between artist and people healed. The main force of this thesis is not that Morris had to discard his romanticism, but on the contrary the stress falls on the inherent compatibility of the two forms:

Morris's moral criticism of society is not only entirely compatible with dialectical materialism, and parallel to the criticisms developed in Marx's early writings, and then in *The Communist Manifesto, Capital, The Origin of the Family* and *Ludwig Feuerbach*; it is also the theme of his most vigorous and original writings within the Marxist tradition.

Owing to the very quality and potency of its own ethical spirit marxism provided the means for the reconciliation of necessity and desire. There was nothing utopian – in the 'bad', idealistic sense – in Morris's thought: 'His approach to socialism was not utopian, but scientific', a 'scientific utopia'.[110]

This conception of science was linked to politics and to the Party ('Were William Morris alive today, he would not look far to find the party of his choice'), and was as hard as Hill's in 'The Norman Yoke'. It was a science that could seek out and eradicate 'errors', from which Morris was not always free. Some passages reverberate in Thompson's account which confirm an orthodox, vanguardist theory of the party as the carrier of truth, and as the materialization of a leadership in symbiotic relationship with the most advanced sectors of the working class.[111] Raphael Samuel is right when he claims that 'The Communist Party historians fought the Cold War under the age-old watchwords of free-thought. They conceived themselves to be fighting a "battle of ideas" . . . defending . . . "the progressive rationalist tradition". They were also the inheritors of a two camp theory of knowledge, in which materialism made war on idealism, and Marxist truth – one and indivisible – was engaged in mortal combat with bourgeois error'.[112]

But this was, exactly, an inheritance. It was one which was increasingly put into question along a number of different lines by the historians. One need only think of Thompson's careful and sustained emphasis on the popular culture from which Morris drew, and on the ethical tenor in which Morris's politics were thought. This sort of recuperation, by no means peculiar to Thompson, began to impose critical strains on the inherited system of scientific marxism. I don't believe that the consequent conceptual *incompatibilities* were resolved by the Communist historians, either by the 'addition' of utopia to science (or desire to necessity, or romanticism to marxism) or by interpreting a science of history as poetic. Similarly the political issue of the relation between party and people was caught in, and limited by, precisely these theoretical ambiguities. Attempts to reconcile these problems never seemed to get very far in achieving an adequate synthesis. The one issue most profoundly resolved, and desperately defended, was the belief in the continuity of radical English populism. It was only due to the sharp break in political conditions in 1956, generating a new complex of imperatives, that there emerged a historiography founded on a more fully reconciled theoretical basis.

The national-popular

The contribution, over two or three decades, by the marxist historians to cultural theory is now generally recognized, although the concentrated attention to Thompson alone has rather obscured the breadth and diversity of this corpus. One of the most particular and distinctive aspects of this contribution, true not only for the period up to 1956, but also for the years since, has been around the theme of the national-popular. Discussion of this concept can be found elsewhere.[113] In brief, the term originated in Gramsci's prison writings and like many of his penetrating theoretical insights is notoriously tricky to disentangle or adequately systematize; and like many abstractions within cultural studies is difficult to pin with sufficient accuracy. Where it is distinct from many other recent advances within cultural theory is in the fact that it is crucially a 'historical' concept, determining a peculiarly historical route through the field of cultural studies, referring to an element – or rather, a complex of elements – *within a conjuncture*, which always needs to be specified, located and historicized. It illuminates and isolates the depth of articulation between nation and people, the degree to which the idea of 'nation' is concretized and universalized, and focuses on the accumulation of popular symbols secured by the full interplay of political forces. As Gramsci forcefully demonstrated by his own studies of Italy, the national-popular is a political goal which has to be achieved. The range of articulations can weaken and diminish, and popular culture can be severed from the national-metropolitan culture (as Thompson implied when he contrasted Britain to Bulgaria); it can be achieved in a reactionary synthesis (as in mass fascist or populist authoritarian movements); or it can be progressive and democratic (most of all, if the working class wins hegemony as the leading class in the transition to socialism). Within all these possibilities the decisive determinations are the conjunctural forms of the popular culture and the modes of struggle which it circumscribes. Predicated on the recognition of the struggles by antagonistic forces for conflicting definitions of 'nation' and 'people', it indicates the unstable and impermanent combination of elements in any one conjunctural moment.

In the historiography this is perhaps at its clearest in the British historians' deep fascination with the seventeenth century as the period of the revolutionary restructuring of the political nation and the climactic formation of a new national culture. (Raymond Williams's etymologies in *Keywords* are revealing here.) To ask the question 'Who are the people?' was also to ask 'What is the nation?', a coupling integral to Hill's reconstruction of the tradition of the Norman Yoke.

It is from within this context of analysing the making of a new 'civilization' from the time of the seventeenth century that the shift to a more nuanced reconstruction of the social totality can best be understood. (Compare Hill's *Puritanism and Revolution* of 1958 to his earliest publication, *The English Revolution*.) This also registers the development of a non-literary theory of culture. In the *Modern Quarterly* of 1948, celebrating a hundred years of *The Communist Manifesto*, Alick West was commissioned to write an essay on 'Marxism and culture'. The essay automatically moved into a discussion of aesthetics and the predicament of artists. By the end of the 1950s such a narrowly thought referencing of the problem of culture would have been far less likely. The Aggregate Conference which the History Group planned for 1957 was devoted to 'Capitalism and culture' and the historiography itself suggests that much more serious attention was being focused on popular mentalities.

But this shift should not be overestimated. The literary inflection was still strong. And no solution adequately bridged the dichotomy between 'high' and 'low' culture. The way round this, however, was neat. Two slightly different but complementary positions were elaborated. The first rested on the assumption that the *authentic* national culture was democratic. This was sustained by historically demonstrating that recognized 'literary' intellectuals (Shakespeare, Blake, Morris etc.) were speaking with the (true) voice of the people. In this version the national culture was national *because* it was popular. This constitutes an important current of Thompson's *Morris* and, perhaps more interestingly, of Leslie Morton's thesis in *The Everlasting Gospel* (1958) which suggested that the very language of William Blake reproduced the 'lost' imagery of the seventeenth-century revolutionaries, a continuity kept alive in the displaced radical and subterranean culture of the antinomian sects of the eighteenth century. The drawback with this sort of interpretation (reflecting, perhaps, the drawbacks imposed by the very discontinuities in popular radicalism itself) was in the neglect of those dominant literary forms which in no way could be thought as 'progressive'. The second position came some way to answering this through a notion of what could be called cultural dispossession, in which the dominant culture fleeces 'the people' of its clear-voiced heroes, closely paralleling the historians' reading of economic dispossession. E. P. Thompson's outrage at those who 'used' Morris is a case in point. A more substantial version can be found in George Thomson's aspirations for reappropriating and transforming the culture of the past. 'This, then, is the first need – to rescue our cultural heritage from the bourgeoisie, to take it over, reinterpret it, adapt it to our needs, renew its vitality by making it thoroughly our own. . . . The English people have not lost their sense of poetry; only their poetry has been taken from them and misinterpreted, so as to lose its appeal. They will recover it with the rest of their heritage'.[114]

The power of this approach was to bring to the forefront of the political agenda the issues raised by the analysis of popular culture, in its peculiarly national and specific forms, in relation to the transition to socialism. Where this project weakened was in thinking the national-popular uncritically as tradition or heritage. Some of the assumptions embedded in this notion were surprisingly unhistorical. The tradition was presented as singular and linear,[115] with the clear implication that Morris or Paine or Winstanley potentially carried equal value for popular cultures of widely separated periods. Emphasis on the singularity of the tradition reinforced the belief that the contemporary popular culture was also singular and homogeneous, unaffected by internal divisions of gender, age or race. The histories of these internal elements were collapsed into the abstract populism of the

English radical tradition, and appropriated to an undifferentiated appeal to a notion of 'the people' which had been culled from a previous age. For this emphasis on tradition – on the achievements of the past – channelled assessment of the present in terms derived from the past, in the sense of measuring or comparing the main-springs of the contemporary popular culture with an 'authenticity' inscribed by the radical tradition itself. At one blow, this cut away the ground on which the historians were standing. The past is not a yardstick by which to *measure* the present. As we argue throughout this book, the conjunctures and struggles of the past *produce* the present. This means that not only the successes of past demo-cratic struggles need to be taken into account, but also their failures and the historic process by which popular cultures have been rendered subordinate. The profound reorganization and transformation of the popular classes by the dominant culture prevents any simple recovery of past traditions. (Indeed, attempts to re-create past traditions may draw socialists into the wrong battles. The blanket reaction of the Communists to the impact of Americanism on British popular culture reproduced prejudices typical of traditional European intellectuals, and in large part was misjudged.) The specific mechanisms by which Morris or his tradition can be incorporated into a dominant culture need precise tracing. To discover the ideological means by which such traditions can be 'dispossessed' marks a crucial precondition for *actively* reconstructing the national-popular on a demo-cratic axis.[116] In this context, popular traditions themselves are double-edged, for at the same time as they inspire collective memories of resistance they can *also* impose the past on the present, 'conjuring up spirits of the past' as Marx put it in *The Eighteenth Brumaire*. It isn't a question of whether Milton or Winstanley, Morris or Mann should be appropriated in a struggle for hegemony, but rather the profoundly more difficult one of making such appropriations effective and popular.

I have already alluded to the inhibitions this imposed on the historians for analysing their own contemporary world, and to the inability actually to reach, in explanatory terms, the present. The most graphic testament to this occurred in 1956 when it was tersely noted in the Group's Minutes: 'Must become historians of the present too.'[117] Hobsbawm mentions some of the overbearing political constraints which discouraged full engagement with the history of the twentieth century – especially with the history of the labour movement and of the Communist Party itself.[118] But this ought not to obscure the conceptual constraints which operated inside the historiography. It is apparent from the Minutes that attempts were made to carry the Group's historical analysis into the twentieth century, but with no lasting success. And it is revealing that later, during the formation of the early New Left, the first *debates* on contemporary culture and the commitment to analyse contemporary issues – such as the separation of ownership and control in advanced capitalism, television and the new structures of communication, youth, racism – came not from the historians but from the younger intellectuals grouped around the *Universities and Left Review*.[119]

In turn, this approach of the Communist historians tended to undermine their attempts to popularize their work. The assertion (which runs through the pages of

The Poverty of Theory) that the divide separating the majority of working people from professionally located 'intellectuals' first became a major block to political advance in the 1960s appears ludicrous on a reading of the papers of the Historians' Group. More accurate would be to see the newly professionalized lower-middle-class or middle-class historians of the 1930s and 1940s as representing the first breach in the traditional intellectual 'aristocracy', a process which accelerated in the 1960s. The Historians' Group is a depressing indicator that voluntarism and a commitment to the people are in themselves quite insufficient for overcoming the complex relations which structure and reproduce the divide between 'mental and manual'. Something of a crisis seems to have come to a head in the Group in 1955: *'bringing history to the people'*, it was realized, needed much more thought.[120] The lack of popular interest in Torr's 'History in the Making' series was not a propitious start. This problem, too, was voiced with clarity in the Minutes: 'one of our chief difficulties now was in establishing and maintaining the channels through which Marxist history could influence the working class movement (cf the decline and purge of the WEA)'.[121] Through the years there was recurrent discussion as to whether a single book, explaining the essentials of marxist history, would have been an appropriate intervention. The details of these discussions cannot easily be reconstructed from the Minutes. But late in 1955 Hill gave his thoughts on what such a text should look like. It

should expose the bourgeois assumptions of the sort of history most people met in popular writing and through the various mass media . . . (eg glorification of the monarchy, great men, the British way of life etc). It should go on to reveal carefully the role of popular forces through history and show not merely the tradition of glorious defeats of successive popular revolts, but also the success (as opposed to the humanitarian or kind ruling class endeavour) of progressive movements in history.

Bourgeois historians should not be directly attacked for bias, but rather the presuppositions which inhibit 'truthful' accounts should be uncovered. Stress should be placed on the role of class struggle and on history as a rational and understandable process; attention must be drawn to the positive aspects of 'our own point of view and its emphasis on people, and on the movement towards the people becoming the prime movers of history'.[122] However, it was finally decided that such a book was not the most urgent requirement, and that the Group's variety of interventions should continue – short articles on English rebels, marxist surveys on recent historiography in *Marxist Quarterly* and *Past and Present*, further essay collections, and the insistence that the Group should increase its production of historical material suitable for teaching. The importance of these interventions ought not to be underestimated, especially in the forbidding political climate of the period. None the less, this programme envisaged little more than the sort of activities the Group had long been practising, and the fundamental problem – expressed evangelically as 'bringing history to the people' – still remained largely unresolved. But in 1956 a new political agenda began to develop.

1956

The rupture in the international communist movement in 1956 falls outside the scope of this chapter, but so far as it affected the Historians' Group some points need to be sketched. There is consensus among those active in the Group that the historians were in the forefront of the critics. Hobsbawm notes: 'It was among the historians that the dissatisfaction with the Party's reaction to the Khruschev speech at the Twentieth Congress of the CPSU first came into the open'.[123] In a letter written at the very height of the crisis by John Saville to E. P. Thompson (his coeditor of the 'revisionist' *Reasoner*) the same argument appears:

It is, I think, significant that of all the intellectual groups in the Communist Party, the historians have come out best in the discussions of the past nine months – and this surely is due to the fact that over the past decade the historians are the only intellectual group who have not only tried to use their Marxist techniques creatively, but have to some measure succeeded. The interesting thing is that the writers as a group have been much more confused – a quite different situation from that in the Eastern countries – and it is precisely the creative writers who should have seen more clearly the heart of things. Of what, otherwise, does their 'creativeness' consist? [124]

The Twentieth Congress was discussed by the full committee of the Historians' Group (with other leading members invited) on 8 April 1956. The main section of the Minutes reads as follows:

Resolutions were passed expressing profound dissatisfaction with the 24th Congress of the British Party for its failure to discuss publicly the implications for the British Party of the 20th Congress of the CPSU (the Group were told in reply that the Congress decided its own procedure); and with the failure of the Party leadership to make a public statement of regret for the British Party's past uncritical endorsement of all Soviet policies and views, the meeting calling upon it to make one as soon as possible, as well as to initiate the widest possible public discussion of all the problems involved for the British Party in the present situation. (This Resolution was passed to the E. C.).

In July Eric Hobsbawm spoke on 'The tasks of historians now' in which he called on the historians self-critically to examine the Party *as historians*; and in November, after the first resignations, he proposed that the rump of the group should form the basis for a broader, independent non-Party grouping of marxist historians so long as Party approval were won, 'which seemed probable'.[125] There is no indication of the fate of this proposal – which in effect argued for the continuation of the Group but without Party affiliation. In the event although the Historians' Group itself continued, it lost those who had resigned from the Party – many of whom gravitated to *Past and Present*. Others became part of a broader movement more self-consciously styled as a New Left.

It may be tempting to see the launching of the New Left, and the subsequent take-off of CND in 1958, as the precarious translation of the intellectual current represented by the Historians' Group into a political force. But this view needs significant qualifications. First, it ignores the differences in politics between the Communist historians which were clarified in the light of the events of 1956 – differences not only defined by the single fracture dividing those who stayed from those who left. Second, it underestimates the diversity of politico-intellectual determinations, dissimilar in orientation, which ultimately fused in the New Left; it is not at all certain that the historians or the *Reasoner* tendency constituted the dominant element. Third, like the War radicalism of the 1940s, the deepening of the popular movement in the last years of the 1950s was not in its origins self-consciously socialist. It may have contributed to that process which, in effect, began to dislodge the political hegemony of the Conservative settlement, but it wasn't the *embodiment* of that popular tradition recuperated by the historians. More accurately, this popular mobilization brought into existence the *conditions* for initiating the strategic perspective implicit in the Group's historiography of the previous ten years. Fourth and last, this view obscures the transformations, politically and theoretically, which occurred under the impact of 1956. Thompson's proclamation in the final issue of the *Reasoner* – 'It is time that we had this out' – is central here. In the historiography one need only contrast the hard-line party emphases which punctuate the *Morris* book, to the later picture of Tom Maguire as the local militant whose politics were only achieved by harmonizing 'the needs and aspirations of his own people'.[126]

But on one point the connections between the Historians' Group and the movement of the New Left seem decisive. The popular aspirations of the New Left and CND – the latter as a force which cut across class lines, claiming its own intellectuals and tribunes – echoed in the minds of some of the historians, at least, the popular radicalism of the 1940s.[127] This is particularly the impression gained from reading the *New Reasoner*, and from this moment Edward Thompson edges to the centre of the stage. It seems as if this reading of the current situation by Thompson and others depended in part on the somewhat shaky supposition that the dormant radical populism of English history was on the point of an explosive reawakening, fulfilling exactly the expectations inscribed in the historiography. This misrecognition may account for some of the extravagance of Thompson's writing in this period. On this critical point Perry Anderson – in what overall was an exceedingly ill-judged attack – was right.[128] Fifteen years later Anderson still holds his ground on this, maintaining that the writings of 1958–61 are among Thompson's weakest.[129] Although many of Anderson's criticisms of a simple populism are still pertinent, what proved defective and destructive in Anderson's own position was the consequent dismantling of the entire problematic, the implicit rejection of all those themes marked by the concept of the national-popular, and what in effect was the uncompromising ditching of the native trad-ition of marxist historiography – the vacuum was filled by Isaac Deutscher, seeded by Anderson 'the greatest marxist historian in the world' – its excesses and mis-conceptions inverted. But the most relevant fact is this. Just as the national struggle against fascism in the 1940s registered inside the historiography and recomposed its conceptual syntax, so too at the end of the 1950s the groundswell of the New Left – the exaggerated claims notwithstanding – provided the conditions for reconciling some of the persistent ambiguities in the historiography of the previous decade.

The free-born Englishman

It was from this interplay of politics and theory that *The Making of the English Working Class* emerged, a definite response to a particular legacy of historiographical problems. This is the subject of a following chapter and only two points need stating here. First, in its centring of the category of experience the *Making* provided a notable resolution to a persistent theoretical difficulty which beset the prior historiography, the oscillation in emphasis between determination and agency. This was paralleled in a more general, quickening retreat from 'scientific' history. (Note the changed mast-head of *Past and Present* in 1958 from 'A Journal of Scientific History' to 'A Journal of Historical Studies'.) Many of the conceptual elements which composed this shift had been long present: in the commitment to understanding history as a creative process (the long lineage back to Torr and Hill in the forties) or as human praxis (as in Hill's contention: 'man's activity in all its manifestations is *one*');[130] in the insistence on the rationality of the plebeian crowd (Hobsbawm, Rudé); in Hill's belief, introducing *Puritanism and Revolution*, that 'No explanation of the English Revolution will do which starts by assuming that the people who made it were knaves or fools, puppets or automata'.[131] These points don't detract from the originality and strength of the *Making*. One need only compare the intervention of the Communist historians in the 'standard of living' controversy in the 1950s (a delegated task initiated by Saville and Hobsbawm, and written up by Hobsbawm) – locked into the debates on affluence – to Thompson's path-breaking, 'qualitative' assessment. (More abstractly, and without short-circuiting the argument, 'culturalism' can be seen as constituting a field of concepts which allowed the theoretical incompatibilities of the 1950s to be reconciled. This is discussed in more detail in the next chapter.) Not all the historians followed the paths opened by the *Making* in equal measure. Many of the other distinctive problems which perplexed the marxist historians were not reworked till much later (such as the relation between romanticism and marxism). Many are still with us in one form or other. And subsequently, those resolutions appearing in the *Making* and elsewhere are now themselves being opened up and put in question, and new theoretical considerations placed on the agenda.

Second, the construction of the English popular tradition reached a kind of crystallization in the *Making*. In his Preface Thompson stressed the specificity of the popular culture in England, and in the opening chapter the connections were traced back to the seventeenth century: 'To read the controversies between reformers and authority, and between different reforming groups, in the 1790s is to see the Putney Debates come to life once again'.[132] But the most sustained reconstruction occurred in the fourth chapter, 'The free-born Englishman', a section which Thompson valued sufficiently in its own right to publish separately in *New Left Review* anticipating the work as a whole.

From the 1790s Thompson noted 'a major shift in emphasis in the inarticulate, "sub-political" attitude of the masses' which was related to

popular notions of 'independence', patriotism, and the Englishman's birthright. The Gordon Rioters of 1780 and the 'Church and King' rioters in Birmingham in 1791 had this in common: they felt themselves, in some obscure way, to be defending the 'Constitution' against alien elements which threatened their 'birthright'. They had been taught for so long that the Revolution settlement of 1688, embodied in the Constitution of King, Lords and Commons, was the guarantee of British independence and liberties, that the reflex had been set up – Constitution equals Liberty – upon which the unscrupulous might play.

Freedom from foreign domination was the very nerve which touched all other aspects:

Freedom from absolutism (the constitutional monarch), freedom from arbitrary arrest, trial by jury, equality before the law, the freedom of the home from arbitrary entrance and search, some limited liberty of thought, of speech and of conscience, the vicarious participation in liberty (or in its semblance) afforded by the right of parliamentary opposition and by elections and election tumults (although the people had no vote they had the right to parade, to huzza and jeer on the hustings), as well as freedom to travel, trade, and sell one's own labour. Nor were any of these freedoms insignificant; taken together, they both embody and reflect a moral consensus in which authority at times shared, and of which at all times it was bound to take account.

The stance 'was not so much democratic as anti-absolutist' and anti-statist, drawing its sustenance from a belief in equality before the law ('each attempt to pack juries aroused an outcry beyond the reformers' own ranks'). Hostility was primarily concentrated against centralized authority from a position made up of a 'curious blend of parochial defensiveness, Whig theory and popular resistance'. This Thompson emphasized, was the tradition articulated by the theorists of the Norman Yoke and, with climactic force, by Tom Paine in his rupturing of constitutional precedent. 'In the years between 1770 and 1790 we can observe a dialectical paradox by means of which the rhetoric of constitutionalism contributed to its own destruction or transcendence.' Paine's egalitarianism effected the bridge between the radical popular traditions of the seventeenth century and the new working-class movement, and it was Paine 'who saw that in the constitutional debates of the 18th century "the Nation was always left out of the question". By bringing the nation *into* the question he was bound to set in motion forces which he could neither control nor foresee. That is what democracy is about'.[133] Thompson picks up this theme in the last pages of the book where this tradition is assessed with full and measured respect:

It was perhaps a unique formation, this British working class of 1832. The slow, piece-meal accretions of capital accumulation had meant that the preliminaries to the Industrial Revolution stretched backwards for hundreds of years. From Tudor times onward this artisan culture had grown more complex with each phase of technical and social change. Delaney, Dekker and Nashe: Winstanley and Lilburne: Bunyan and Defoe – all had at times addressed themselves to it. Enriched by the experiences of the seventeenth century, carrying through the eighteenth century the intellectual and libertarian traditions which we have described, forming their own traditions of mutuality in the friendly society and trades club, these men did not pass, in one generation, from the peasantry to the new industrial town. They suffered the experience of the Industrial Revolution as articulate, free-born Englishmen.[134]

Although this is clearly a formidable depiction, advancing upon many of the earlier discussions, its roots reached well back into the historiography of the Communist Group. To recap, four areas of difficulty have been identified in this body of work: the obliteration of discontinuities; the strong implication that the forward march of the people is necessarily democratic; the belief in an 'authentic' radical popular culture, resilient or impervious to dominant interventions, such that it can be called upon as unambiguously 'ours' (as in the defence of Morris); and the elevation of the past over the present. Together, these established English popular culture as the tradition of the Good Old Cause or the Free-Born Englishman.

In hindsight, the most glaring weakness in this presentation is the supremely masculinist structuring of this tradition. Its rhetoric is of the liberty-loving Englishman as master of his household, the threshold of which defines his power in the 'private' sphere. This structuring was all but unchallenged, the single exception being an intervention by Bridget Hill. She observed that 'bourgeois history is mainly the history of male society', and went on to suggest that in this respect radical histories had been uncritically cast in the image of the dominant historiography. She argued for the need to study the resistances of working-class women *and* of feminist movements, the economic exploitation of proletarian women *and* 'the terrible degradation of women under bourgeois marriage'. In consequence, she urged a return to a *different* tradition of socialism, specifically to the more consciously feminist politics of Owenism.[135] Not only did this intervention challenge the 'absence' of women, but also the very selectivity, and construction, of the radical tradition as presented by the male historians. By asking different political questions, a rather different 'tradition' emerged. Theoretically, this illuminates the extent to which the popular was a *construction* within the historiography, and not a self-evident reality which could be scooped up from the past.

In addition, in a similar vein, it is clear from Thompson's account that the tradition of the free-born Englishman is open to a number of differing, and potentially conflicting, readings. As Thompson himself noted, the stance of the common Englishman 'was not so much democratic' as anti-absolutist. However this is not a mere historiographical qualification, a mere gesture. The distinction between a

tradition which *is* democratic, and a popular tradition resonant in its desire to
be free from state interference – one which may under certain conditions *become*
democratic – is surely all-important. Despite this formal recognition, in *The Making
of the English Working Class* this distinction continually threatens to become
dissolved in the reconstruction of the tradition in its democratic and heroic heights.
The full theoretical consequences of the historical fact of an anti-democratic
Church and King crowd became truncated from an early point. There was no
whisper concerning what Geoffrey Best called the 'flag-saluting, foreigner-hating,
peer-respecting side of the plebeian mind', or what Perry Anderson has identified
as 'the depth of the ideological capture of the "nation" for conservative ends'.[136]
In the light of these observations both continuity and epochal coherence need to
be questioned.

The source of an enduring difficulty in the legacy of the Communist historians
was their initial conflation of a popular tradition (which framed a number of very
different ideologies in different conjunctures) with the determinate ideologies
themselves. As Laclau shows, 'popular traditions do not constitute consistent and
organized discourses but merely *elements* which can only exist in articulation with
class discourses'.[137] In the main, the populism of the historians' politics forced
attention on to the abstract 'elements' of a long, popular tradition. When these
were linked together at their high points (John Ball to William Morris) they
appeared, precisely, as abstract. There were exceptions. Hill's emphasis on the
conflicting appropriations of the theory of the Norman Yoke was an insight
insufficiently developed within the mainstream of the Group, for it indicated with
precision the range of articulations which could cohere around a single popular
tradition. More often, the temptation was to lift or extrapolate ideological elements
from their determinate, conjunctural contexts. In consequence these elements can
indeed come to signify abstract political forces (as Anderson rightly recognized
in his critique of Thompson's 'cult of 1956'). For these elements remain abstract
and indeterminate until articulated to other political forces. The 'free-born
Englishman defending his home' is abstract until we know who he is defending it
from – Nazi invasion and fascism, or Asians who have moved in next door.

The possibilities for a right-wing populism to develop, building on the libertarian
and anti-statist traditions of English thought, undoubtedly register on the mind with
more resonance in our contemporary era than in the 1950s. Today we do not have
to look very far to see an aggressive and radical Conservatism rummaging in the
past in order to produce its own coherent and organized conception of 'history',
recasting the individualist elements of the free-born Englishman into a new
reactionary populist ideology. This again is an observation from hindsight. But this
privileged vantage point should not be exaggerated. Thompson for example has
been explicit (on two occasions) that the most coherent development of the radical
popular ideology of the early nineteenth century was in the politics of Lloyd
Georgeism. Alternatively, it could be shown how from the onset of the imperial
crisis in the 1890s the notion of the Englishman's birthright (and the veneration of
'the English stock') has developed as a consistent refrain in the radical right and

(later) the proto-fascist fringe.[138] The implications of these shifts to the right, and the consequent reworking of the popular iconography, were never confronted by the historians. Taken further, it can be argued that the concept of the (national) popular, as it was constituted within the historiography of the period, effectively disintegrated in the face of such questions.

Thus the tradition of English populism can be constructed in a number of different ways: feminist or masculinist, left-wing or right-wing. In other words it is absolutely pivotal to be able to explain how the notion of 'the people' or of 'the popular' is conceptually constructed. Different constructions imply different politics. The problem lies in the various ways of organizing the concept of 'the people' as an object of knowledge. This premise was hardly recognized by the historians. For them, the people were transparently *the people in history*, and popular culture the tradition of previous generations. In 1965 Thompson wrote: 'We will not understand the intensity of the conflict (of the seventeenth century), the tenacity of the authoritarians, nor the energy of the Puritans, unless we understand the kind of people they were and *hence* the socio-economic context. But the mediation between "interest" and "belief" was not through Nairn's "complex of superstructures" but *through the people themselves*'.[139] Here is encapsulated, with absolute clarity, the theoretical premise not only for Thompson's reconstruction of English populism, but for the dominant Communist historiography of the 1950s as well. To argue against this, in full theoretical engagement, is not necessary here. Such a critique can be found later in this book, and in parallel pieces elsewhere.[140] It need only be said that, of necessity, 'the people' and 'popular culture' are concepts within historiography; they will only be advanced by resisting the conflation which collapses them back into 'the people in history'; and it is *precisely* attention to the 'complex of superstructures' which promises an end to this conflation.

It is possible to see why the Communist historians adopted their position. On the one hand they were committed to take up and develop the 'people's history' of the radical and liberal traditions. In effect, this was the Popular Front at work in the historiography. Their precursors on this terrain were radical liberals. In Christopher Hill's words, 'Tawney fired the imagination of my generation',[141] and in the days of the Cold War the Communists spent much energy in defending Tawney from his detractors. Similarly, Thompson's dialogue with the Hammonds has been ever-present and he too, time and again, has felt impelled to argue their defence, attempting to win back ground which in earlier engagements seemed secure. On the other hand, for the Communist historians the sort of theorization and abstraction necessary actually to develop and redeploy radical liberal 'people's history' smacked of 'science', anti-humanism, and, by default, class reductionism – smacked, in sum, of an *anti-populism*. This is the paradox in which the historians were caught. To avoid the collapse of 'the people in history' required just this commitment to the conceptual *transformation* of the radical liberal tradition, but in turn this theoretical endeavour was resisted because of its perceived anti-populist drift. This is where the one-sided appropriation of Dobb was so debilitating. By eclipsing his concern with the relation between 'knowledge' and 'history', the space which would allow the active transformation of 'people's history' contracted.

It is this need to transform radical and liberal 'people's history' which is at issue for socialists. In an important article, Raphael Samuel has recently drawn attention to the varieties of 'people's history': conservative, liberal and socialist. It is an argument which is parallel to Laclau's on popular traditions, emphasizing the concrete political and conceptual forms to which histories of 'the people' are articulated. Samuel claims that: 'The notion of "people's history" is not one which Marxists find themselves at ease with, even though in Britain they make up a large part of its present-day practitioners . . . it has in the past been appropriated by the Right as well as by the Left, while its philosophic roots are pre-Marxist'.[142] The very openness, the indeterminate nature, of 'people's histories' which Raphael Samuel points to implies that there exists no pre-given conjunction between 'people's history' and socialist theory. To effect this conjunction requires the reordering of the liberal, or liberal radical traditions. That this continues to raise profound intellectual and political tensions is evident from the Ruskin History Workshop Conference in 1979, devoted to this precise issue, and from the papers subsequently published as *People's History and Socialist Theory*. The fact that the Communist Group of the 1950s placed this problem so centrally on the agenda is a clear tribute to their initiative. But at the same time it is important to be clear that in this Communist historiography the earlier traditions of 'people's history' were insufficiently reworked and that politically this resulted in an 'untransformed' populism.

The incompleteness of this transformation of radical historiography can be illustrated by looking at the slide between the concepts class and people. Despite its title, in *The Making of the English Working Class* the terms are frequently interchangeable. But perhaps the most succinct formulation comes from Hill: 'People, social classes, are the instruments through which social change is effected'.[143] Not only is the word 'people' ambiguous here (suggesting both 'the people' and human individuals) but it is directly equated with social class. Once more, it can be seen how Dobb's contribution to a marxist historiography, thinking class relations at different levels of generality and premising his histories on the need to specify distinct levels of abstraction, was far too easily shunned. This was the price paid for ditching his economism and what was perceived as his residual rationalism. In its place, the historians adopted the very language of the radical liberal tradition, of Paine and Cobbett themselves. Oppression comes to be represented by the 'French Bastard', 'Old Corruption' and 'The Thing'. At times this looks less like an attempt at transformation and rather more like capitulation to the older traditions.

Partly as a consequence, the theoretical conditions for thinking that transformation of popular traditions (discontinuities) diminished. 'The People' and 'The Thing' appeared as continuous and fixed elements in the history of England, and in this the marxists curiously mirrored the Whiggish assumptions of many of their antagonists. Clearly, of course, the struggles of the people against oppression were not unchanging. We are told of these changes; they may even be dialectical. But no means is presented by which to explain the shift from one articulation of people/nation to another.

This leads to the final point. When contemporary forms become the object of the histories the analysis threatens to become, literally, anachronistic. In a recent summation of his work, George Rudé completes his Introduction by saying: 'Moreover, the last of the "English" chapters, being concerned with the entirely new problems of an industrial society, is rapidly sketched and leaves readers to puzzle out for themselves the answer to the question, "What next?".'[144] The rhetoric of the question is symptomatic. Within marxist historiography in Britain nearly all of the most valuable contributions to cultural history, all the histories which penetrate and can best depict popular cultures, have their object located in pre- or proto-capitalism. In this sense the 'stop in the mind' in which continuity was superimposed on discontinuities has generated a long-lasting legacy. The historiography has concentrated on the formative, heroic or democratic moments of 'people's history': the seventeenth-century Revolution and the formation of the bourgeois nation under pressure from below; the *making* of the English working class. Again, the need to extend the history of popular cultures into the modern period has registered in the historiography. Hill emphasized the anachronism of the theory of the Norman Yoke in an age of the industrial working class, socialist movements and marxism. A similar point is made in an essay he 'presented' to Dobb: 'The acceptance of wage-labour as a permanent system was accompanied, significantly, by the abandonment of the backward-looking idea of the birthright, and even of the concept of the free-born Englishman.'[145] Yet this makes the contrary pull, back to continuity, look even more bizarre. What is more, it resulted in a historiography which offers surprisingly few clues, given its empirical depth, for concrete engagement, in theory or politics, with contemporary popular cultures. The impact of the transition to 'industrial' society for a study of contemporary cultural forms has usefully been outlined by Tony Bennett.[146]

In asking 'What next?' Rudé had the weight of the whole intellectual tradition of marxist historiography pressing against him. A strenuous theoretical effort is required to locate within historical studies that cultural transformation which Rudé leaves his readers to 'puzzle out for themselves'.

It is not that this central problem has been ignored. The controversies surrounding the remaking and recomposition of class relations are directly relevant and need much greater consideration. But the fact still remains that histories of the later nineteenth century and the twentieth century tend to be emptied of such imaginative reconstructions of cultural formations in comparison with those of the earlier periods. Characteristically (and here I'll exaggerate to press home my case) the histories of the formed working class, fully inserted into the capital-labour relation, having 'learned the rules of the game' and 'seeking time-and-a-half', have been organized around the concept of the labour aristocracy, which until recently has generally been conceptualized quite aculturally. In fact, part of the problem with the concept of the labour aristocracy is that it has had to carry the burden of explaining *all* that differentiates the industrial working class from its plebeian forerunners, all the changes within the structure of the cultural field that Bennett illuminates. (And it is interesting to see how it has subsequently become stretched to cover the whole period from the mid nineteenth century to the 1920s and beyond, most especially by John Foster.) That this is not just a consequence of personal idiosyncrasies of the historians can be judged from the fact that this dichotomy operates within the work of one historian. In *Primitive Rebels* Eric Hobsbawm gave a superb anthropological account of 'pre-modern' social movements, a dimension which disappears from the defining concerns of *Labouring Men*. The language, ritual and symbols of contemporary proletarian life are only very slowly becoming constituted as objects within historiography.[147]

Histories and memories

It is undeniable, whatever qualifications one makes, that the histories produced by the members of the CP History Group in the decade from 1946, and the theoretical paths opened by this collective intellectual project, have permanently reconstructed our knowledge of the past. I have only been concerned with the first ten years of the Group and with some aspects of the immediate aftermath of 1956. In the subsequent historiography, although some of the deepest problems encountered in this earlier period continue to resurface, the themes first placed on the agenda in the 1940s have become immeasurably more sophisticated. Following the themes of the national-popular one could note Thompson's 'Peculiarities of the English', perhaps the most cogent theoretical restatement, and a subtle development of familiar territory. The abiding interest in plebeian movements and resistances, in the meanings and rituals of subterranean cultures, has become much more finely specified, etching in a whole dimension of bandits, foresters, machine-breakers, poachers, rick-burners, smugglers, food rioters, arsonists. Hill's essay on 'The many-headed monster', his studies of *Anti-Christ in 17th Century England* and *The World Turned Upside Down*, Thompson's *Whigs and Hunters*, Hilton's *Bond Men Made Free* and Hobsbawm's *Bandits*, for all their differences, present a remarkable picture of popular movements, opening up a very rich seam of concepts – custom, common sense and good sense, moralities, changing categorizations of property, crime and justice, symbolic forms of domination – focusing the internal cultural constitution of the dominant and subordinate fields of political forces.

The connections between nation and people continually intersect in Hill's work on puritanism, an output over the years which is more reminiscent of Stakhanovism than the usual pace of the tramping, artisanal historian. *The Century of Revolution*, written soon after Hill left the Communist Party (and at last achieving the History Group's frustrated aspirations for a student textbook) is framed by its Gramscian analysis of 'the conflict between two conceptions of civilization' from which emerged as victorious puritanism as way of life – Parliament, property and nation fused in a new historic bloc. *Puritanism and Society* and *The Intellectual Origins of the English Revolution* specified in much greater depth the internal determinations of the cultural or 'mental' revolution of the sixteenth and seventeenth centuries, both in terms of its 'philosophers' (scientists, theologians, artists) and in the dramatic reconstitution of the popular culture. Notable is how Hill's feel for popular mentalities has, over the years, moved to the very forefront of his histories. In *Intellectual Origins*, the familiar identification of the influence of the common people on the poets and dramatists becomes widened to include the scientists (Bacon pre-eminent amongst them): 'the triumph of science saw the triumph of the standards of the common man over those of his social superiors'.[148] By the time of *The World Turned Upside Down* the reconceptualization of the popular culture of the seventeenth century is so sharp it forces a revision of the original 'two conceptions' thesis. Here he reconstructs the radical alternative as a 'third' culture in its own right, pitted against both Court and ascendant Puritanism, composed by a profoundly democratic libertarian strain, and resistant to the imposition of disciplinary, external constraints. Hill concludes that, in crucial respects, in the latter half of the twentieth century 'we haven't caught up with the 1640s'.

This delineation of antagonistic cultural formations also theoretically structures his *Milton and the English Revolution*. Here Milton appears as a political thinker straddling the puritan and radical cultures, 'in permanent dialogue with the plebeian radical thinkers of the English Revolution', and whose epitaph Hill writes in familiar terms: 'He would not want his personal fame to be separated from his Good Old Cause'.[149] Again this rehearses the characteristic popularization of national literary figures. It is an analysis which has caused a good deal of controversy, and not only by provoking the smouldering hostility of literary critics. Many have found his historicization of Milton too headstrong. But what is interesting in the response of the literary critics was that resentment was caused neither by the radicalization of Milton, nor – against the 'dislodgement' effected by Leavis and Eliot in the 1930s – by his reinstatement as poet. Rather, Hill's approach cut into the discipline of literary criticism itself, threatening to dislocate its very joints. Theoretically, the *Scrutiny* terrain – the metaphysic of the text, the primacy of aesthetics, the dehistoricization and abstraction of the 'literary', the reverence for standard English – has become more securely translated into a cultural history (or Raymond Williams's 'materialist cultural analysis') in a way that was only ever anticipated by the historians in the 1950s.

It would be a fruitless task to chart the impact of the historiography of the Communists on subsequent historical analysis, only because it has been all-pervasive. *History Workshop Journal* for example, developing as a real alternative to the dominant apparatuses of historical scholarship (and whose first editorial committed the journal to its 'concern with the common people in the past'), is by and large unthinkable without the prior interventions of the Communist historians. To close this chapter, therefore, I'll return to one last aspect of the national-popular.

The objective of creating a democratic national-popular culture involves much more than revising the historical knowledge of the academies. The national-popular is decisively constituted by historical *memory*[150] – by the multiplicity of 'everyday' (non-academic) representations of the relations connecting the past to the present. It is here most of all that conceptions of the past are ordered in the field of struggle. At its most common this can be observed in the institutionalized commemoration of a nation's past, materialized in street names (working-class districts inscribed with the legends of imperial battles; housing blocks bearing the names of poets), postage stamps, banknotes, museums and so on. But such commemorative landmarks can be bureaucratic and imposed, in the sense of remaining disconnected from personal and popular memories. The defining problem therefore is not simply to rearrange the elements of the iconography but to ensure that a democratic perspective on the past connects with people's contemporary conditions of existence and 'becomes popular'. This may be stating the obvious. Within the History Group,[151] we can see that three interconnected responses emerged to cope with this and with the problem of how to justify historical practice, all of which were ranged against the notion of the people as a 'paralysed mentality' - which had afflicted early Communist thinking in Britain.[152] All these versions are of value - indicating different moments in the historiography–politics complex - and, to different degrees, they were all shared by the individual historians.

The first is the most familiar: history as lesson, the belief in learning from the past to understand the present. It is a persistent refrain in socialist historiography, and rightly. In the Preface to the *Making* Thompson hoped that 'In some of the lost causes of the people of the Industrial Revolution we may discover insights into social evils which we have yet to cure. . . . Causes which were lost in England might, in Asia or Africa, yet be won'. And in a recent interview Hobsbawm has stated: 'I am increasingly coming back to the old-fashioned opinion that it is useful in politics to have historical perspective if you want to know what is new in a situation. You've got to know how it's different from what's gone on before'.[153] In this version historical analysis is a necessary component in the elaboration of political strategy. But to take this further, to specify more concretely requirements of historical practice, is difficult; nor does it really offer much rationale for studying drama in ancient Greece or the Rising of 1381. The limitations of this approach derive from the separation of historical practice from politics - such that one is brought *into* relation with the other, diminishing the political structuring of historical knowledge as a practice.

A second explanation is history as exhortation: the *appeal* to class or people to hear its own history (propaganda, in an orthodox sense). This may have been the dominant political impulse in the Communist History Group in the 1950s. A variant of this is history as a moral example, the partisan recuperation in historiography of resistances to past injustices in order to build confidence to act today. If the first justification is 'Andersonian' in temperament, then this would be 'Thompsonian' - the compassionate practitioner seeking out the poacher or bread rioter, the anonymous letter writer or the rick-burner. In a similar vein is the urge to keep *faith* with the past. Again, Thompson's recovery of the 1940s against its contamination by bureaucratic detractors is relevant. A similar belief concludes Raphael Samuel's long survey of marxist historiography: 'As the women's movement has shown, one does not need to be a triumphalist in order to keep faith with the past, or use it as a critical point with which to view the present'.[154] This conception is important too, and has been too easily demeaned. But again, the limitations of keeping faith with the past need to be recognized for it is difficult to know how, in analytic and strategic terms, this can be sufficiently developed. As I have implied in this chapter, an appropriation of history, if couched only in these terms, can become loosened from its anchorage in contemporary conditions, and its strengths misdirected.

Third is the study of history *as* politics, fully grasping the measure to which conceptions of the past have a hold on, and organize, *contemporary* 'memories' and ideologies. At one point Hill (and it was Hill who most developed this position) expressed this formally, with a visible debt to his early Party training in dialectics: 'We ourselves are shaped by the past; but from our vantage point in the present we are continually reshaping the past which shapes us'.[155] But in the content of his own historiography more adequate clues can be found than in this elegant formulation. Hill persistently returns to the central fact that a new sense of historical time developed in the seventeenth century. At the heart of this development lay the emancipation from the past – from 'history' – and the belief in the possibilities of 'making' the future. Hill identifies this transformation as a shift from mythological to historical time, suggesting that this conditioned the emergence of a new paradigm of knowledge, the science of politics. The extent to which history and politics are unified in his own mind can be gauged from his judgement that Ralegh 'trembled on the edge of a science of politics, which would be dominated by history'.[156] But aside from this intellectual revolution in the dominant culture Hill insists (in 'The Norman Yoke' and elsewhere) that the popular conception of past and present was decisively recast as a new 'popular memory'. Some of Hill's sharpest insights concern the interconnections between these two modes of conceptualizing history, and their respective political effects.

What distinguishes this third approach of history *as* politics is the commitment to the conditions of the production of historical knowledge as a political question. It centrally locates 'making histories' and the production of 'memories' as a constituent moment in the struggles within ideology and culture. This is vital in order to understand the *active* construction of conceptions of the past as a continual and defining moment in political practice, engaging with and deconstructing reactionary 'memories' and histories. The distinction between this and other approaches may often be a fine one, as the practice of the British historians proves. But it is decisive for all that, because it includes as a site of struggle, and thus as problematic, popular culture itself. It stresses the need to theorize the connections and disjunctures between professional or academic histories and the complex amalgam of public and private 'common-sense' conceptions of the past. For notions of history and memories are themselves constituted as the earthworks and fortresses of civil society, of which Gramsci wrote.[157] It is in this, non-reductionist sense, that Hill claimed 'history as politics'.

3 E. P. Thompson and the discipline of historical context

Gregor McLennan

Introduction

E. P. Thompson's work over the last thirty years or so has been a remarkably wide-ranging, consistent and challenging presence in socialist intellectual life in this country. Forged in the heat of argument, his writings typically generate counter-polemic or adulation. Readers and listeners are never left in any doubt that important practical problems of the day lie behind even his most specialist interests. It is this embattled, political, and even rhetorical mode of historiography which Thompson exemplifies that demands our attention. And even in moments of open provocation, Thompson's work enforces *self*-examination on those who seek to assess his contribution.

There are also drawbacks in a focused analysis of this kind, the foremost of which is the relative inattention which the discussion must commit upon historians of the calibre of Hobsbawm, Hill, or Hilton. It is worth stating that these writers do not necessarily suffer by comparison with Thompson.[1] Eric Hobsbawm's comparative surveys of feudal crisis and the ages of revolution and capital are commanding theoretical grids. They have a sharp, 'objective' quality which Thompson's accounts lack. Rodney Hilton's dominance of the historiography of feudalism is due at least in part to the fine balance he strikes between 'structural' analysis and the emphasis on the decisive role of class struggles. Thompson tends to prise struggle and structure apart and chooses between them. Christopher Hill's books display as much as Thompson's a concern for literary sources and forms, and for the rationality of popular or 'deviant' action in pre-capitalist society. The point here is to emphasize – as Edward Thompson himself insists – that his work forms part of a kind of informal collective of socialist historians, each contributor to which is aware that his or her work complements that of others.

This account of E. P. Thompson's contribution has the following shape.[2] I begin by looking at how Thompson mobilizes his status and stature as a historian, with a view to indicating the range of his concerns and their political purpose. His defence of the historical mode is then discussed in detail, first in its critical opposition to social theory and philosophy, then in its positive elaboration as 'the logic of process'. After examining the methodological aspects of his major historical works, I take up more general issues to do with Thompson's marxism and the controversial but cloudy question of 'culturalism'. Thompson's political standpoints are then evaluated. Obviously, the questions broached here are of key significance, yet owing to the scope of the essay they perhaps receive, in terms of space, less direct attention than they merit. However, I hope that, throughout the piece, I have shown how historical research and reflection are closely entwined with the relative shifts in Thompson's political practice – from Communist activist and teacher; to socialist intellectual and commentator; to the principal spokesperson on the urgency of opposing nuclear arms escalation. Finally, I briefly consider Thompson's characteristics as a writer and polemicist, pointing to the typical blend of impressive and distracting qualities.

The objective of the assessment is twofold. I try to grasp the distinctive features of Thompson's historiography, theoretical inclinations, politics and style. In doing so I argue that in spite of his persuasive and combative confidence in debate, Thompson's views are, in important respects, inconsistent. This judgement is critical, but not derogatory, since it also registers Thompson's awareness of the intellectual problems and moral complexities which all socialists (and especially 'intellectuals') at some point have to come to terms with. Second, I hope to make the case that, shorn of its overstatements and convolutions, and despite some of his own pronouncements, E. P. Thompson's work provides a rich and instructive illustration of the necessary interdependence of theory, historiography, and politics.

The uses of history

Nothing captures E. P. Thompson's convictions better than his use of the figure of 'the historian', and his defence of the category of 'history'. We would naturally expect any historian to deploy professional competence in general argument. But even amongst socialist historians, Thompson is unusually militant about history as an intellectual force. In theoretical or political debate, he uses it as a rhetorical weapon against all-comers. The variety of contexts and the variable force of the tactic are worth exemplifying.

'The state of the nation'[3] is a critical analysis of the growth of statism in Britain today. The essay is conducted from the point of view of the observing historian, flown in from the past specially for that purpose. Only part-artifice, this strategy is effective and ingenious: Thompson is allowed to make a vigorous contemporary critique of authoritarian ideology through the voice of History itself. Ideology is exposed simply by putting the record straight.

As a historian I can say that I know of no period in which the police have had such a loud and didactic presence, and when they have offered themselves as a distinct interest, as one of the great 'institutions' and perhaps the first in the realm.[4]

Yet

In a broad secular view there has never been a time when public disorder in the streets has been less.[5]

Here, the concept of 'order' is neatly turned against its proselytizers. Similarly, Thompson refers to the 'muggers of the constitution' who propose to abandon the jury system.

I must ask myself, what is the revolution of the times which struck us suddenly ten years or so ago, like a typhoon, and swept seven hundred years of practice and of precedent away.[6]

But the stance of the historian can become a posture. Too much is made of precedent: the figures of a reincarnated Burke (now on the Left), and the dogged but virtuous free-born Briton become distracting, and their creator presumptuous.

I cannot allow that, in this ancient realm, the office (i.e. of Director of Public Prosecutions) has yet qualified as an 'institution of this country'.[7]

It is arguable too that, historically, this insistence upon the progressiveness of the institutions of British liberty concedes too much to formal rather than real democracy. For example, the idea that the spirit of the jury system has only recently been overthrown is misleading. In the first years of the last century Sir Samuel Romilly's long and 'moderate' campaign to reform the law was persistently impeded, then soundly defeated. He had proposed that juries be invested with some of the supreme and unaccountable power which the judges had in practice wielded, and were to continue to wield, for many decades.

In his notable argument with one of the intellectuals who presides over the rightward turn today (though in an appropriately liberal manner), Thompson taunts Conor Cruise O'Brien with being a knowledgeable historian who should know better than to flame 'The great fear of Marxism'. Again, one is bound to say that Thompson's tactic succeeds, especially when exposing the paucity of demonstration in O'Brien's article.[8] However, there is just a hint that O'Brien should *really* know better. The implication is that if it were only realized that marxism need not harbour 'readers of Lukacs or Althusser', if it were only allowed that workers could be well-ordered and good-humoured, then all would be well, and the *Observer* might in return be applauded for its libertarianism and sense of history. That is, perhaps, to read too much into what is otherwise a fine rejoinder by Thompson. But he has appeared as keen to lambast the Left as he has to contest conventional wisdom.

In 'The secret state',[9] Thompson taxes what he calls the 'unofficial' Left for its ambivalence towards civil liberties. And he is right to do so. However, not *all* of the Left have by any means been blind to the question, and even amongst those who have, we would be pushed to find proponents of

the soppy notion that all crime is some kind of displaced revolutionary activity.[10]

To 'a historian in a libertarian marxist tradition' such 'half-truths . . . degenerate into rubbish'.[11] Thompson is justified in warning against gestural sympathies for terrorism and the like, even if it requires stretching a point. On the other hand, we might consider that his own work on the eighteenth century is apt to leave us with the uneasy feeling that any possibly semi-criminal aspect of popular riot has been (almost) explained away by Thompson himself as perfectly rational political protest, or even revolutionary activity.

I have so far focused on the essays collected in *Writing by Candlelight* in order to suggest that in Thompson's valuable recent political commentaries are tensions and issues which are germane to his broader historical and theoretical work. We have also already caught sight of the co-presence of sharp refutation and overstatement, of historical richness and a 'rhetoric of history'.

History, sociology, and philosophy

Thompson is by no means a friend to anyone who qualifies as a historian. Rather, it is the *category* of history and the typical concerns of sensitive historians which he is eager to defend. There are two sides to Thompson's thought here. First, his approach to history is one of affirmation, of commitment to humanist values. In his historical books and articles, Thompson tries to place indelibly in the imagination of his reader the sense that people – particularly those of the 'lower' classes – *make* their own history. His emphasis on the particularity of agency and struggle is not so much a disembodied respect for 'facts' as fellow feeling for groups of people who, against the odds, assert their right to individual and collective self-determination. Though such struggles may in some eyes have appeared to take strange forms, Thompson champions the validity of historical experience in the face of contemporary class oppression, or in the light of the condescension of posterity. His intention is always to combine historical accuracy with socialist humanist values. If, on the one hand, Thompson is increasingly driven to defend the historian's 'craft' in a narrow sense, he is at the same time proud to publish his writings

in places where no one works for grades or for tenure, but for the transformation of society.[12]

The second general aspect of his work is polemical criticism. Generous in affirmation, Thompson is unscrupulous and often bitter in debate against those whom he suspects of undermining a fully humanist history or libertarian socialist politics. It would be wrong to say that this impulse comes from either his historiography or his dissident Communism alone, for in Thompson these mutually imply and support one another. Indeed, just because of the intrinsic connection between the two, he conceives of marxist theory 'as critique, theory as polemic'.[13]

I will lay aside some of Thompson's positive, substantive ideas for the moment, and develop an account of his critical precepts. It is important to note that despite the length and fierceness of Thompson's critique of Althusser in 'The poverty of theory', his severity with modes of work which to him smack of anti-history is not at all new. What is new, or at least is fuller, in that essay, is an elaboration of the notion of 'the logic of process' or 'historical logic'. We can discuss these in turn, for they lead to a series of problems to do with Thompson's marxism, and his histories.

Thompson charges Althusser with a static sociologism as well as philosophical idealism. These fallacies are related but separable: the one involves insufficient consciousness of change and conflict; the other imagines that Theory can take on a life of its own, outside its socio-historical context. Thompson has consistently exposed the former, as he sees it, whether its source be socialist or conservative. For example, in 'Commitment in politics',[14] he chastened Stuart Hall for dwelling on the 'negative aspects' of relative affluence in the working class in the post-war boom. Thompson attributes the fault to the infiltration of sociology, and as a counter-measure recommends 'a sense of history' in order to return conflict and change to the foreground. The dual purpose of 'history' in Thompson's outlook is well illustrated here. The historical perspective is intended to modify our perception of apparent social novelty by reflecting on *other* periods of 'affluence'. But it is also a means of dwelling – as a matter of principle – on positivities rather than regressions in the assessment of 'consciousness'. One difficulty with Thompson's counsel here is that it comes close to morally prohibiting the recognition that some changes do have significant 'negative aspects'.

In *The Making of the English Working Class*[15] Thompson again disputed that 'the finest-meshed sociological net' could provide us with a 'pure specimen' of a historical phenomenon such as class. But in fact, it is the crudity of sociology, not its purity, which most riles him. In 'Anthropology and the discipline of historical context',[16] Thompson takes Alan Macfarlane to task for his 'lumpish and unsubtle' sociological categories. And it is with an eye to irony that Thompson suggests (in the same essay) that Keith Thomas, an advocate and practitioner of a more anthropological approach to history, is 'too good a historian to be indoctrinated by social science'.[17]

The main culprit, for Thompson, is a pseudo-scientific sociology which posits trivial generalizations or 'laws' across time and place, or which kneels at the 'totem pole of the computer'.[18] Nevertheless, one gets the sense that (as Thompson sees it) if a historian is *intuitively* up to 'his' task, the arduous labour of conceptualization is unnecessary. It is certainly not to be treated outside of specific historical presentation. Indeed, in general, Thompson seems to favour an intuitive and emotive mode to a more analytic one, as is indicated by the prominence of poets in his pantheon.[19] But the merits of anti-philistinism should not be taken to the point of downgrading the attempt to analyse where analysis, not intuition, is appropriate. In many of his rasping critiques, Thompson tends to encourage the view that only the particular is worthy of attention and that it is fully grasped through empirical familiarity as against rational abstraction. By posing the issue in this way, quite different theories are tarred with the same brush, and marxism itself appears to be criticized not for the adequacy (or otherwise) of its abstractions, but for the fact that abstraction is thought necessary. Again, it is important to say that this is the logic of Thompson's statements rather than what in practice he does. For example, his vocal anti-Stalinism is also a theoretical critique of the ill-used base-and-superstructure model in marxism. Yet the rather cryptic view that theory is polemic indicates Thompson's own indecision about the value of abstraction.

One of the weaknesses of 'The poverty of theory' is that it does not aid a balanced solution to this important question. The charge of 'static' and crude generalization appears to be levelled at *any* attempt to elaborate a conceptual approach to history. The sins of sociologism and philosophical idealism are thus merged. Sometimes adopting the strange terms of a socialist phenomenology, Thompson warns against 'the reification of process entailed by the very vocabulary of analysis'.[20] In Smelser's structuralism, for instance, sociology is 'only to be understood as a moment of capitalist ideology'.[21] In Althusser's structuralism, there is also 'an identical reification of process',[22] and similarly, it too is held to be an ideology: that of Stalinism. We will see that neither Thompson's position nor his criticisms are quite so simple. As early as 'Outside the whale'[23] Thompson rejected as unhistorical the kind of 'alienation' theory which so commonly accompanies the vocabulary of 'reification'. And 'The poverty of theory', for all its instant appeal, must now be acknowledged to be a deeply problematical set of arguments.

However, even if in some form 'theory' survives, Thompson will not entertain the prospect of a sociology untransformed by history. On this score, Thompson is surely right to remain intransigent: a great deal of time and resources are wasted in social science on projects which are historically illiterate and methodologically barren. Yet – to use one of his own favourite expressions – Thompson's irresistible tendency to 'lump together' different kinds of work into clear-cut 'disciplines' can be misleading. This is not to defend sociology as such; but some sociological work does indeed merit defence. The point is that exactly the same criticisms as Thompson levels against sociology could be made against a lot of history – or any other academic 'discipline'. Thompson knows this and has strenuously criticized exponents of 'modernization' theory – which is a historical paradigm as much as it is a sociological one. In America, H. G. Gutman (whose work shows affiliation to Thompson's) has conducted an excellent theoretical demolition of the 'new history' as exemplified by Fogel and Engerman's *Time on the Cross*. Gutman's refutations cut across the whole field of the socio-historical disciplines. Thompson's arguments, while similar, are weakened by the impression conveyed that important common problems boil down to the irreparable opposition of one set of faculty members to another.

Thompson's other *bête noire* is the philosopher. The term is derogatory both in its general sense of the wide-eyed speculator, and in its specialist sense of someone who lays down or questions the criteria governing substantive kinds of knowledge.

Once again, Thompson's animosity is particularly aimed at marxists who have tried to reverse Marx's own strictures against philosophy as such. Thompson draws especially on *The Poverty of Philosophy*. If the distinction is tenable, the philosophical fallacy is more dangerous (in Thompson's accounts) than that of sociologism. The latter error has more to do with the denial of social change than with the systematic abstraction of ideas from the historical agents who are responsible for them. In other words, sociology is anti-humanist, as it were, by accident. Philosophy is *in principle* contemptuous of ordinary mortals, whose thought, in reality, is more in practical gestation than delivered to the world in pristine clarity. That, at least, has been Edward Thompson's perception over the years:

Always life is more unexpected than the thoughts of the philosophers who abstract and make conceptual patterns.[24]

people are not so stupid as some structuralist philosophers suppose them to be.[25]

That kind of statement registers well enough a healthy mistrust of the arrogance one often encounters in the more academic species of philosophizing. Notwithstanding Thompson's penchant for point-scoring by means of mock self-effacement, there is also here an oversimplified appeal to the green fields of life as against the grey tones of abstraction. Thompson's jibes often work best when it is also clear that he knows more philosophy than he is prepared to admit.

In the old days (one supposes) . . . the philosopher, labouring by lamplight in his study . . . set down his pen, and looked around for an object in the real world to interrogate. Very commonly that object was the nearest one to hand: his writing table. 'Table,' he said, 'how do I know that you exist, and if you do, how do I know that my concept, table, represents your real existence?' The table would look back without blinking, and interrogate the philosopher in its turn. It was an exacting interchange, and according to which was the victor in the confrontation, the philosopher would inscribe himself as idealist or a materialist.[26]

This is brilliant, knockabout stuff, and the objective of the barbs is not necessarily to discount the importance of all philosophical issues. It is rather to criticize the *pretensions* of philosophers (like Althusser) and to remind them that those issues are *limited* ones. Further, it is to insist that historians too are qualified to deal in ideas. The task of showing the conditions and contexts from which ideas gain currency is, in the long run, more important than logical dissection.

Thompson is therefore opposed to an excessively a priori mode of philosophy not in order to deprive some academics of an immoral living, but because of its effects in history and in politics. For example, he keeps in sharp focus the connections between the brutality of Stalin's practice and the latter's attempts to appear as an omniscient philosopher. That Althusser should have on occasion propagated that image of Stalin is anathema to Thompson.[27] Similarly, historiography can be contaminated by apriorism, and many examples of past Communist tracts could be cited. What is perhaps more worrying for Thompson is that today, when marxist historiography has become a major intellectual force, dogmatic modes resurface. Thus he roundly criticizes John Foster's historical work for excessive 'platonism' in handling class consciousness.[28]

One of Thompson's strategies in 'The poverty of theory' is to equate all philosophy with 'platonic' or 'rationalist' philosophy, and to condemn both together for the sake of history. It is important to say that this strategy does not work. This is partly because of what I have said already: outside polemic, Thompson would probably not sustain – nor could he – a blanket anti-philosophy. In 'Poverty' and elsewhere, he cites with respect and approval Alisdair MacIntyre and Charles Taylor. Those familiar with these writers will know that, although they are humanists, they confront central theoretical and philosophical issues. I refer to questions about 'structure' and agency, the 'science' of society or history, the need for a philosophical space within substantive knowledge, and so on – questions which Althusser (amongst others) also wrestles with.

The other reason why Thompson's dismissal of philosophy fails is that he attempts to set out his own epistemological preferences. Thompson does not only insist on the contextualization of abstract ideas, however indispensable that task might be. A sociology of knowledge does not entail that the subject matter of epistemology – the formal aspect of all knowledge – is thereby rendered irrelevant. In fact they can and should be regarded as complementary. To be fair, Althusser was well aware of this. Thompson, on his side, also has ideas about the necessary form of knowledge, some of which he discussed in earlier work. Adopting his approving term for Caudwell's outlook, Thompson advocates 'epistemological interactionism'.[29]

As formulated in 'Peculiarities of the English',[30] epistemological interactionism is the 'equilibrium between the synthesising and the empiric modes.' Specifically, a theoretical model (and *some* such model is inescapable) confronts an 'irreducible' reality. There is 'a quarrel between model and actuality. This is the creative quarrel at the heart of cognition.'[31] In 'The poverty of theory', that quarrel becomes softened into a *dialogue* between hypothesis and evidence. It is true that Thompson usually limits himself to the forms of *historical* knowledge, but his central propositions carry wider implications. Indeed, the 'dialogue' epistemology has clear affinities to mainstream philosophers such as Karl Popper, and, when articulated in terms of 'experience', the American thinker John Dewey.

How persuasive is Thompson's epistemology? Frankly it is hard to say, because it is not elaborate enough to be unambiguous. And it is not so general as to prohibit general criticism. For example, when moved to defend the primacy of reality over theory in terms of 'facts', Thompson does get close to denying the reality and specificity of conceptual elaboration. This is his 'empiricist' vein, in the sense of an account which takes 'facts' as given entities (usually defined in terms of sensible qualities) to which theoretical terms can be reduced. Empiricism, stated thus bluntly, is a general epistemology the variants of which have been (in my view) decisively criticized, not only by Althusser and other 'conventionalists', but by marxist and non-marxist 'realists'.[32] The other side of the emphasis on irreducible facts is the implied artificiality of 'models'. It is true that Thompson allows the indispensability of models, and in that sense the latter are not wholly artificial. But Weber also held to that view, yet both from his account and from Thompson's it is difficult to rescue the notion of scientific *theory* – something which in its own way articulates real structures. The epistemology of models leaves theory as no more than suggestive, and reality as an imponderable panoply of appearances.

However, at other times, Thompson's formulations may be said to be of a *realist* kind. Here the emphasis tends to be *against* the idea that real processes or 'facts' are *wholly* constructed, rather than slapping a prohibition on theorizing in the name of the empirical data. In fact, Althusser himself was never altogether a 'constructionist', though his epistemology teeters on the brink of conceptual idealism. The main complaint against Althusser must be that in his uncontrolled critique of positivism, what I have termed realism seems similarly condemned as irremediably empiricist. It is, then, understandable if unsatisfactory that Thompson's hackles should rise in defence of the 'empirical mode' to the point of empiricism 'proper'. But at least some part of that stance was for a realist epistemology in its rather blunt but persuasive sense that while theory is indispensable, it refers to real processes, some elements of which must be irreducible to the conceptual apparatus.

The logic of process

I want now to move on to Thompson's own conception of 'historical logic', and thence to his historiographical achievement. However, the issues involved in previous sections will continue to emerge, especially in relation to Thompson's marxism. For the moment, we can say that his broadsides against sociology and philosophy are both more complex and less consistent than they appear. His arguments for and within *history* are similarly uneven.

In what he ironically describes as a philosophical 'intermission' in 'The poverty of theory',[33] Thompson conducts a discussion of what he terms the logic of process or historical logic. I have indicated that such reflections cannot qualify as an alternative to, or refutation of, 'formal' logic or even a general epistemology. But they do constitute an important survey of conceptual issues as they pertain to historical methodology and practice. The general tenor of the argument is that historians have their own protocols of enquiry and disputation, that there is in historiography

a *distinct* logic, appropriate to the historian's materials.[34]

Part of Thompson's case is, as we might expect, the reiteration that philosophers have neither the proper credentials nor the patience to appreciate the peculiarities of historical research. On the whole, this is right, and the point militates against pontification in the philosophy of history. On the other hand, just because he is right to assert the 'epistemological legitimacy' of historical knowledge, Thompson is confusing when he makes the hazy claim that historians occupy 'the ground of any objective (as distinct from theoretic) notion of causation'.[35] If history is epistemologically legitimate, what force or meaning is there in the puzzling antithesis objective/theoretic causality? One meaning which suggests itself is that the logic is inscribed in history itself, not reflection about history. However, this is unlikely given Thompson's repeated objections to metaphysical patterns in historical theory. Similar problems of interpretation arise over the decipherment of assertions to the effect that

historical knowledge may depart from other paradigms of knowledge, when subject to epistemological enquiry.[36]

Again, if this means that history is not physics or philosophy, then we can agree. (The statement also supports Althusser's principle of the internality of criteria of validity to each scientific 'continent'.) If, on the contrary, it means that history is inherently unavailable for rational scrutiny at a fairly general level, then the argument for epistemological legitimacy itself falls.

The positive elaboration of the historians' 'discourse of the proof' is given in Thompson's six points about 'interrogating' facts, and in eight 'propositions' about historical logic. Thompson thinks that his sixth point – unlike the other five – might be controversial in the eyes of other historians: that discrete facts may be interrogated for 'structure-bearing evidence'.[37] He defends the point by means of a critique of nominalism (a kind of methodological individualism in history), since from the latter perspective (fairly common among historians) structure-bearing evidence might be thought to be impossible. However, in my view, various historians would disagree with Thompson's other points too. Some would hesitate over the idea that historians, through certain forms of evidence, can supply a provisional 'section' of past economic and political social forms (Thompson's fifth point). As to point four, Thompson accepts the centrality of a 'narrative of contingent events'. But Braudel (for one) has vigorously contested that assumption, and recent debates about the 'narrative' form reveal that the relation between facticity, story-telling, and analysis is not a simple one.[38] Thompson's first three points are, respectively, to do with value-bearing evidences, those which are value-free, and the authenticity of historical data. Here, of course, is a 'bread and butter' basis for agreement amongst historical practitioners.[39] Yet it must be said that the points are about *sources*, not discrete facts; and if history were 'essentially' about the authentication of sources only, it would be methodologically equivalent to antiquarianism, or, more interestingly, to espionage.

The eight propositions are epistemological rather than methodological in a more technical sense. They are more prosaically presented than the six points, but it is not just for that reason that they are difficult to encapsulate. In effect, Thompson's propositions conflict with each other. This can be seen in three ways. First, let us consider the relation between facts and meanings. On the one hand, Thompson gets close to positivism:

facts are *there*, inscribed in the historical record.[40]

[facts] are determining.[41]

Later, and by contrast, when the 'other half of the dialogue' is added, Thompson finds himself in a relativist mood, saying

that these values, and not those other values, are the ones which make this history meaningful *to us*. . . . If we succeed, then we reach back into history and endow it with our own meanings.[42]

The second way of interpreting Thompson's propositions is in terms of *theory* and facts (rather than values and facts). Contrary to appearances, Thompson is not entirely hostile to 'theory' in preference to the facts. The 'court' of history has, in the end, two benches, one of which is

the coherence, adequacy, and consistency of the concepts.[43]

Finally, and in summary, we can say that epistemologically, Thompson's case is unclear. He has succeeded in showing the epistemological legitimacy of history, but for that reason cannot sustain the notion of a special *logic* for history. (This is not the same thing as specific research methods, which every 'science' has.) We can agree with him that evidence is determinate, that knowledge is provisional, that its object is 'real', and that categories are themselves subject to historical change (these being the core of his eight propositions). But that is not to say that history is unique. Rather, it means that history must hope to share with other 'scientific' disciplines the related criteria of objectivity and theoretical fecundity. Thompson argues well that 'notions of causation, contradiction, of mediation, and of the systematic organisation (sometimes structuring) of social, political, and intellectual life, . . . "belong" within historical theory.'[44] However, the sentiment surely undercuts other things he has to say. Also, and ironically, from berating philosophers for theorizing beyond 'what most historians *think* they are doing',[45] Edward Thompson finds himself in the same boat.

History from below

It is easy to take for granted nowadays how profoundly Thompson's work has transformed our understanding of the nineteenth and eighteenth centuries. Contemporary historiography is obliged to draw from, and respond to, his seminal theses about early working-class culture and movements, about 'the standard of living', and about the relation between law and popular agitation in the period of 'patrician' society. To sandwich a discussion of this achievement between more general 'theoretical' questions might therefore be thought to be a scandalous reversal of priorities. Two things can be said to allay such fears. First, it would be presumptuous for someone who is not a specialist historian to engage in lengthy substantive debate. Second, the general theme of our book is the relation between theory, politics, and research in historiography. From that perspective, much *can* be said about Thompson's substantive work without necessarily encroaching on clear-cut specialist ground. Persisting with the methodological issues of fact/value and theory/history, we can draw some connections between the histories – especially *The Making of the English Working Class* and *Whigs and Hunters* – and Thompson's general theoretical standpoints.

I suggested that Thompson's defence of historical 'facts' was not a question of 'empiricism' in any hard sense. On the other hand, he will not abide the idea that one can draw up historical 'laws' in any 'pure' theoretical form. We can bring these two 'refusals' together by saying that in the first instance, Thompson's 'method' is to attend to and to rationalize the particularity of historical experience.

If you want a generalization I would have to say that the historian has got to be listening all the time.[46]

This generalization takes us some way towards the deep respect which Thompson holds for the people he studies. In a much-quoted passage in *The Making*, Thompson announces his intention to 'rescue' the 'casualties of history'. He asserts that 'their aspirations were valid in terms of their own experience'.[47] The 'data' of Thompson's craft are human values and experiences. We are thus immediately confronted, in the history, with the problem of values, interpretation, and 'hard' facts. And it *is* a problem. Historians must always be listening, to be sure, but the ear of the conservative historian G. M. Young (a good listener) was selective:

history is the conversation of people who counted.[48]

So *who* we listen to, and what we make of what they say, raises the question of the principles of interpretation, a matter about which the historian cannot be so passive. Thus,

The meaning isn't there, in the process; the meaning is in what we make of the process.[49]

Here is where Thompson's political conception of history comes into its own. It is linked to his empathetic and factual methodology, but it goes beyond those things. In many ways, Thompson's 'middle period' mode is akin to that of the slightly earlier generation of Communist and socialist historians. 'Homage to Tom Maguire'[50] belongs with *Tom Mann and His Times* (by Dona Torr), for like *The Making* and *William Morris*,[51] it is history-as-moral-lesson as much as history-as-record. A more analytical piece such as Hobsbawm's 'General crisis of the seventeenth century' strikes us as a rather different vein of marxist historiography:

though the latter appeared before *Tom Mann*, it is altogether less 'engaged', more *Annaliste*.

Another crucial illustration of the coexistence – and tension – between homily and receptiveness in Thompson's historiography is *William Morris*. Although he has said that 'the material took command of me, far more than I ever expected',[52] Thompson was not quite swept off his feet. The first edition was written before Thompson became a 'dissident' Communist. This is reflected in many asides and arguments which were later omitted. Here is an aside:

All roads lead to Communism.[53]

Here is a conjecture:

Were William Morris alive today, he would not look far to find the party of his choice.[54]

And one of the main arguments embodies an orthodox Leninist view, in that the index of Morris's political maturity, Thompson maintains, was his

firm contact . . . with the advance guard, the most conscious section, of the revolutary proletariat,

who, in turn, 'trusted, loved, and respected' Morris.[55] Thompson now thinks of these sentiments as unfortunate Stalinist pieties. And it is true that the principal foci of the text – Morris's 'moral realism' and his 'crossing the river of fire' as a committed artist and man – are not much altered in the later edition. Nevertheless, the meaning and significance of Morris's moral realism has changed to the extent that Thompson himself has: from being 'entirely compatible with dialectical materialism',[56] Morris's 'prevailing note' is now

the appeal to the moral consciousness as a vital agency of social change.[57]

This is more than just a change in formulation. It reveals the visible shift in Thompson's practice, one from Communist activist to socialist scholar. Thompson remains among the most political of historians, but the effects of that relative change in public identity, for good or ill, should not be overlooked, even in the 'middle period' of *The Making of the English Working Class*.

The Making is Thompson's most read and sustained historical work. It is also a teeming nest of problems about moral interpretation and historical receptiveness, empirical recovery and methodological reconstitution. The somewhat over-used term 'history from below' captures something of these problems. Thompson, we have seen, is concerned to establish the intrinsic validity of early working-class experience. His intention is to put the historical record straight: popular life before 1830 had a rich cultural and political unity without an awareness of which historians cannot understand those decades. *The Making* is therefore history from below because that culture has hitherto been under-emphasized in the record. But it is also history from below in a moral and theoretical sense. The making of the class was its own doing, and to recognize the validity of its varied experiences requires the assertion of its conscious agency. The book is therefore pitted against two orthodoxies. The first is empiricist historiography, which ignores both the qualitative dimension of 'industrialization' and the real political presence of the working class. Second, Thompson challenges those marxists who would consider that material determinations are logically prior to matters of historical initiative and the complexities of consciousness. In order to fully register the marxist view that 'men make their own history', Thompson severs that motto from its over-stressed counterpart in marxist doctrine: that they do so in circumstances not of their own choosing. For Thompson, the latter dictum (in some hands) can imply that history is *never* made by conscious choice.

This deeply held and vividly expressed commitment to a certain kind of historiography and politics is mobilized through an extraordinarily wide and sensitive control of the sources. Such a combination of skill and intellectual challenge has been acknowledged on all sides as perhaps the most stimulating single work by an English historian in recent times. Today, perhaps inevitably, *The Making* is beginning to receive a more critical examination. Quantitative historians have (naturally) been long sceptical of Thompson's provocative defence of the Hammonds' perspective to the effect that living standards cannot be measured by monetary averages. (Actually, it is mistaken to think that Thompson argues that calculations are irrelevant: his main chapter is 'Standards and experiences', and his argument is about their incommensurability, not their identity.) It is probable, however, that in vehemently debunking 'orthodox empiricist postures',[58] Thompson has gone too far. For he tends to argue from the justified rejection of 'any automatic, or over-direct, correspondence between the dynamic of economic growth and the dynamic of social or cultural life',[59] to the rather more dubious celebration of 'a working class structure of feeling'.[60] Thus we may agree that the academic and barely conceptualized question of 'the standard of living' of empiricist historiography leads to 'the fragmentation of our comprehension of the full historical process'.[61] However, the questions raised by those historians (as Hobsbawm has accepted) do connect to further questions about material exploitation. Thompson would probably not disagree, but the problem is not fully recognized in *The Making*.

The other major issue about *The Making* is the question which the title poses: was the working class made by 1830? Perry Anderson has taken up this and other theses of Thompson's in what amounts to an impressive critical assessment. I can do little more than to refer the reader here to the second chapter of *Arguments Within English Marxism*. The comments which follow are intended to buttress Anderson's theme by picking up on related points which he does not especially highlight. Adopting a view which I would subscribe to, Anderson argues that the point of Thompson's admirable stress on consciousness, agency, and tradition defeats itself. This is because he overestimates the progressiveness and continuity of the radical tradition of the 'free-born Englishman'. Simultaneously, Thompson underestimates the structural determinations of class formation. Anderson's simple but effective reminder has large consequences:

It comes as something of a shock to realize, at the end of 900 pages, that one has never learnt such an elementary fact as the approximate size of the working class, or its proportion within the population as a whole, at any date in the history of its 'making'.[62]

Much has been said about Thompson's lack of an 'objective' criterion of class.[63] More generally, what is missing in *The Making* is a conception of *capitalism*. Anderson has remarked that industrialization is only a grim backcloth in the book. But its effects are nevertheless felt. What is lacking is the sense that the formation of a 'working class' is not so much the coalescence of antagonisms in conditions of industrialization (though it may be that too), as the dominance of a capitalist production process and its concomitant social relations. This is not a fine point of marxist dogma; it is rather a question of historical assessment. E. J. Hobsbawm's work often suggests that we cannot speak of a fully formed capitalism much before 1850.[64] To set a date for such an 'event' is obviously pedantic, but it does usefully indicate that the 'making' of the English working class was a long, multifaceted part of the *transition* to industrial capitalism.

Part of the problem with Thompson's thesis is that transitional forms, both economic and ideological, are invested with the characteristics of the finished process. Thus handloom weavers and artisans (as Anderson notes) are presented *as* the working class, while factory hands receive no attention. On the 'consciousness' side, the democratic tradition of English dissent and radicalism is presented as the common content of working-class aspirations. That there is something to this idea is undeniable (cf. the 'Good Old Cause' of Hill and others). Yet *The Making* encourages the implausible impression that it is the whole story.

Anderson aptly comments that these 'meta-historical' questions allow the non-specialist to come in on the debate. But as with the 'standard of living' argument, they are inseparable from issues of historical method. For example, the teleology of a conscious political working class 'present at its own making'[65] leads to possible anachronism. There are many comments and descriptions which (however qualified) together project on to weak or defeated or transitional movements the full unifying weight of the attribution 'working class'. Thus the Pentrich rising may well have been a 'wholly proletarian insurrection', but it had 'no hope of success'.[66] The actions of the yeomanry at Peterloo were the product of 'class hatred',[67] but the military also panicked in the circumstances. Peterloo itself was a 'class war', though it was 'pitifully one-sided'.[68] However true all these things are, the end point of the making process (itself perhaps posited too early) is questionably presented as the main characteristic of what were highly complex popular struggles in a transitional period. Obviously, these events were transitional *to* some further social state, but the 'end' cannot easily be read into the events of its formative process.

My point is not to suggest that Thompson of all people is not sufficiently aware of the complexity of motives. It is to take issue with the idea which he sometimes implies that historical agents, and especially collectivities, have a unified consciousness which is realized or evinced in particular actions. Again, this is not just a 'theoretical' denial of humanism, but a matter of historical import. In a recent useful book, John Stevenson has systematically worked through popular disturbances in the 'Thompson period'. Stevenson's conclusions are cautious but firm, that while

it is clear that there were several insurrectionary attempts in the years between the French Revolution and the Great Exhibition; it is also clear that many . . . disturbances continued to follow earlier patterns without embracing a radical ideology.[69]

Stevenson's work is inconceivable without the precedent of Thompson's, but it provides a salutary qualification to the latter. Together with indications like those made by Hobsbawm, it reminds us that the continuities of popular movements in the 'making' period are perhaps as much throw-backs to pre-capitalism as they are prefigurations of the 'working class'.

One final comment on the methodological implications of *The Making* seems in order. The book accorded Thompson the status of a major 'technical' historian, and he has responded in due course by defending the technical aspects of the historian's craft. Nevertheless, *The Making* irrevocably ties 'external' criticism of sources to moral and theoretical theses. For example, in the chapter 'An army of redressers', Thompson boldly argues for the existence of political consciousness in the Luddites on the basis of the *non-existence* of certain kinds of sources (e.g. to do with oath-taking). If the Luddites were organized with revolutionary purpose, they would not leave around such obvious traces. This clever and simple case is a 'counterfactual' one, and it will impress socialist readers perhaps more than scrupulous orthodox historians. But Thompson's marvellous common-sense explication reveals a lot about his 'craft':

Anyone who has conducted a raffle or organized a darts tournament knows that scores of men cannot be assembled at night, from several districts, at a given point, and armed with muskets, hammers, and hatchets . . . all with the organization of a spontaneous college 'rag'.[70]

Moreover, it is from assumptions like this that Thompson discounts some of the evidence that *does* exist, and which implies that Luddism was devoid of political content (e.g. the testimony of spies). That the case was a daring methodological gambit can be seen by the fact that other historians still either vigorously deny its hypotheses (Thomis and Holt), or heavily qualify them (Stevenson, Dinwiddy). One might also point out that when *The Making* and a book like M. I. Thomis's *The Luddites* are put side by side, the ideological, argumentative, and inferential structure of the most factual historiographical questions is plain to see.[71]

The interpretation of Whig history

The Making seems to me a more morally charged work than Thompson's more
recent investigations into the eighteenth century. The latter cluster of interests is
marginally less politically contentious from the point of view of socialist debate
today. For reasons which will emerge, it is more appropriate to discuss Thompson's
account of eighteenth-century society from the perspective of the theory/history
relationship, rather than the (closely related) one of values/facts. On the other
hand, there are clear similarities.

First, there is a sense in which the object of the later work is the same as that in
The Making. Thompson has moved from reconstituting the proletariat to the period
of 'class struggle without classes'.[72] However, if the latter term can be translated
into questions about popular movements and 'public order', then (as I have
suggested) so can the period of 'the making'. And Thompson himself holds the
general view that abstract 'class interests' are not fought over by classes *as* classes.
So despite his own tendency to impose some of the language of 'class' on to
popular movements, it is one major purpose of even the later work to dispute
that political and cultural issues are ever matters of class first, and class struggles
second.

Actually, the aphorism 'class struggle without classes' is unwieldy: it seems to
require permanent inverted commas. In 'The poverty of theory',[73] Thompson
supposes that Althusser and others have done both marxism and history a wrong
by divesting the category of class of its content as class struggle. In fact,
Poulantzas[74] defines classes as the *product* of a range of political, ideological, and
economic relations and practices. And Althusser explicitly argues against the
view that 'classes exist *before* the class struggle'.[75] Althusser counterposes to that
view his own assertion that 'it is therefore the class struggle which constitutes the
division into classes'.[76] The relation between class struggle conceived as social
conflict and class relations in the more technical sense is a vexed problem which
cannot be resolved here. Marx himself (in *The Eighteenth Brumaire*) could no more
than hint at a compromise by distinguishing between a more structural criterion
and a more political criterion of class membership and identity. But the fact is
that Thompson, Althusser, and perhaps even Marx, are misleading. If non-economic
practices are held to be constitutive of class (as, for example, in the versions of
Poulantzas and Carchedi), the 'definition' of class becomes arbitrary – it depends on
one's own perception of what constitutes 'working-class consciousness' and the
like. 'Class struggle' in this wider sense is dislocated from the only possible *precise*
(though certainly *limited*) criterion of class: an 'economic' one. Anderson, following G. A. Cohen, has re-emphasized the point; but it was always a bone of
contention in debates about Poulantzas's theories. And in fact, some 'theoreticists'
were to be found defending the epistemological legitimacy of history.

The second area of continuity between Thompson's phases is the nature of his moral and historical judgements. In what is something of a *tour de force*, Anderson accuses Thompson of anachronism and moral distortion. This is because Thompson, in *Whigs and Hunters*,[77] makes clear his virulent contempt for Whig 'parasitism', and especially for Walpole. He seeks interpretatively to reach out to 'shake Swift by the hand'.[78] Anderson is sharply critical of such 'moral affiliation beyond the task of causal explanation'.[79] He valuably suggests that too often the 'dignity of the discipline itself' is (questionably) thought by its practitioners to be 'saved' by means of retrospective identification with historical protagonists. Anderson provides ample historical argument for the backwardness and spitefulness of the Tory humanism to which Thompson gives his allegiance. For Anderson, Walpole 'calls for no exceptional indignation'.[80] Swift, for his part, is characterized in terms of his personal 'impulse to brutalize' while remaining representative of the Tory 'reversions' to 'bigotry, hierarchy, authority'.[81]

To judge this disagreement is beyond my competence: it certainly provides the terms of a fruitful and potentially fuller debate. Still, it is a pity that through the smoke of his riposte, Anderson did not say more about what makes *Whigs and Hunters* 'a magnificent feat of historical retrieval'.[82] 'Old Corruption' certainly plays its part in the scenario of *The Making*. But that drama had only one character: the 'working class'. When he turns his attention to the earlier period (though we must remember that they are adjacent in time and themes), Thompson takes a more 'societal' view. Here, the theatre is not in the telling of the story, but in the object of analysis. In the eighteenth century, class interests are not superficially clothed in ideological and cultural 'forms'. The law, deference, customary rights and obligations – these are the very fabric of proto-capitalist social relations. Political power and economic change are together convened in them.

Thompson's later work, then, is about class struggle from above as well as from below. But it is also an affirmation of the superiority of 'struggle' over 'class'. He is concerned to stress the subtle reciprocity of ideas which contributes to the 'popular mentalities of subordination', and at the same time to indicate how that hegemony was at times seriously undermined.[83] The complexities of the subject are thus reflected in Thompson's concepts and methodology. His reluctance to deploy 'orthodox' marxist notions of class and surplus labour is indicated in his distinction between 'patrician society' and 'plebeian culture'. Thompson suggests that the principal social groups are the popular masses (not a proletariat) on the one side, and on the other the ruling oligarchy. (The latter is a 'secondary complex of predatory interests' rather than a 'proper' ruling class.[84]) The objects of this displaced class struggle were material enough (the price of bread, poaching). But Thompson also persuades us that the disruptive actions of the crowd in defence of popular standards and rights amounted to a *'moral* economy'.[85]

Two comments can be made about the categorial aspect of this work, both of which are at once theoretical and substantive. First, Thompson's use of Gramscian terminology is notable. 'Hegemony' is a concept which is geared to thinking about the balance of class forces and about the *educative* role of the state. It combines the sense that ideological forms are at one and the same time functional and constitutive. It is thus eminently suited for analysing, say, the shift between 'riot' and 'deference', or the unique pre-eminence of the law. However, the phrase Thompson adopts misleadingly implies that 'class' is inapplicable to these social struggles. It is, of course, difficult to describe the period with confidence in the terms of 'modes of production'. Still, it was then that certain fundamental features of modern capitalist society were laid down (property law, state 'regulation' of trade, banking and agricultural capital). Similarly, the 'interests' of a definable propertied class, as Hay[86] shows, can be directly linked to the majesty and mercy of the judicial process. Once again, it is Thompson's authority which allows us to assert such things with confidence, but he himself tends to overdo the 'moral' component of hegemony. Also, the fact that a social formation might not transparently reveal a single mode of production or class structure does not entail that such analysis cannot be undertaken, or will not be helpful. The work of Poulantzas and others in developing Gramscian concerns seems relevant here, especially the notions of 'power bloc' and 'class fractions'. Thompson with some justice shies clear of such 'structuralist' tools because they may be no more than phrases which tend to prohibit historical research. But in this case (as in that of the 'articulation' of different modes of production) abstruse structuralist terminology perhaps points up real issues worthy of closer specification. While Thompson assures us that class analysis is 'valuable and essential',[87] the thrust of his arguments is to suggest that a notion of struggle can thrive without that encumbrance.

My second comment is less directly about Thompson's concepts than about an approach to which – possibly – his ideas contribute. That approach is to do with the 'rationality' of the process of customary negotiation. The rejection of the historiographical tradition in which popular movements are equivalent to random violence and straightforward crime is a major advance. That conservative tradition seems likely to be permanently displaced as a consequence. Yet, I am uneasy about the assumption of 'rationality' outside of that kind of polemic. Similar difficulties, in my view, confront Christopher Hill's work on the sectarian tradition in an earlier period, so the point can be put generally. Popular protest and violence is undoubtedly a matter of normative 'standards' and cultural practices. The disruption of the latter is likely to elicit a motivated response which can be causally understood whatever the form taken by the response. In that sense, popular protest is always 'rational'. But protest is also often organized with specific objectives in mind, and so may be 'rationally' conducted, that is, in a *strategic* manner. It may be helpful to hold these related senses apart, for they are not quite the same. The rationality of the agents (in the strong second sense) does not follow *just because* their dissatisfaction is readily understandable (the first sense). Specifically, 'riot' or 'crime' may be the product of social disintegration, but not all riots and crimes are socially motivated protests. Defences of customary practices (poaching or smuggling) differ in important respects from 'spontaneous' price riots, which differ again from petty or organized thieving. Sometimes popular cultural forms, even where 'progressive', involve unnecessary brutality or plunder. Sometimes the violence of the *menu peuple* gets close to the 'mindless' stereotype beloved of conservatives (e.g. Church and King riots). In short, the problem of the border-line between protest and politics recurs throughout modern history, and it seems advisable to be wary of the conception that cultural practices or popular disorder are governed by an indirect but uniform moral purpose.

Methodologically, Thompson's eighteenth-century writings are extremely interesting. In particular, *Whigs and Hunters* breaks new ground in its ambitious but multilevelled 'discourse of the proof'. In Thompson's own estimate, it is 'an experiment in historiography'.[88] As part of the general project of the 'social history of crime' out of which the admirable *Albion's Fatal Tree* also emerged, Thompson investigates the obscure origins of the remarkable Black Act which in 1723 added innumerable new capital offences to the statutes.

What made this exercise more hazardous was that I had neither read nor researched very much on any aspect of social history before 1750.[89]

Putting aside any 'general description' of the society at large, and in keeping with the philosophy of *The Making*, Thompson

started with the experience of humble foresters and followed up, through sketchy contemporary evidence, the lines that connected them to power.[90]

Thompson easily identifies with the likes of 'William Shorter, the Berkshire farmer, or John Huntridge, the Richmond innkeeper'. (Actually, many Blacks were not as humble as we might expect.[91])

But the sources, as much as the sympathies, 'forced' Thompson to

see English society in 1723 . . . from 'below'.[92]

The starting point – experience – is by no means a given datum. Thompson has to reconstruct parish economies and forest bureaucracies in order to get to that point. The result is a series of chapters which will probably not be noted for the Thompsonian eloquence, but they are painstaking comparative observations which reveal more of the author's celebrated 'craft' than homilies about agency.

The story which emerges is a complex one which is difficult briefly to summarize. The Blacks were

armed foresters enforcing the definition of rights to which the 'country people' had become habituated . . . resisting the private emparkments which encroached upon their tillage, their firing and their grazing.[93]

The forest officialdom represented, and was part of, a new class of

incomers with greater command of money and influence, and with a ruthlessness in the use of both.[94]

Thompson carefully argues that the emergency in which this 'class' antagonism played a large part cannot be put down (as some thought) to Jacobitism.[95] His own account shows how untenable it is to separate local cultures and economies from matters of state and society.

What appears as crisis was a conflict in the broadest sense political.[96]

Thompson argues that the Blacks, who 'for two or three years achieved a hegemony in the forest', did not resort to disruption for 'simple economic reasons'.[97] Similarly, the politics of the Black Act has no direct economic causation:

It was this displacement of authority, and not the ancient offence of deer-stealing, which constituted, in the eyes of Government, an emergency.[98]

But perhaps uniquely in Thompson's work, there is no *antithesis* between political and economic causation here. Rather, there is a deep complementarity. When the material foundations of social organization seem structurally threatened as a matter of policy, then questions of immediate 'interest' become articulated as cultural principles and sometimes political strategy.

Substantively, *Whigs and Hunters* is a fundamental and challenging thesis. Theoretically (leaving aside for a moment Thompson's controversial discussion of law), the book lends considerable support to those marxists who would stress that the determination of politics by material interests is real enough, but necessarily indirect. As historiography, *Whigs and Hunters* is on some counts more satisfactory (if less epic) than *The Making* or *William Morris*. As a piece of empirical research, it is innovative and evidently cautious where caution seems called for. Yet it is a thoroughly theoretical book with recurrent central threads (as my rather dispersed quotations will indicate). Thompson, as always, defends his 'literary' sources,[99] but there are plenty of numbers too. Lastly, Thompson's own judgement reflects the double-sided convenience of his 'logic of process':

The structure of historical explanation which I have offered depends in part upon logic, and only in part upon fact.[100]

Marxism and culturalism

It is appropriate at this point to confront more directly the central characteristics of E. P. Thompson's marxism. His typical approach and dislikes have been the subject of much recent controversy, some of which has been conducted from the Centre for Contemporary Cultural Studies. These controversies range over both Thompson's general perspectives in historiography, and his specific disagreements with 'orthodox' marxism on questions of 'class', 'base and superstructure', and the marxist tradition itself. The key terms of the debates are 'culturalism' and 'humanism'. How useful are they? On the one hand, it must be said that they can be confusing as general categories of analysis, and so there is also a danger of doing Thompson's work a disservice. On the other hand, they focus – however hazily – on real problems of theory and interpretation.

The danger in using 'humanism' as a term of critical appraisal is that it invites counter-accusations of *ethical* anti-humanism, and this in my view seriously skews discussion between socialists. Since this is not an essay on Althusser, I will not try to unravel the pros and cons of his emphasis on *theoretical* (not political) anti-humanism. But clearly the term is provocative and perhaps dangerous, since it has widespread connotative resonances of a somewhat 'elitist' nature. With regard to *Thompson*, it has been understressed that his work has been consistently *socialist* humanist. Whether in epistolary form (to the 'philistines',[101] to Kolakowski[102]) or in straightforward argument, Thompson has explicitly remained contemptuous of those for whom humanism has been an excuse to leave the socialist camp altogether for the softer environs of 'tolerance' and social democracy. This is insufficiently recognized by his critics.

Nevertheless, 'humanism' constrains the clarity of analytical and political assessment. It is one thing (and a good one) to defend literary sources and to insist that marxists can benefit from their meanings. Thompson's histories are not just about human testimony, they involve substantial amounts of literary criticism, and this is useful. The bulk of *William Morris* is practical criticism, and the ghosts of Blake and Wordsworth stalk the pages of his texts. At the same time, Thompson has been careful to criticize a 'literary' retreat from socialism (as in 'Outside the whale', where he takes Auden and Orwell to task).

There is a point where the emphasis on sensibility, on the moral consciousness, on the validity of human experience becomes the sole object, and the subject, of historical disclosure. As I have indicated, this overestimates the transparency of sources and the purposive integration of human subjectivity and agency. Experiences are not unities which necessarily cohere. Nor do they confer upon historians (or poets) privileged access to the nature of social reality. One might even say (with Paul Hirst) that it is a metaphysical assumption – with historical counter-instances – that human subjectivities either individually or collectively always display historically purposeful agency.

Thompson has had occasion to dispute the accuracy of his critics' complaints against him. He has recently[103] distinguished between two senses of 'experience' in order formally to comply with a more 'materialist' criterion. One sense does indeed refer to the self-perception of individuals. The second is the wider sense that 'experience' is also whatever socially impinges on self-perception. The distinction is appropriate, but its very validity suggests that the single term 'experience' is likely to perpetuate some confusion (rather like Althusser's 'Generalities'). The truth is that the second sense requires, in a way the first does not, a materialist and causal analysis of society. The different senses are related, but they are incommensurable. And marxists have with some reason accorded analytical priority to the second.

Thompson's humanism – in its theoretical sense – is therefore hedged with difficulties, and this is partly because his own work and his marxism ultimately breaks the logic of moral and experiential self-reference. What of 'culturalism'? Here, again, we must register some problems for those who use the term in critique. Richard Johnson, for example, has said that Thompson's work is 'fully "culturalist" in its presuppositions'.[104] If the" "register some hesitation, there remains decisively negative weight in the attribution. In like manner, Perry Anderson diagnoses the Thompson malady as an involuntary 'creeping culturalism'.[105] One part of this question has led to a rather fractious debate in *History Workshop Journal*.[106] It is important, therefore, to work through some of the relevant formulations. What is culturalism, and in relation to what is culturalism a fallacy?

If the sense of 'culturalism' is taken to be theoretical humanism, then it refers to the irreducibility of the experience of human agents and implies a strict analytical relativism. Where Thompson *does* imply this, the pejorative connotations of 'culturalism' are, I think, appropriate. But culturalism might (more plausibly, in Thompson's case) refer more to a concern with cultural forms, ideas, and institutions which are not wholly within the reach of 'strict' economic causality. Here the problems of interpretation are complex.

For the 'orthodox' marxist (or so the parody runs), any form of culturalism is a fallacy, since experiences are given by class location, and institutional forms are derivative from the economic base. The derogatory slant of the term 'culturalism' takes something from this orthodox impulse, and both Johnson's and Anderson's arguments are the weaker for the implied 'correctness' of their own assumptions. In any case, Thompson is not 'fully culturalist' in that 'incorrect' sense. We have seen how cultural forms are materialistically interpreted in *Whigs and Hunters* while yet remaining 'relatively autonomous'. In his fine critique of Raymond Williams,[107] Thompson explicitly refuted the idea that culture (or 'communications') determine social being, and that to imply as much (as Williams did) is to abandon crucial notions of struggle, of power, of ideology, and of materialism. In another 'early' piece, Thompson criticized *Universities and Left Review* for their preferences for 'the uses of literacy' rather than of history; and for their (alleged) naive belief in 'a way of life'.

Let us keep steadily in view the realities of class power.[108]

In a recent interview, Thompson has said that his dislike of structuralist marxism is not a rejection of structural marxism.[109] It is in the light of these statements and writings that the charge of 'culturalism' can become a blunt instrument of criticism.

However, on the question of his own consistency, Thompson, especially in polemic, is not a reliable source! And if he has been consistent about the primacy of social being, Thompson has, in dwelling on the limitations of the marxist concepts of 'class' and 'ideology', at the same time deprived himself of their basic utility. His discussions of cultural forms (the law, for example) are sometimes deliberately aimed against those who do indeed keep class power steadily in view. Moreover, he does hold that a definition of class as a matter of cultural self-definition is superior, and opposed, to the notion of the relation of groups and individuals to the means of production.[110] Similarly, to deal with experiences in terms of 'ideology' or from the point of view of more general causal factors is, for Thompson, to deny historical agency and to affirm elitism. Finally, Thompson does give undue prominence to literary and qualitative materials *as if* they were necessarily antithetical to less vivid evidential resources. As in other aspects of Thompson's work, these contrasts are sometimes complementary, but often they are contradictory. A more general point to be made here is that 'class' and 'class consciousness' – however fraught with difficulties – remain central to a marxist *political* strategy. If the concept of class is replaced by social being and cultural agency, the narrow but (in my view) still important boundary between marxism and social democratic theory and practice tends to disappear. That is certainly an option for socialists today, but its problematical consequences ought to be more openly addressed.

On theoretical and political grounds, then, disagreement must be expressed where 'culture' slides into 'experience' in its more limited sense. The accusation of culturalism is not so much an assertion of the validity of structuralism, as a refusal to embrace a 'subjectivist' approach to social theory by sustaining a false antithesis between 'structure' and 'experience'. Richard Johnson's critics in *History Workshop Journal* no. 7 unaccountably thought the belief in such a synthetic perspective phoney. If the *extent* to which Thompson has been a 'culturalist' has been exaggerated, and requires public redress, the tendency in his work to discourage synthesis provides some reason for the currency of the term 'culturalism'.

Thompson's long-standing anti-economism is now joined by an obsessive anti-structuralism. Together, these impulses have resulted in a partial withdrawal of confidence in marxism on his part. Of course, few marxists are today untouched by the need to rethink or develop in new ways some of the received wisdoms. But Thompson's declarations strike me as unnecessarily sharp, and too bitter. Two examples can be given of where Thompson's experience and inclinations prohibit a more positive response. To take first a minor but illustrative case, Thompson speaks of the need for 'junction concepts' which span or join the material and subjective aspects of experience. He mentions 'mode of production', 'needs', and 'class' as possible candidates.[111] I have suggested that to conceive of two separate realms as requiring unification is already too severe. Even so, some of Thompson's work might be thought of as 'junction history' (for example his essay on 'Time, work-discipline and industrial capitalism'[112]). Here, an important avenue of theoretical dialogue has opened up which might reveal how much Thompson shares with the younger marxists he seems intent on pillorying. Unfortunately, this fleeting proposal for dialogue is followed up by the declaration in 'The poverty of theory' of 'unrelenting intellectual war'[113] against those who deal in concepts like 'mode of production' and 'class'.

The second case concerns Thompson's discussion of law in *Whigs and Hunters*, where his identification of structuralism with economic reductionism appears to become myopic. Thompson argues that the law does indeed, on balance, serve ruling classes, but that its modalities require some element of *real* justice. Moreover, law is a requirement for, and condition of, *any* civilized society. Thus, socialists should respect the need for order and justice, and recognize that humane precedents from even repressive eras can be found and defended. But none of this is a denial that legal institutions and ideologies do have structural causes; the book investigates precisely that connection. Rather, Thompson is protesting against undue reductionism. But here Thompson just gets Althusser and others wrong, because these 'structuralist philosophers' have argued (albeit in colder terms) for the recognition that the law is necessarily 'relatively autonomous'. (Thompson's remarks on relative autonomy and 'last-instance determination' in 'Poverty' do not reduce the substance of those concepts, though they aptly criticize the pretence in the formulations.) In view of these apparent inconsistencies, it is to be hoped that Thompson will elaborate his suggestive remark that his perspective now converges with Raymond Williams's recent and cogent statement of 'cultural materialism'.[114]

Perhaps the most problematical assertions in 'The poverty of theory' occur around the question of Marx's own economism, and of the marxist historical tradition. These passages I find distorted as arguments, but they clearly show Thompson's sharpened sense of a 'break' within British socialism. There have been signs that this has for some time been Thompson's view (the 'break' is set up in Thompson's 'Open letter of Kolakowski'). However, the comments on the 'two Marxisms' are also the product of quite recent embroilments in polemic.

First, Marx. The shift in emphasis can be gauged by comparing 'Poverty' with Thompson's 'Open letter to Leszek Kolakowski'). However, the comments on the 'two Marxisms' are also the product of quite recent embroilments in polemic. tentatively) some fundamentals. By the time of 'Poverty', Marx's major work has become an index of economism and theoreticism.

There is something in Marx's encounter with Political Economy which is obsessive.[115]

He had been sucked into a theoretical whirlpool.[116]

Thompson goes on to stress the historical parts of Marx's writings, and especially those of Engels. Here, perhaps for the first time in his work, 'history' seems to become an autonomous category, without connection to theory or to marxism. As I tried to say earlier, the strategy does not succeed, and partly because Thompson's own standpoint is contradictory. But also, Thompson's view of Marx is unconvincing. He sets up the argument in terms of an inevitable choice between theory and history. Yet it was Marx's achievement systematically to reject that dichotomy (while continuing to prize real history above all else). Moreover, if Marx was marked by his 'obsession' with Political Economy, then we still have cause to celebrate it. For it definitively dismantled the ideological function of the separation of 'economy' from its historical and political conditions. One does not have to be an 'economist' in either sense of the word to find at best ungenerous Thompson's resurrection of that separation for critical purposes.

With regard to the two traditions of marxism, between which Thompson urges us to choose, it is similarly possible to cavil. Of course, as a matter of tactics (and perhaps not even then), marxism can be presented as historical common sense as opposed to pretentious academic theorizing. Thompson uses this tactic (just) to good advantage in 'The great fear of Marxism'. But as a matter of both historical and theoretical accuracy, Thompson's distinctions are wild. On one side, the 'tradition' which carries so much moral burden in 'Poverty' appears to date from approximately 1956 – a gross truncation. Before that Thompson, along with all the other marxist historians, was bound in some way to the doctrines of 'diabolical and hysterical materialism'.[117] Hobsbawm, Hilton, and Dobb, for example, did not give up the concern for theoretical conclusions and premises of a fairly orthodox marxist kind. Thompson also tries to carry along other figures such as Morris and Caudwell (the latter in an essay where the search for common ground with Thompson actually dominates the assessment – to mixed effect[118]). We cannot even say that Thompson's own work provides a pure sample of the 'historical' tradition. I have argued this at some length, but in any event, Thompson explicitly refuses to accept his break with the 'Dobbian' approach.[119]

So Thompson's preferred tradition is neither hallowed nor does it unambiguously enlist anyone in its ranks. The 'real' tradition is in fact rather older and messier. On the other side, the 'new' marxists are posited by Thompson as being the (unwitting) carriers of reductionism and Stalinism, though their very existence in theoretical and political terms is inconceivable without the rejection of both. Moreover, as Gavin Kitching[120] has pointed out, many are keen to learn from, and critically to contribute to, history and other 'concrete' work. It is true and disturbing that many of us have at times been subject to 'theoreticism' of an Althusserian kind. Actually, theoreticism was a relatively short-lived phase, and its demise has not seen a noticeable decline in the enthusiasm for a theoretically-informed historiography. The absurd and pretentious excesses of theoreticism are now not in doubt, but even so, the big guns of Thompson's wrath have possibly proved less effective against it than his more considered advice might have been. This is because 'theoreticism' is not, and never was, the whole story in the more widespread historical and political changes of the 1960s and 1970s. The marxist tradition is therefore certainly one of inner conflict and heterogeneity. While it may have an overall social and theoretical shape, it is not a pre-given entity outside political and historical conditions. Having said that, Thompson's idiosyncratic division of marxism into the camp of 'theology' on the one side, and that of 'active reason' on the other[121] is unacceptably schematic.

Survival and the critique of Stalinism

This essay is not the proper context for overt political discussion, since it is mainly historiographical in focus. But as can be gathered from the previous section, issues of history and theory (especially in Thompson) are simultaneously political. There are three main areas in which Thompson's politics show continuity and renewed vigour. The first is the critique of Stalinism. In a series of essays written shortly after his resignation from the Communist Party, Thompson outlined, 'through the smoke of Budapest',[122] his credo of socialist humanism. Stalinism as an ideology, he argued, rested on a dogmatic 'productivism' and scholasticism which in his assessment rendered marxist theory no more than the rationalization of repressive state socialism. Its key features, as Thompson lists them, are anti-intellectualism, moral nihilism, and the denial of creative agency.[123] He went on to question sharply the abstract schema of 'Revolution' which he saw as also disfiguring the ultra-leftist alternative to Stalinism.[124]

It is in this context that Thompson's 'libertarianism' is to be understood. For, despite the verbal association, Thompson's values are not those of the more anarchist varieties of anti-statism. We have noted his respect for the law, and he would probably not find an accountable police force an excessive imposition. Similarly, in calling for the 'reaffirmation' of socialism,[125] Thompson had in mind less a visionary Communist utopia than a responsible popular democracy pledged to the safeguard of civil liberties. The latter is the second major strand in Thompson's political writings.

Nowadays, Thompson's outspoken opposition to the growth of authoritarian statism is much less directly connected to his affirmation of socialism. As a set of arguments, his call for greater police accountability, for the defence of the jury system, for the opening up of state procedures and an end to systematic surveillance, seem to have commanded the interest, and perhaps the support, of many who would not normally describe themselves as socialist. However, these democratic campaigns and the broad audience which is required for their success in an age of increasingly narrow communication channels, do raise fundamental questions of *socialist* policies. They also relate to the question of Thompson's attitude to Stalinism in Britain today.

To take the second point first, Thompson has insufficiently understood the political changes on the Left in the last decade or more. Among many Communists, the rights and wrongs of '56 are still difficult to broach in the way in which Thompson himself confronted them. That is certainly a problem. However, Thompson's sense of history deserts him when he reads through Althusser, or young intellectuals, or today's CPGB, the 'essence' of the debates of 1956. (He has more than once acknowledged how difficult he finds it to approach the contemporary era as a historian.) I pointed out certain theoretical affinities linking Thompson to more recent 'revisions' in marxism. A case could be made for the view that politically too there are significant correspondences. It is impossible to sustain the thought that after Czechoslovakia, 1968, feminism, and the shifts in the composition of the working class, Communist Party strategy remains 'Stalinist' in all but appearance. What is remarkable about the Postscript to 'Poverty of theory' is not Thompson's perception that despite talk of 'inner party democracy' and 'broad democratic alliances', CPs retain aspects of economism and bureaucratic management of debate. That is evident to all but apologists. Rather, it is his reluctance to admit the real developments of a 'popular democratic' strategy (caught in the paradoxical term 'Eurocommunism'). And this is strange even for a reluctant contemporary historian.

The other side of the coin is that after 'Wilsonism', 'Thatcherism', and the Social Democratic Party, the need for a broad perspective on *socialist* democracy is of some urgency. One might even say that, 'objectively', questions of civil liberties cut deep into the fabric of contemporary capitalism and social democracy. As a 'Marxist fragment within the Labour Party',[126] Thompson's outstanding work in this area inevitably raises the question of a socialist alternative. Preconceptions about the wasteland of Stalinism to his left will not greatly contribute to necessary 'alliances' here.

Perry Anderson has noted that some of Thompson's key sentiments from his CP days have not changed much, and Anderson uses this fact to ironic effect. A discussion of *William Morris* is the occasion of Anderson's political disagreements with Thompson. It is conducted in the somewhat standard Trotskyist terms of genuine revolution versus social reformism. Indeed, it turns out that Morris himself constructed 'the first Marxist scenario for *dual power*',[127] and that Morris scripted 'the Chilean tragedy nearly a century in advance'.[128] However, the main point of the argument is about Thompson's political conceptions:

their degree of continuity with the main strategic perspectives of the CPGB from the mid-50s onwards is unmistakable.[129]

The illusion which Thompson is stated to share with the CP is the naive belief that by adopting the 'parliamentary road', and by couching socialist politics in the language of bourgeois rights only, the institutions of democracy can be shifted peacefully into socialism. These issues need only be mentioned for their centrality to become obvious, though they cannot be further pursued in this context. Anderson's interpretations are similar to the points I have offered, but while his doubts about creeping reformism are important, they do not necessarily show the stark and simple Trotskyist alternative to be a cogent or feasible strategy in its own right.

Anderson's case is, of course, linked to another important debate between Thompson and himself. Anderson and Tom Nairn took Thompson to task for his uncritical stance towards the 'labourist' ideology of the English working class. Thompson's response to these and many other charges formed one of his best pieces, 'The peculiarities of the English'. The achievement of the English working class (and its bourgeoisie), the *naïveté* of an approach based on the model of 'other countries', the heavy-handedness with which theorists conflate 'empirical' and 'empiricism' – all this was skilfully set out by Thompson. It is true all the same that the relation of socialism and marxism to the working-class movement was not publicly seen as a problem by Thompson. As with some parts of *The Making* and *William Morris*, 'Peculiarities' was too vocally English in idiom to be wholly convincing. I say this not to cite an absence for the sake of it, but to suggest that today, perhaps more than ever, socialists need critically to discuss the nature of labourism, and the role of economic struggle in a socialist strategy. Within the CPGB, Eric Hobsbawm has inaugurated an important debate along these lines.[130] Those issues should also exercise Edward Thompson, and his view on them would be valuable.

The third main theme of Thompson's politics is the real possibility of nuclear war.

Serious politics today, in any worthwhile scale of human values, commences with nuclear disarmament.

These words were not written in 1980, but in 1959.[131] That they might have been is a tribute to Thompson's consistency on this overwhelming issue. In fact, it is depressingly true that to keep Cruise missiles off British soil, and to oppose the replacement of Polaris by Trident, are difficult enough, but crucial, first objectives today. Thompson has committed his considerable energies to the renovation of the constructive anger which fuelled the original CND, and which, in part, gave purpose to the New Left. As a consequence, this has meant the postponement of Thompson's eagerly awaited study of 'customs in common' and of Blake. In a more rarefied atmosphere, that would be cause for regret. But for obvious and urgent reasons, that commitment and that postponement will be welcomed. On the question of nuclear war, above all, we are all indebted to Thompson for his contribution.

Thompson's renewed activism around this grave issue again suggests that his own inclinations and qualities are oriented towards moral questions of a universal character. As has been shown by the huge and successful meetings which accompanied *Protest and Survive*, and by the public debate around the BBC's refusal to allow his proposed Dimbleby Lecture, Thompson continues to thrive on open protest and polemic, most effectively against the Establishment. That fundamental principles of humanism are at stake hardly requires saying. But 'neutralism' and disarmament also enable Thompson to take a critical stance against hawkish and bureaucratic tendencies in the 'Socialist' bloc. By encouraging links between protesters throughout Europe, Thompson again stretches out a hand (to use one of his favourite phrases) to 'dissident' socialists in the Warsaw Pact countries.

Thompson's appeal, in the context of the massive growth of CND and END, poses major questions for socialists. He has argued that 'exterminism' has a disastrous logic of its own, unexaminable in the traditional terms of 'class analysis'. This is a salutary reminder to those leftists who might hope to manoeuvre CND in the direction of their own organizations that the campaign against the arms race is not, directly at least, a matter of pro-socialism. Nor can it be won by anything other than a genuinely broad and democratic alliance. It also internally scrambles an easy 'party line' approach by refusing the equation that Soviet policy equals Peace, and above all puts the case against the frightening argument about the need for a 'workers' bomb'. Nevertheless, the suggestion that 'exterminism' is the independent category best suited for analysing the build-up towards nuclear warfare seems to me unjustified. Political analysis, to be sure, is in part about the internal dynamic of configurations of power and their moral consequences. But political strategies, motives, and military expressions are not, in a broad sense, separable from economic interests and class struggles. The advent of Reagan, the contrast between Thatcher and Foot in this context, the relation between hawks and doves in the Kremlin – these things cannot be seen simply in terms of power, morality, or military inevitabilism. But something in Thompson's category of 'exterminism' allows that possibility.[132]

The bustard and the kangaroo

Thompson's style of writing on both history and theory is part and parcel of his beliefs and arguments. The words often used to describe his literary talents reflect an uncommon range and blend: 'passionate', 'accessible', 'funny', 'committed', 'literary', 'sour', and so on. It is not surprising, therefore, that many of Thompson's admirers support his basic arguments just because his writing has a 'human' quality which is lacking in the dry, factual approach of many historians, or in the arid jargon of many marxist theorists. It seems worthwhile to look in a little detail at the Thompson 'style', by which I mean his characteristic literary tropes, and also the way in which he argues a case.

There are two reasons why this analysis is not simply incidental relief. The first is to acknowledge the relevance of recent work on modes of expression in the fields of 'meta-history' (for example, Hayden White's[133]), and in 'discourse theory'. The content of historical and other work, and its acceptance, is not some (wholly) abstract meaning which flits in and out of writers' heads and books. Similarly, the form in which propositions are made or stories told is not the province (simply) of logical validation or literary criticism. The opening of one of Thompson's essays[134] declares that it is an argument rather than an article, and that captures some of the paradoxes linking form and content.

The second reason is that in common with the *substance* of his views on many things, Thompson's 'style' is not a uniform or uniformly effective thing. It does not follow from the fact that he is a very good writer that everything he says is well said. Moreover, it is not true (in my experience) that non-academics find Thompson particularly easy reading. If these thoughts seem a little ungenerous, it is not because we have failed to learn a great deal from his way of putting things. Rather, it is to enter a caution, here as in other matters, against the uncritical reception of his work, in comparison to which other marxists are sometimes automatically thought to be dull or incomprehensible.

In many ways, Thompson's traits are akin to that figure who dominates many of his pages: the free-born Briton. This is not just to do with what Thompson says about the common law or enshrined civil liberties, the radical character of which has always troubled those who occupy the constitution. It is about typical *attitudes* and manner too. Thompson, ever independent, is sometimes idiosyncratic, and (like his Englishman) occasionally patriarchal. The consistency of his writing is also a belief in the virtues of stubbornness. After a certain point, he 'refuses' to accept something, even if the argument is unfinished. A sense of basic rights and wrongs accompanies his theoretical humanism and historical listening. But he is as good at closing his ears. This commonsensical English approach is defensive of traditions, hostile to theory, and loyal to popular common sense itself.

There are countless illustrations of these values in Thompson's work. They are present in what he 'rescues' from history and how he takes responsibility for ensuring that what is rescued is seen to be valid. Here, the 'incoherent wrath' of the impotent authors of threatening letters ('The crime of anonymity'[135]) is on a par with the articulate revolutionaries of the Corresponding Society.[136] They are present too in his defence of the achievement of the English working class, so much so that his loyalty to popular traditions allows him to skate over the political problems connected with that achievement, that Englishness ('Peculiarities'). And they are present in his contempt for 'the philosophers' today who appear to be dismissive of ordinary people, seemingly duped by 'ideology' ('Poverty of theory').

Against the 'platonists', Thompson poses 'history' as a system of values as much as an intellectual discipline. History is the appropriate medium for an awareness of popular politics. Even academics must hear 'the voices (which) remain in one's inner ear'.[137] But stubborn moral awareness is on no account, for Thompson, stupidity; it may not (must not) be 'abstract', but it is *reasonable*. 'Reason' like 'history' is a mode which Thompson aims to defend, and in defending, to practise. Reason here is practical reasoning, not logical proof and refutation. For Thompson, one can be (as many are who are not 'intellectuals') stubborn, bitter, and affirmative, and be the more reasonable for it.

The political and moral resonances of these modes are obvious. Often brilliantly, Thompson bridges the gaps between theory and practice, logic and morality. Like Gramsci, he assumes that everyone is an intellectual, and that those who have the privilege (and the burden) of serving in the social function of 'the intellectuals' should acknowledge it. Moreover, when theoretical disputes shrink in the glare of basic moral questions (such as the escalation of nuclear arms), Thompson is well suited to rise to the occasion.

Some of the negative aspects of these modes of understanding have been discussed in relation to the absences and inconsistencies in Thompson's work. I refer to the problems of 'history and theory', of the validity of 'experience', or ideology, labourism, and the marxist tradition. In this context, Thompson's manner can be trying. For there is much that is contrived in his Englishness, his humble plea for reason, and his anti-theoretical defence of popular modes of consciousness.

I commenced to reason in my thirty third year, and despite my best efforts, I have never been able to shake the habit off.[138]

Thus begins the preface to *The Poverty of Theory* (Volume I of *Reasoning*), and of course, since the book is a lampoon as well as an argument, we might expect irony and sarcasm as well as gravity. Some of this works:

M. Marchais, as we know, has promised that when he comes to power he will be kind to animals. My cat, who read this over my shoulder, laughed.[139]

And we laugh too. This small aside in the argument is combined with the jacket photograph – Thompson, head in hands, in mock-anguish; the cat confidently challenging the photographer and reader. However, here the jibe becomes less an aside than an end in itself. As such, it intrudes and complicates our response (my response anyway) to a book which belligerently proposes the break-up of marxism. The style noted for its passion and moral seriousness often slips into a stilted self-referentiality: rhetoric in the pejorative sense of the word.

This dialectic between openness and contrivance encourages hit-and-miss literary flourishes, as in the case of the cat. Indeed, Thompson has a penchant for animation. In 'Poverty', the 'sublime gestures' of 'theoretical practice' are encapsulated in 'the kangaroo factor'. After some graphic description, Thompson summarizes:

The analogy is grossly unfair to kangaroos, which bound forward with a purposive air to an objective, keep their paws tidily in place, and every now and then stop, eat, and survey the world. Theory hops on for ever, even through the Stalinist night.[140]

Thompson is also wary of whales,[141] but he likes bustards. In fact, he is a bustard.[142]

I remain on the ground like one of the last of the great bustards, awaiting the extinction of my species on the diminishing soil of an eroding idiom, craning my neck into the air, flapping my paltry wings. All around me my younger feathered friends are managing mutations; they are turning into little eagles, and whirrr! with a rush of wind they are off to Paris, to Rome, to California.[143]

If there is an engaging persuasiveness in these metaphorical tactics, there is also a point where a law of diminishing returns comes into operation. Sometimes it is clear that Thompson's aim is as much to test and demonstrate his wide historical and literary knowledge as it is to make a political statement. 'An Elizabethan diary'[144] is a case in point; important as the themes that it deals with are, it is appropriately placed in *Vole*. Where, on the other hand, the art is intended to serve the argument, but oversteps its function, the integrity of the case being made becomes more problematical. The extended metaphor of the state as an inky aquarium ('The secret state') probably helps the journalism and its reception; but the Burkean tone of 'The state of the nation' detracts. The caricature of Althusser as puppeteer and impresario is excellent,[145] but the 'Orrery' transformed for the purposes of illustrating Althusser's Errors is tedious. I am not sure whether Thompson's use of what happens to the girl in the orchestra – to illustrate how a number of structures intersect[146] – makes too many concessions to sexism. But his laboured account of 'that very gracious lady, La Structure à Dominante' does.[147]

As Thompson has allowed,[148] the 'Open letter to Leszek Kolakowski' is particularly prone to dubious gesture. Thompson's transposition of Kolakowski's pet figure, the jester (itself overdone by Kolakowski), is one example.

> I proceed by digressions, and that is an idiom also – an essayist's contrivance. Never mind, we proceed, if circuitously, and there is perhaps more logic in the progress than I mean, as yet, to show. I have been jesting with you, you indomitable and seasoned jester, because I am the product of a jesting culture. If you come before us to ask us questions, I will ask questions of your questions.[149]

Especially in the light of Kolakowski's reactionary but perfectly 'reasonable' refusal to correspond, this long, tortuous piece of self-definition is the least likeable of Thompson's writings. It highlights the risks involved in seeking a distinguished 'literary' presentation.

Thompson's arguments themselves are typically about what someone else has argued. This is inevitable, and is particularly suited to Thompson's temptation to combine focused polemic with occasioned general reflection. But the focus can become blurred from a too-general viewpoint. Thus Thompson too readily (and too repetitively) convicts individual opponents of every crime on the Thompson statutes in any given year. Althusser, for example, gets a merited thrashing for some things, but Thompson makes many unclear or misdirected attributions and equations. Those who have a natural feeling of discomfort about 'isms' will not object to the fine print. Yet for those who have paid attention to both Thompson and Althusser, the latter might even appear sometimes (as Thompson says of the forest Blacks) not as aggressor but as victim. One might even suggest that in *Protest and Survive*[150] too much is said in relation to Professor M. Howard, FBA. Readers of that fundamental pamphlet, I guess, are more interested in the general issue than the peg found to hang it on.

Substantive political problems can be read through, or read into, Thompson's figurative expressions. In *Whigs and Hunters*, he sees himself as a historian stranded

> on a very narrow ledge, watching the tides come up.[151]

When his disagreements (as he sees it) with marxism are also clear, Thompson accepts his situation:

> I therefore crawl out on to my own precarious ledge.[152]

Another – more explicitly political – case in point occurs at the end of 'The poverty of theory'.

> My dues to '1956' have now been paid in full. I may now, with a better conscience, return to my proper work and to my own garden. I will watch how things grow.[153]

What a contrast these essentially passive self-images are to the other Thompson: the embattled, polemical, resilient socialist intellectual! It is a strange combination; but not an illogical one. Often, Thompson's defence of the progressive radical tradition and popular politics has a peculiarly *intellectual* ring to it. It is as much an image of reality as a reflection of it. I am not saying that Thompson has no experience of the *real* working class, nor that his histories have not earned him the right to speak on 'their' behalf. But a sense of popular democracy and solidarity sometimes approaches a 'populism', that is, a political outlook in which the goodwill and innate progressiveness of the masses are assumed to be behind one's own perceptions of the tasks of the day (or those of the past). Oddly enough, populism often comes loudest in the context of isolation: beleaguered revolutionary parties (including the CPGB), 'post-marxist' politicians, guilt-racked socialist academics.

In Thompson's historiography, in his writings on leaving the CP, and even in *Protest and Survive* ('Prepared for the people of England by E. P. Thompson'), his manner is to assume that his ear is closer to *vox populi* than his deluded opponents. Yet Thompson's adoption of the mantle of Burke, or of Swift, or of the Free-born Briton is a highly interpretative political *persona*, arising from his position as a (too) independent socialist writer.

If there is some truth in the foregoing, Thompson's recent activism and public presence is doubly heartening. First, because of the intrinsic importance of what he is saying. Second, because it would have been a major loss to all had Thompson remained tending his Worcestershire garden. It is therefore apposite to conclude this critical assessment with a reminder that at his best, Thompson's polemical style and historical imagination strike an impressive and distinctive note. This is true of the essays collected in *Writing by Candlelight* as a whole. But the essay 'A state of blackmail' is especially good from our point of approach.

From a review of Chapman Pincher's *Inside Story*, Thompson builds up an important protest against Rightism, which he sees as growing from 'steady, vegetable pressures from within the state itself'.[154] The demolition is both crisp and emotive. And while the thick metaphor (now more organic than mammalian) adds to the atmosphere, its aptness may be left, so to speak, as a matter of taste.

this platter-full of 'secret' excreta, some of it still warm from the bowels of the state.[155]

Thompson also enters one of the extended scenarios we have come to expect of him, concerning the imagined leak of his 'file' to the press.

Historian Linked to Bulgarian Embassy
Exclusive by Filchbag Peeper.[156]

All this is nevertheless part of a crushing critique which communicates a real sense of urgency about the defence of civil liberties. But what makes the essay memorable as well as effective is its 'spontaneous' conclusion. Thompson picks up on the coincidence that Pincher and himself were officers in the same wartime regiment. He therefore has a *personal* interest in the way in which Pincher mobilizes a conception of popular sacrifice in those years, for support of rightist ideology *now.*

I walk in my garden, or stand cooking at the stove, and muse on how this came about. My memories of that war are very different.[157]

So different, in fact, that 'musing' hardly captures Thompson's barely-controlled anger as the full, complex meaning of the distortions dawns on him.

I am not even clear what I am trying to say, except that it has to do with the betrayal of the past and the calumny of the dead.[158]

Thompson gives his own version of the politics and aspirations of the wartime working class. He is generous about the potentiality of popular socialism, but even looking back he is prepared to 'leave it at evens'.[159] 'Pincher's people', on the other hand, are treated to an onslaught. And they are the people who still today

lay claim to the whole inheritance of that war as their own private asset, and who today hold the public state and the private citizen in their blackmail.[160]

In broad outline, this judgement is undeniable, and is powerfully expressed. The richness of the piece results in the coalescence of its themes, and is difficult to convey in terms of each. Between the lines it is about the complex texture of personal and popular memory; about the relation of socialist strategy to civil rights and the means of communication; about the analysis of history and its political reconstitution; and about the moral complexion of the drift into the logic of 'exterminism'.

Stylistically, there are chunks of Thompsonian eloquence, but no unearned intrusion. There is plenty of sentiment (Thompson relates how he found himself with tears on his cheeks), but it is extremely moving, not pathetic. And what sometimes appears in his work as a sort of political generation gap disappears here at the very moment when Thompson proudly defends his own contemporaries. His hope that 'younger people' will understand these issues will not, let us hope, go unfulfilled. In sum, 'A kind of blackmail' is a fine example of Thompson's energies as a libertarian socialist, and of his best qualities as a writer and historian.

Part Two
Marxist theory and historical analysis

4 Philosophy and history: some issues in recent marxist theory

Gregor McLennan

Introductory

In this part of the book, we consider some problems about the general connection between marxist theory and historiographical practice. Some of what follows is rather more abstract than the topics of the other two parts. But problems of a 'philosophical' kind often underpin the more 'concrete' questions of empirical research, methodology, and substantive historical judgement. What is the status of historical facts, or theories, or adequate socio-historical explanation? This type of question arises in any consideration of the relation of historiography to other intellectual and political problems.

Our discussions have largely been about marxist or socialist historiography, and marxism is particularly prone to epistemological debates about its forms of explanation. Two good reasons for this are, first, that marxists have typically claimed to be more 'scientific' than rival theorists, and second, marxism's scientific character is held to better the prospect of changing historical development in a socialist direction. In a sense, then, marxist historiography is inevitably tied to issues about 'science', 'theory', and facts, partly because of the ultimately practical object of the marxist enterprise.

In fact, there has been an endless series of important debates in which marxists have questioned or stipulated the role of presuppositions in historical enquiry. Marx and Engels broke with their 'erstwhile philosophical conscience' in *The German Ideology*, where they first seriously proposed an empirical approach to history. Yet even that text was a sketch or generalization about historical method, and so in the very moment of abandoning a speculative *philosophy* of history, they confirmed that a level of abstraction which deals with the status of theory, generalization, and evidence is inescapable. And in important substantive arguments, marxist historians appeal to, and develop, that level. In the now-famous debates in the 1950s about the transition from feudalism to capitalism, a large and crucial part of the dialogues was taken up by notions of what a 'proper' marxist explanation should be. For example, the Japanese historian K. Takahashi firmly reasserted the 'logical development of the categories' as against P. Sweezy's allegedly non-marxist historical revisions.[1] No one would, I think, challenge Takahashi's credentials as a specialist historian, yet his arguments were also of a manifestly theoretical or philosophical sort.

The problems of a 'meta-historical' level of abstraction continue to worry and divide marxists, as is indicated by the responses to E. P. Thompson's *Poverty of Theory*, or in recent numbers of the *History Workshop Journal.*[2] When abstract questions appear to displace historical particularity, fierce antagonisms can flare up between otherwise like-minded people. This is understandable, and perhaps to a degree inevitable, but as the useful editorial to *History Workshop Journal* no. 6 reminds us, theory and history should not be seen as mutually exclusive categories or practices – least of all by marxists.

Today it is common to hear of the 'crisis of marxism', and, certainly, if this refers to the move towards a more questioning and subtle historical materialism than was held even in the 1950s, then the currency of the phrase may be justifiable. Since the rediscovery of the 'early Marx' there have been a great number of reinterpretations of marxism as such. In the forefront of debate has been the question of whether marxism is a science or an ideology; whether it is history or philosophy; a theory or a methodological guideline. Many people are disturbed by the proliferation of such issues, as if marxism, almost by definition, should eschew the self-examination characteristic of the 'bourgeois' traditions. However, political developments today cannot but affect the character of marxist thought, and, in turn, intellectual issues continue to have a broader relevance. So when Althusser proposes a revamped marxist science; or when Hindess and Hirst reject 'history' altogether; or when Thompson defends the empirical mode; or when Gramsci is invoked by many sides as their theoretical patron, there *is* some point in returning to Marx himself, and in asking what the main contemporary problems are for marxism on the more philosophical plane.[3]

This chapter begins with a general account of the problem of marxism and philosophy and a summary of three important options, which are then considered in detail and in turn. They are: the rejection of marxism, marxism conceived as a methodology rather than a theory, and the search for a marxist epistemology. Prominent amongst candidates for the third option are marxist 'rationalism' and marxist 'realism'.

One final introductory comment concerns the relation between current interpretations and Marx himself. Recent books dealing with Marx (especially his philosophy) have been marked by an unprecedented academic care to be precise and definitive. In some cases, this has led to grand (sometimes grotesque) terminological systems, while in others the preference is for short, dissective (perhaps pedantic) commentary. Either way, the analysis of Marx's theories has seemed ever less motivated by political issues assessed independently of a programme of study. This phenomenon is not necessarily to be regretted, and its causes are large social and historical changes which cannot be put down simply to the personal choices of the marxist intellectuals. But two problematical theoretical observations can be made. First, the interpretations of Marx have sought to be 'rigorous', to excavate the *real* Marx, his inner theoretical essence, in contrast to rival interpretations. Second, this process of competitive dissection is paradoxical: the closer we get to what Marx really said, the more difficult it seems to assess what he really meant.

Does it matter that Marx was not – in crucial respects – a precise analytical philosopher, or is this very judgement the product of a misreading of Marx's propositions? Such conundrums multiply. The search for the real Marx may be unavoidable, and may be in some ways decidable. But we should be clear that it is as much an intervention in contemporary marxism as it is a disembodied exercise. To go further, these debates are historical and intellectual *products*, and their claims are inescapably stamped by their conditions of production – conditions increasingly distanced from those of Marx.

Marxist theory has long been distinguished by its historical and political orientation, and marxist politics by its claim to be scientifically or theoretically derived. Undoubtedly, this dialectic of theory and practice has been a source of strength. To recognize the centrality of this *nexus* of philosophy, history, and politics is one thing; but it is extremely difficult to clarify the relation between its elements. Often, marxists allow phrases such as 'dialectical totality' to stand in for clearer conceptual exposition. It is also easy to lay excessive emphasis on just one aspect of the marxist enterprise. Some have elevated the 'science' to absurd heights, thus slipping into 'theoreticism', while others have sought relief from difficult intellectual issues by ritualistically asserting the primacy of 'practice'.

Our main concern is with historical materialism – a marxist or Marx-influenced *history* – but there is no obvious escape from the problems thrown up by the relative weight marxism confers upon theoretical abstraction and apparently abstruse philosophical reasoning. But didn't Marx, after all, decisively criticize theory's posture above history and its apparent freedom from economic determination? This understandable reaction finds expression in the distrust which socialist and other historians feel for (especially academic) marxist philosophy. Thus E. P. Thompson rails against philosophy's encroachment (in the person of Althusser) on the only legitimate site of marxism: history. Setting aside the difficulties which Thompson reproduces, his appealing conclusion is that marxism is historical analysis (in a fairly conventional methodological sense), or it is nothing.

We can sympathize up to a point with such views intended to establish the empirical character of historical materialism. But theoretical argument directing us to historical research – or to current political problems (Hindess and Hirst) – can turn out to be self-defeating. This is because they typically employ philosophical arguments to refute philosophy. In other words, what is often being rejected is not so much epistemology *per se* so much as one brand in favour of another. In E. P. Thompson's case, the anti-philosophical impulse is combined with his own account of both marxism and history. But the characteristics of his alternative are mixed. A Popperian notion of a 'dialogue' between fact and hypothesis, and a 'realist' conception of theory, are at least two of the possible elements. They cannot be said to produce a coherent theory, but they are epistemological propositions.[4]

It seems, then, that the debates as to which brand of epistemology best suits Marx and/or marxism today need not be thought of as just an esoteric side-show (though that is how it often finishes up). In any case, it is artificial to enlist Marx himself in the ranks of blanket anti-abstraction. The meaning of his most famous aphorism on the subject is not that the philosophers have only *interpreted* the world (and not changed it); it is rather that many philosophers have *only* been concerned to interpret it. Theory may not be separable from practice, but it is not the same thing as practice.

Central questions arise when we consider what the principal contents of historical materialism are, and how (not 'if') they are connected to philosophical presuppositions. To most people, perception of the connection has been strongly conditioned by the dominance of Soviet marxism in the twentieth century. Historical materialism was conceived as a fairly rigid schema whereby the forces of production (labour power, science, but prominently technology) strongly determine relations of production (ownership relations). In turn, this complex of factors (the economic 'base') determines the political and cultural 'superstructures'. Diachronically, the model posited a succession of modes of production governed by productive forces, characterized by definite forms of property, and culminating in Communism.

This version of marxism was no doubt something of a politically motivated caricature. Typically, Marx did not employ such a template. However, the Soviet models did have answers to the charge of 'mechanicism', namely, that the social elements posited, like those of the natural world, are intrinsically interpenetrative, though materially caused. In this sketch of 'dialectical materialism' Engels, and Plekhanov, could be cited as founders, and Marx at least invoked in support. The formula for historical development, however, came to rely on a conception of the necessary forms of being-in-general, and the way in which society and thought corresponded to, or exemplified, those forms.

The two complaints commonly levelled against this approach (sometimes termed 'diamat') are its heavy philosophical burden, and (despite the 'dialectic') its determinism. Social science and politics seemed to depend on rather vague metaphysical generalities such as dialectic, matter-in-motion, or relative interpenetration, reflection, correspondence, and the like. However, apart from its philosophical ambiguities, diamat encourages the view that by a 'scientific' analysis of economic formations couched in the proper vocabulary, social development can be rigorously plotted and verified. Here, it seems that real social and intellectual complexities cannot be registered. And cast as an a priori system, diamat undermines both historical specificity and human agency. In the (academic) marxist revival of the 1960s and 1970s, it almost became a working assumption that 'productive forces' and 'dialectics of nature' were relics of an unsophisticated (and inhuman) marxist past. However, some marxists are again maintaining that, shorn of the Hegelian or Darwinian context, and prised from a Stalinist politics, these concepts must still do service if marxism is to remain viable.[5]

G. A. Cohen,[6] in particular, has rigorously defended the productive forces position as a historical theory. Significant social and intellectual changes happen as and when they do, because they serve the development of the productive forces. Despite its deceptive simplicity, Cohen's argument is not merely the revitalization of a discarded theory. Its far-reaching effects can be summarized in three points.

First, Cohen disputes the view that marxism involves a distinct philosophy (even 'dialectics'), since the theory of history can be stated in the 'straight' philosophical language of causal and functional relationships. Second, he defends the primacy of the forces of production over social and cultural relations, but refuses the criticism that the theory is (in any harmful sense) an economic or technological determinism. This is because, while social relations are functional for the development of the forces, the precise *content* of social relations is not 'given' by the forces. Indeed, the *rate* and *form* of that development are governed by the social relations of production.[7] Third, historical materialism, as Cohen elaborates it, is not logically joined to what have been taken to be the main concepts of *Capital*, namely value and surplus value, which Cohen believes to be false.[8]

In sum, Cohen's 'traditional' theory effectively and originally dismantles the idea that there are necessary connections between historical materialism, dialectical materialism, and the orthodox theory of capitalism. To judge Cohen's brilliant and controversial case fully would take us too far afield for present purposes.[9] In general, concern might be expressed that his theory of history is either too broad (referring to very general stages), or unacceptably narrow, since it seems to tie specific historical struggles to a teleology of productive power. Moreover, it is not clear that Cohen has refuted a view of 'mode of production' in which forces and relations are more closely bound up with one another than he allows. Finally, we may note that 'functional relations' and value-theory continue to arouse controversy amongst philosophers and economists. One sure effect of Cohen's contribution is to shake up traditional and more recent orthodoxies concerning causality and determinism, philosophical critique and history.

Rejections of marxism-as-philosophy

Anxiety about determinism and causality have typically led to epistemological claims for marxism which aim to overcome central dilemmas, or to wholesale rejections of marxism because these dilemmas are thought to be intractable. The most self-conscious and radical recent example of the former approach has been Louis Althusser's epistemology of 'structural causality'. At times one has to gasp at the lengths to which he goes in order to implicate Marx in person in Althusser's own distinctive enterprise. But the spirit of the attempt has much in common with classical attempts to overcome problems by systematically employing an epistemological perspective in dealing with the problems of theory and fact, necessity and relativity, forces and relations of production, and the connection between economy and social totality. The relation between philosophy and substantive analysis in Althusser's work is therefore not especially eccentric.

Perhaps it is just the characteristically marxist task to secure a 'fit' between epistemology, historical method, and political knowledge which is naive or hopeless? The endless trickle of the disillusioned from the mainstream waters of marxist theory begins with this question. Leszek Kolakowski's detailed rerun of Popper's 'demolition' of marxism is one notable example.[10] He argues knowledgeably, and with some justice, that 'hard' versions of marxism are untenable, and (more questionably) that softer versions are trivial. They are trivial, according to Kolakowski, because they are so general as to arouse no opposition. Aside from exaggerating both the generality of marxism and the absence of opposition to it, the implication here that triviality and generality are equivalent in meaning is surely illegitimate. And on Kolakowski's own admission, it is due to the truth and success of Marx's insights that the basic tenets of marxism have become widely supported.[11]

Barry Hindess and Paul Hirst would, perhaps, have no truck with Kolakowski's donnish liberalism, but their critique of marxist theory is substantially similar. They have argued[12] that determinism and the 'relative autonomy' of the superstructures from the economic base are contrary principles which are simply yoked together in marxism. Hindess and Hirst suggest that this can be rationalized only by erecting a philosophical doctrine (such as dialectical materialism) in which that union is given special status, protected from refutation. Marxism thus requires and provides an epistemology in virtue of which opponents' discourses are condemned to fail the test of validity when confronted by the privileged marxist presuppositions. Unlike Kolakowski, Hindess and Hirst's attack is aimed at all epistemological argument, the essential circularity of which is shared and perpetuated by marxism.

Three points can be made in partial response to these fundamental criticisms. First, and most substantively, the argument hangs on the alleged incompatibility between determination by the economic base 'in the last instance' and the relative autonomy of the superstructures. However one chooses to characterize these theoretical poles (and the terms used here may not be the best), it is just not the case that X's being determined deprives X of causal status in its own right, including the propensity to substantially affect the determining conditions. It may be that marxists haven't themselves followed this insight, and that there are no set rules for the degree or scope of the determining relations. But that is not a logical point about the concept of causality.

Second, Hindess and Hirst maintain that any epistemological argument is fatally flawed because, being epistemological, it is necessarily dogmatic. This characterization, however, is itself a form of 'essentialist' critique: different kinds of position are reduced to a necessary form ('epistemology'), and are thereby condemned. Hindess and Hirst thus deploy precisely the kind of privileged critique that they find intolerable in epistemologies.

Third, they refuse any bifurcation of reality into the non-discursive and discursive realms (the comparison of which is held to be the root fallacy of epistemological dogmatism). Yet they continue to make reference to what is, at least in part, non-discursive, especially political and economic states of affairs. It can be said, therefore, that Hindess and Hirst have not, as promised, 'bracketed out' ontological questions about what exists (these being closely linked to epistemological questions about what can be known).[13] However, Hirst[14] has rebutted this charge by stating that discourses do indeed have referents, but that the latter are not in a realm distinct from discourse. Now it is true that this is a defence: to posit discursive definitions of the non-discursive avoids the question of the *really* non-discursive. But apart from driving those without a penchant for philosophical niceties to give up in despair, this is still a common philosophical argument, not one against epistemology. S. Gaukroger, whom Hirst favourably cites, is one recent example in the philosophy of science. His argument is that the entities of a discourse are constructs of the discourse itself, the discourses do not necessarily 'compete for reality'.[15] But Hirst, and I think Gaukroger, want also to hold that no idealist deductions can be made from this: the objects of a discourse are not *purely* discursive. Hirst:

What is subject to calculation in our position is certainly not purely discursive.[16]

However, it *is* true, for Hirst, that 'the potentiality of *difference* in the constructs of practices and the referents discourses speak of explodes the "non-discursive" as a unitary category'.[17] This view is not, as it stands, logically untenable, but further pedantic investigation into the meaning of such terms as 'unitary category' or about the exact force of terms like 'potential' might render the thesis a weak or trivial one. After all, why not just forget about the non-discursive, and argue that entities are 'purely' discursive? Hirst, it seems, still hesitates over that final commitment.

Hirst's points against marxism seem to work by positing (and condemning) epistemological discourses *as such*; that is, ones whose substantive content is transparently ordered by its epistemological premises or structure. However, this is rather artificial, because all substantive discourses have some kind of epistemological premises, and those which are (relatively) conscious about them are not necessarily any more dogmatic than those discourses that prefer to remain object-oriented. Moreover, there are discourses which are *about* the general structure of theories, i.e. which deal in general theoretical assessment rather than substantive elucidation. Such second-order activities would be a more accurate sense of 'epistemological discourse', and despite their anti-epistemological cast, Hirst's own arguments form an exemplary instance of the practice. Hindess and Hirst have important things to say about the limitations of epistemology and its sometimes damaging effect on more 'practical' questions of economic calculation, legal forms, and political strategy. But they cannot be said to have fought clear of epistemological argument.

Marxism as method

One alternative to a philosophically-based marxism has been the idea that it is principally a *method* rather than a theory. This option is appealing because it suggests a middle road between a full-blown materialist cosmology and the abandonment of marxism altogether.

The classic exponent of the marxism-as-method view is Georg Lukacs. If research disproved all of Marx's theses *in toto*, Lukacs argued, the serious 'orthodox' marxist would have no cause for concern. This is because 'orthodoxy refers exclusively to *method*'.[18] This formulation was intended to counter or evade the perennial charges brought against marxism by non-marxists on the question of empirical prediction – notoriously on the falling rate of profit, on the immiseration of the proletariat, on the timing of the transition to socialism, and so on. In addition, the emphasis on method seems to free us from the clutches of a 'speculative' marxism, be it in the form of Soviet diamat or Althusserian structuralism. In justification of this perspective, we can call upon certain key clarifications or caveats in Marx, Engels, and Lenin. For example, marxism should not be thought of as an *'a priori* construction' or a 'lever for construction' or a 'compulsory schema of history'. Rather it is a 'guide to study' and action, a hypothesis about specific historical phases: 'what else but the dialectical method?'[19]

However, the assertion that dialectical method is not only distinct from, but is a safeguard against, philosophical apriorism and a general theory of history is problematical. Quotations alone will not do the trick, since many formulas implying just such a transhistorical schema are littered throughout the texts of the marxist classics, often on the same page as the 'favourable' references cited above. In any case, there is something strange about the idea that marxism is no more than a doctrine-free methodological toolkit. In fact, when one examines claims for method, it is often to find an inextricable combination of substance and heuristic. There is something prima facie unacceptable about absolving method from any unfavourable consequences it may result in when 'applied'.

No sooner has Lukacs made his quotable claim on behalf of method, than he ties it irrevocably to the very movement of history:

It might appear as if the dialectic relation between parts and whole were no more than a construct of thought as removed from the true categories of social reality. . . . If so, the superiority of dialectics would be purely methodological. The real difference, however, is deeper and more fundamental.[20]

It seems that, after all, dialectic and the provability of substantive theses are intimately connected. What Lukacs attempts in *History and Class Consciousness* is to so tie up the internal bonds between dialectic, history, and revolutionary consciousness that to state an empirical objection to the theory is, necessarily, to fail to understand its distinctiveness. Such an objection requires a division between external fact on the one hand, and value or inner movement on the other – a division which is definitively abolished 'from the standpoint of the proletariat'. History (with a capital 'H') thus appears in and through the dialectical categories which grasp the unfolding pattern of its disclosure. In short, Lukacs's claims for marxism-as-method are certainly as philosophical, and therefore as transhistorical, as the orthodoxy he sought to replace.

A modern analogue of Lukacs can be detected in arguments put forward on occasion by social historians. Fired by their belief that an Althusserian concern for philosophical elaboration within historical materialism is a disaster, historians sometimes adopt Lukacsian views. For example, contributors to *History Workshop Journal* no. 7[21] objected to any separation of the historical process which would allow any distinction between economic and cultural spheres. Similarly, analytical categories which appear to abstract from the totality of social life are thought to entail the belief that real processes show divisions which correspond to theoretical categories. Where the categories have a philosophical tinge, Stalinism or theoreticism is suspected, because philosophy appears to stand on its own, in 'dominance' over real processes and other enquiries. Moreover, since abstraction invites a series of artificial cuts into a historically homogeneous process, theoretical separations do no more than reflect the 'reified' nature of social spheres in capitalism, and therefore may be considered 'bourgeois'.

As with Lukacs, these arguments are implied, but are difficult to elucidate or sustain. One problem, for example, is that the labour theory of value (which Gavin Williams, for instance, espouses in a didactic form) authorizes the kind of abstraction which modern Lukacsians abhor. It will be said that the whole point of that theory is that it is not simply economic, but that it highlights social relations of production as well as technical productive forces. However, as E. P. Thompson has recognized, marxian economics still requires a fundamental causal principle about the primacy of material production and the 'nature-relation'. Second, value-theory is *highly* abstract, entailing severe theoretical distinctions and licence for historical truncations. In other words, even if they are adequate (which is not a given assumption here), marxian economic categories do not easily comply with strictures aimed to condemn abstraction and to espouse the essential unity of all social processes.

Moreover, the general idea that History has priority over philosophy can itself be a philosophical position. To say that theory has historical conditions is one thing, and a very important one, to insist upon. But to argue that it is of the essence of historical understanding to grasp reality as a uniform whole in its dynamic movement by refusing 'artificial' theoretical distinctions, or distinctions between social practices: that view is an a priori one about the necessary disclosure of history through a separate and privileged mode of cognition. It is a view which Hegel systematized and which Lukacs encouraged marxists to adopt. But it is still a (rather obscure) metaphysical injunction, which though oriented around the concept of 'praxis', is not necessarily any closer to real practice.

Another way of trying to oust philosophy is to assert that marxist theory is not a philosophy of *history*, but a critique of capitalism only. Korsch[22] took this standpoint, arguing that the historical and conceptual relevance of marxism was to capitalism and not other social formations. Like any other theory or philosophy, marxism is the product of specific social relations. So, for Korsch, marxism (properly conceived) has nothing to do with general materialism either as a metaphysic or as a theory of history. This position is indeed radically historical, so much so that Korsch is happy to deny that even such conceptions as 'base and superstructure' have a special bearing on problems of specific social analysis. I have introduced Korsch because he seems to me to be the 'limit case' of the argument against philosophy and for empirical method,[23] and Korsch too has contemporary parallels. For example, Derek Sayer[24] and P. Corrigan *et al.*[25] have developed a view of Marx's method which shares many of Korsch's concerns. We would also suggest that the rational core to the points made by historians and others tempted by Lukacs is probably encompassed by the kind of position Sayer adopts.

That position can be characterized as follows. Marx's objects of explanation are particular social forms. While it is true that very general transhistorical categories (such as 'production') are required in order to make sense of change and continuity, those categories have no independent content. In addition, there can be no meaningful separation between the forces and the relations of production, so no overarching, technologically inclined theory of history. Each historical epoch has specific social forms of production and social relations within which production takes place. Consequently, marxism places a premium on historical as opposed to analytical modes of thinking, and social rather than just economic relations. Above all, then, marxism is empirically open-ended: an a posteriori methodology, not an a priori doctrine.

There is much to applaud in this view, and it is helpful for an understanding of many aspects of Marx's procedures. But there are also some difficulties with it. One lasting problem (as with most texts on 'what Marx really meant') is that although the position squares well with parts of Marx, it is clearly not the whole story. Those writers who favour the 'productive forces' theory[26] provide more than enough evidence to invoke the 'real Marx' in their support. Substantively, the concept of social relations which is advanced is almost without determinate content. If social relations are themselves productive forces (and vice versa), and if the notion of superstructures is illegitimate (as it would have to be), then just about everything counts as a 'social relation'. And in leaving such concepts historically variable as well as conceptually broad, close *empirical* control on their employment and instantiation is (ironically) discouraged. Although Sayer for one is not generally open to charges of vagueness, it is part of the logic of the stance he adopts.

Also, like Korsch, Sayer relies heavily on the theory of value at the expense of a theory of history, and that is problematical. Since it is capitalist commodity-forms which are responsible for the real and categorial separation of social spheres, the role of marxist theory is exclusively thought to be a vigorous *critique* of the consequent theoretical and practical ideologies. Above all, marxism must avoid becoming a general philosophy. We have already noted the complex question of the relation of historical materialism to the critique of value, but it is an urgent theoretical problem. Many marxists feel that the theories of value and of surplus value are weak or dispensable. Further, in Sayer's account it is implied that the 'laws' which govern one historical mode of production will differ in both form and content from those which characterize others. Here, the empirically open approach makes for a principle of discontinuity in the modes of production, something which Marx's undeniable stress on historical 'laws' seemed intended to combat.

To sum up this section, we can conclude that whatever Marx or others have said against 'speculative' philosophical constructs, most claims for a practical marxist methodology which shed that metaphysical weight are less than convincing. In so far as theory and method are inseparable, substantive commitment cannot be evaded. In so far as theory is attached to some general protocols of explanation, the idea of a marxist epistemology cannot, as yet, be taken to be obviously faulty or idealist.

Marxist epistemologies

We can now turn to the issue, what kind of epistemology did Marx subscribe to? For our purposes, this question would be better expressed as: what epistemology is implicit in marxist procedures? Virtually all important contributions to marxist philosophy in recent years have been attempts to overcome the difficulties apparent in the kind of dialectical materialism suggested in the work of Engels, and systematized by theorists such as Plekhanov, Bukharin, and Stalin.[27] It is generally accepted that these attempts to formalize a marxist world-view often discredited marxism in the eyes of even sympathetic critics. There are many reasons for this, not all of which fit together.

One objection has been that dialectical logic seems to diminish, or even to replace formal logic (on the one hand), and inductive criteria of empirical research (on the other). Part of this criticism is that marxist dialectics has been given a privileged cognitive role over and above both natural and historical science. 'The laws of dialectic' tended to become the final court of appeal in intellectual dispute, despite the fact that they are of an exceptionally high level of generality. The 'laws' of the transition from quality to quantity, the interpenetration of opposites, and the negation of the negation: almost any piece or process of knowledge, if one chooses, can be slotted into these categories. And it is easy to see how leaders of the orthodox Communist movement – especially in the Soviet Union – could come to employ the same 'laws' as little more than rationalizations for their own practical ends. The intellectual content of dialectical materialism seemed to have no independent explanatory capacity: it was wide open to 'interpretation', and the dominant ('correct') readings became in effect those of Communists in political power.

Yet it is important to be careful about the relation between the particular Stalinist hue of diamat and the kind of theory dialectical materialism was. One can give an 'overpoliticized' reading of the political uses to which the doctrines were put. Some aspects of its 'scientific' aspirations might still be defended, though preferably in clearer terms. And there is something about the inherent oscillation between 'dialectic' and 'materialism' which seems to lend itself to pragmatic mobilization. For example, it is common to criticize Bukharin, Plekhanov, and Stalin on the grounds that they were insufficiently dialectical owing to certain 'mechanistic' tendencies. But alternative accounts and politics are equally open to the charge of practical manipulation if dialectics implies both causality and ceaseless interpenetration. In the work of continental dialecticians,[28] any principle of determination seems to stand condemned as reductionist. In Mao's version of dialectic, the identification of 'principal aspects' of contradictions, or the 'primary' and 'secondary' contradictions is largely an *ad hoc* business, especially when the particularity of social contradictions is frequently emphasized.[29] The point here is that we have to decide whether dialectical materialism can in principle be saved by the ever-more-precise balancing of its two constituent parts. Marxists in the past have stressed now one side, now the other, and either the dialectics or the materialism, according to context, have often been only gestural. There are grounds for suggesting that neither the parts nor the compound are ultimately satisfactory.

In the light of such apparent inconsistencies, the following options seem to be open. First, we could re-read Marx, hoping to construct from his work a more adequate epistemology or method. Second, we could find there a number of considerations which fall short of an epistemology, but which furnish a set of conceptual premises for substantive work. The first raises the problem of whether it is Marx or us that holds the epistemology systematically (in opposition to rival interpretations). The second approach acknowledges that, after a point, it is a mistake to demand from the multifaceted work of Marx a systematic philosophy. We propose that the second view is preferable, partly because of the problems with other implicit epistemologies.

Rationalism

By 'rationalism' we refer to Althusserian versions of marxism. Since much has been written lately on the fallacies involved in this epistemological trend, I will be brief. A word on the possible origins of the Althusserian 'system' may be useful here. Two main factors, we might speculate, were involved. First, dialectical materialism was unsatisfactory in itself. For academic philosophers of the Left (for example Colletti and some British marxists), the unrigorous, dogmatic cast of argument standard in marxism, and its reluctance to take seriously developments in 'bourgeois' philosophy was something of a burden. In particular, a dialectical materialist ontology seemed inevitably to produce a simplistic account of the epistemological mechanisms of scientific knowledge. It was often connected to a facile and rigid social analysis, increasingly difficult to square with the details of advanced bourgeois democracies and (potential) de-Stalinization in the Western Communist Parties. Second, recourse to a showdown with bourgeois critics, given the weak position of academic marxism, was problematical: such a confrontation risked making concessions to 'empiricism', compromising marxism's stance as a quite independent theoretical practice. Althusser displays an entrenched fear that marxism might absorb the 'softer' bourgeois tones present in humanism, and in so doing embrace social democratic politics.

If this scenario is in part accurate, it explains the defensiveness and determination with which an Althusser or a Della Volpe[30] maintained the scientificity of marxism against opponents, though their own contributions were in respects 'revisionist'. Dismissals of the currents they represent as being theoreticist, as if that is all one has to say about them, are rather simplistic and (ironically) unhistorical. That elements of theoreticism resulted, and demand criticism, is undeniable.[31]

For Althusser, both dogmatic marxism and bourgeois philosophy performed erroneous reductions. The former, whether as diamat or histomat (the 'application' of dialectical materialism to the 'stages' of historical evolution), required that the mechanisms of knowledge be derived from the make-up of the basic constituents of the natural or historical world. Dialectical alternatives to this rather mechanical conception succeeded only in dispensing with causality itself, and therefore with science: for Althusser, an intolerable proposition. For its part, bourgeois epistemology, whether idealist or empiricist, 'reduced' from the other side: *because* of the constitutive role of the subject, criteria for knowledge can be drawn up, but we cannot have independent means of knowing how *things* are, or that they really exist 'objectively', i.e. independent of the knowing subject.

Althusser's strategy was to assume both *that* we have knowledge, and that knowledge is of an independently existing world. So there is no 'problem' of knowledge. This is Althusser's gesture towards materialism. But the task of epistemology is to elaborate the differential mechanisms of the knowledge process, and a marxist epistemology must be possible here, because Marx himself (according to Althusser) decisively contributed to and clarified the nature of a scientific 'break' from the non-scientific hinterland of knowledge. A proper understanding of marxist *philosophy* is thus the precondition of the correct comprehension and application of the marxist science of history.

Because of the 'neutral' status accorded to both science and philosophy by Althusser, the typically marxist contention that philosophy was analytically and in reality derivative from socio-historical considerations seemed quite overthrown. The grounds and conditions of social knowledge, and therefore practice, became by definition the Althusserian norms. What is more, this sequence of theoretical self-generation – from the definition of science to the conceptual status of historical 'modes of production' – involves little independent or sustained argument. Beginning with the healthy desire to rid marxism and science of dubious metaphysical bogeys, Theoretical Practice once more erects philosophy as the key to the sciences and science to the highest social eminence. The accusation of 'idealism' in this context certainly seems justified, though we need to say something about the criterion of knowledge here as well as its exalted status.

Althusser argued that the knowledge-mechanism of each science is a matter for the science in question. This proposition has two rather different implications. On the one hand, Althusser refuses to set up a universally valid single model for scientific explanation – the temptation and fallacy of the 'philosophy of guarantees'. On the other hand, scientific criteria are the products not of the practitioners of science (Althusser is not a Kuhnian), but of the logic of the categories and methodologies produced. These, in turn, prescribe – for any science – the kinds of empirical evidence and conceptual 'proof' available to a theoretical 'problematic'. Consequently, just as Althusser has a formal place for materialism at the back of his epistemology, so he need not deny the significance of empirical or experimental verification. But his caveat is always that such verification be regarded as a theoretical product of a specific kind. Again, the disembodied *logic* of science appears as the general foundation and justification of knowledge.

As far as historical analysis is concerned, there are many things one could say about Althusser's risky operation.[32] On the one hand, his attempts to reformulate the causal relation between base and superstructure were important. Now that some of the dust has settled over the debates again, we can acknowledge – as Perry Anderson has – that Althusser's project was not necessarily anti-historical, and that his discussions have been in some ways very fruitful for 'concrete' work.[33] 'Relative autonomy', 'overdetermination', and 'structure in dominance' are useful ways of thinking complex causal relationships in history. The last is an especially awkward term, but it is helpful in cases where the possibility of superstructural dominance does not seem to replace economic exploitation (for example, the place of religion in some feudal formations). Finally, Althusser has stimulated an awareness of the need for better and fuller conceptualization in historical argument. True, the Althusserian penchant for theory seems simultaneously to demand an impossible rigour and insufficiently respects real empirical constraints, but the goal of a theoretical history need not generate undue animosity between marxists.

The major problems arise when the concern for a conceptual science of history serves only to legitimize philosophical abstraction, thus constituting a rationalistic approach to real history. The principal culprit concept here is 'structural causality', referring to the mutual dependence of a cause and its effects. In fact, structural causality goes beyond other Althusserian concepts such as 'overdetermination', and his application of this formal notion to history involves intractable problems, especially from a marxist point of view. For one thing, it is an obscure rather than coherent account of causality. The idea that a cause, to be a cause, must have an effect seems reasonable. But Althusser argues, implausibly, that causality consists of a structure which is only present in and through its effects, such that they form a unified conceptual totality.

Applied to the base/superstructure model, structural causality is open to a number of less pretentious translations. The most familiar of these might be that superstructural elements are not wholly or in every respect determined by the base, and that they have a 'reciprocal' effect upon the economic structure. Applied to history, structural causality is conceived by Althusser as 'mode of production'. The latter is a social totality, or 'state of the structure' (Balibar) rather than just an economic base (for example, capitalism rather than capitalist production). This expanded notion seems to have advantages when linked with a critique of teleological or linear time – which Althusser regards with some justice as an uncritical assumption of the various schools of bourgeois historiography. Structural causality is intended to ensure that a formal, content-less 'time' could no longer be the dominant organizing principle of historical thought and research. It also seems to provide at least a heuristic whereby an account of specific social phenomena can be systematically linked to, and thus be explained by, the nexus of social relations of which they are the necessary effect. However, it must be said that such an aim is by no means a novelty to marxist historians.

The concept of mode of production as a social totality has further disadvantages.

History tends to become divided according to marxist theory into large slabs, each of which has its own internal logic, derived from their theoretical principles of 'articulation' and logical conditions of existence. Like continental plates, these modes, structurally defined, bump corners with each other, but do not grow into, or become transformed into, one another. Balibar in particular got into all sorts of difficulties in attempting to build a theory of transition between modes, something that the theorization intrinsically hindered.[34] Critics objected that history became static and severed, allowing little place for the active, transformative role of class struggle and human agency.

Attractive in its apparent unification of philosophy, history, and social theory, 'structural causality' was eventually doubted even by those marxist anthropologists who, more than most, were initially excited by its effect on their discipline.

Realism

Are the excesses of diamat or structural causality due to the illusions of philosophy as such, or are they only idealist snares which philosophers must risk as an occupational hazard? Radical philosophers, especially in Britain, have refurbished an epistemological realist outlook on the basis of the second interpretation. Realism is a philosophical position which grasps many of the features of marxist explanation. The advantage of realism over other views is its acknowledgement of the theoretical moments in science, together with an emphasis on the independence of empirical evidence. Before examining realism, it is as well to distinguish it from empiricism, because some marxists, in arguing for the one, have defended the other. Historians in particular tend to do this when confronted with what they see as an extraneous glut of theory.

This is one main strand in E. P. Thompson's 'Poverty of theory'. Thompson does not critically or in detail examine empiricism as a philosophical position, but assumes that if there is a choice between empirical facts and static theory, and if by choosing the former he is to be considered an empiricist, then empiricist he must be. However, by pinning his colours to the mast in this way, Thompson commits the same mistake as the rationalists who argue that those who defend the empirical mode must be intrinsically hostile to theory. Because of this reciprocal tactic of guilt by association, neither side advances clear discussion. Thompson for his part is forced into defending the 'historical discipline' as such, as if it was some unitary practice based on something called 'the facts' and immune to larger theoretical contentions. Of course, Thompson's own historiography and the elements in his critique of Althusser which are more properly of a realist character render such a defence uneven and inconsistent rather than all-embracing.[35]

Marxists are unlikely to be straightforward empiricists, because in its positivistic forms empiricism is the doctrine that all knowledge is reducible to atomic propositions which correspond to discrete impressions, sense data, and the like. Similarly, the positivist conception of scientific laws depends on the view that statements of empirical regularity constitute the logical basis of genuine explanation. Neither idea is compatible with the belief that there are systemic or hidden causes of empirical phenomena – this being the basis of the marxist claim, for example, to reveal the true nature of exploitation.

Even so, marxists have often seemed to argue that the facts and reality declare themselves, whether in the experience of classes or in the correspondence of thought or perception to reality. And marxists are sometimes quick to deduce from any and every piece of evidence that marxist laws have been corroborated. Barry Hindess[36] has persuasively argued that Lenin's tome of statistical support for his thesis about *The Development of Capitalism in Russia* is the opposite of empiricism. But in *Materialism and Empirio-Criticism*, Lenin's account of knowledge (mixed as it certainly is) gets close to simple empiricism. Part of that book is one kind of defence of the independence of objects, but Lenin sometimes argues (against 'fideism' and 'subjectivism') that the objects of knowledge are directly known, and that the material world alone causes our thoughts and perceptions to 'copy' reality. He virulently denounces Plekhanov's notion (in my view, a reasonable proposal) that ideas and sensations are 'hieroglyphics' rather than mirror-images. Lenin's polemic thus trades on an equation between knowledge and perception, and gives the latter a rather mechanical-materialist treatment. In effect, Lenin rules out the possibility of real processes being opaque rather than transparent.

Ernest Mandel is one marxist whose tendency to empiricism compromises the argument of his *Late Capitalism*, which

attempts to demonstrate that the 'abstract' laws of notion of this mode of production remain operable and verifiable in and through the 'concrete' history of contemporary capitalism.[37]

This statement is ambiguous as between a realist and an empiricist meaning. I would not wholly support Hussain[38] who argues that Mandel simply interprets all evidence as confirmation of Marx's (or Mandel's) 'laws'. But Mandel's thesis is limited because it is open to criticisms of this kind. The empirical moment in research and proof may be indispensable, but the process of abstraction need not be pinned point for point to the data to be theoretically viable. Indeed, as Fine and Harris[39] point out, Mandel takes 'laws' – especially that of the falling rate of profit – to be those of the 'secular development of capitalism'. In fact, Marx's laws concern only the cycle of production, and even in that domain movements in the rate of profit, etc., cannot be simply explained by the law. This example also shows how reverence for the facts and theoretical intransigence can often go hand in hand.

A realist theory cannot be cognitively assessed primarily on empirical evidence, though it must explain relevant empirical phenomena. Realism is the philosophical view that knowledge is of objects or processes which exist independently of thought. In the terminology of one of its prominent spokesmen, Roy Bhaskar,[40] science discovers the 'generative mechanisms' which, when known, afford causal explanations. Natural science works by creating artificially 'closed' conditions in which decisive tests of theories can be carried out. But the natural world itself is an 'open' system, a system which cannot be adequately grasped in terms of the constant conjunction of observed phenomena (the latter being the dominant empiricist criterion).

Society too, for realism, is an open system, but unlike natural science, social science cannot construct decisive evidence. This is due to the fact that human beings change their social practice in the light of knowledge and self-consciousness. Agency and thought are thus constitutive of the object of study. As a consequence, social theory is necessarily historical, because the relations of social structure to knowledge and practice are, necessarily, relations over time.

Realism, stated in this way, retains many of the central interests associated with humanist and hermeneutic traditions. The latter, including many marxist thinkers, have resisted the very concept of social science, its apparent aping of natural science, and its abstraction from historical reality. Bhaskar, for example, agrees for the above reasons that social science must be incomplete, critical rather than definitive, and intimately bound up with social practice. But the recourse to irrationalism or intuition often encouraged by beliefs of this kind is refused by Bhaskar and others. Important arguments here would be that, for example, theoretical abstractions are as important and inescapable in social as in natural investigation; that theoretical explanations in social and historical enquiry must be coherent at a number of levels; and that while empirical or experiential controls are indispensable, phenomena of that kind are explained by causal and other sets of propositions, they do not themselves embody a privileged reference point for explanation.

For the new realists, historical materialism, as a major component of the social scientific enterprise, follows these criteria. By means of theoretical abstraction, marxism postulates generative mechanisms at the level of the mode of production, which helps explain the nature and development of historical and empirical problems and phenomena. Social forms, conjunctures and strategies are thus to be understood in terms of theoretically-expressed tendencies which have a real, structural status but which are not empirically transparent.

The development of such tenets is conducted by the new realists with novel cogency and care. The Preface to an important collection, *Issues in Marxist Philosophy*, proudly (if a bit pretentiously) announces its kinship with British analytical philosophy, at least in the concern for clarity. The arguments are indeed competent and persuasive: but the tones of the British university should warn us against an easy identification of these ideas as being Marx's own.

The labour of precise philosophical statement was (rightly) not Marx's priority. The whole fracas about 'symptomatic readings' of Marx arises because his general protocols are implicit rather than explicit. Accordingly, while we can agree that Marx's presuppositions were of a realist sort, it is important to be aware that they form a cluster of recommendations and prohibitions, not a philosophical *theory*.

Realism, for all its intuitive appeal, is such a theory. It is a philosophical position – a metaphysic, even – which does not begin with Marx and goes beyond him. And its contemporary formulations are cultural products of a very different kind from Marx's classic texts. So although it may be preferable to rationalist or empiricist constructions of the 'essential' Marx, realism must also abstract from parts of his work, must make a case about the spirit of his enterprise rather than the letter.

The point is belaboured here because there is a danger that realism, for all its advantages, might perpetuate current wrangles rather than materially advance discussion. For example, we have seen that Derek Sayer advocates marxism-as-method. He constructs this view of Marx along realist lines. (This is a little inconsistent: realism must substantially wed method to theory or doctrine, but the point is a small one.) But in his haste to burn out the Althusserian heresy, Sayer overplays two things. First, he exaggerates the extent to which Althusser's Marx is sheer invention, as opposed to one (perhaps extreme) interpretation. Second, Sayer argues that Marx – *contra* Althusser and great irony – was the empiricist *par excellence*. It seems to us that a more self-critical presentation of realist tenets and less concern to appear as the spokesman of the real Marx would have been more helpful here. As it is, substantial points are clouded by the kind of terminological sophistry which is supposed to be the trade mark of the tradition Sayer opposes. In general, however, the debate is indicative: those who object to philosophy in marxism will find no solace in realism.

As a philosophical position, there are a number of problems with realism. First, one may doubt whether it *is* a single position. Even amongst the marxist realists there are clear divergences. Bhaskar, for example, is committed to the view that generative mechanisms, powers and agents are the things that make up the basic structure of the world. Such an ontology, and the necessary form of its appropriate science, for Bhaskar, can be established by philosophical argument alone. These claims are contested by another realist, David-Hillel Ruben.[41] Derek Sayer, in his realist account of Marx, relies heavily on the American philosopher N. R. Hanson. But as other realists R. Keat and J. Urry[42] suggest, Hanson is in key respects a 'constructivist' – he does not allow that objects, even those of everyday perception, are theory-independent. Finally, Ted Benton[43] states realism in a more general way. This is persuasive, but as a fairly general standpoint, realism might be far less contentious. Benton, for example, uses Althusser in drawing out some realist arguments. In addition, realism is today a common position within mainstream philosophy of science and in theories of meaning, and it is sometimes thought to be irrelevant to the specific details of theoretical positions.

This leads to a second important problem. Realism need not be a *materialist* philosophy. Benton, Ruben, and others rightly say that 'material' should not be construed as simply 'physical'. But in that case, materialism must be defined in terms of objectivity, structures, and science. Here it seems to be more appropriate to subsume materialism under realism rather than vice versa. Yet it then becomes rather more difficult to rule out of court *idealist* conceptions of 'the real'. The latter have a long pedigree in philosophy, and in *Marxism and Materialism*, Ruben, for instance, cannot withhold the term 'realism' from thinkers such as Hume and even Bishop Berkeley: no materialists. Similarly, there is some question about whether philosophers today who have done much to advance the realist standpoint (for example, Hilary Putnam) are nevertheless idealists.[44]

The third and overarching difficulty with realism is whether transcendental arguments are essential to it, and if they are, whether it matters. By 'transcendental' is meant, roughly, a priori: arguments about the necessary make-up of the world, or knowledge, and so arguments which are not dependent on any particular body of knowledge. Bhaskar says, yes, they are necessary and important, and his view of science depends upon them. He argues that science is possible only if the world is structured in a certain way and if certain objects and powers endure. Ruben shares Bhaskar's *belief* in structured objects, but maintains that this is impossible to prove adequately. For Ruben, transcendental realism cannot be the only possible explanation of science, even though we may think it is right. Ruben insists that transcendental arguments are circular and so insignificant: they state what they presuppose. Furthermore, to expect a priori arguments to deliver a non-circular definition of science is to undermine the common marxist and materialist point that science, and not philosophy, tells us what exists and in what way. When we consider social science, Ruben argues, we want to know about particular societies, and cannot be satisfied with generalizations about the necessary form of the social *per se*.

We have condensed these debates a great deal, since the details of the positions require much closer philosophical argument. And this itself, together with the fact that these are general issues in modern philosophy (the debate about 'positivism' having been to a large extent superseded), should reinforce our point that while realism is an important advance, it is not specifically marxist. Ruben, to his credit, is aware of this, and tries to hold only to what is distinctive about marxist materialism. He argues that a 'reflection theory of knowledge' is crucial here. Despite his militant labels, however, Ruben fails to show that 'materialism' is any different from realism broadly conceived. Nor does he convincingly establish that 'reflection' is the only, or most appropriate, way of thinking the relation of knowledge (including historical knowledge) to being. He does not intend it to mean a 'copy' theory, or to give support to an empiricist reading. Rather, the broad sense of 'reflection' is more akin to a 'correspondence' between ideas and the world.[45] However, while 'correspondence' seems a fairly basic and defensible notion, it is compatible with a generous view of theory-formation and different criteria of explanatory adequacy. The category of reflection is therefore too restrictive, and seems neither a necessary nor an especially useful one for marxists to defend.

Conclusion

The purpose of this discussion has been to outline a number of central issues in marxist thinking about the role and status of philosophy, and how they connect to problems of historical theory and methodology. Obviously, not every problem appears to be directly relevant; but by and large, there are important consequences for marxist historians in arguments about the nature of marxist explanation and social science. Similarly, the character of historical research and methods form the groundwork of the philosophers' attempts to formalize and defend marxist conceptions of theory and explanation.

In conclusion, it seems reasonable to argue that the philosophical basis of marxism is indeed of a realist kind, but is more a set of presuppositions than an epistemological theory. Philosophical conceptions play an indispensable role in historical materialism and can be made relevant to more substantive questions at the same time as striving to maintain high specialist standards. However, it is also important to say that there is no specifically marxist epistemology and so the desideratum of being tied to socio-historical analysis is the more important. One reason for the vehemence and unproductiveness of much inner-marxist debate throughout its history has been the very belief that marxist knowledge was of a unique kind.

This belief has generated a number of attempts to codify and proselytize marxism as a philosophical system. And *those* attempts have in turn frequently produced an anti-philosophy lobby within the marxist camp. Paradoxically, the legitimate concern for the primacy of history has at times taken on a mysteriously philosophical air. The ups and downs of these debates and their development are very much historical and political questions. But there should also be space for the evaluation of marxist philosophies in their own right, partly because even in apparent grand isolation, they have been intimately connected with the way in which historiography has been conceived and practised. If this conclusion is acceptable, more co-operative projects involving marxist historians and philosophers should replace the mutual suspicion which sometimes divides them. Some of these tasks would be methodological in character. For example, marxist realists might be expected to contribute guidelines to the debates about historical 'narrative', or about the status of subjective evidence, or to comment in detail on the assumptions and coherence of arguments within specific empirical fields. Other questions will have a more substantive aspect: the relation between popular beliefs and theoretical ideologies; the conception of long-term social transformation; the historical 'relative autonomy' of intellectual, scientific, or aesthetic movements and ideas; the problems of 'agency and structure' in particular cases. Within these broad areas lie many key and politically pertinent problems for socialist theory. They cannot be properly tackled as long as the blinkered contraposition of the theoretical and empirical modes, of philosophy and history, persists.

5 Reading for the best Marx: history-writing and historical abstraction

Richard Johnson

Introduction

Marx's work is a point of reference for many of the historians discussed in this volume and for our own contributors too. The book would be incomplete, therefore, without a more direct look at his 'historical' practice. How did Marx combine history, theory and politics? If his theory is historical and his history theoretically organized, how is this fusion or relation achieved? And how were Marx's historical explanations related to his politics – his hopes and struggles for a communist future?

These questions are closely related to the debates discussed in the previous chapter. I very much agree with Greg McLennan's argument that both marxism and history-writing are clarified by being brought into a relation to realist philosophy.[1] Yet with some notable exceptions, including McLennan's work, the history/theory questions have tended to be evaded. Ted Benton has put this still more sharply:

> But nowhere in the corpus of Marxist literature is there any sustained attempt to give theoretical expression to the logical conditions, rules and constraints involved in the employment of these concepts in concrete analysis.[2]

He points to this area as one in which 'much important philosophical work in Marxism remains to be done'.

This deficiency has not really been supplied in more recent debates about history and theory. As we have seen, *The Poverty of Theory* does not discuss the relation between historical research and the more general categories very satisfactorily.[3] More surprisingly, perhaps, Perry Anderson's reply, though contesting the categories themselves and insisting upon rigour, leaves history-writing and research relatively unquestioned. He finds in Thompson's formulations, indeed, a 'superb vindication of historical evidence'.[4] Following McLennan's insistence on the interrelation of philosophy and historical practice, it seems worth pursuing these questions a little further.

But why choose the writings of Karl Marx as the ground on which to pursue them? Why, indeed, return to Marx at all, and, if so, in what spirit? For readers who stand 'outside' marxism – even if they argue still for a hopeful and progressive politics – a sense of indebtedness will hardly be sufficient explanation. A major tendency in recent debates is not so much a recovery or a renovation as a shredding of 'marxism' into a thousand pieces. Some currents are proud to announce 'we are no longer marxists now!' So it is important to say why, for others, Marx remains a resource, and within what limits.

The answer has to be somewhat retrospective and autobiographical. Most of the work on which this essay was based, the first group readings and discussions, took place some years ago. They were one way in which we attempted to work out the conundrums posed in the polemics of the 1970s. It was plain, from what we already knew of Marx, that our own dilemmas did not appear in quite the same form as in the early development of historical materialism. Marx's own work did not show the same inhibiting polarities of history and theory, structure and struggle, intellectual work and politics. We did not expect to find easy answers in Marx's work, but perhaps the questions would be posed in more manageable and more fruitful ways. So we returned to Marx looking for helpful clues to modern dilemmas. Ours was not a philosopher's reading in the manner of Althusser's circle in the 1960s. Nor was it quite the historian's reading, in the manner of Edward Thompson. It was precisely the *relation* between history and philosophy that interested us, whether approached from the historical or the philosophical side. This was to occupy an awkward space: too commonsensical for some, too abstruse for others.

We called the product of this reading, at first mainly in fun, 'the best Marx'. But it was a tag which stuck. I retain it now because it sums up an important difference between the eventual reading and other returns to Marx, including our own earliest forays.[5] Since much of the 1970s' debate was posed in terms of 'marxism', it was tempting to treat Marx as an authoritative court of appeal, reading him to recover *the* Marx, even the *real* Marx. As we have argued, there are problems with such readings,[6] preferable though they are to those that place marxism, relativistically, as only one form of sociological theory. They overestimate the unity and transparency of Marx's texts, they minimize the *parti pris* of the reader and they may run against the spirit of much of Marx's own practice, especially his practice of criticizing theories *historically*. Marx or marxism cannot be allowed to forgo the same test. We cannot ignore the host of new developments, problems and needs thrown up by social movements since the 1870s and 1880s. One reason for remaining 'a marxist' is that many of these *were* anticipated in Marx's writing. There *was* something strategic about his time and place (mid-nineteenth-century Britain) and something particularly effective about his way of working that gave his thinking an unusually long historical reach, and as realized prediction, not mere prophecy. This is why reading Marx today remains so exciting. Large parts of his account of the tendencies of capitalist development remain valid despite the fact that he did not investigate the full range of historical determinations. Capitalist development *has* been Promethean, *has* acquired 'a world-historical dimension' and *has* remained ridden with contradictions and crises. But on many modern developments Marx is quite silent and remains, in some legitimate readings, quite mischievous in his influence. The centrality, today, of struggles over gender and over race require a stretching and transforming of marxist ideas and the production of whole new areas of useful knowledge, some of which may challenge Marx's most general premises. Similarly the increasing importance of the struggle over the cultural and political definition of 'needs' necessarily poses questions for the fundamental tenets of 'materialism'.[7]

Our title – 'the best Marx' – represents our response to these problems. We acknowledge that Marx's own accounts are not unified. We recognize that readings take sides – though not arbitrarily, not released from *disciplines* of reading. We insist that Marx's weight is relative: relative to historical circumstances, to particular needs, and to rival theorizations. We are obliged to recognize that the best Marx is partly our own construction or that of our time and place. And if, in this reading, there is a 'best' Marx, there must also be a 'worst' Marx too!

In what follows I draw heavily on this collective mulling over and also upon the individual writing, published and unpublished, of other members of the group.[8] First I sketch the main stages in Marx's method, noting the place he accorded to research, to abstraction and to historical reconstructions. Like other commentators, I suggest that Marx's method as a whole resembles a kind of circuit: a movement from the concrete to the abstract and back again from the abstract to the concrete. In the rest of the first part, I look more closely at the first points on this circuit, those that represent Marx's method of research, analysis and inquiry. In the course of this discussion, 'abstraction' emerges as a big issue. It is, therefore, the main subject of the second part of the essay where I look more closely at what Marx means by 'adequate' or 'historical' abstractions and at his criticisms of other ways of thinking. Finally, returning to the later points on Marx's circuit, I discuss the way in which he presents his results. It is in this context that I look at Marx's most detailed historical writings. The essay ends by noting some limits to 'the best Marx' and by drawing out some implications for historical practice today.

The circuit as a whole and the method of inquiry

Sources

Marx's reflections on ways of working are cryptic, partial and often obscure. Perhaps the most extended text on method is the 1857 Introduction to the *Grundrisse* (Marx's first draft of parts of *Capital*).[9] This text is certainly very rich and I will refer to it often. But it is also the most difficult Marx text of all. A good case can be made that it is self-contradictory. Certainly it was suppressed by Marx himself and was never used in the Prefaces to *Capital*.[10] Large claims have been made for the notebooks themselves, as being of 'inestimable value for the study of Marx's method of inquiry'.[11] But this promise does not seem to have been realized in subsequent commentaries. It may be that the questions put to the *Grundrisse* have been too narrow, overwhelmingly concerning Marx's debt to Hegel and to dialectics.[12] None the less there are some wonderfully revealing passages in which Marx discusses the nature of abstraction. Other statements of 'method', the Preface to the *Contribution to the Critique of Political Economy*[13] or *The German Ideology*,[14] are not really about the way of working at all. They sketch, rather,

Marx's general sociology or social ontology. Of course, Marx's method cannot be divorced from his premises, especially from his view of the social character of thinking, but these two texts announce some general results, not the ways they were reached.

I have found Marx most revealing about his method in passing: in practical contexts, in criticizing others and in replying to his own critics.[15] His methods, after all, were forged in the process of critique: first of Hegel, the neo-Hegelians and early socialists, then of Scottish and English political economy. They were often consolidated in this form too as in the much later *Notes on Adolph Wagner* (1879-80) which are particularly interesting for Marx's views of language and abstraction.[16] But the most useful 'practical' texts of all are the Marx-Engels letters which sustained a rather intellectual correspondence about political events, discoveries and writings, more or less as they happened.[17] All this imposes a certain discipline on the commentator. It is necessary to use a wide range of sources, to connect up diverse references, and to expand on some very cryptic formulations.

For Marx's method of inquiry, it is necessary to make the most of limited materials. In the case of 'presentation', however, there is less difficulty. Obviously, it is possible to analyse all of Marx's major texts from this point of view, seeing how he chose to present his results, at what level of abstraction, in what order and so on. I have drawn particularly on the structure of presentation of *Capital* (mainly volume I) and to a lesser degree, on the 'historical' or 'political' essays, especially *The Eighteenth Brumaire of Louis Bonaparte*. These essays really require a separate study.[18]

Marx's way of working: an overview

A uniquely complete but typically condensed account is to be found in the Postface to the second edition of *Capital*. The context is a discussion of reviews of 'the method employed in *Capital*'. Some reviewers dub the method 'metaphysical', others 'the critical analysis of the actual facts'. Marx responds - apparently in a very roundabout way:

Of course the method or presentation must differ from the method of inquiry. The latter has to appropriate the material in detail, to analyse its different forms of development and to track down their inner connection. Only after this work has been done can the real movement be appropriately presented. If it is done successfully, if the life of the subject matter is now reflected back in the ideas, then it may appear as if we have before us an *a priori* construction.[19]

Marx distinguishes two broad domains of method: 'the method of inquiry' and 'the method of presentation'. He insists that the methods for each are very different. But they are also mutually dependent. Adequate inquiry is essential to appropriate presentation, even though the process of finding out disappears in the result. Evidently, 'presentation' is more than just 'writing up', more than the mere 'communication of results'. It is an essential part of scientific activity, of discovery and explanation in the larger sense. It is through the process of presentation that the material finds its appropriate forms of expression, and 'life' is reproduced in 'ideas'.

In more detail, Marx defines five main stages/aspects. (Typically, I think, Marx would have called them 'moments', his own use of a Hegelian term, to indicate that they are necessary stages or forms through which a practice must pass to be fully developed.) I list them here:

1. 'appropriate the material in detail': which we may call 'research';
2. 'analyse its different forms of development': 'historical analysis';
3. 'track down their inner connections': 'structural analysis';
4. 'presenting the real movement': 'presentation';
5. 'the life of the subject matter reflected back in ideas': 'validation'.

Of these distinctions, that between 2 and 3 is the most problematic, though all the 'moments' are dependent on the others and may not occur in simple sequence. In the case of 2 or 3, however, a form of 'analysis' which is both historical and structural might better be termed, as Marx termed it, 'dialectical'. Below, I make the separation, but for convenience of presentation only.

The whole sequence can also be presented as a diagram (Figure 1).

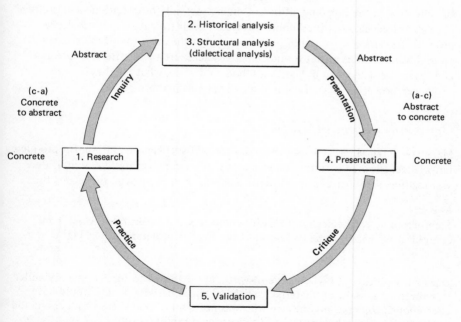

Note. In 'reading' the diagram you should start at point 1, research, then follow round the circuit, but note the caveat about 'moments' in the text.

Figure 1 *Marx's method of working*

I have added several elements to Figure 1 not present in the quotation from the Postface. They are worth noting here, but only as an agenda to which we will return, in a more careful way, later.

The first addition concerns the poles marked 'abstract' and 'concrete' and the movements between them (from concrete to abstract on the top left quarter of the circuit; from abstract to concrete on the top right). This is an attempt to represent Marx's argument that the movement from research to analysis (from 'appropriating the material in detail' to 'analysing its different forms of development') is also a movement from a concern with dense and specific particulars to relatively more abstract thinking. Inquiry involves abstraction. Conversely, 'presenting the real movement' means moving, in thought, from abstractions of different kinds to something like the real complexity of the world which we are trying to understand. Presentation (including history-writing) involves 'concentration' or, to coin a term to oppose to abstraction, 'concretion'.

The point of noting these movements at this stage is to describe the circuit as a whole. It can be described in the formula concrete–abstract–concrete (or c–a–c). For Galvano della Volpe, the Italian marxist philosopher, it is this circuit rather than any one element along it that distinguishes Marx's method. Indeed, for della Volpeans, it distinguishes the scientific method as such.[20]

Second, I have added the terms 'critique' and 'practice' to indicate the means of validation in the bottom half of the circuit. Actually both critique and political practice belong also to other moments in the circuit (research, as we shall see, involves the *critical* appraisal of phenomena), but the inclusion of these terms around 'validation' is meant to indicate a problem: are there criteria of practical and 'scientific' adequacy in Marx's method, and, if so, what are they?

We can now look at each point along the circuit in more detail.

'Appropriate the material in detail'

Marx saw detailed research as a necessary but not sufficient condition for producing knowledge. His own practice was exemplary; the references in *Capital* indicate a vast reading. A monstrous appetite for 'material' comes through the letters too.

Engels:
I am buried up to the neck in English newspapers and books from which I am compiling my book on the condition of the English proletarians. (1844)[21]

Marx:
During my illness . . . I was unable to write, but managed to force down my gullet an enormous amount of 'material', statistical and otherwise, which would have been enough to make anyone sick who was not used to that sort of fodder and did not possess a stomach accustomed to digesting it rapidly. (1868)[22]

Nor was this an occasional activity in special periods of 'research'. It continued after discoveries were made. Understandings were subjected to further material.

Often, in the later stages of writing *Capital*, the effect was confirmatory:

As for Chapter IV it cost me much hard toil to ascertain *the things themselves* i.e. their *interconnection*. Then, after that had all been done, one Blue Book after another arrived while I was in the midst of the *final elaboration*, and I was delighted to find my theoretical results confirmed by the facts.[23]

But research also promised new developments. Like all good historians of the contemporary, Marx kept a sharp eye on those events which threatened to outrun his ideas:

I should under no circumstances have published the second volume before the present English industrial crisis had reached its climax. The phenomena are this time singular, in many respects different from what they were in the past. . . . It is therefore necessary to watch the present course of things until their maturity before you can 'consume' them 'productively', I mean *'theoretically'*.[24]

This stress on 'observation' also informed Marx's critiques. The trouble with many philosophers' was that they knew no history. They commented in thinner and thinner ways on ideas.

Mr. Proudhon, incapable of following the real movement of history, produces the phantasmagoria which claims to be dialectical. He does not need to speak of the seventeenth, the eighteenth or the nineteenth century, for his history proceeds in the misty realm of imagination and is above space and time. In short, it is not history, but trite Hegelian trash.[25]

Even Ricardo, whom Marx respected more, was sometimes judged at the court of 'facts':

Statisticians and practical men . . . have been maintaining the existence of absolute rent for the last 35 years, while the (Ricardian) theoreticians have been trying to demonstrate it out of existence by very arbitrary and theoretically feeble abstractions. Up to now, in all such quarrels I have always found that the theoreticians have invariably been in the wrong. (1862)[26]

Though Marx was certainly a very 'bookish' person, he neglected neither the political experience of contemporary socialist movements, nor the practical common sense of the bourgeoisie. The fact that his friend Engels was a capitalist was quite a help here:

Now, you as a manufacturer must know what you do with the returns you receive for the fixed capital *before* it has to be replaced *in kind*. And you must give me an answer on this point (without theory, *purely as a matter of practice*).[27]

This is enough to gladden the hearts of practical persons the world over – including 'practical' historians – but it is only part of 'appropriating the material in detail'. It is important to look at Marx's language again, especially his metaphors. The favourite figures are of eating or consumption. Though he sometimes uses the language of 'testing',[28] the relation between 'objective' source and the observer who remains external to it is foreign to Marx's way of thinking. The sources are actually stuffed into the mind, so to speak, and there masticated and 'digested'. In the wonderful phrase, they are 'consumed . . . "productively", I mean *"theoretically"* '. They are taken in, made your own, possessed mentally, re-emerging rethought and perhaps transformed. Omnivorous ingestion is a condition for this, of course; the sources must actually enter the mind and its mental extensions of notes and sketches. But this elementary condition, certainly neglected by some who think they are wise, is treacherous none the less if supposed to deliver knowledge, just like that.

A further clue is Marx's term 'appropriation' which also expresses activity, labour. The elementary process of labour is the active appropriation and transformation of nature. It involves the use of tools. In mental labour, the main tool is the human brain itself, and the concepts, premises and habits of mind already developed there. It is important to remember this when we are being bullied for being 'theoretical'. There is no mental act which does not depend upon prior conditions of this kind, no 'innocent' observation. In Marx's case we have to remember the whole sequence of critical thinking marked by texts from the *Paris Manuscripts of 1844*[29] to the *Contribution to the Critique of Political Economy* (1859). It is true that one major strand, here, was the critique of philosophy, whether of Feuerbach's humanism, the idealism of the neo-Hegelians or the unending tussle with 'the colossal old chap', Hegel himself;[30] but these critiques were themselves philosophical. They form part of a search for adequate foundations of study, the basis of a new, critical science.[31]

By the time Marx started to work on *Capital*, then, he had settled accounts with the main philosophical positions of the day and battled for close on twenty years with political economy. It is sometimes forgotten that the main object of attack in the *Paris Manuscripts* of 1844 was *already* political economy even if the critique was, at first, philosophical and moral.[32] (If political economy really does describe capitalist society, Marx asks, what, then, are the human consequences?) His labour on, for example, the British Blue Books, was undertaken with tools long prepared. It is only if we cut through the continuities of his thinking (which are, on the whole, quite striking) that we can ignore the dependence of the *Grundrisse* and *Capital* on the earlier work. Althusser manages this by exaggerating the break from Hegel;[33] Thompson by imagining the springing of a trap of 'economy' (from which Marx is rescued by 'history') in the preparatory work for *Capital*.[34] Actually it is difficult to conceive of the achievements of *Capital* (including its narrowly 'historical' insights) without the examination of 'social forms' in the notebooks, and difficult to think of all this without, say, the starting points of *The German Ideology*. In this case, as in all others, research was guided by tools, premises and interests which already had a lengthy history of their own. 'Appropriation' was critical: already a process of critique.

'Analyse its different forms of development'

I cannot manage a full account of Marx's way of working on materials so appropriated. It is enough to stress three main features, each signalled in Marx's own
phrase. First, Marx's procedure of inquiry is *analytic* ('analyse', 'different forms').
It is designed to produce categories that allow us to grasp differences. The method –
the stress on 'different forms' – is, to put it rather abstractly, anti-reductionist.
There are of course many forms of reduction but they all amount to a radical
mental simplification of social life. The stress on complexity means that Marx
refuses to *reduce* 'the material' to the workings of a few simple general principles
or real identities. Similarly he is suspicious of procedures which 'generalise' by
seeking in different forms only the common elements.[35] Second, it is not only
formal difference which the categories must express but also movement or tendency ('its different forms of development'). This is why Zelený, who is concerned
to dig out the general 'logic' of Marx's method, refers to it as 'a unified structural-
genetic analysis' or, in a similar couplet, 'dialectical-logical derivation'.[36] Stuart
Hall, in his careful reading of the 1857 Introduction, makes the same point in a
different way.[37] It is not merely that different forms of social life are distinguished
but that the dynamic of their movement and their further capacity for change are
also revealed.

It is plain that this procedure requires historical knowledge in the more usual
sense: it depends on appropriating the materials of 'the present English crisis' and
indeed of 'the seventeenth, eighteenth and nineteenth century'. How else could
the forms of development of social life be uncovered? But it also depends, and this
is our third important point, on what Marx calls 'abstraction'.

'Abstraction' is as important as 'research'. It is a further condition of analysis.
Marx insisted on its centrality; some of his largest claims to 'science' were based
upon its power. In the Preface to the first edition to *Capital*, he wrote:

Beginnings are always difficult in all sciences. The understanding of the first
chapter [of *Capital*, volume I], especially the section that contains the analysis of
commodities, will therefore present the greatest difficulty. . . . The value-form,
whose fully developed shape is the money-form, is very simple and slight in content.
Nevertheless, the human mind has sought in vain for more than 2,000 years to get
to the bottom of it. . . . Why? Because the complete body is easier to study than its
cells. Moreover, in the analysis of economic forms neither microscopes nor chemical
reagents are of assistance. The power of abstraction must replace both. But for
bourgeois society, the commodity-form of the product of labour, or the value-
form of the commodity, is the economic cell-form. To the superficial observer,
the analysis of these forms seems to turn on minutiae. It does in fact deal with
minutiae, but so similarly does microscopic anatomy.[38]

This is partly Marx's justification for starting *Capital* with a peculiarly difficult
passage (which has, indeed, put off many readers!). But there is a more general
argument too. Adequate knowledge depends upon the close investigation of the

internal structure of natural or of social processes. There are, however, real differences between natural materials or biological organisms and human societies including capitalist ones. In natural science physical or biological states may be isolated, controlled and experimented with. Social processes cannot be isolated in this way. The solution lies in the mental equivalent of the physical isolation of matter. A social phenomenon, already appropriated mentally by (theoretically-informed) observation, may be mentally isolated from the complex of determinations, effects and contingencies that surround it. It may be mentally appropriated, as it were, 'pure and simple'. 'The force of abstraction' is a process of *abstracting from* the 'real concrete', from complicated social and historical processes in their totality, which remain, however, the ultimate object of study. Abstraction is a *temporary* simplification of the social world in order to render it intelligible. It involves 'dropping' some elements of a situation in order to concentrate, for the moment, on others. It is not reductive, because each set of determinations is abstracted in turn and then, as it were, recomposed. As Zelený puts it:

In dialectical-logical derivation there is an abstraction from the numerous factors and conditions which have played a role in the historical realization of the forms under investigation. This abstraction . . . is necessary as a first step in understanding historical development and real forms in their complexity, their essence and their particularity. Otherwise the 'conceptual knowledge' of real activities could not be worked out.[39]

Abstraction was not, for Marx, a unique feature of his method. Rather, it was a feature of systematic thought as such. It was normal in the natural process of thinking. It occurred in thought whether the thinker was aware of this or not. As we shall see, this was one of Marx's fundamental premises concerning the character of thinking and of its relation to other practices:

Men who produce their social relations in accordance with their material productivity also produce *ideas, categories,* that is to say the abstract ideal expressions of these same social relations.[40]

Abstraction, *per se*, did not depend therefore on a particular exercise of the will. What matters is not the *fact* of abstraction (which happens anyway as the medium of thinking) but a self-consciousness of this process and *the choice of the form of categories, and their derivation*. On the other side, inadequate or ideological categories are flawed not because they are 'abstract' but because they are abstract in the wrong way or form. We will return to these questions in the second part of this essay, but it is important to stress this, because it is often assumed, especially by empiricists, that very abstract categories are *ipso facto* ideological and that only complex concrete descriptions of real social processes are really 'materialist'. This contrasts with Marx's insistence that abstraction is a condition of really concrete studies. It is only by making abstractions of the different economic forms that it is possible to distinguish them, analyse them and trace their development. Before we write a history of money, or understand its function in bourgeois society, we have to grasp the money form itself, what this strange medium is capable of achieving and what its possibilities of development, limits and contradictions are. The opening sections of *Capital*, based on the abstraction of the commodity form,[41] are a classic instance of this method at work. It is for these reasons that the initial movement of the method is from the concrete to the abstract, from the complex 'material' already appropriated in research to the simpler abstractions and distinctions. Only later, having understood how key processes and determinations may work, is it possible to return, in thought, to a complexity that resembles that of the real world.

'Track down their inner connections'

The abstraction of social forms and an analysis of their development does not fully satisfy Marx's criteria of adequate inquiry. We can take Marx's description of his object of study in *Capital* as an example:

What I have to examine in this work is the capitalist mode of production, and the relations of production and forms of intercourse that correspond to it.[42]

But this 'examination' involved more than a description of these relations and forms, it meant tracking down 'the natural laws of movement' or 'the economic law of motion of modern society'. Leaving aside that contentious term 'law', Marx is saying that he seeks a *critical and explanatory* knowledge of modern society. Certainly he starts from everyday life ('the forms of intercourse'). In *Capital* he starts from the commodity, from buying and selling, and from money, the 'magical' medium. But the analysis cannot stop here. After all, this is the starting point of bourgeois apologetics too; but they stay on the surface of things:

There it will be seen how the philistine's and vulgar economist's *way of looking at things* arises, namely because it is only the immediate phenomenal *form* of these relations that is reflected in their brains and not their *inner connection*. Incidentally, if the latter were the case what need would there be of science?[43]

The best political economists go further. They grasp the conditions on which practical activity in bourgeois society rests:

The code of modern political economy, in so far as it has been drawn up accurately and objectively by the economists, is to us simply a summary of the laws and conditions under which alone modern bourgeois society can exist – in short, its conditions of production and exchange expressed in an abstract way and summarised.[44]

One index of this limitation is the way economists treat history. They either 'smudge over all historical differences and see bourgeois relations in all forms of society'[45] or, if thinking historically, do so conservatively. They construct retrospective histories in which 'the latest form regards the previous ones as steps leading up to itself'.[46] The effect is to read the past uncritically and one-sidedly and to sanction present arrangements as the culmination of 'development'. This is to treat the 'steps leading up' to bourgeois society as real history, but stop time and change once it is reached. Bourgeois society itself has, in this sense, no history.[47]

To trace 'the different forms of development' retrospectively is not enough. Modern society is not just a summation of previous development: it is still undergoing change; still has a characteristic *dynamic*. It develops under its own specific 'laws'. Similarly there are *limits* to its development: just as the feudal regime was transformed into a capitalist one, so capitalism itself may change its specific laws and character. Under what conditions will this occur?

Answering this question (or indeed posing it) involves a different political standpoint and different intellectual tools to those offered by political economy. It means going beyond the immediate 'obviousness' of the given social order. This is what Marx means by 'tracking down the inner connections', a phrase most often used to distinguish his approach from vulgar economics. Understanding the rules and tendencies of motion of contemporary society involves unearthing the 'inner connections' of its economic forms.

To say more, at this stage, about the character of Marx's own categories would be to anticipate the second part of this essay, but there are an important set of connected issues around the problem of Marx and 'dialectics'.[48]

Since some recent discussions of Marx, Hegel and dialectics have not been particularly sensible,[49] it is worth pointing to the unambiguous character of Marx's own statements. On the one hand Marx constantly criticized Hegel for attempting to derive the real forms of the social world from the process of thinking itself. (We will look at this in more detail under the heading of idealist abstractions.) On the other hand, it is clear that Marx found in dialectical thinking a general form of categories much more appropriate to his object than other modes of logic. Dialectical thinking allowed him to specify the 'inner connections' of forms – contradictions, metamorphoses, 'moments', immanent tendencies – in a way that structurally specified the possibilities of future development. In its idealist form, dialectics seem 'to transfigure and glorify what exists'. In its 'rational' (i.e. materialist) form

it includes in its positive understanding of what exists a simultaneous recognition of its negation, its inevitable destruction; because it regards every historically developed form as being in a fluid state, in motion, and therefore grasps its transient aspect as well; and because it does not let itself be impressed by anything, being in its very essence critical and revolutionary.[50]

The whole cast of Marx's thinking is dialectical in this sense. But dialectics was not some ready-made schema which provided a priori truths and recipes. Marx was extremely scornful of such uses. Of Lassalle he wrote:

He does it like a school boy who has to prove in his exercise that he has got his 'essence', 'appearance' and 'dialectical process' down pat.[51]

Dialectics, rather, was a 'method of dealing with the material':

Lange is naive enough to say that I 'move with rare freedom' in empirical matter. He hasn't the least idea that this 'free movement in matter' is nothing but a paraphrase for the *method* of dealing with matter – that is, the *dialectical method.*[52]

Dialectics, in other words, was a mode of analysis, a useful form of thought or logic. It was not a set of formulas that could simply be 'applied'. Marx's reason for adopting an Hegelian form of categories was that *real social movements could not be grasped in any other way*.

Historical abstractions

History and theory: a reformulation

It is useful to restate, at this point, one of the opening questions: what is the relation in Marx's work between theory and history-writing? The question takes on new implications in the light of the importance of abstraction. When we speak of 'history' and 'theory' in this context what do we mean?

The answer is by no means self-evident, for most of the commonsensical definitions of history are unsatisfactory: that the object of history is 'the past', for instance, or that history typically takes the narrative form. Some of these issues are discussed later in this book:[53] it is enough, for the moment, to uphold the range of historical practice. It includes work as broad and as 'structural' as Dobb's *Studies,* Marc Bloch's *Feudal Society* or the geophysical dimensions of Fernand Braudel's *La Méditerranée et le Monde Méditerranéen* but also as detailed, 'close in' (and narratively organized) as Edward Thompson's *Making*, Ronald Fraser's *Blood of Spain* and Le Roy Ladurie's *Montaillou.*[54] In other words, historians too write in ways that are more or less abstract. Sometimes they are concerned with the broad character of epochs or transitions. They write about feudal ties, forms of rent, or ways of organizing production: they develop historical categories. At other times, they seek to get as close to the complex, lived tissues of everyday life as ingenuity and sources will allow, employing categories to present 'real history'. It is typical of this side of historical practice that discussion of the more abstract categories remains attenuated or hidden; but is it useful to think of one side as 'historical' and the other as not?

There are really *two* sets of questions here. The first concerns the nature of 'theory'. It makes some sense to retain a distinction between 'theory' and historical re-creation if there is really something about theoretical categories that distances them from history. If, however, theoretical categories already express historical conditions (only more abstractly than concrete histories) this distance vanishes or narrows. We are 'doing history' all the time, only in more or less abstract ways. The categories themselves are more or less historical. In Marx's case the search certainly *was* for 'historical' categories in this sense. One implication of this is that for historical materialism at least, the theory–history distinction itself may sometimes mislead. It is better to speak not of 'history' and 'theory', but of *historical categories and accounts at different levels of abstraction*. The best practice breaks the distinction itself.

'Levels of abstraction' constitutes the second set of questions. Even if categories *are* historical, rooted in historical inquiry and abstracted thence, there are still some problems about 'levels'. How do we move from relatively abstract historical accounts to the detailed reconstitution of something like the complexity of the real historical world, past and present? If the historical (or unhistorical) character of the categories is a problem for the process of inquiry, 'levels of abstraction' is a problem concerning the process of presentation. It is a question of how more abstract categories can be presented and be put to work in more complex accounts, demonstrating their explanatory power.

The rest of this essay deals with these two sets of questions: with problems of 'inquiry', reformulated as the nature of abstractions; with problems of presentation, reformulated as 'levels of abstraction'.

Unhistorical abstractions

And now, indeed, in opposition to these socialists there is the stale argumentation of the degenerate economics of most recent times . . . *which demonstrates* that economic relations everywhere express *the same* simple determinants, and hence that they everywhere express the equality and freedom of the simple exchange of exchange values; this point entirely reduces itself to an infantile abstraction.[55]

Poor Frederick Bastiat, the 'classic representative' of this degenerate economics, 'as regards insipidness, affection of dialectics, puffy arrogance, effete, complacent platitudinousness and complete inability to grasp historic processes'![56] The label 'infantile' seems to be Bastiat's unique privilege, but Marx's writings are chock-full of similar epithets. Abstractions may be 'chaotic', 'thin', 'violent', 'arbitrary', 'feeble' as well as 'infantile'; they may also, more positively, be 'rational' or 'historical'. They may be 'mystical' or 'sacred': 'formulas which have been sleeping in the bosom of God the Father since the beginning of the world', 'entities of Pure Reason'. But they may also be 'profane', originating in actual human activity, capable of grasping real historical movements.[57]

What is the force of these epithets? It is tempting to regard them as polemical merely. Yet Marx's satirical or ironical modes are not stylistic or political flourishes tacked onto substantive arguments. Often they are one way in which theoretical points are elaborated. Satirical figures, after the laugh, yield points of theory. With the *possible* exception of 'infantile' (Marx's attitude to children?), they need to be read technically, theoretically. When Marx says a particular abstraction is 'thin' or 'violent' he has in mind a set of features and effects. If time allowed, it would be possible to go through the whole catalogue and show this in detail.

More summarily, I shall group Marx's epithets into three main classes: 'chaotic' abstractions, 'sacred' abstractions and 'thin' abstractions. Categories with these forms, however, share a common feature – their 'arbitrariness' – and tend to produce common effects. They reinforce the existing social relationships by presenting them as natural and eternal, immune to historical change. This 'naturalization' is the distinguishing feature of ideological thinking but may be reached in different ways: hence the need to specify *different* ideological forms, hence the range of epithets. Thus Proudhon's abstractions, partly 'chaotic', partly 'sacred', and produced in the name of Socialism, tend none the less to the same effects as the 'thin' abstractions of the economists:

he shares the illusions of speculative philosophy for he does not regard *economic categories as the theoretical expression of historical relations of production, corresponding to a particular stage of development in material production*, but arbitrarily transforms them into pre-existing *eternal ideas*, and that in this roundabout way he arrives once more at the standpoint of bourgeois economy.[58]

Let us look more closely, then, at abstractions, 'chaotic', 'sacred' and 'thin'.

Chaotic abstractions and common-sense thinking

Chaotic abstraction is the form of thinking found, typically, in the practical common sense of the bourgeois class and in 'vulgar' economy – those economists who simply theorize the immediate concerns of capitalists in their respective countries. They work from the immediate experience of capitalist exchange relations and stay within this viewpoint. Of course, all knowledge starts from 'experience', from the chaotic impressions of everyday life; but in empiricist modes of knowledge (for that is what they are) 'real life' is supposed to yield up knowledge unproblematically. This corresponds to the forms of abstraction, to the sorts of categories employed. Often these categories abstract whole chunks of real life. These lumps are 'chaotic' because they contain great internal complexity and many determinations. None of these is properly distinguished and analysed (let alone understood dialectically). To return to an earlier formulation: 'it is only the immediate phenomenal form of these relations that is reflected in their brains and not their inner connections'.

One common form of empiricist abstraction is to mistake a complex historical product or result for an adequately analytical starting point. Proudhon is chastised by Marx for taking 'machinery' as a category of this kind. In one sense, 'machinery' is not a 'category' at all:

The machine is no more an economic category than the ox which draws the plough. The contemporary use of machines is one of the relations of our present economic system, but the way in which machinery is utilised is totally distinct from the machinery itself. Powder is powder whether used to wound a man or dress his wounds.[59]

Adequate categories grasp the changing socially determined uses of things. To treat 'machinery' as an analytic or explanatory concept is to fall into a fetishism, the fetishism of the 'concrete'.

Marx used similar arguments against two of the starting-points of political economy: 'population' and 'the individual'.[60] He pointed out that the Robinson Crusoe-like figure of 'the Natural Individual', the starting-point of classical liberal theories, was actually a complex historical product, thinkable only after the break-up of bonds of personal dependence and the appearance of 'the society of free competition'.[61] Adequate historical categories would have to untangle this complexity. To take the individual not as 'historical result' but as 'history's point of departure' is to make a chaotic abstraction which lumps all the complexities in together as an undifferentiated premise. The specific bourgeois form of individuality is represented as something 'posited by nature', therefore not modifiable.

But perhaps the best example of Marx's discussion of empiricist abstractions is his critique of William Carey, a true predecessor of Milton Friedman, and 'the only original economist among the North Americans'. Carey has a Marx-like appetite for 'material':

As a genuine Yankee, Carey absorbs from all directions the massive material furnished him by the old world. . . . Hence his strayings and wanderings through all countries, massive and uncritical use of statistics, a catalogue-like erudition.[62]

But he never recognizes 'the inherent soul of this material'; he never concedes to it 'its right to its peculiar life'. Instead he conducts massive research as 'inanimate documentation for his theses'.[63] Since Carey lacks categories that would cut into and organize his (European) material, his treatises consist of

a couple of general theses in schoolmasterly form. Following them, a shapeless material, compendium, as documentation – the substance of his theses by no means digested.[64]

It is, indeed, a familiar phenomenon, not least in Anglo-American academia today! 'Chaos', a particular empiricist chaos, is the result of failure really to 'appropriate the material' and to use it as the basis for determinate abstractions. Marx noted this tendency in other contexts too: in certain kinds of opponents of political economy 'who accuse them of barbarically tearing things apart which belong together'[65] (e.g. production and distribution) and in critics of his own work. The trouble with those who want to retain the 'wholeness' of concrete situations is that they imagine that separations (abstractions) are only made by the economists, with no corresponding forms in reality:

As if this rupture had made its way not from reality into the text books, but rather from the text books into reality, and as if the task were the dialectical balancing of concepts, and not the grasping of real relations.[66]

Similarly his own critics want to promote the concrete *over* the abstract as though the two are rival rather than complementary ways of thinking:

All objections to this definition of value are either derived from less developed relations of production, or are based on the confused idea of setting up the more concrete economic determinations (from which value is abstracted and which, on the other hand, can therefore also be regarded as a further development of it) in opposition to value in this abstract unqualified form.[67]

If abstractions are adequate, correct, historical, it will not do to cite more concrete situations in disproof, for the abstraction simply expresses one side of this situation anyway. The idea that value is abstract labour power, realized in exchange and embodied in the different 'moments' of capital, cannot be disproved by a recourse to empiricist common sense: 'we all know that capital is really stocks and shares, machinery and plant'. For value can be abstracted from these concrete (or 'developed') forms too.

What, then, are the political effects of such thinking? It may certainly express the typical viewpoint of a social group, class or country. Carey interests Marx because he tells him a great deal about the American conditions from which, unconsciously, he generalizes: 'Carey's generality is a Yankee universality'.[68] But Carey's thinking remains inside this perspective, expressing the interests of American commerce. He cannot develop the categories for a critical account of North American society. Instead he presents a picture of fundamental harmony, finding the sources of difficulty only in British international domination.[69] He projects antagonisms onto the world-historical scene, refusing to see them at home. Carey is, therefore, a 'vulgar' economist – albeit an interesting one.

In the absence of systematic and historical abstractions, common-sense thinking merely fixes the obvious necessity of existing social relations. It remains close to the practical thinking of the dominant class, the ideas necessary, that is, for the reproduction of its dominance. Marx gives many examples of this practical complicity; perhaps the most famous is 'Senior's last hour'. Again we should note the theoretical status of Marx's satire:

One fine morning, in the year 1836, Nassau William Senior, who may be called the Clauren [a writer of sentimental novels] of the English economists, a man famed both for his economic science and his beautiful style, was summoned from Oxford to Manchester, to learn in the latter place the political economy he taught in the former. The manufacturers chose him as their prize-fighter, not only against the newly-passed Factory Act but against the Ten Hours' Agitation which aimed to go beyond it. With their usual practical acuteness they realised that the learned professor 'wanted a good deal of finishing'; that is why they invited him to Manchester.[70]

Sacred and profane: the character of idealism

The classic texts for Marx's critique of 'sacred' abstractions are *The German Ideology* and the texts on Proudhon. The theme is, however, a recurrent one; the target is not, of course, religion but idealist or speculative philosophy. To refer back to Greg McLennan's argument, if 'chaotic' abstractions are the butt of Marx's critique of empiricism, 'sacred' abstractions constitute the critique of 'rationalism'. Since much of this argument is familiar from the *Poverty of Theory*, I can be relatively brief.

The best starting-point is a passage in *The German Ideology* where Marx and Engels criticize idealist history-writing. This follows the laying out of their own materialist premises (to which we will return). Very little history, they argue, is written from the standpoint of human productive activity. It is written, instead,

according to an extraneous standard; the real production of life seems [from this point of view] to be primeval history, while the truly historical appears to be separated from ordinary life, something extra-superterrestrial. . . . The exponents of this conception of history have consequently only been able to see in history the political actions of princes and States, religious and all sorts of theoretical struggles, and in particular in each historical epoch have had *to share the illusion of that epoch.* [71]

Such historians believe in the primacy of political or religious motives as expressed in the intentions of contemporaries. This is, in fact, to derive explanations from the political ideologies of the time. But we have not yet reached the intellectual movement characteristic of 'sacred' thinking; we are still in the relatively 'mundane' world of the practical ideologist:

While the French and the English at least hold by the political illusion, which is moderately close to reality, the Germans move in the realm of the 'pure spirit', and make religious illusion the driving force of history. [72]

Philosophers abstract further from political ideologies and represent *these categories themselves* as the principles of movement of real history.

The 'idea', the 'conception' of the people in question about their real practice, is transformed into the sole determining, active force, which controls and determines their practice. [73]

The beginnings of such a process can be seen in histories which centre on the ideas and historical 'authorship' of 'great men'; its intermediate stage in histories of ideas, inattentive to the social content of thinking. But, for Marx, it was Hegel's philosophy of history which represented 'the last consequence . . . of all this German historiography', 'for it is not a question of real, nor even of political, interests, but of pure thoughts', stripped of their historical content. [74] In the neo-Hegelians and again in Proudhon and Bastiat, such thinking becomes entirely 'phantasmagoric', 'sacred' or 'mystical'. The thoughts or categories themselves, now divorced from the complex situations they once expressed, perform their ghostly dances on the special stage of 'theory'. They become 'a series of "thoughts" that devour one another and are finally swallowed up in "self-consciousness" '.[75] So it is that in the place of 'a vast, prolonged and complicated movement' of history, someone like Proudhon can put 'the whimsical motion of his own head'.[76] As Marx hints here, this is indeed the characteristic delusion of the 'philosopher' (or of the professional intellectual or academic):

It is therefore the men of learning that make history, the men who know how to purloin God's secret thoughts. The common people have only to apply their revelations.[77]

It is easy to smile! But the smile should at least be an uncomfortable one. For in the critique of idealism we certainly can see the characteristic thought forms of modern marxist rationalism, not to speak of a whole history of self-sustaining dogmatisms of other kinds, certain 'vanguard' conceptions of politics and a *permanent tendency*, while the social divisions of knowledge-production remain, for thinking to take an idealist or rationalist direction.

Once again, Marx is concerned to indicate the political effects of such thinking. The original ideological cast of practical thinking is now entombed in the dialectical movements of Pure Reason. Only it now acquires the additional immunities and powers of 'absolute' knowledge. Thus Hegel, despite the 'absolute' historicity of dialectics, ended up sanctifying the forms of the Prussian state.

Thin or simple abstractions: their rationality and limits

One further way of abstracting from the real complexity of social life is by generalization. We abstract a few common elements from a range of situations that are, in other ways, diverse. 'Thin' or 'simple' abstractions of this kind have a peculiar status for Marx. They have a legitimate place in scientific thinking; they are 'rational abstractions':

all epochs of production have certain common traits, common characteristics. *Production in general* is an abstraction, but a rational abstraction in so far as it really brings out and fixes the common element and thus saves us repetition.[78]

Now political economy characteristically depends upon such abstractions. In its early 'scientific' moments, political economists made, on this basis, some essential advances:

Political economy has to do with the specific social forms of wealth or rather of the production of wealth. The material of wealth, whether subjective, like labour, or objective, like objects for the satisfaction of natural or historical needs, initially appears as common to all epochs of production. . . . What it is customary to say about this in general terms is restricted to abstractions which had a historic value in the first tentative steps of political economy, *when the forms still had to be laboriously peeled out of the material*, and were at the cost of great effort, fixed upon as a proper object of study.[79]

Marx himself adopts a similar method, but as part of his whole repertoire of abstractions. It is not true that he avoids simple abstractions altogether.[80] He too 'peels out' of the whole historical range a few 'general-historical' features:

Labour is, first of all, a process between man and nature, a process by which man, through his own actions, mediates, regulates and controls the metabolism between himself and nature. He confronts the materials of nature as a force of nature. He sets in motion the natural forces which belong to his own body, his arms, legs, head and hands, in order to appropriate the materials of nature in a form adapted to his own needs. Through this movement he acts upon external nature and changes it, and in this way he simultaneously changes his own nature.[81]

Marx is concerned here with absolutely general features of human labour, though he speaks of them in terms that imply a whole history of the *development* of human and non-human nature. He recapitulates, in a more historical form, some of the leading 'humanist' themes of his earliest work, especially *The Paris Manuscripts* of 1844.[82] These historical generalizations then provide the *basis* for the specification of the successive forms and conditions of labour.

Marx's major premises are all of this kind. Similar, for instance, is the statement that human beings 'possess consciousness', a 'simple' abstraction but the basis for elaborating historical forms of consciousness as they are influenced by the social divisions of labour. As conscious, thinking producers, human beings certainly make history – but the conditions have then to be specified.

We see at work here one of Marx's major procedural devices: the making of distinctions between more or less abstract categories and the recognition that the level of abstractness should be related to the historical range of the categories themselves. Some features of human history really *are* of a general kind, others characteristic only of particular times. The categories, in their simplicity or abstractness, in their density or concreteness, must express this too. Simple abstractions are rational when they really correspond to general transhistorical features: they are ideological when they *stand in for* detailed historical specification. So while 'production in general' is a 'rational abstraction', 'this common element sifted out by comparison'[83] merely indicates a space or ground for further categories that correspond to more particular determinations. Actual situations are ordered ensembles of determinations, some held in common with other situations, others particular and even unique.[84] It is important not to forget these 'essential differences': they are just those features which mark, determine and explain historical development and change.

On this basis Marx launches a devastating critique of the political economists' deployment of simple abstractions. Here rational abstractions are pushed beyond their legitimate use; the concern with essential differences is 'forgotten'. Political economists start by laying out 'the general preconditions of all production', a limited but useful task liable to degenerate, however, into 'flat tautologies'.[85] They distinguish the forms of human society, at best, by their *degrees* of productivity. In this process, however, they 'smuggle in' determinations that are specific to capitalist or bourgeois societies. They then represent these 'as inviolable natural laws on which society in the abstract [i.e. human sociality or productivity as such] is founded'.[86] In Adam Smith's hands, for example, 'capital' (a particular historical form of production, involving particular kinds of possession and dispossession) takes on the form of a simple abstraction, within which distinctions can be made only by degree.[87] Capital is 'accumulated labour which serves as a means for new labour'. There is no basis for qualitative historical distinctions here, and Marx shows the unhistorical character of the starting-point by reducing it to absurdities. A stone that is thrown at a bird counts as capital under this definition. The stone must first be 'appropriated by some sort of activity before it can function as an instrument, as a means of production'. As a tool it therefore represents 'accumulated labour'. But this is even true of the physical capacities of human arms and legs, for the body must be 'nourished, reproduced, in order to be active as an organ'.[88] Capital becomes 'something altogether unhistorical'. As in the case of 'individuals', a whole process of categorial specification and historical development is suppressed. *What began as 'peeling out' the common elements ends as 'abstracting away' everything else!*

Again we have a conservative result. This way of thinking about social relationships cements their necessity and limits the possibilities of further change:

> If, then, the specific form of capital is abstracted away, and only the content [accumulated labour] is emphasized, *as which it is a necessary moment of all labour* [sic] *then of course nothing is easier than to demonstrate that capital is a necessary condition of all human production.* The proof of this proceeds precisely by abstraction from the specific aspects which make it the moment of a specifically developed *historic* stage of human production.[89]

The 'catch' lies in Smith's definition. Certainly, one feature of capital is 'accumulated labour'. It shares this feature, however, with other less developed economic forms. Not *all* objectified labour (stones, arms and legs, human brains) which serves as a means for new production, is capital. The *specific* characteristics of capital remain to be analysed: a work of great complexity.[90]

It is useful to take a second case. This concerns the general concept 'society'.[91] Marx criticizes Proudhon for regarding 'society' as 'a subjective abstraction' existing only in the consciousness of individuals. Proudhon reduces society to a general psychological standpoint or need. For Marx this is another example of 'abstracting away', though now, in addition, in an idealist or contemplative mode:

This so-called contemplation from the standpoint of society means nothing more than the overlooking of the *differences* which express the *social relation* (relation of bourgeois society). Society does not consist of individuals, but expresses the sum of interrelations, the relations within which these individuals stand. . . . As if someone were to say: seen from the perspective of society, there are no slaves and no citizens: both are human beings.[92]

Actually, Marx insists, we can only grasp societies by specifying social relations:

To be a slave, to be a citizen, are social characteristics, relations between human beings A and B. Human being A, as such, is not a slave. He is a slave in and through society. What Mr. Proudhon here says about capital and product means, for him, that from the viewpoint of society there is no difference between capitalists and workers, a difference which exists only from the standpoint of society.[93]

As the case of Proudhon makes clear, the different forms of bad abstraction may occur in combination: a particular account may combine elements of transhistorical abstraction, empiricist 'chaos' and rationalist idealism! It may well be that poor Bastiat's peculiar 'infantilism' consists precisely in this. We might end this section, as we began, with Marx's assault on his 'twaddle' since it sums up what we have teased out in detail. It is also a reminder that, at its most general, Marx's critique concerns ways of thinking that are *reductive* of complex differences and radically *dehistoricizing* in their effects.

Marx points out that Bastiat reduces everything (wages, profit, capital, interest) to the simple exchange of exchange values. He ends up with one huge tautology:

Thus, after first taking from the empirical world the fact that exchange value exists not only in this simple form but also in the essentially different form of capital, capital is then in turn reduced again to the simple concept of exchange value. . . . In so far as I abstract from what distinguishes a concrete from its abstract, it is, of course, the abstract, and does not differ from it at all. *According to this all economic categories are only so many names for what is always the same relation, and this crude inability to grasp the real distinctions is then supposed to represent pure common sense as such. The 'economic harmonies' of Mr. Bastiat amount au fond to the assertion that there exists only one single economic relation which takes on different names, or that any differences which occur, occur only in name.*[94]

The grins on latter-day marxist faces should now speedily change to blushes. For some currents in marxist theory do certainly resemble Bastiat's in two important respects: they reduce and they eternalize. Thus Bastiat reduces all social relations to simple commodity exchange; some marxists tend to reduce all social relations to 'class'. Some even contrive a simple 'materialist' inversion of Bastiat's reductions: the reduction of all social relations to one – 'the capital relation'. This then finds expressions (under different names) in the different social spheres.[95] Similarly, much marxist thinking has tended to eternalize: this holds especially for those who continue to believe in entities called 'social formations' which grimly reproduce themselves in perpetuity. This is not so very different from the political economist's time-warp of bourgeois social relations.[96]

Intelligent thinking as a natural process: Marx's own premises

I want to look, now, at the positive side of Marx's view of historical theory. What were his own premises in making abstractions? What, indeed, are the main features and political effects of *really historical thinking*?

I think that the best way of approaching this is to consider the premises which guide the critiques. It is best because it conforms to Marx's own way of working. Marx's critiques are never (or rarely) simply negative. Not only do they always 'win' some real knowledge from the positions critiqued, they are also part of Marx's own theoretical development, and one of the ways in which his theoretical positions are validated. This is most obviously true of a work like *The German Ideology*, perhaps the prime source for Marx's own premises in their most abstract form. It is at once a critique of German philosophy and a statement of historical materialism. It grounds the second in a critique of the first. It is an attempt to demonstrate the superiority of materialist thinking over self-reproducing idealist categories.

But what kind of premises are they that guide Marx's critiques? They are certainly not simply methodological rules; they amount, rather, to a description of the conditions of thinking, from which prescriptions can then be made. It is worth saying a bit more, in advance, about the relation between these two sides: description and prescription, Marx's view of thought as a social-natural process and its implications for 'intelligent thinking'.

Despite Marx's stress on ideology, he is fundamentally optimistic about knowledge. The possibility of real knowledge is present in the natural organization of human beings (their 'consciousness', their 'thinking heads'), in the relation between human and non-human nature (as an active, appropriating, producing relation) and even in the nature of social organization, under capitalist conditions. Indeed social organization and the relation to nature constitute incitements to knowledge even as they shape its forms and govern its distribution in alienated and oppressive ways. This corresponds, we might add, to the classic form of the knowledge relation in modern conditions: the desire to know; the encounter with knowledge in alien forms.[97]

Recent debates have usually focused on one side of this relation, its negative side, the side concerned with ideology. In the face of what has been seen as the weight of ideological determinations, the search for genuine knowledge has often assumed a tone of desperation. If ideology is so pervasive, then 'science' must be a very special and difficult practice. It is in this context that Marx's optimism is so striking. He has an extremely relaxed attitude to the possibility of knowledge, quite different from the modern epistemological agonies. Here he is, for example, explaining to Ludwig Kugelmann why it is that the theory of value has changed rather little over time:

On the other hand, as you have correctly assumed, the *history of the theory* certainly shows that the concept of value relations has *always been the same* – sometimes clearer, sometimes hazier, more hedged around with illusions or scientifically more precise. Since the reasoning process itself proceeds from the existing conditions, and is itself a *natural process*, intelligent thinking must always be the same, and can vary only gradually, according to the degree of development, including the development of the organ by which the thinking is done. Everything else is drivel.[98]

There are no epistemological dramas here! The possibility of knowledge does not lie in some special procedural guarantee, but in the way in which the natural and social worlds are organized. It is often argued, quite rightly, that Marx's discussion of *capitalist* social organization is an exceptional case so far as the knowledge relation is concerned: the forms of capitalist society are peculiarly opaque and mystifying. But this is only *part* of Marx's view: it shows why 'science' is *necessary*, but not why it is *possible*. Capitalism also offers some *privileges* to knowledge which are uniquely its own. The developed form of money, for example, is certainly the very paradigm for fetishistic thinking. But money also realizes, in a special symbolic form, the real abstraction of value and exchange and can reveal the secret of abstract labour power. Intellectual practice must work on the tendency of social processes to throw up *significant phenomena*, signs, symbols or symptoms that can 'read', critically, realistically, materialistically.[99] It is for these reasons that Marx uses terms like 'violent' and 'arbitrary' when discussing inadequate abstractions. These ways of thinking misuse the resources available in the natural and social world. They produce knowledges artificially, by mere act of will and interest. Historical or determinate abstractions, by contrast, conform to the possibilities of knowledge which social processes themselves may offer. They are 'real abstractions' already given in nature or in history. Marx's premises, then, describe these social-natural conditions of thinking and involve prescriptions about resourceful intellectual activity within the possibilities and the limits so revealed.

We may abstract from Marx's critiques and from his practice four main premises and an essential rider. Each premise describes a condition of knowledge production (Figure 2). Each premise is especially alive in Marx's critique of a particular form of inadequate knowledge: idealism, empiricism, reductionism, etc. Each premise involves prescriptions about method, about the actual practice of investigating the world. One way of defining 'historical abstractions' in Marx's method is to say they conform to all four premises. Inadequate abstractions, by comparison, breach one or more of them.

Marx's essential rider concerns the role of 'practice' in the validation of knowledge. It is no mere addition or afterthought. It is inscribed at the heart of Marx's view of intellectual practice; it is inextricably connected with the historical nature of his abstractions. I will refer to the association of socialist politics and historical thinking shortly, but a fuller treatment of this theme must await the third part of this essay.

The premises, except the last, are neatly encapsulated in a passage from the letter to Annenkov:

> Thus, Mr Proudhon, mainly because he lacks the historical knowledge, has not perceived that as men develop their productive forces, that is, as they live, they develop certain relations with one another and that the nature of these relations is bound to change with the change and growth of these productive forces. He had not perceived that *economic categories* are only *abstract expressions* of these actually existing relations and only remain true while these relations exist.[100]

Premise	Summary form	Critique of	Implications
1 Rationalist premise	'Thought is distinctive'	Empiricism	Systematic abstraction
2 Materialist premise	'Thought expresses social relations'	Idealism	Research/critique 'real' abstractions
3 Historical premise	'Social relations – and categories – are transitory'	Eternalizing/ naturalizing	'Really historical thinking'
4 Structural premise	'Social relations are complexly structured'	Reductions	The concern with 'forms'

Figure 2 *Marx's premises for really historical thinking*

Marx's 'rationalism'

Thinking is a form of production or appropriation: it is the way we grasp reality mentally, 'ideally', that is in ideas, categories, abstractions:

> The ideal is nothing but the material world reflected in the mind of man, and translated into forms of thought.[101]

'Ideally' or 'the ideal' in this usage has no necessary connection with ideal*ism*. Marx is saying that thought is a human social practice, but one which has its own forms of raw material, tools and product. It occurs *in a particular medium* into which the 'material world' is 'translated'.

Marx is a 'rationalist' by virtue of this stress on the particularity of thinking – not in any more developed sense. He also tended to underemphasize this premise because his main enemy (philosophically) was not an empiricism (which neglects the specific features of thinking) but the full-blown rationalism or idealism of German philosophy (which regards thought or 'the concept' as 'the real act of production').

On most of these matters it seems to me that Marx's discussion in the 1857

Introduction is quite decisive.[102] Marx affirms *both* his distance from all idealist traditions *and* his understanding of the peculiar nature of mental products. For the 'philosophical consciousness' conceptual thinking is 'the real human being'; the conceptual world is the only, or the privileged, reality. There is a very limited tautologous sense in this: it is true that we can only grasp relations in thought and that they only fully exist for us when we 'think' them:

This is correct in so far as the concrete totality is a totality of thoughts, concrete in thought, in fact a product of thinking and comprehending; but not in any way a product of the concept which thinks and generates itself outside or above observation and conception; a product, rather, of the working-up of observation and conception into concepts.[103]

Thought *is* distinctive but not as some independent reality: it is a 'moment' or aspect of human productive activity as a whole:

The totality as it appears in the head, as a totality of thoughts, is a product of the thinking head, which appropriates the world in the only way it can, a way different from the artistic, religious, practical and mental appropriation of this world.[104]

As mere thinking, moreover, it is a practice with distinct limits. It does not change society, its 'real subject':

The real subject retains its autonomous existence outside the head just as before; namely as long as the head's conduct is merely speculative, merely theoretical.[105]

But to recognize the limitations of thinking is essential to 'the theoretical method' too. We must not *substitute* the products of our thinking for 'society'. The independent existence of society 'must always be kept in the mind as the pre-supposition'.

Several problems remain. Marx never spelt out (to my knowledge) the difference between conceptual thinking and the other ways of understanding the world. Is it only systematic thinking which employs abstractions or are they characteristic (in different forms perhaps) of consciousness and language more generally? The gaps here are huge and significant not least for political-intellectual practice today. The relation between worked-up critical analysis and the practical knowledges of everyday life remains an issue of the utmost political magnitude.

The materialist premise

Thought is distinctive, but it *expresses social relations*. Social relations – 'society' – is the raw material of thinking. The determination of social consciousness by social being is therefore 'internal' to the practice of thinking itself: it is not an external imposition on thought. Language itself arises from the needs of subsistence and of social intercourse:

Men begin, as a matter of fact, by appropriating certain things from the external world as the means of satisfying their own needs . . .; later they *also* come to designating them linguistically as what they are for them in practical experience.[106]

This can be traced in the histories of individual words and their usages:

But what would old Hegel say if he heard in the next world that the *general* (*das Allgemeine*) in German and Norse means nothing but the common land, and the particular (*das Sundre, Besondre*) – nothing but the separate property divided off from the common land? The logical categories are in that case damn well arising out of 'our intercourse'.[107]

The 'illusory' independence of ideas (or of language in general) can also be explained historically, through the division of mental and manual labour, through the constitution of specialized thinkers and through the idealist forms of abstraction.[108] But even the most 'phantasmagoric' ideas can be traced to the social situation they express, to the original abstraction: Proudhon's speculations to his French *petit-bourgeois* existence, Adolph Wagner's to German professorhood.[109] As Marx put it in *The German Ideology*:

Consciousness is, therefore, from the beginning a social product and remains so, as long as men exist at all.[110]

Marx's materialism has important implications for method. If his limited rationalism implies attention to the specific forms of thinking, his materialism means that all forms of human consciousness constitute a resource for more adequate knowledge. His intellectual critiques are always vigorous and sometimes savage, but they have another main characteristic: they always rescue *something*, albeit transformed, from what is critiqued: Carey tells us about the USA; Senior and others, though 'wrong', provide a way into bourgeois common sense. These thinkers express something of the real, willy-nilly; hence the importance of critique as the realist interrogation of categories. This kind of critique is both formal and historical: it digs out assumptions and contradictions, but also the historical content of ideas, the situations they actually express.

The historical premise

Thought is distinctive, it expresses social relations, *but social relations are themselves transitory*. We come here to the heart of Marx's thinking about abstractions. In what sense, to be adequate, do categories have to be 'historical'?

There are two senses of 'historical' that Marx certainly rejects. Abstractions are not 'historical' simply by virtue of referring to past events or epochs. 'Historical' cannot be equated with 'old'. Marx was not an historian in this sense: his study was not 'the past'. His subject, rather, was 'modern bourgeois society'. This necessarily *involved* historical study (in the usual sense), but was also about the current state of the society and its future. History – as the contemplative study of the past 'for its own sake' – was very low down on Marx's own agenda. Engels, who thought Marx should have used more 'historical sketches' in *Capital* mainly to ease the problems of reading so abstract a text, put it like this:

At most the points here arrived at dialectically might be set forth historically at somewhat greater length, to furnish the historical proof, so to speak, although what is most necessary in this respect has already been said.[111]

Second, 'historical' abstractions are not those which are identified in the thought of past epochs themselves. The standpoint in modern bourgeois society constitutes, for Marx, a real scientific privilege. In a famous passage he wrote:

Bourgeois society is the most developed and the most complex historic organization of production. The categories which express its relations, the comprehension of its structure, thereby also allow insights into the structure and the relations of production of all the vanished social formations out of whose ruins and elements it built itself up, whose partly still unconquered remnants are carried along with it, whose mere nuances have developed explicit significance within it etc. Human anatomy contains a key to the anatomy of the ape. The intimations of higher development among the subordinate animal species, however, can be understood only after the higher development is already known. The bourgeois economy thus supplies the key to the ancient.[112]

Marx went on to criticize the abuses of this historical privilege of the more developed forms but his insistence on the benefits of hindsight distances him decisively from those historians who argue that past epochs can only be understood 'in their own terms'. This, for Marx, was simply to 'share the illusion of that epoch'.[113]

Underlying Marx's stress on the benefits of modernity is a twofold argument. First, abstractions are historical, in the fullest sense, because they are found in the actual forms of social organization. Historical thinking expresses real abstractions. Second, such abstractions must also grasp the possibility, immanence, direction or tendency of *further* development. Since thinking cannot run arbitrarily ahead of social development, or only on the basis of the real abstractions already made, a strategic location within the most developed forms is an important condition for the advance of knowledge. Marx believed mid-nineteenth-century Britain con-stituted such a privileged location: it was the '*locus classicus*' of the capitalist mode of production and, therefore, of thought upon its forms. In Germany, by contrast, 'the living soil from which political economy springs was absent'.[114] It was an imported product, and remained, until further German development, 'the theoret-ical expression of an alien reality'. It followed that Germany's capitalist future could best be studied from Britain.

More generally Marx put it like this:

Although an abstraction, this [value as abstract labour] is an historical abstraction which could only be evolved on the basis of a particular economic development of society. . . . The most abstract definitions, when more carefully examined, always point to a further definite concrete historical basis. (Of course – since they have been abstracted from it in this particular form.)[115]

Every adequate category, in other words, has a specific historical origin and continuing point of reference. This applies even to 'the most abstract definitions'. Take, for example, the category 'capital in general' (as distinct from individual capitals). Marx argues that although this is an abstract category, it is 'not an arbitrary abstraction, but an abstraction which grasps the specific characteristics which distinguish capital from all other forms of wealth'.[116] It corresponds to a process of development by which capital itself is generalized, universalized, rendered social or collective between different capitals:

Capital in general, as *distinct* from particular real capitals, is itself a *real* existence. This is recognized by ordinary economics, even if it is not *understood*, and forms a very important moment of its doctrine of equilibrations etc. For example, capital in this *general form* . . . forms the capital which accumulates in the banks or is distributed through them, and, as Ricardo says, so admirably distributes itself in accordance with the needs of production. Likewise through loans etc., it forms a level between the different countries. . . . While the general is therefore on the one hand only a mental mark of the distinction, it is at the same time a *particular* real form alongside the form of the particular and individual.[117]

It is only when capital is developed in this general universal form that the general category 'capital' can itself be fully developed. The category applies, in addition to its general usage, to a quite particular phase.

Marx also develops this argument in relation to labour. In two pages in the 1857 Introduction,[118] he sketches a theoretical and social history of 'labour' as a conception. Of course 'labour seems quite a simple category' and the idea of labour as such is 'also immeasurably old'. None the less its full development as a simple abstraction is as modern as are the relations which create 'abstract labour' in real life. Abstract labour is actually a tendency of modern societies, a category *and* a historical development:

Indifference towards specific labours corresponds to a form of society in which individuals can with ease transfer from one labour to another, and where the specific kind is a matter for chance for them, hence of indifference. Not only has the category, labour, but labour in reality has here become the means of creating wealth in general, and has ceased to be organically linked with particular individuals in any specific form.[119]

In contemporary USA especially, 'labour as such' has become 'true in practice'. Whereas in the guild and craft system labour always took specific forms depending on the concrete character of the product, under capitalist relations of production the labourer is reduced, more and more, to the mere bearer of human activity, of 'labour as a *use value* for capital'.

This economic relation . . . therefore develops more purely and adequately in proportion as labour loses all the characteristics of art; as its particular skill becomes something more and more abstract and irrelevant and as it becomes more and more a *purely abstract activity*, a purely mechanical activity, hence indifferent to its particular form . . . activity pure and simple, regardless of its form.[120]

As Marx concludes:

This example of labour shows strikingly how even the most abstract categories, despite their validity – precisely because of their abstractness – for all epochs, are nevertheless, in the specific character of this abstraction, themselves likewise a product of historic relations, and possess their full validity only for and within these relations.[121]

Marx's deployment of abstractions, then, is different from that employed by the best political economists. They move from the complexity of real situations to thinner and thinner abstractions, often rendering situations eternal to the mind by radically simplifying them. By contrast Marx discovers even behind legitimate general abstractions further concrete historical forms which the abstractions also express. The effect of this procedure is to *render back into history* relations which bourgeois thinking had *naturalized or eternalized.* There is, in other words, a deep complicity between the critique of ideology (ideas which tend to cement the existing social order) and *really historical thinking.* Since historical thinking has this critical dimension, it is associated too with a political standpoint on the side of the groups and classes who are exploited or oppressed under existing social relations. On the other side, there is a close association between the surface or obvious appearance of things in bourgeois society, a belief that they are, in fundamentals, unchangeable, and the interests of those groups that benefit most from existing arrangements. There is a further complicity, therefore, between really historical thinking and a hopeful and progressive politics. As Marx puts it, rather optimistically, 'once the interconnection is grasped, all theoretical belief in the permanent necessity of existing conditions collapses before their collapse in practice'.[122]

The structural premise

The premise of 'complexity' comes into play as soon as we consider not merely the nature of particular categories and their origins and degrees of development, but their forms of combination in more complex (and in this sense 'concrete') historical accounts. In his reading of the 1857 Introduction, Stuart Hall has insisted on the 'structural' as well as the 'developmental' elements in Marx's deployment of categories.[123] Relations are understood in their *degrees of development*, but *also* in their historically specific *arrangements* and combinations. A simple developmental model favours an evolutionism which is foreign to Marx's most sophisticated thinking. Some of this argument may be problematic (it is not clear for instance whether Marx embraces a 'complexity' of an Althusserian type or one that owes more to Hegel's dialectics – a complexity of 'moments' not 'structures') but the stress on complexity, on 'ensembles' is of huge importance. Marx is very pre-occupied with 'placing' categories in their dominant or subordinate place in a struc-ture or process. Bourgeois society is not a 'pure' economic form. It contains 'partly still unconquered remnants' from previous formations; these have in turn developed a 'specific significance within it', different from their place in earlier formations. They may appear 'entirely stunted', even 'travestied'.[124] The 'same' or similar form may occupy an altogether different position in a new ensemble. Again, Marx's 'formalism' – his concern with structure and difference – is not an anti-historical principle: it is a way of making historical distinctions. It stands *against* general evolutionist theories. As Marx puts it most trenchantly:

Thus events strikingly analogous but taking place in different historical surroundings led to totally different results. By studying each of these forms of evolution separately and then by comparing them one can easily find the clue to this phenom-enon, but one will never answer these by taking as one's master key a general historico-philosophical theory, the supreme virtue of which consists in being supra-historical.[125]

Many examples could be given of this 'structural' strand in Marx: his comparison, for example, of the (subordinate, limited) place of money in the ancient world and its omnipotence or symptomatic dominance in bourgeois society. The same form occurs but in completely different relations to other social categories. But to follow this further we need to turn to Marx's mode of presentation.

Presenting the real movement: history, validation and critique

Presentation: what's at stake?

It is important, first, to draw out the full range of issues involved in the practice of 'presentation', using Marx's *Capital* as an example. Obviously, in *Capital*, one main purpose of presentation is the systematic exposition of the historical categories themselves, their formal elaboration. Marx seems to privilege this aspect when he writes:

Volume I comprises the 'Process of Capitalist Production'. Besides the general scientific exposition, I describe in great detail, from hitherto unused *official* sources, the condition of the English agricultural and industrial proletariat *during the last 20 years*. Ditto *Irish* conditions. You will, of course, understand that all this serves me only as an *argumentum ad hominem*.[126]

From this point of view, *Capital* may be read as a three-volume definition of the capitalist mode of production (using English and Irish illustrations). Read thus, it has its own formal structure: it proceeds from the elementary forms (the commodity, exchange value, use value and value, labour power, the capital–labour relation), to the 'inner connections' of capital's circuits of self-expansion (the main concern of volume II) to the overall tendencies of the accumulation process (the 'laws of tendency', their contradictions and crises, the countervailing tendencies).

But there is more going on in *Capital* than this. Marx is also concerned to validate his (historical) categories, to demonstrate their explanatory force. This involves presenting and explaining 'the real movement' in whole passages of historical change. In this sense, presentation involves history-writing. As we have seen, Marx is not committed to presenting the categories in the order in which they appeared historically; he does not write strictly chronological history. But he is concerned to ground the categories in accounts of historical change of different magnitudes and time scales.

But this is still an inadequate account of presentation. Marx's mode of validation – 'presenting the real movement' – is also a process of critique, as the subtitle 'a critique of political economy' reminds us. Critique involves pitting the historical and materialist way of thinking against the most powerful explanatory systems of the day, in order to establish the competitive advantage of Marx's own political and intellectual premises. Premises are necessary philosophical starting-points, but they are also tools for concrete analysis which must prove their power in practice. This power can only be relative, not abstract or absolute. Nor are the theories or premises themselves in any way immune to these struggles. Marx is concerned to explain the tools of rivals too. He is concerned not only with the inadequacy of economic thinking, but with its historical origin, development and reasons for existence. He claims to tell us more about political economy than economists know themselves! Marx's 'science', then, is intimately connected to critique, not as polemic or satire alone, but as a struggle to assert the superiority of really historical thinking.

A fuller reading on these lines of *Capital* would be useful, but still incomplete. It would remain overly epistemological, caught in a discourse of science. It would gut *Capital* of its politics. I do not mean by this what Marx once described as winning 'a victory for our Party in the field of science',[127] a description around which a whole history of subsequent pragmatisms and uneasy negotiations could be written. I mean political in a broader sense. Marx sees the presentation of *Capital* as part of a labour of transforming the social world. The clearest formulations on this are in his earlier work, especially in *The Theses on Feuerbach*, but they roll right through Marx's intellectual-political project.

The 1857 Introduction puts the problem, or its negative side, quite cryptically:

The real subject (society) retains its autonomous existence outside the head just as before; namely as long as the head's conduct is merely speculative, merely theoretical.[128]

This echoes the second Thesis on Feuerbach:

The question whether truth about the objective world is attained by human thinking – is not a question of theory, but a *practical* question. In practice must man prove the truth, that is reality and power, this-worldliness of his thinking. The dispute over the reality or non-reality of thinking – that is isolated from practice – is a purely *scholastic* question.[129]

Or, still more familiarly, in the last Thesis:

The philosophers have only *interpreted* the world in different ways, the point is to *change* it.[130]

The apparent lucidity of these declarations is a bit misleading. More is involved than an injunction to those who think, also to act, though this injunction is certainly there. But this isn't enough if the thinking and the 'practice' thereby remain unchanged! More interestingly, Marx is saying that the thinking itself will be inadequate unless it is practical. He is not criticizing thinking as such (a not unheard of pragmatist reading!) but particular ways of thinking – speculatively, philosophically, or in ways that are 'merely theoretical' or 'contemplative'. The nearest modern equivalent is, revealingly, 'academic', as in the proverbial phrase 'it's an academic question'. Thinking must itself be practical, capable of informing practice because informed by it. And since we are talking of a relation, there are implications for 'practice' too. Practice is a way of testing the truth of our understandings, demonstrating their realism, their 'this-worldliness'. There is no suggestion here that 'practice' is some inert, ready-formed party or programme, to which thinking must then conform. Political premises too are the object of thinking, or continuous evaluation. Marx is describing a 'dialectical', or a two-sided moving relation between politics and thinking, between transforming social relations and producing ideas, between practice and theory. It is only in this relation that the realism of thinking, especially of thinking that concerns immanent tendencies and possible futures, can finally be proved or disproved.

In this context, presentation takes on a still greater importance. It is the production of really useful knowledge based on really historical thinking. This knowledge, its usefulness, is to be tested in relation to transforming the world in the interests of the oppressed and exploited majorities. So far as the political work of *Capital* is concerned much could be summed up in the theme of the *historicity* of the capitalist mode. *Capital* is an attempt to show how this system of social organization arose, how and under what conditions it is maintained, why it is no more eternal than the formations it replaced, and how it generates, within its very structures, the conditions for further transformations.

I don't want to imply that in *The Theses* or practically in *Capital*, Marx provides the modern paradigm for presentation. I actually find Marx less helpful here than in the realm of 'inquiry'. There are several problems. First, in the case of *The Theses*,

Marx's discussion of 'theory' and 'practice' is itself very abstract. Though he redefines the philosophical figure 'man' in terms of 'the ensemble of social relations',[131] 'man' remains the referent, ungendered, unclassed, unplaced in the divisions of labour. Similarly, in *Capital*, Marx seems insufficiently attentive to the conditions of readership – as much a process of knowledge-production as the writing. Whose practice, whose experience precisely, was *Capital* meant to illuminate and in what ways?

Second, *Capital*'s form, its individual authorship, is definitely a problem, both in inquiry and presentation. It is one of the most taken-for-granted aspects of marxology that Marx's work is radically incomplete, a fact to be ascribed, no doubt, to the average human life-span. But Marx's individual authorship, even allowing for his collaboration with Engels, is very relevant here, especially in the case of *Capital*. Marx himself, despite the fundamental 'humility' of his realism, is a classic study in the pride, anxiety and struggles of individual authorship, complete with intimations of premature death and the part-conscious exploitation of wife, family and friend. The fact that this was 'all in a larger cause' (and that the cause was an important one) makes it no less ambiguous. It nearly always is!

Well, why didn't I answer you? Because I was constantly hovering on the edge of the grave. Hence I had to make use of every moment when I was able to work to complete my book, to which I have sacrificed health, happiness and family. I trust that I need not add anything to this explanation. I laugh at the so-called 'practical' men with their wisdom. If one chose to be an ox, one could of course turn one's back on the sufferings of mankind and look after one's own skin. But I should have really regarded myself as *impractical* if I had pegged out without completely finishing my book, at least in manuscript.[132]

Poor Marx – and he didn't even manage it in the end! It seems unkind (if not impious) to question this (uneven) sacrifice. But what if it had been a *group* that had worked on *Capital* instead of an individual 'thinking head', serviced and helped by others? Certainly the manuscript would have been less likely to break off. . . . The skills which Marx developed, which now have to be excavated from his texts, could have been shared, generalized. They partly *were* in Engels's case, but history, if not Marx, has cast Engels in the uncomfortable and deferential role of Marx's mediator, only secondly, his coworker. Marx's monopolization of intellectual effort (and self-development) was peculiarly inappropriate for the political-intellectual project on which they were engaged. This is true, too, of the form of presentation. How easy it is, reading *Capital*, to be intimidated by Marx the genius, Marx the patriarch or Marx 'the Word'!

The mode of presentation of *Capital* is, then, no ideal model for intellectual-political practice today. A work of a fraction of its scope would have to be, should be, a collective project. Yet Marx's view of what is involved in presentation and the levels at which he attempts to operate in *Capital* remain valuable resources none the less.

Levels of abstraction: 'logical' aspects

One main feature of Marx's writing is that it is more or less abstract, more or less concrete. Whole texts differ in this respect. The historical or political essays on France which Marx wrote in the early 1850s, his more sketchy studies of English politics, or the analysis of the Commune in 1871 are concrete enough to satisfy the most scrupulous historian, though they were actually written as instant retrospective political analysis. *The Eighteenth Brumaire of Louis Bonaparte*, the finest of these texts, is Marx's attempt to make sense of the detailed blow-by-blow development of political struggles in France from the July Revolution of 1848 to the coup of Napoleon III in 1851. It certainly does not spare detail; indeed it threatens all the time to be swamped by the complexity and muddle of it all:

The period we have now to deal with contains the most variegated mixture of crying contradictions . . . passions without truth, truths without passion, heroes without deeds of heroism, history without events; a course of development apparently only driven forward by the calendar, and made wearisome by the constant repetition of the same tensions and relaxations.[133]

Compare all this density with the laying out of general historical premises in *The German Ideology* or the *Preface to the Contribution to the Critique of Political Economy* or, though they refer more narrowly to a particular epoch, 'the arid steppes' of *Capital*, volume II, all formulae and hypothetical cases in the study of the capitalist circulation process.[134] Somewhere in between one might place *The Communist Manifesto*, with its large-scale historical sweep ('The history of all hitherto existing society is the history of class struggles') and its focus on bourgeois society and 'modern industry' only in their *general* social dynamic, especially the polarization of classes.

It is more interesting to consider movements of level within texts. Most of them are multilayered in this sense. *The Eighteenth Brumaire* is not short of generalizations about the relation between social being and consciousness;[135] *The German Ideology* is not short of (very sketchy) references to Rome, Athens, German tribes, serfdom, crafts and modern industry.[136] But the most interesting case from this point of view is the first volume of *Capital* which contains much greater density of historical reference than the other two. Since it is not possible to comment on the whole volume, I have taken Chapters 7 to 15 as the main source of examples. These chapters deal with the basic forms of the labour process and with the different ways of increasing the rate of extraction of the surplus. Chapters 7 to 11, which together comprise Part III, deal with the production of absolute surplus value, by increasing the length of the working day; Chapters 12 to 14 (Part IV) deal with the various ways in which the productivity of labour can be raised, especially the use of machinery. These chapters are especially rich in movements between levels of abstraction, from the discussion of human labour in general to the detailed account of the struggle over factory legislation in Britain in the 1830s and 1840s. How can we understand these levels and the movements between them more systematically?

It is partly a matter of clarity of exposition. The reader's attention is focused on one set of relations or on one point in a process at a time. Other relations or points are held in abeyance, blocked out, dropped, suspended, but not forgotten. In the next stage of argument, other relations or moments are supplied or our original object is looked at from another point of view. The model is increasingly made more complex. The discussion of the labour process at the beginning of Chapter 7 provides excellent examples. Marx starts his whole sequence of chapters on ways of working by insisting that he wants to disregard most of the determinations on actual historical forms of labour: 'we shall . . . in the first place, have to consider the labour process independently of any specific social formation'.[137] Later he says, 'we presuppose labour in a form which is an exclusively human characteristic'.[138] At the end of the eight-page discussion of the labour process 'pure and simple', he sums up as follows:

> The labour process as we have just presented it in its simple and abstract elements, is purposeful activity aimed at the production of use-values. It is an appropriation of what exists in nature for the requirements of man. It is the universal condition for the metabolic interaction between man and nature, the ever-lasting nature-imposed condition of human existence, and it is therefore independent of every form of that existence, or rather it is common to all forms of society in which human beings live.

He then stresses just what has been *missing* from this description:

> We did not, therefore, have to present the worker in his relationship with other workers; it was enough to present man and his labour on one side, nature and its materials on the other. The taste of porridge does not tell us who grew the oats, and the process we have presented does not reveal the conditions under which it takes place, whether it is happening under the slave-owner's brutal lash or the anxious eye of the capitalist, whether Cincinnatus undertakes it in tilling his couple of acres, or a savage, when he lays low a wild beast with a stone.[139]

In the very next passage Marx starts to supply some of these *social* determinations: 'let us now return to our would-be capitalist'. An elementary description of the distinguishing features of labour under capitalist conditions then follows:

> The labour process, when it is the process by which the capitalist consumes labour-power, exhibits two characteristic phenomena. First, the labourer works under the control of the capitalist to whom his labour belongs. . . . Secondly, the product is the property of the capitalist and not that of the worker, its immediate producer.[140]

But this too remains very simple and abstract with many presuppositions made. Marx deliberately suspends consideration, for example, of the dynamic relationship between capitalist relations of production and the development of new forces for the appropriation of nature. He assumes, for the sake of argument, that the capitalist takes 'labour-power as he finds it in the market' adopting existing organization and technique.

> The transformation of the mode of production itself which results from the subordination of labour to capital can only occur later on, and we shall therefore deal with it in a later chapter.[141]

In fact we have to wait to Chapter 15, the last long chapter in this sequence, before something like the full complexity of the specifically capitalist forms of the labour process is explored, but the chapters in between involve the slow, systematic accumulation of key features in their relations to each other, organized around the central dynamics of the system: the capitalist's unending pursuit of control and of valorization (the expansion of value or accumulation of capital), the resistances and struggles of the labourer to make the proletarian position habitable.

Abstractions of this kind organize the whole of *Capital*. Indeed, there is one major simplification which crucially limits the whole text. *Capital* is not intended as a study of bourgeois society as a whole even in its mid-nineteenth-century British form. It looks at capital only from certain points of view, therefore abstractly. The nature, the real limits of such a perspective emerge in the preface to the first edition in the form of an argument about real concrete social individuals.

> To prevent possible misunderstandings, let me say this. I do not by any means depict the capitalist and the landowner in rosy colours. But individuals are dealt with here only in so far as they are the personification of economic categories, the bearers of particular class-relations and interests. My standpoint, from which the development of the economic formation of society is viewed as a process of natural history, can less than any other make the individual responsible for relations whose creature he remains, socially speaking, however much he may subjectively raise himself above them.[142]

In other words Marx abstracts from real living individuals too. He abstracts only what is characteristic of these persons in their economic activity. In the main body of *Capital* people are awarded occasional theatrical appearances, especially as authors, but we quickly fix on their *representative* features. Nassau Senior is briefly a flesh-and-blood person (with 'a beautiful style' unlike other 'economic mandarins'), but quickly becomes a mere personification of the common sense and short-term interests of Manchester millowners. Real capitalists with actual names make their appearances in these pages, but Marx's characteristic move is to write of 'the capitalist' and 'the labourer', acting in 'typical' but often hypothetical situations. We can actually watch Marx refining away complexities in this way. A certain flesh-and-blood capitalist 'E. F. Sanderson, of the firm of Sanderson Bros & Co., steel-rolling and forges, Attercliffe' appears in the chapter on the working day to oppose the regulation of night work for boys under 18.[143] But Marx really treats Sanderson's person, his industry and his firm as incidental. Sanderson is interesting because he represents capital: he speaks 'in the name of all the Sandersons', even of 'the Sanderson clan'. This is not a reference to E. F. Sanderson filial and patriarchal relations (unfortunately) but to the brotherhood of capital:

But Messrs Sanderson have something else to make besides steel. Steel-making is simply a pretext for profit-making.[144]

The ubiquity of this device of personification is most obvious when Marx works the other way: he actually invents (or so it seems) imaginary or composite personages to represent whole social categories. One example is the double personification involved in Marx's magical passage on 'the voice of the worker' in the chapter on the working day.

Suddenly, however, there arises the voice of the worker, which had previously been stifled in the sound and fury of the production process.[145]

This 'voice' addresses the capitalist in the only way 'he' will understand, according to 'the law of the exchange of commodities':

You pay me for one day's labour-power, while you use three days of it. . . . I therefore demand a working day of normal length, and I demand it without any appeal to your heart, for in money matters sentiment is out of place. You may be a model citizen, perhaps a member of the RSPCA, and you may be in the odour of sanctity as well; but the thing you represent when you come face to face with me has no heart in its breast. What seems to throb there is my own heartbeat. I demand a normal working day because, like every other seller, I demand the value of my commodity.[146]

'The thing you represent' is present too in the case of the glass manufacturers who oppose lunch breaks for children for fear of losing heat from their furnaces. They acquire a collective or structural personality:

Meanwhile, late at night perhaps, Mr Glass-Capital, stuffed full of abstinence, and primed with port wine, reels home from his club, droning out idiotically 'Britons never, never shall be slaves'.[147]

Again, Marx is not concerned to do justice to the motives of individuals. Nor is he concerned to understand how whole human subjectivities are formed in actual living people. To do this we would have to breach the fundamental organizing abstraction of *Capital* and look at determinations which are normally beyond its reach. We would have to start by recognizing, for example, that 'Mr Glass-Capital' is a man, a father, husband, patriarch, an active member of the local Independent congregation, a believer in 'the progress of the nation' and in possession of elaborate personal justifications for unscrupulous money-making. As for Marx, he is using abstraction (in the form of personification) to insist on key features of the economic system, including the moralities that are implied by conformity to its main pressures.

Levels of abstraction: historical aspects

Movement through the different levels of abstraction is a way of 'presenting the real movement', clearly, logically. But it is also a method that expresses Marx's historical premise, his insistence that social arrangements are 'transitory'. Levels of abstraction are linked to the historical status, the historical scope of reference of the categories which are being elaborated. Movements through levels are not just a matter of logical simplification or concretion; they are movements from the historically general to the historically specific. Two main questions are kept continually in view: from what real social histories do these categories derive and to what real situations do they apply? This is the way of avoiding the political economists' sleight of hand of rendering historically specific ideas natural or eternal. As Engels puts it:

The logical method of treatment was the only appropriate one. But this, as a matter of fact, is nothing but the historical method, only divested of its historical form and disturbing fortuities.[148]

This use of levels can be illustrated from the same chapters of *Capital* which we have already used. Consider again the movement we described from the discussion of the labour process in its simplest elements to labour under capital. Certainly this is a formal movement to greater complexity, but it sums up a series of historical movements too: from the simplest forms of labour (the savage and his stone; 'Cincinnatus' and his two acres), to more elaborate class societies (slavery) to the classes of modern society. Marx moves, in carefully signalled stages, from *universal categories* (true of all history), to *trans-epochal* categories (true of all class societies), to categories with a narrower scope of reference, true of a *particular epoch* or social regime of labour, usually the capitalist epoch. Here some features of earlier phases are preserved but reworked; but there are also specifically capitalist features in the new ensemble which must also be understood. As Marx puts it later:

What distinguishes the various economic formations of society – the distinction between for example a society based on slave-labour and a society based on wage-labour – is the form in which this surplus labour is in each case extorted from the immediate producer, the worker.[149]

It is the third level of abstraction – the epochal – which is the *characteristic* level of *Capital*, though Marx frequently makes excursions into other epochs, especially slavery (in its *relations* to the capitalist mode) and feudalism (in comparisons and in discussions of origins). He focuses on what is specific to the capitalist organization of labour and to capital's peculiar dynamic of accumulation, contradiction and crisis. The logical elaboration stays mainly within this level, divested, as Engels says, of its detailed historical forms or 'disturbing fortuities'.

Engels none the less simplifies *Capital*'s complicated architecture. Certainly, the critique of political economy caused Marx to take special pains to disentangle universal and epochal categories, but he works at other levels too. It is not only economic categories which he criticizes but what capital does to the everyday life of mid-nineteenth-century British workers. The key here is what Marx repeatedly describes as his 'historical sketches'. These parts always interest historians most, but I want to argue that they are integrally geared into the main drive of the argument, depending upon categories developed in the more abstract ways. It is not a coherent reading, in my view, to play off the 'theoretical' and the 'historical' Marx, to reject the trammels of 'political economy' and rescue the more concrete bits.[150] The movement through levels means that the sketches are integral to the critique and the method.

I think it is useful to distinguish three main forms of 'historical sketch'. The first form might better be described as the 'historical example'. Here Marx refers, often in passing, to very particular cases, firmly rooted in time and place: not features of the capitalist mode in general (still quite an abstract level) but particular exemplifications. Such examples do not have a very elaborate life in the text, but they are important for grounding Marx's more abstract arguments in the 'materials' from which they were drawn. Here 'presentation' does, to some extent, reflect the processes of inquiry. Even the most abstract discussions are punctuated with examples of this kind. Unlike the hypothetical cases which Marx also uses, they are real historical instances. Very commonly they are contained in the footnotes to the main text – but not, for that reason, to be neglected. Marx, in fact, is a skilful user of the footnote in a way different from the usual academic reference.

In the sections which follow the labour process chapter but precede the details on the working day,[151] Marx frequently refers to works of bourgeois political economy and criticizes particular arguments. He summarizes a report from *The Times* to illustrate the impact of crises on the attitudes of manufacturers,[152] and he quotes extensively from the reports of Factory Inspectors.[153] These chapters also contain two passages we have already commented on – 'Senior's last hour' (described as 'the following famous example') and 'the voice of the worker'. If we look at Marx's footnotes at this last point, we discover that 'the voice of the worker', a personification of great imaginative power and theoretical pertinence, was also derived, in part, from a particular historical case. Marx properly acknowledges the contribution of the struggles of real historical workers:

During the great strike of the London building workers (1859–60) for the reduction of the working day to 9 hours, their committee published a manifesto that contained, to some extent, the plea of our worker. The manifesto alludes, not without irony, to the fact that the greatest profit-monger among the building masters, a certain Sir M. Peto, was in the 'odour of sanctity'.[154]

So to paraphrase Marx himself on 'old Hegel', the categories 'damn well arise out of our intercourse', complete with something of the moral trenchancy of working-class judgements too![155] This system of double reference – the elaboration of categories and a kind of pegging down to real historical materials – is typical of Marx's method of presentation and could only be missed in the most theoreticist of readings.

But this is only the minimal form of 'historical sketch'. The second form is more developed and we may term it 'historical comparison'. This is the characteristic move, for example, of the second section of the chapter on the working day, which Marx entitled 'The voracious appetite for surplus labour: manufacturer and boyar'.[156] Marx is here concerned to show that there is something very particular about capital's use of labour – its tendency to extend the hours of labour, unless checked by law or workers' resistance, beyond the point that flesh and blood can endure. The point is first established by lightning transepochal comparisons. Capital does not invent surplus labour. Wherever the means of production are held by a class of non-producers, the direct producer must produce both her own subsistence and that of her master. This is true for the Athenian aristocrat, the Etruscan theocrat, the Roman citizen, the Norman baron, the American slaveholder, the Wallachian boyar or the modern landlord or capitalist. Overlabour may occur under the earlier forms too but it must be secured by legal means or by overt coercion. Under slavery 'the recognised form of overwork is forced labour until death'.[157] Under capitalist conditions overlabour is secured by the sheer force of economic disciplines; it is part of the dynamic of accumulation. It is only by external regulation that the process may be curtailed.

To secure this point more firmly, Marx makes a longer comparison between feudal exactions in the Danubian Principalities and the English factory system.[158] There are several things going on in this rich passage. Marx is establishing what is peculiar to capital's 'thirst' for labour, elaborating the level of epochal categories. He is also developing a profound and detailed critique of the English factory system in terms of its effects on workers young and old, men and women:

Hence it is self-evident that the worker is nothing other than labour-power for the duration of his whole life, and therefore all his disposable time is by nature and by right labour-time, to be devoted to the self-valorisation of capital. Time for education, for intellectual development, for the fulfilment of social functions, for social intercourse, for the free play of the vital forces of his body and his mind, even the rest time of Sunday (and that in a country of Sabbatarians!) – what foolishness! But in its blind and measureless drive, its insatiable appetite for surplus labour, capital oversteps not only the moral but even the merely physical limits of the working day. It usurps the time for growth, development and healthy maintenance of the body.[159]

Such an indictment requires great detail, much of it from Blue Books and inspectors' reports, but it also yields a further theoretical-historical point of great importance: that early capitalist strategies of accumulation, the pattern of absolute surplus value extraction, are grossly contradictory. Capital actually maims, cripples, destroys its very source of wealth. It destructively consumes its labour power. It shortens lives; it increases the cost of replacing labour. Paradoxically, then, it is in capital's general interest to limit its own gargantuan appetite.[160]

But there is a third, still more developed form of historical sketch: accounts of key historical *transitions*. These passages are, methodologically, the most instructive of all. They show, once more, the mutual dependence of levels of abstraction – of theory and history in the old nomenclature. On the one hand, Marx approaches 'history-writing' in something like its conventional sense: he employs narrative, thick description, supplying more and more determinations. He often breaches the self-imposed limitations of *Capital*'s main line of argument: he is concerned not only with the 'naked' labourer and capitalist, but with the workers and their masters and others as political forces, acting through state power and through the law, pursuing this strategy or that, becoming conscious of larger interests. He is concerned with the everyday forms of struggle and oppression: the forms in which people become conscious of their social existence and seek to change it. On the other hand Marx has already established, more abstractly, what is at stake in such struggles and how they form part of a larger pattern of change and transformation. The more extended historical sketches seem often to 'stand free' from the larger architecture: they certainly function less as illustrations of arguments already made. But I want to insist, once more, on the complementarity of Marx's accounts of process, conditions, tendency and his detailed history-writing: the one establishes the conditions and the possibilities of change, the other examines actual outcomes in the only way this can be done – by the detailed, blow-by-blow analysis of politics, giving fuller weight to the forms of organization and consciousness.

There are three main parts of *Capital* volume I that approach this level of concreteness, the level not of the epoch in its 'classic' instances, but of the particular phase, transition or conjuncture. None of these rival the conjunctural particularity of the historical or political essays but they all, in different ways, illustrate the method of concrete analysis. The first is Marx's account of the struggle over the Factory Acts which immediately follows the discussion of the length of the working day.[161] The second is the sequence of chapters on the various ways of increasing the productivity of labour –'co-operation', 'manufacture and the division of labour' and 'modern industry'. The third is Marx's discussion of 'the so-called primitive accumulation' towards the end of volume I, his own account of the genesis of the capitalist mode of production in the dissolution of the feudal social order.[162]

There is not space to discuss all three passages. I will concentrate on the first, but it is important to stress just how fertile the other two have been. The notes on 'primitive accumulation' played a key part in founding the modern tradition of marxist history-writing which is discussed in the second chapter of this volume: without Marx, without *this* Marx, no Dobb's *Studies*; without Dobb's *Studies*, the problematic of the Communist Party Historians' Group would not have been conceivable. The chapters on the forms of the labour process have been no less important. A vital link here is the work by a modern American marxist, Harry Braverman, whose *Labor and Monopoly Capital* brought Marx's tools to bear on the subsequent development of labour under capitalist conditions. The modern critical study of work (and of the cultures of work) derives very largely from the Marx–Braverman contributions. There is still a need, indeed, to return to the substance of Marx's chapters with a more historical eye and a method more informed by national peculiarities and transitions.[163]

We left the chapter on the working day, at the point where Marx noted that the legal regulation of hours of labour was, potentially at least, in the interests of capital as a whole. But at this level of abstraction regulation could only be envisaged as an immanent tendency. To understand how this outcome was actually achieved, Marx is obliged, by his own method, to move to a more concrete analysis. The shortening of the working day is not inscribed in some inexorable logic of progress. Individual capitals, indeed, strenuously resisted regulation and sought subsequently to evade it.[164] Moreover the practice of the legal shortening of hours involved a direct reversal of inherited forms of regulation. By an historical comparison Marx shows that up until the eighteenth century the state had intervened to lengthen hours, not to shorten them.[165] Factory legislation can only be properly understood as the result of political processes and especially as a response to the demands of organized workers. 'The normal working day' was the product of 'centuries of struggle between the capitalist and the worker'. This was intensified after the massive encroachments of capital in the early years of the Industrial Revolution.

As soon as the working class, stunned at first by the noise and turmoil of the new system of production, had recovered its senses to some extent, it began to offer resistance first of all in England, the native land of large-scale industry.[166]

The history of the struggles that followed is re-created in some detail. The strategies of each party – of the Factory Movement, of manufacturing interests, of Whigs, Conservatives and political economists and of the factory inspectors – are traced in their shifting relations and alliances. The patterns of pressure, containment, concession, evasion and ultimate triumph are shown in their contingencies. It is certainly arguable that this account is still not detailed enough, especially on the ideological dimensions of the struggles. But the nature of the argument is clear enough. Working-class struggle was a major determinant on the outcome:

The establishment of a normal working day is therefore the product of a protracted and more or less concealed civil war between the capitalist class and the working class. Since the contest takes place in the arena of modern industry, it is fought out first of all in the homeland of that industry – England. The English factory workers were the champions, not only of the English working class, but of the modern working class in general, just as their theorists were the first to throw down the gauntlet to the theory of the capitalists.[167]

The story of the Factory Acts, then, is also part of another parallel history which is conditioned by the development of the capitalist mode, but also acts as a determination within or upon it. This is the history of formation of a working class:

For 'protection' against the serpent of their agonies, the workers have to put their heads together and, as a class, compel the passing of a law, an all-powerful social barrier by which they can be prevented from selling themselves and their families into slavery and death by voluntary contract with capital. In the place of the pompous catalogue of 'the inalienable rights of man' there steps the modest Magna Carta of the legally limited working day which at last makes clear 'when the time which the worker sells is ended, and when his (sic) own begins'.[168]

As Marx makes clear in the chapter on 'Modern industry', the limitation of the working day is, however, a victory won on a capitalist terrain. Having been forced to abandon the ungoverned extension of working hours, capital compensated by intensifying labour, especially through machinery, in the hours available to it. This change in the use of labour-power is seen by Marx as a shift of great significance. A major modification in capital's working is forced through by working-class struggles. The episode plays a major part in the structure of Marx's own argument too, for it links the sections on 'absolute' and 'relative' surplus value. Thus this historical sketch is no mere footnote or illustration: it occupies a central point in the presentation of Marx's main argument.

The best Marx as a resource: some conclusions

None of the historical sketches in *Capital* are developed enough to test our best Marx in really concrete studies. The nearest we have to such a test are Marx's political writings on France and Britain produced in the years following the failure of the 1848 Revolutions.[169] There are definite limits of these texts for our purpose: their writing predates the discoveries of *Capital* and, probably, much of Marx's own developed thinking on method. But in texts like *The Eighteenth Brumaire of Louis Bonaparte* we certainly find Marx working with the very tissue of historical sources and changes presupposing or abstracting much less, holding more of the determinations in view. It is worth noting some key features of this long essay, though it would require a fuller study to do proper justice to its importance for history-writing today.[170]

The Eighteenth Brumaire is a theoretically organized account of a political conjuncture. It is organized, like *Capital*, on different levels of abstraction but unlike *Capital* is concerned, primarily, with analysing and explaining a three-year history of detailed political struggles. Centrally it poses the question of how, in France, the 1848 Revolution failed, not only as a social revolution, but as an assertion of parliamentary forms of government too. As Marx put it, referring to the favourite French explanations of Bonaparte's coup:

It remains to be explained how a nation of thirty-six millions could be taken by surprise by three swindlers and delivered without resistance into captivity.[171]

Theoretically *The Eighteenth Brumaire* draws on Marx's previous thinking about society, state and politics as formed in the critique of Hegel's theory of the state and expressed in *The German Ideology* and *The Communist Manifesto*. But it is even less of a mere illustration of truths already arrived at than the more developed sketches in *Capital*. As several commentators have stressed, it marks a considerable break in Marx's thinking, especially about the relation between the class basis of politics and the political and ideological forms of representation.[172] The materials of the conjuncture are the basis for theoretical innovation; they force Marx to stretch and develop his categories further, from the relatively simple optimism of *The Manifesto* (in which revolution is inscribed in the uninhabitable position of the modern working class) to *The Eighteenth Brumaire*'s attention to other conditions. It is a false trail, in my opinion, to look for a 'theory of representation' in *The Eighteenth Brumaire*, but Marx certainly explores *a whole repertoire of representative forms and strategies* characteristic of politics at a particular moment of the development of class forces and the forms of the bourgeois state. He shows, moreover, how the pursuit of these strategies in the blow-by-blow struggles, actually forms the institutions, builds up, in this case, the highly centralized and autocratic machinery of the French state.

In the case of the dominant classes of French society – the different fractions of capital – the relation between economic interests and political organizations is quite direct, at least as the story begins. The Orleanists and Legitimists represent big capital of different kinds. Together they constitute the Party of Order, representing the interests of capital as a whole.[173] But this is not a necessary or a constant relation. A major theme in *The Eighteenth Brumaire* is the transfer of power and of legitimacy from the parliamentary parties to Bonaparte, the guarantor of order and of the material interests of 'the extra-parliamentary mass of the bourgeoisie'. Marx describes this dramatic change as follows:

Similarly, the extra-parliamentary mass of the bourgeoisie invited Bonaparte to suppress and annihilate its speaking and writing part, its politicians and intellectuals, its platform and its press, by its own servility towards the President, its vilification of Parliament, and its brutal mistreatment of its own press. It hoped that it would then be able to pursue its private affairs with full confidence under the protection of a strong and unrestricted government.[174]

For other classes access to the political order is less direct. The proletariat is a real force in the streets of Paris. It fuels, while its power remains, the whole revolutionary sequence. The complicated movements of dominant parties and fractions are always in some part a response to the threat of popular control. But, in this phase of development, the working class can only find a subordinate place in formal politics, as part of 'the people' in an alliance of a predominately *petit-bourgeois* or 'social-democratic' kind, concerned with the harmonization of classes, not the overcoming of class society as such.[175] The peasantry, though a class in its social being and cultural distinctiveness, has acquired no political organization of its own and so may be 'represented' passively, partially, treacherously, by Bonaparte himself, who cultivates the popular Napoleonic legend.[176] Other political groupings have no extensive social basis but are constituted solely from groups of intellectuals and politicians. The 'pure republicans' are a 'coterie' of this kind, inheritors of a political tradition, the tradition of French Jacobinism.[177]

More generally, *The Eighteenth Brumaire* is a fuller realization of the ambitions I sketched in the Factory Act case. It examines the conditions of political organization and struggle, the raw materials in the nature of French society for the practice of politics. France is not a fully developed capitalist social order. Its working class is too weak and localized to become the basis of a new form of society. Its bourgeoisie is heavily weighted towards the traditional sectors of land and commerce, less actively transformative than the industrial capitalists of Britain. It is a largely rural and peasant society. This sets limits both to bourgeois rule and proletarian transformation. It underpins the Napoleonic solution, a kind of historical compromise that secures the bourgeoisie's material interests while robbing the bourgeois parties of direct power. (Marx's treatment of English arrangements is not, in some ways, so dissimilar: there too a particular agency, in this case Whig aristocracy, tends to rule *for* capital.)

Marx is concerned to show, however, not just the 'logic' of this outcome, but *exactly how it was secured*, with all the mistakes, muddles and 'fortuities' that this necessarily involved. In terms of our argument about abstraction this involves supplying much that is characteristically absent in *Capital*, especially the specifically political and ideological conditions of major social transformations. *The Eighteenth Brumaire* is wonderfully rich here. It is a key text, for example, for what is discussed as 'popular memory' in the last two articles of this book: for the force of a national political culture, for the importance of national historiography, and for the way in which 'the tradition of the dead generations weighs like a nightmare on the minds of the living'.[178] It also employs the full range of levels of abstraction. Some of its most memorable passages are pitched at the level of a universal or general-historical discourse:

Men make their own history, but not of their own free will; not under circumstances they themselves have chosen but under the given and inherited circumstances with which they are directly confronted.[179]

Others belong to the level of the epoch, but employing political rather than economic categories:

Bourgeois revolutions . . . storm quickly from success to success. They outdo each other in dramatic effects; men and things seem set in sparkling diamonds and each day's spirit is ecstatic. . . .Proletarian revolutions, however, such as those of the nineteenth century, constantly engage in self-criticism, and in repeated interruptions of their own course.[180]

But most of the essay deals with the detailed swing and feel of events. Here Marx uses to the full a series of devices which we noted also in *Capital*: personification and theoretically-organized satire and irony for example. It also uses methods of presentation which I cannot fully discuss here, especially a form of narrative in which the taken-for-grantedness of 'the story' is undermined by the continuous use of terms like 'it appears' or 'seems', which reference determinations not fully conscious for contemporary participants. In writing of the outcome of the Napoleonic regime for example:

France therefore *seems* to have escaped the despotism of a class only to fall back beneath the despotism of an individual, and indeed, beneath the authority of an individual without authority. The struggle *seems* to have reached the compromise that all classes fall on their knees, equally mute and equally impotent, before the rifle butt.[181]

Marx writes 'seems' because he wants to say that this real appearance is only part of 'the story'. Bonaparte's coup may actually guarantee bourgeois interests in the best way possible; certainly classes are not 'equally impotent'. 'The compromise' continues to involve *relations of force* between them. Moreover we have to ask how the coup and the centralization of power effects future possibilities, especially, for Marx, the possibilities (or certainty) of proletarian revolution.

If *The Eighteenth Brumaire* is the exemplary Marx text for 'concrete studies', it is not free from difficulties. Underneath the complexity of the struggles, Marx seems to preserve another almost independent 'motor' whose dynamics are not really explored.

But the revolution is thorough. It is still on its journey through purgatory. It goes about its business methodically. By 2nd December 1851 it had completed one half of its preparatory work; it is now completing the other half. First of all it perfected the parliamentary power, in order to be able to overthrow it. Now, having attained this, it is perfecting the *executive power*, reducing it to its purest expression, isolating it, and pitting itself against it as the sole object of attack, in order to concentrate all its forces of destruction against it. And when it has completed this, the second half of its preliminary work, Europe will leap from its seat and exultantly exclaim: 'Well worked, old mole!'[182]

It is clear enough what Marx is doing here. He is saying that the centralization of the French state is a condition for proletarian revolution. He is also offering socialists and communists a version of the future in which history is on their side even at a moment of conspicuous defeat. Such visions are enormously important (and always related to views of the past). But Marx breaches his best practice here. 'The Revolution' becomes a (familiar) idealist category, the internal complexity of which is not indicated and which 'realises itself in history'. All historical complexities are submerged within its onward march. The actual conditions on which such a transformation might depend, centralization aside, are not illuminated.

It would be possible to give other examples of this 'worst Marx', in each of which Marx breaches one of his central premises. Nor is *Capital* immune from this tendency. There are points in volume III in particular in which Marx presents capital's laws of tendency as laws in the strongest possible sense: forces working independently of human wills to produce necessary outcomes.[183] But Marx forgets here the nature of his own abstractions: in order to come to such a conclusion he would have to supply many other determinations. The worst Marx *is* reductive, does tend to functionalist or determinist explanations, does simplify 'real history'. Abstraction emerges not as a resource, but, definitely, as a problem.

It is not difficult to see how this arises. It has to do with the immense ambition of Marx's project and the difficulty of realizing it. The method implies that every major social determination at work in specific social situations be abstracted thence, properly analysed and then recomposed, as it were, in a concrete model or mental approximation to 'the real movement'. Marx made a start for some of the social situations of his own time. His most developed achievements were tightly limited, however, by his chosen standpoint: the economic foundations of the social order. It was tempting to breach his own (quite self-conscious) abstraction, to read *the whole history* from the economic forms. Usually, I want to stress, Marx does *not* do this; marxism is not necessarily a reductive or functionalist system of thinking. But the temptation to short-circuit the whole programme, to cash the findings politically, was often overwhelming. Some of the difficulties of using Marx as a resource derive, then, from his large-scale ambitions – 'the economic law of motion of modern society' no less! Others derive from the standpoint of the users, who are in the position of legatees. What was an historical abstraction for Marx or a premise to be grounded in practice may become in marxology an a priori truth or test of orthodoxy. Materialist categories with a particular historical origin and legitimate scope of reference may be treated idealistically as political or intellectual touchstones. Equally, to escape the grip of 'the master' the critique of marxist categories may acquire a rather fey adolescent air with orthodoxies 'demolished' at random as though this dismissal too could be achieved without serious and detailed research. As we have seen these ways of encountering Marx (as marxists or ex-marxists or not-marxists-at-all) run against every principle of Marx's own best practice. They annul the built-in benefits of the standpoint in the present, now *our* present. They treat Marx's mid-nineteenth-century findings as finished doctrines, true or false. They do not criticize the inherited categories *historically*, only, at best, 'logically'. They divert attention from the really urgent intellectual tasks – researching the modern social world and making *fresh* abstractions from these researches.

It is in suggesting ways of doing this that the best Marx seems to me most useful, though this is not to deny the force, adequately criticized, of the more substantive concepts too. Certainly, I have found the return to Marx useful in relation to current dilemmas, or the dilemmas of a few years back. The best Marx is helpful in sorting out what is sensible in rival positions, and in breaking false polarities by suggesting altogether different solutions. From the perspective developed here the Althusser–Thompson debate involves some ridiculous oppositions. Of course the 'rationalist', Althusserian camp is right to stress the systematic development of categories or concepts. There *are* some basic conditions for clear, explanatory thinking. But it is also the case that without research and the direct labour of abstraction the categories acquire a fixity and universal application which tips over into an idealism. Marx's old antagonists – Hegel, Proudhon and the idealist historians – *are* recognizable in much 'post-Althusserian' thinking.

Similarly the choice between 'theory' and 'history' is evidently no choice at all. There is no necessary tension between general categories and concrete studies. It is not a question of abandoning the first in favour of the second. It is much more useful to reformulate the problem in a way that actually corresponds better to the practice itself. The problem of theory in inquiry is better formulated as the problem of the character of abstractions. All systematic thinking abstracts: the question is how? Are the abstractions 'chaotic'? Do they present historically specific relations as everlasting shackles on human development? Do they reduce complexities to a few simple elements or principles? Do they exaggerate (in an understandable pride of the intellectual) the power of thinking and of the categories themselves? Are the abstractions made self-consciously or are there huge half-conscious absences?

The problems of the role of 'theory' in presentation or in history-writing can be similarly reformulated. All accounts work on different levels of abstraction: they simplify the historical detail, more or less. The question is not whether to present histories abstractly, but how to handle the different levels of abstraction, explicitly, carefully, clearly. Solutions will depend partly on the requirements of intelligibility and partly on the historical scope of the study. But most if not all studies should work at different levels. It is hard to imagine a detailed account, for example, that does not make *some* assumptions about the nature of human beings in general. On the other hand, there are some social determinations that can only be reached by a close consecutive study of events that re-creates the conditions and the stratagems. We cannot, it seems to me, understand the particular determinacy of class or other social struggles in any other way: re-creating them in the past, necessarily living them in the present and the future.

Part Three

Autobiography/memory/tradition

6   Popular memory: theory, politics, method

Popular Memory Group

> Must become historians of the present too.
>
> Communist Party Historians' Group Minutes, 8 April 1956

In this article we explore an approach to history-writing which involves becoming 'historians of the present too'. It is important to stress 'explore'. We do not have a completed project in 'popular memory' to report. We summarize and develop discussions which were intended as an initial clarification. These discussions had three main starting-points. First, we were interested in the limits and contradictions of academic history where links were attempted with a popular socialist or feminist politics. Our main example here was 'oral history', a practice that seemed nearest to our own preoccupations. Second, we were attracted to projects which moved in the direction indicated by these initial criticisms. These included experiments in popular autobiography and in community-based history, but also some critical developments with a base in cultural studies or academic historiography. Third, we tried, as in the case of all the articles in this book, to relate problems of history-writing to more abstract debates which suggested possible clarifications.

What do we mean, then, by 'popular memory'? We give our own provisional answers in the first part of this essay. We define popular memory first as an *object of study*, but, second, as a *dimension of political practice*. We then look, in the second part, at some of the resources for such a project, but also sketch its limits and difficulties. These are discussed in turn and at more length in the third and fourth parts. They range from problems of theory and method to the social organization of research and writing.

On its own this essay is incomplete in another way: though it sketches the field as a whole, it explores one side of the popular memory relation, the side nearest to oral history as a practice. The larger argument is extended, in important ways, in Chapter 7. Although this has a different authorship it grew from the same discussions.

---

* This essay is based upon the collective work of the Popular Memory Group in the Centre for Contemporary Cultural Studies which met between October 1979 and June 1980. The group consisted of: Michael Bommes, Gary Clarke, Graham Dawson, Jacob Eichler, Thomas Fock, Richard Johnson, Cim Meyer, Rebecca O'Rourke, Rita Pakleppa, Hans-Erich Poser, Morten Skov-Carlsen, Anne Turley and Patrick Wright. This piece was written by Richard Johnson with Graham Dawson.

Defining popular memory

Popular memory as an object of study

The first move in defining popular memory is to extend what we mean by history-writing (and therefore what is involved in historiographical comment). The other essays in this book have not drawn too formal a distinction between academic history and more popular or politicized kinds. Such a distinction makes little sense if applied to Marx, or the Hammonds, or the early years of the Communist Party Historians' Group, or to much feminist history. We have tended to use some loose notion of 'the history-writer', who works under the sign of history as art or science, and even so flexible a definition does set limits. This is especially true for the present time. The looser, potentially amateur notion of 'the history-writer' has hardened into 'the historian' as specialist academic. Left historiographies have not been immune from this process. Socialist and feminist histories have developed with at least one foot in universities or polytechnics. The expansion of a radicalized college-going constituency, characteristic of the 1960s and 1970s, has created a kind of specialized readership. Some of the contradictions, and two different ways of handling them, can be seen in the contrasted strategies of two recently founded historical journals, *Social History* and *History Workshop Journal*: the one pursuing a cautious historical avant-gardism, the other avowedly socialist and committed to the idea of a genuinely 'popular' history.[1]

For the modern period there is a real problem of the implicitly non-popular effects of focusing on formal history-writing, a practice largely colonized by academic and professional norms. (As we shall see this is also the case with new methodologies, especially 'oral history', which are sometimes seen as intrinsically 'popular' and democratizing.) If we retain this focus, we risk reproducing some very conservative forms: a closed circle of comment between left social historians and what Marx would have called 'critical critics'. Ken Worpole has pointed out the effects of this in justly sceptical terms:

It is obvious to anyone that the last two decades have produced an outstanding growth in the range of work done in the field of Labour studies and the more informal modes of working-class self-organisation and forms of cultural identity. . . . There has been a proliferation of research papers, published essays and full-length books emerging from this powerful intellectual current. Yet . . . I seriously wonder whether we could with any confidence suggest that we have a more historically conscious labour movement now than we have done at previous periods of crisis in the past. I would think not.[2]

He suggests 'two observable trends' that might account for this: the concentration of history in higher education (the move from 'draughty Co-op Halls and Trades Halls to modern Polytechnic lecture rooms') and the expense of commercially published books ('expensive hardbacks for the higher education libraries, rather than pocketbooks for the people'). What is so important about these comments is that they direct attention to the *form* of historical works and the social conditions within which they are produced, distributed and (sometimes) read. These questions are completely taken for granted in the ordinary run of critical reviewing, though the problem of the accessibility of language and of 'jargon' sometimes stands in for the larger problems.

Worpole's comments show the need to expand the idea of historical production well beyond the limits of academic history-writing. We must include *all* the ways in which a sense of the past is constructed in our society. These do not necessarily take a written or literary form. Still less do they conform to academic standards of scholarship or canons of truthfulness. Academic history has a particular place in a much larger process. We will call this 'the social production of memory'. In this collective production everyone participates, though unequally. Everyone, in this sense, is a historian. As Jean Chesneaux argues, professionalized history has attempted to appropriate a much more general set of relationships and needs: 'the collective and contradictory relationship of our society to its past' and the 'collective need' for guidance in the struggle to make the future.[3] We have already noted a similar stress in Christopher Hill's work: the recognition of a larger social process in which 'we ourselves are shaped by the past' but are also continually reworking the past which shapes us.[4] The first problem in the pursuit of 'popular memory' is to specify the 'we' in Hill's formulation or 'our society' in Chesneaux's. What *are* the means by which social memory is produced? And what practices are relevant especially outside those of professional history-writing?

It is useful to distinguish the main ways in which a sense of the past is produced: through public representations and through private memory (which, however, may also be collective and shared). The first way involves a public 'theatre' of history, a public stage and a public audience for the enacting of dramas concerning 'our' history, or heritage, the story, traditions and legacy of !the British People'. This public stage is occupied by many actors who often speak from contradictory scripts, but collectively we shall term the agencies which construct this public historical sphere and control access to the means of public-ation 'the historical apparatus'. We shall call the products of these agencies, in their aggregate relations and combinations at any point of time, 'the field of public representations of history'. In thinking about the ways in which these representations affect individual or group conceptions of the past, we might speak of 'dominant memory'. This term points to the power and pervasiveness of historical representations, their connections with dominant institutions and the part they play in winning consent and building alliances in the processes of formal politics. But we do not mean to imply that conceptions of the past that acquire a dominance in the field of public representations are either monolithically installed or everywhere believed in. Not all the historical representations that win access to the public field are 'dominant'. The field is crossed by competing constructions of the past, often at war with each other. Dominant memory is produced in the course of these struggles and is always open to contestation. We do want to insist, however, that there are real processes of domination in the historical field. Certain representations achieve centrality and luxuriate grandly; others are marginalized or excluded or reworked.

Nor are the criteria of success here those of truth: dominant representations may be those that are most ideological, most obviously conforming to the flattened stereotypes of myth.

Historical constructions are most obviously public when linked to central state institutions. The governmental and parliamentary systems, especially in their 'Englishness', are historical apparatuses in their own right. Aided (*sotto voce*) by BBC pomposity, they 'breathe' a sense of 'tradition', guaranteeing the inviolability of the broad ground-rules of formal politics, 'our democratic constitution'. Actually (and contradictorily) it is not parliamentary institutions that are the important foci for most pageantry, the main form of historical theatre. The monarchy and the military are much more closely involved here, providing the very stuff of tradition. Both loom large in the regular metropolitan spectacles and in the more occasional shows: jubilees, royal weddings, state visits, state funerals and commemorative events. Nor are the historical interventions of the monarchy and the military only metropolitan, appropriated by visiting tourists (though they certainly benefit the tourist industries). Loudly amplified through the media, they intersect with everyday life in the localities. 'Our Royal Family' may be cosily consumed at the fireside. Children may learn about a militaristic past at the war museums, through handbooks of military strategy and technology and through the local airshow or open day, commemorating, perhaps, the Battle of Britain. Historical recreations (popular now in the grounds of the better preserved local castles) may figure military moments (the Civil War) or pugnacious popular myth, robbed, however, of political significance (Robin Hood versus the Sheriff of Nottingham perhaps). Such events produce too their own historiographies of brochures, guides, official (e.g. regimental) histories and massive academic and popular literatures on royal and military personages and themes. Despite their official origins such representations have a real life within the patterns of popular leisure and pleasure.

Other institutions, though linked to the national or local state, have a greater degree of autonomy, operating with high-cultural, educational, preservational or archival purposes. We include here the whole world of museums, art galleries, record offices, the Department of the Environment's official preservation orders, the 'National' Trust, the 'National' Theatre, and in general the sphere of history as 'cultural policy' – much of what is explored in Chapter 7 as 'National Heritage'. Perhaps the educational system itself belongs here too: the academic producers and all those definitions of historical significance carried in the formal curricula, in O and A level syllabuses and examinations, and in the texts that are widely used in schools. In this 'cultural' field, the relations between scholarly and dominant historiographies are especially intimate; the historian's criteria of truthfulness are more likely to prevail here than in the more overtly politicized versions.

History is also business. It is important for the whole range of publishing activity, especially since historical writing retains much more of an amateur or 'lay' public than other social sciences. Best-seller lists commonly contain items that are marketed as 'historical', especially biographies and autobiographies, historical fictions and military histories. In Britain, more than in Europe, World War II has provided an inexhaustible supply of historical fact and fiction, much of it in heavily militaristic guise and reinforced by the close convergence of war, fighting and a boy culture in men, young and old.[5] (The historical paradigm here is definitely not academic history but the tradition of masculine romance that runs from *Boy's Own* to the Super-hero comics of today.) To popular fiction and the modern form of the glossy illustrated documentary book, we have to add the historical movies, somewhat displaced in the block-buster market by the contemporary salience of science fiction. More interesting because less remarked on is the massive contemporary growth of 'historical tourism'. We mean the way in which historically significant places become a resource, physically or ideologically, for the leisure and tourist industries. The way is led there by the owners of palaces, mansions, castles and other 'country houses', and, in its own discreet way, by the Anglican Church. But the last decade or so has seen the commercial colonization of many lesser sites with historical or mythical capital. The guide books, also commercially produced and with very large and expertly promoted circulations, point us to these places, encapsulating their historical meaning.

The public media too – especially radio, television and the press – are a principal source of historical constructions. We include the intersections of history, journalism and documentary, but also the media arts, especially historical drama. The media certainly produce their own historical accounts – they produce a contemporary history daily, for instance, in the form of 'news'. But they also select, amplify and transform constructions of the past produced elsewhere. They increasingly draw, for example, from oral history and 'yesterday's witness'. They give a privileged space to conceptions of the past which accompany the party-political battles. Of all parts of the historical apparatus the electronic media are perhaps the most compelling and ubiquitous. Access here may often be decisive in gaining currency for an historical account.

More removed from the patronage of state and of capital are the voluntary associations of the world of history. Most counties and many towns have their own historical and archaeological societies, often with a long nineteenth-century pedigree. Like the Historical Association which links schoolteachers and academics, these societies draw on a fund of amateur historical enthusiasm, bounded by a strong sense of locality. To these we must add newer growths: the preservation societies and community-based groups and WEA classes, including those with socialist and feminist purposes. The growth of 'oral history' and of the History Workshop movement has added whole layers, sometimes of a radically new kind, to these local and participatory forms.

As this last set of examples suggests, the various sites and institutions do not act in concert. To make them sing, if not in harmony at least with only minor dissonances, involves hard labour and active intervention. Sometimes this has been achieved by direct control (censorship for example) and by a violent recasting or obliteration of whole fields of public history. More commonly today, in the capitalist West, the intersections of formal political debates and the public media are probably the crucial site. Certainly political ideologies involve a view of past and present and future. Ranged against powers such as these, what price the lonely scholar, producing (also through commercial channels) the one or two thousand copies of the latest monograph?!

There is a second way of looking at the social production of memory which draws attention to quite other processes. A knowledge of past and present is also produced in the course of everyday life. There is a common sense of the past which, though it may lack consistency and explanatory force, none the less contains elements of good sense. Such knowledge may circulate, usually without amplification, in everyday talk and in personal comparisons and narratives. It may even be recorded in certain intimate cultural forms: letters, diaries, photograph albums and collections of things with past associations. It may be encapsulated in anecdotes that acquire the force and generality of myth. If this is history, it is history under extreme pressures and privations. Usually this history is held to the level of private remembrance. It is not only unrecorded, but actually silenced. It is not offered the occasion to speak. In one domain, the modern Women's Movement well understands the process of silencing and is raising the 'hidden' history of women's feelings, thoughts and actions more clearly to view. Feminist history challenges the very distinction 'public'/'private' that silences or marginalizes women's lived sense of the past. But similar processes of domination operate in relation to specifically working-class experiences, for most working-class people are also robbed of access to the means of publicity and are equally unused to the male, middle-class habit of giving universal or 'historic' significance to an extremely partial experience. But we are only beginning to understand the class dimensions of cultural domination, partly by transferring the feminist insights. Nor is this only a question of class or gender positions. Even the articulate middle-class historian, facing the dominant memory of events through which he has actually lived, can also be silenced (almost) in this way. One telling example is the difficulty of writers of the New Left in speaking coherently about the Second World War:

> One is not permitted to speak of one's wartime reminiscences today, nor is one under any impulse to do so. It is an area of general reticence: an unmentionable subject among younger friends, and perhaps of mild ridicule among those of radical opinions. All this is understood. And one understands also why it is so.
>
> It is so, in part, because Chapman Pincher and his like have made an uncontested take-over of all the moral assets of that period; have coined the war into Hollywood blockbusters and spooky paper-backs and television tedia; have attributed all the value of that moment to the mythic virtues of an authoritarian Right which is now, supposedly, the proper inheritor and guardian of the present nation's interests.
>
> I walk in my garden, or stand cooking at the stove, and muse on how this came about. My memories of that war are very different.[6]

This is followed by a reassuringly confident passage which is a classic text for studying the popular memory of the 1940s, but the struggle is intense, the victory narrow, and the near-silencing of so strong and masculine a voice in the shape of its domestication is very revealing.

It is this kind of recovery that has become the mission of the radical and demo-cratic currents in oral history, popular autobiography and community-based publishing. We will look at these attempts to create a socialist or democratic popular memory later in the argument. But we wish to stress first that the study of popular memory cannot be limited to this level alone. It is a necessarily *relational* study. It has to take in the dominant historical representations in the public field as well as attempts to amplify or generalize subordinated or private experiences. Like all struggles it must needs have two sides. Private memories cannot, in con-crete studies, be readily unscrambled from the effects of dominant historical discourses. It is often these that supply the very terms by which a private history is thought through. Memories of the past are, like all common-sense forms, strangely composite constructions, resembling a kind of geology, the selective sedimentation of past traces. As Gramsci put it, writing about the necessity of historical consciousness for a Communist politics, the problem is ' "knowing thyself" as a product of the historical process to date which has deposited in you an infinity of traces, without leaving an inventory'. Similarly the public discourses live off the primary recording of events in the course of everyday transactions and take over the practical knowledges of historical agents. It is for these reasons that the study of 'popular memory' is concerned with *two* sets of relations. It is concerned with the relation between dominant memory and oppositional forms across the whole public (including academic) field. It is also concerned with the relation between these public discourses in their contemporary state of play and the more privatized sense of the past which is generated within a lived culture.

Popular memory as a political practice

Socialist, feminist and radical historians have always understood that history matters politically. History-writing has sometimes been seen as a way of fighting within one branch of 'science', an attempt to dislodge 'bourgeois' history from its predominant place within the professional intellectual field. Left historians have shared a general, often vague, sense that a history informed by marxist or socialist premises must serve the politics of the present and future. Only rarely, at least in contemporary debates, has this general association been challenged.[7] The intrin-sically 'historical' character of marxism, as science or as critique, has usually seemed to guarantee the connection.

The political uses of history do seem to us more problematic even from a marxist perspective. This is especially the case when history is defined as 'the study of the past'. We have come to see this as one of the key features of professional history, and indeed, of historical ideologies. Certainly it is deeply problematic from the viewpoint of 'popular memory'. For memory is, by definition, a term which directs our attention not to the past but to *the past–present relation*. It is because 'the past' has this living active existence in the present that it matters so much politically. As 'the past' – dead, gone or only *subsumed in* the present – it matters much less. This argument may be clarified if we compare a number of approaches to the political significance of history, returning to some of Bill Schwarz's formulations in Chapter 2 on the Communist Party Historians' Group.[8]

We may follow Schwarz in distinguishing three main approaches to the political relevance of history. The first approach, while retaining in a strong form the notion that the object of history is 'the past', seeks to link past and present in the form of salutary 'lessons'. These may have a negative force, warning, for instance, against returns to past disasters. The contemporary argument about 'the 1930s', which draws on a conventional left historiography of that decade, is a case in point.[9] But this argument may also work more positively, typically by identifying 'traditions' which then become a resource for present struggles. Raymond Williams's *Culture and Society* tradition, Edward Thompson's tradition of liber- tarian socialism or communism, formed in the junction of marxism and romanti- cism, and the socialist feminist succession uncovered in the historical work of Sheila Rowbotham are salient examples here. An even better case is that already discussed by Schwarz: the Communist Historians' construction of a long lineage of popular democratic struggles from the Levellers and Diggers to the socialisms and communism of the twentieth century. More generally still, and the move is typical of Edward Thompson's history, the re-creation of popular struggles shows us that despite retreats and defeats, 'the people', 'the working class' or the female sex *do* 'make history' even under conditions of oppression or exploitation. In the same way, especially if we are conscious of this lineage, *we* can make history too.[10] The link between past and present, between history-writing and the construction of historical futures today, is in essence an exhortatory one.

A second way of conceiving the past-present relation is to employ historical perspectives and methods as an element in strategic analysis. We start from the need to understand contemporary political problems. We seek to examine the conditions on which contemporary dilemmas rest. In looking at the nature and origins of current oppressions, we trace their genesis as far back as it is necessary to go. Here the relation between past and present is necessarily more organic, more internal. The past *is* present today in particular social structures with determinate origins and particular histories. This cooler, 'scientific' evaluation of the past is best exempli- fied, as Schwarz suggests, in Perry Anderson's historical project, from 'Origins of the present crisis' to his sequence of major studies in the origins of the modern capitalist world. It is characteristic too of Marx's own historical projects, *Capital* itself but also the essays on French and English politics, though in Marx it is allied with a more inspirational or agitational mode of history-writing, closer to the first of our own categories and with a similar risk of triumphalism.

A stress on popular memory adds something to both these conceptions, though it does not displace them. The construction of traditions is certainly *one* way in which historical argument operates as a political force though it risks a certain conservatism; similarly any adequate analysis of the contemporary relations of political force has to be historical in form as well as reaching back to more or less distant historical times. It must also attempt to grasp the broader epochal limits and possibilities in terms of a longer history of capitalist and patriarchal structures.

What we may insist on in addition is that all political activity is intrinsically a process of historical argument and definition, that all political programmes involve some construction of the past as well as the future, and that these processes go on every day, often outrunning, especially in terms of period, the preoccupations of historians.[11] Political domination involves historical definition. History – in particular popular memory – is a stake in the constant struggle for hegemony. The relation between history and politics, like the relation between past and present, is, therefore, an *internal* one: it is about the politics of history and the historical dimensions of politics.

Some examples may make the implications of this argument clearer. It can be argued that conceptions of the past have played a particularly central role in political life in Britain especially in popular conceptions of nationhood. The intersections between a popular conservative historiography and the dominant definitions of British (but especially English) nationalism have been especially intimate. One problem of left historiographies in Britain that retain 'the nation' or 'the national-popular' as a major affirmative category is precisely the thoroughness of this conservative appropriation of nationhood and the more structural conditions, especially the long history of Empire and of cultural separation from Europe on which it rests.[12] The dominant memory of the Second World War (in which the 'island race' was united under a great leader, Winston Churchill), and its recurrent re-evocation (they/we really can pull together when it's absolutely necessary) is a case in point.[13] Similarly, contemporary racism feeds upon a memory of a nation and of a working class that was white, chauvinistic and dominant on a world-wide scale. Indeed 'the British People' (to whom the legacy of Alfred, Drake, Wellington and Churchill is bequeathed) is, often half-consciously, a racist construction. The dominant nationalist themes, grown cosy and thoroughly naturalized by repetition, disguise or celebrate the actual history of imperial and colonial domination. They define what it means to be British, to 'belong' today. In so doing they marginalize and oppress black people in Britain whose history is precisely the reverse side of the conservative chronicles.[14]

More particular political questions are fought out on this ground too. Each major political settlement involves its own historiography, academic and popular. The dominant social-democratic and liberal-conservative post-war tendencies, for example, constructed their own history of the 1940s as a period of massive social transformation. For Labour Party 'revisionism' particularly, the 1950s were a post-revolutionary era, to which traditional left analyses of a marxist kind were quite irrelevant. The dominance of this historical account (classically expressed in the political writing of John Strachey and Anthony Crosland) marginalized socialist and marxist explanations in this period.[15] We can see similar processes at work today. Contemporary Thatcherism has constructed its own historical account that centres on the failure of the whole arc of post-war politics and the growth of a bureaucratic statism. Similarly, attempts to create a new liberal and social-democratic centre in British politics are pursued, as Dave Sutton has suggested, partly by historical means, including an extensive re-evaluation of the 'new

Liberalism' of the late nineteenth and early twentieth centuries.[16] The historiography of the Labour Party, too, has taken on new dimensions in the light of the
growth of socialist currents within it. The historical debate about the 1930s has
acquired a new urgency with the growth of unemployment and the constant
referencing (sometimes in very conservative terms) of this decade by Labour
politicians and trade union leaders. Here again one finds a significant 'revisionist'
project, now launched from a position right of centre in British politics, that
discovers that the 1930s were not really so bad after all![17] If we remind ourselves
of the centrality of history-writing and teaching for a long succession of left
intellectuals in Britain, the fact that marxism has taken characteristically historical
forms and the strength of a feminist, especially a socialist-feminist historiography,
the importance of history as a ground of political struggle seems confirmed.
Explanations of this cultural centrality of history are evasive and need a proper
comparative context: do all nation-states with long histories develop an extensive
historiographical culture? Perhaps the very early formation of the nation-state and
the long subsequent continuities, unbroken by revolution except in the seventeenth
century, is one part of an explanation. If we are looking to fill the 'absent centre'
of British national culture, history and the sense of the past might prove a very
strong candidate.[18]

The formation of a popular memory that is socialist, feminist and anti-racist
is of peculiar importance today, both for general and for particular reasons.
Generally, as Gramsci argued, a sense of history must be one element in a strong
popular socialist culture. It is one means by which an organic social group acquires
a knowledge of the larger context of its collective struggles, and becomes capable
of a wider transformative role in the society. Most important of all, perhaps, it is
the means by which we may become self-conscious about the formation of our own
common-sense beliefs, those that we appropriate from our immediate social and
cultural milieu. These beliefs have a history and are also produced in determinate
processes. The point is to recover their 'inventory', not in the manner of the
folklorist who wants to preserve quaint ways for modernity, but in order that,
their origin and tendency known, they may be *consciously* adopted, rejected or
modified.[19] In this way a popular historiography, especially a history of the
commonest forms of consciousness, is a necessary aspect of the struggle for a
better world.

More particularly, the formation of a popular socialist memory is an urgent
requirement for the 1980s in Britain. Part of the problem is that traces of a
politicized memory of this kind chart, on the whole, a post-war history of dis-
illusionment and decline. In particular, there is a sense of loss and alienation so
far as the Labour Party is concerned. But the problem is deeper than this difficulty
(which, even now, the socialist revival within and outside the Labour Party may
be lessening). For what are to be the forms of a new socialist popular memory? A
recovery of Labour's past will hardly do; nor is it helpful to chart the struggles only
of the male, skilled, white sectors of the working class who have formed the main
subjects of 'labour history' to this day. We need forms of socialist popular memory

that tell us about the situation and struggles of women and about the convergent and often antagonistic history of black people, including the black Britons of today. Socialist popular memory today has to be a *newly constructed enterprise*; no mere recovery or re-creation is going to do. Otherwise we shall find that nostalgia merely reproduces conservatism.

Resources and difficulties

Resources

The resources for such a project are great but they are also, in important ways, very disorganized, systematically disorganized that is, not merely 'lacking organization'. This has much to do with the diverse social origins of different kinds of resources and the immense difficulties of their combination. For many resources have, in the last two decades, been created through the critical work of academic practitioners – especially, in our field, historians, sociologists, philosophers and so on, dissatisfied with the limits and ideologies of their professional discipline. 'Cultural studies' has developed along these lines, but belongs to a very much wider field of radical and feminist intellectual work where much of the stress has been, till lately, upon theoretical clarification and development. But there have been important breaks outside the academic circles too, or in a tense relation to them. They have been most commonly connected to adult education (especially the WEA) or to schoolteaching or to post-1968 forms of community action. The principal aim of these tendencies has been to democratize the practices of authorship; in the case of 'history' to lessen or remove entirely the distance between 'historian' and what Ken Worpole has called 'the originating constituency'. The characteristic products of this movement have been popular autobiographies, orally based histories, histories of communities and other forms of popular writing. But it has also developed a characteristic critique of academic practice that stresses the inaccessibility even of left social history in terms both of language and price, and the absorption of authors and readers in the product (book or journal) rather than the process by which it is produced and distributed. Partly because of the stress on 'language' and the commitment to 'plain speech', oral-historical or popular-autobiographical activists are often deeply critical of the dominant forms of theory. It is this division that is, in our opinion, a major source of disorganization. The tensions between the 'activist' and 'academic' ends of radical historical tendencies are explosive to a degree that is often quite destructive. They are often qualitatively less productive than directly cross-class encounters in which working-class people directly interrogate academic radicals. Even so there is a beginning of useful connections between academic 'critics' and community activists (who are not always different persons); where patience holds long enough on either side there are the beginnings of a useful dialogue. Some of this can be traced in the pages of *History Workshop Journal*, the conference volume to History Workshop 13 and in the writings, especially, of some authors whose experience spans an 'amateur' and 'professional' experience.[20] In general History Workshop (as journal and as 'movement') has been distinguished by its attempt to hold together these two unamiable constituencies along with other groups under the banner of 'socialist' or 'people's' history. In this sense History Workshop is the nearest thing we have to an *alternative* 'historical apparatus', especially if its own recently-formed federation is placed alongside the older Federation of Worker Writers and Community Publishers.[21] In what follows we want simply to note some developments, within and outside the History Workshop movement that seem to us already to point towards the study of popular memory.

It is oral history – the evocation and recording of individual memories of the past – which seems, at first sight, nearest to the popular memory perspective, or one aspect of it. In fact the term oral history embraces a very large range of practices only tenuously connected by a 'common' methodology. What interests us most about oral history is that it is often the place where the tension between competing historical and political aims is most apparent: between professional procedures and amateur enthusiasm, between oral history as recreation (in both senses) and as politics, between canons of objectivity and an interest, precisely, in subjectivity and in cultural forms. Later, we want to illustrate these tensions by looking at the early work of the oral and social historian Paul Thompson. There are good reasons for choosing Thompson's work. He is both a socialist and a professional historian. He has done more than anyone to introduce and codify the use of oral methods in this country. With Thea Vigne, he organized the first large-scale SSRC-funded oral history research project.[22] He is also author of the first lengthy 'introduction to the use of oral sources for the historian'.[23] He is editor of *Oral History*, the main medium of communication between oral historians, and is closely associated with History Workshops.[24]

In focusing part of our argument around Thompson's work, we do not mean to imply that there are not alternative models.[25] Other adaptations of oral history are, indeed, much nearer to our own concerns. We would cite for example the critique of oral history, in its more empiricist forms, to be found in Luisa Passerini's work.[26] Her pursuit of the structuring principles of memory and of forgetfulness, her concern with representation, ideology and subconscious desires, her focus on 'subjectivity' as 'that area of symbolic activity which includes cognitive, cultural and psychological aspect',[27] and her understanding of subjectivity as a ground of political struggle, all bring her work very close to British traditions of cultural studies, especially where they have been influenced by feminism. Her critique of oral history seems to us much more radical than its sometimes guarded expression might suggest. And we agree absolutely with her criticisms of English debates for the failure to connect oral history as a *method* with more general theoretical issues.[28] The beginnings of her analysis of popular memories of Italian fascism in Turin mark a large advance on most thinking about the cultural and political (as opposed to merely 'factual') significance of oral history texts.

Although there is a beginning of a more self-reflexive mood in Britain, the strengths here lie more in a developed practice of popular history, often building on the social and labour history traditions. This is the case, for example, with the most stunning single work drawing on evoked memories of participants – Ronald Fraser's *Blood of Spain*.[29] The lessons of this book for future practice lie more in the way it is written than in any self-conscious prescriptions by the author, a long-time practitioner of oral history or 'qualitative sociology'. What we found interesting in *Blood of Spain* was the use of oral remembered material in something like the form in which it is first evoked: not as abstracted 'facts' about the past, but as story, as remembered feeling and thought, as personal account. The whole book is woven from such stories and retrospective analyses, sometimes quoted, sometimes paraphrased, clustered around the chronology of the Spanish Civil War or the make-or-break issues that were debated and literally fought out in its course. There is a sense in which Fraser's interviewees actually 'write' *Blood of Spain* by providing the author with the cellular form of the larger work: innumerable tiny personal narratives from which is woven a larger story of heroic proportions and almost infinite complication. *Blood of Spain* is history through composite autobiography, the re-creation of experience in the form of a thousand partial and warring viewpoints.[30]

But is arguable that the most significant development has been the growth of community history, popular autobiography and working-class writing more generally, where the terms of authorship have been more completely changed. In one sense, *all* these texts and projects are evidence for the forms of popular memory; they are all about the relation of past to present, whether self-consciously 'historical' or not. Some projects, however, have specifically focused on these themes: the chronologically-ordered sequence of accounts of work in Centreprise's *Working Lives*, part of the *People's Autobiography of Hackney*, is one example;[31] the work of the Durham Strong Words Collective, especially *Hello Are You Working?* (about unemployment) and *But the World Goes on the Same* (about past and present in the pit villages) is another.[32] The Durham work is especially organized around contrasts of 'then' and 'now', often viewed through inter-generational comparisons. As the editors put it:

The past exerts a powerful presence upon the lives of people in County Durham. The pit heaps have gone but they are still remembered, as is the severity of life under the old coal owners and the political battles that were fought with them. As they sit, people try to sort things out in their minds – how *were* things then? How different are they now? And why?[33]

Different from either of these projects are the politically located, culturally sensitive projects around history and memory that have developed within the contemporary Women's Movement. There is already a strong past–present dialogue at work within contemporary feminism as Chapter 8 shows. Much feminist history also draws on oral materials, sometimes using them in innovative ways.[34] The autobiographies evoked by Jean McCrindle and Sheila Rowbotham, and published as *Dutiful Daughters*, are framed by the editors' feminism and by a distinctive politics of publication. The aim is to render private feminism oppressions more public and more shared, thereby challenging dominant male definitions and the silencing of women.[35] Works like this continue a long feminist tradition of writing about past and present through autobiographical form. We might also note in this collection, in the Durham work, in Jeremy Seabrook's *What Went Wrong?* and elsewhere the beginnings of an interest in a specifically socialist popular memory. It was interesting that both *Dutiful Daughters* and *What Went Wrong?* were the subjects of 'collective reviews' at History Workshop 14.[36]

Not all relevant practices and debates belong to what would usually be thought of as 'historical' work. Indeed, there is a real danger that 'History', who is often a very tyrannous Muse, will draw the circumference of concerns much too narrowly. That is one reason why the broader categories – black, or women's or working-class 'writing' for example – are sometimes preferable. Even here, though, there are unhelpful limitations: the commitment, for example, to the *printed* word and the tendency to neglect other practices including the critique of dominant memory in the media. It is here that debates on 'popular memory' which come out of a completely different national and theoretical tradition are so important, especially debates in France around Michel Foucault's coinage of 'popular memory' as a term.[37] French debates focus on such issues as the representation of history in film and around the 'historical' policies of the French state – for example the Ministry of Culture's promotion of popular history and archival retrieval during the official Heritage Year of 1979.[38] Another important French voice for us has been Jean Chesneaux's *Pasts and Presents: What is History For?*, a militant and sometimes wildly iconoclastic attack on French academic history, including academic social history written by marxists.

One importance of the French debates is that they have directed attention to the possibility of radical cultural practice of an 'historical' kind outside the writing of history books.[39] It is important to note developments of this kind in film, community theatre, television drama and radical museum work. The film 'Song of the Shirt', the television series 'Days of Hope', the television adaptation of Vera Brittain's *Testament of Youth* and the strong historical work of radical theatre groups like 7:84, Red Ladder and The Monstrous Regiment are examples of 'history-making' often with a real popular purchase, yet usually neglected by historians. Innovations in this area are intrinsic to popular memory both as a study and a political practice. They should certainly receive as much interest and support from socialist and feminist historians as the latest historical volume, or the newest issue of 'the journal'.

Difficulties and contradictions

What, then, are some of the difficulties in realizing the potential of these resources? Oral history and popular autobiography have, after all, now been around for some time, initially generating a real excitement. Why have the political effects been fairly meagre? What are the remaining blocks and inhibitions here?

There are, perhaps, four main areas of difficulty. Very often these have to do with the tensions that exist between the academic or professional provenance of new practices and their adaptation to a popular politics. We will summarize the four areas of difficulty briefly here, then in the rest of the article consider each at more length.

The first set of difficulties is epistemological in character. They arise from the ways in which 'historical' objects of study are defined. They revolve around the empiricism of orthodox historical practice. They are not purely technical matters for philosophers to adjudicate. The historian's empiricism is a real difficulty. It blocks political progress. That is why it is so important to return to these questions once more, showing the political effects of this persistently empiricist stance.

The second set of difficulties derive initially from the form in which the 'raw material' of oral history or popular autobiography first arises: the *individual* testimony, narrative or autobiography. This poses, in a very acute form, the problem of the individual subject and his or her broader social context. In what sense is individual witness evidence for larger social changes? How can these changes themselves be understood, not as something that evades human action, but also as the product of human labour, including this individual personality? This difficulty runs through the oral history method and through the autobiographical form. It is also reflected in larger divisions of genres: history, autobiography, fiction (with its particular experiential truth). Such divisions in turn encapsulate hierarchies of significance. The oral-historical witness or the autobiographer, unless held to be a personage of exceptional public power, speaks only for herself; it is the historian who, like the Professor in *Lucky Jim*, speaks literally for 'History'. Some resolution of this persistent problem, some way of thinking the society of individuals, would be an important additional resource.

We have already touched on a third set of difficulties: the tendency to identify the object of history as 'the past'. This largely unquestioned feature of historical common sense has extremely paradoxical results when applied to oral history or popular autobiography. Indeed it shows us that this definition cannot be held without a radical depoliticization of the practice of research. What is interesting about the forms of oral-historical witness or autobiography are not just the nuggets of 'fact' about the past, but the whole way in which popular memories are constructed and reconstructed as part of a *contemporary* consciousness. In this section we will look at some of the characteristic ways in which a sense of the past has been constructed in private memories.

The fourth set of difficulties is more fundamental. It concerns not just the manifest intellectual and theoretical blockages, but the social relations which these inhibitions express. In oral history and in similar practices the epistemological problem – how historians are going to use their 'sources' – is also a problem of human relationships. The practice of research actually conforms to (and may in practice deepen) social divisions which are also relations of power and of inequality. It is cultural power that is at stake here, of course, rather than economic power or political coercion. Even so research may certainly construct a kind of economic relation (a balance of economic and cultural benefits) that is 'exploitative' in that the returns are grossly unequal ones. On the one hand there is 'the historian', who specializes in the production of explanations and interpretations and who constitutes himself as the most active, thinking part of the process. On the other hand, there is his 'source' who happens in this case to be a living human being who is positioned in the process in order to yield up information. The interviewee is certainly subject to the professional power of the interviewer who may take the initiative in seeking her out and questioning her. Of course, the problem may be solved rhetorically or at the level of personal relations: the historian may assert that he has 'sat at the feet of working-class witnesses' and has learnt all he knows in that improbable and uncomfortable posture. It is, however, *he* that produces the final account, *he* that provides the dominant interpretation, *he* that judges what is true and not true, reliable or inauthentic. It is his name that appears on the jacket of his monograph and his academic career that is furthered by its publication. It is he who receives a portion of the royalties and almost all the 'cultural capital' involved in authorship. It is his *amour propre* as 'creator' that is served here. It is his professional standing among his peers that is enhanced in the case of 'success'. In all this, at best, the first constructors of historical accounts – the 'sources' themselves – are left untouched, unchanged by the whole process except in what they have given up – the telling. They do not participate, or only indirectly, in the educational work which produces the final account. They may never get to read the book of which they were part authors, nor fully comprehend it if they do.

We have deliberately overdrawn this case, to make the point polemically. But we do not describe an untypical situation for the more professionalized types of oral-historical practice. The question is what are the wider effects of such social divisions? Are they transformable? To what extent, locally, fragilely, have they already been transformed? And what are the difficulties and opportunities involved in further transformations? Much is at stake here. We are discussing a particular form of class relation (that between working-class people and sections of the professional middle class) and how it can be transformed into a more equal alliance. It is an alliance that happens to have been a crucial one in the history of left politics and one which is certainly central to the future of socialism and feminism today.

The problem of empiricism

By empiricism we mean the epistemological doctrine that holds that the test of true knowledge lies in observation, 'experience' or the collection of 'facts'. This may be understood in a classically inductivist way, factual accumulation producing know-ledge in a more general form, or it may rest on more strictly positivist procedures: the validation or falsification of particular hypotheses by experiment or observa-tion. When professional historians describe their research procedures they almost always employ empiricist formulations. But the historian's empiricism takes particular forms, influenced by the elementary experiences of archival research.

Research is seen as a dialogue between the historian and 'his evidence'. In this, the historian takes the active part but represents also the subjectivity of inquiry or hypothesis. It is the 'source', the product of a now unchangeable past, that provides the possibility of a knowledge that is objective if it is honestly and critically interrogated. Indeed in some justifications of historical research this procedure is seen as *more* objective than those of natural science:

As a matter of fact, in a very real sense the study of history is concerned with a subject matter more objective and more independent than that of the natural sciences. He [the historian] cannot escape the first condition of his enterprise, which is that the matter he investigates has a dead reality independent of the inquiry.[40]

Although Elton's formulations are perhaps extreme and were developed in a polemic against what he saw as E. H. Carr's relativism,[41] we also think they still accurately represent the common sense of historical professionalism. It is this sense of the facticity and determinancy of the source which unites a discipline otherwise fragmented into thematic and period subspecialisms. This is even reflected in what, not entirely in jest, one might call the small talk of the historical subculture. How do you start a conversation with a historical researcher? Why by asking, of course, 'What's your period? What are your sources?' Or, 'What are you *working on*?'

Oral history as it has developed in Britain within a professional historical practice has conformed very much to this historical common sense. The tensions that have resulted are very well illustrated in the early work of Paul Thompson, especially in *The Voice of the Past* (1978) which is Thompson's authoritative introduction to oral history method and in *The Edwardians* (1975) which is the first fruit of the Essex Project, a national interview study of the family, work and community life before 1918. In what follows we will use the *Voice of the Past* in particular to suggest ways in which an historian's empiricism may limit the radical potential of oral history practice. We should stress that we are not concerned to criticize Thompson himself as author or as historian, recognizing the necessary limits of pioneering projects. But the example *is* a particularly salient one for some *typical* historian's dilemmas.

Oral history – the wrong defence?

The Voice of the Past is addressed to 'the practitioner' who emerges as a curious composite figure. On the one hand it is addressed to professional historians who are to be persuaded that the use of oral sources is 'perfectly compatible with scholarly standards'. On the other it is addressed to a popular socialist audience with which Thompson himself identifies:

I myself believe that the richest possibilities for oral history lie within the development of a more socially-conscious and democratic history.[42]

From this perspective oral history is a transformative socialist practice in terms of purpose, content and the social relations of its production:

(History) should provide a challenge, and understanding which helps towards change. And for the historian who wants to work as a socialist the task must be not simply to celebrate the working class as it is but to change its consciousness. . . . (Oral history) provides the means for a radical transformation of the social meaning of history.[43]

Like all texts *The Voice of the Past* is susceptible to different readings. Our own reading, developed in detail elsewhere, is that these two aims are inherently contradictory and are mainly resolved in a conservative direction. It is professional history, not history as a popular socialist practice, that remains in dominance in this text.

There are two main ways in which this happens. In the end both depend upon the adoption of empiricist solutions, hardened, here and there, by a reliance on borrowings from a more narrowly positivist social science, especially a quantitative sociology and an experimental psychology. The first empiricist move is to rest the case for the radicalism of oral history less upon a theoretical and political standpoint, more upon the method itself. *The Voice of the Past* does not develop political and theoretical criteria for a socialist practice; indeed its political content remains quite unspecified. In a typical empiricist move, it is the method itself which guarantees, or at least encourages, the political effects. Oral history makes available a new and untapped source in the testimony of living people.

The historian's traditional sources are administrative and other records of authority. In Chesneaux's characterization: 'Our memory is that of the power structure which functions as a gigantic recording machine'.[44] Thompson provides an interesting critique of such sources and argues that, by contrast, oral history makes possible 'a much fairer trial' – 'witnesses can now also be called from the underclasses, the unprivileged and the defeated'.[45] This may provide a challenge to the established account. But this is not all. Oral history also demands of the historian an altogether different mode of working:

Historians as field-workers, while in important ways retaining the advantages of professional knowledge, also find themselves off their desks, sharing experience on a human level.[46]

Tempted out of the record office into the living room, the historian finds that the process of research no longer involves working on inert material. We are in face to face contact with living people, asking them to talk about their experiences and share their understandings. The process of research is necessarily interpersonal and depends on human rapport. The straightforward *human* contact implicit in oral history works against any tendency to 'objectify' the material:

For the historian comes to the interview to learn: to sit at the feet of others who, because they come from a different social class, or are less educated, or older, know more about something.[47]

Oral history, by main force of the method, provides the means to deprofessionalize history: 'it gives history back to the people in their own words'.[48] According to this view, then, oral history will transform the social relations of research because it is inherently democratic. It will transform the content of history because it necessarily provides an alternative viewpoint, a viewpoint 'from below'.

These formulations are empiricist because they rest on argument about alternative content and transformative practice on the nature of the historical source itself. They neglect the relations of power that enter into the method, unconsciously because not theorized, at every point from the devising of an interview schedule to the presentation of the final explanatory account. Something more than method is needed, in other words, to render oral history into socialist practice. But this conservatism is greatly strengthened by the other coexisting discourse in Thompson's text, the discourse of 'professional standards'. We can best understand this strand by recalling some of the criticisms made of oral sources from a stance more firmly within orthodox history.

These criticisms amount to a two-pronged attack. The first points to the 'fallibility' of memory. Memory is a highly selective process which registers some processes and discards others. Stephen Koss, reviewing *The Edwardians*, supported this familiar point with an example. He once interviewed a woman about an episode in her life which, during the course of his research, he had read about in a letter. She could remember nothing about it and denied that the episode had taken place as he described it. Such comparisons, Koss argued, testify to the incompleteness of memory, its gaps and absences. But Koss raised another set of problems:

His Edwardians, after all, have lived on to become 'Georgians' and now, 'Elizabethans'. Over the years certain memories have faded or, at very least, may have been influenced by subsequent experience. How many of their childhood recollections were in fact recalled to them by their own elders? What autobiographies or novels might they have since read that would reinforce certain impressions at the expense of others? What films or TV programmes have had an impact on their consciousness? It would be interesting to know whether Lady Violet Brandon (a character quoted in *The Edwardians*) had read Vita Sackville-West's *The Edwardians*, or whether Grace Fulford watched *Upstairs Downstairs*. More generally, to what extent might the rise of the Labour Party in the post war decade have inspired retrospective perceptions of class status and conflict?[49]

These are tricky questions indeed, but there is more than one way of responding to them. Within an empiricist framework in which sources are used to re-create a given factual past, the continuous transformations of memory under the force of subsequent experience and shifting interpretative frameworks, do indeed pose major difficulties. For Koss these difficulties are adjudged insuperable; oral witness provides at best ungeneralizable, vivid, poignant insights that are usually impossible to validate. Factual reality – what did happen as opposed to what people might believe happened – can only be known if the necessary limits, biases and distortions of the source material are located and taken into account by the tried and tested methods of the craft. The problem then becomes how to apply such methods to a new type of source, to show in fact, that it is as reliable as any other.

It is this route that Thompson takes in his defence of oral history against the professional historians. He adopts two main lines of argument. He shows first, rather convincingly, that all historical sources are biased in this sense, since they share a specifically human provenance and social purpose.[50] But he also develops a whole battery of methods designed to safeguard the accuracy of oral history practice. These involve the careful comparison across sources, the demonstration, from experimental social psychology, of certain regularities in patterns of memory and forgetfulness, an excursion into the biochemistry of the brain in processes of ageing, guidance on the proper forms of questioning to avoid 'retrospective bias', and the adoption of norms of 'representativeness' drawn from the sampling methods of quantitative sociology, and the adequate (sociological) classification of the statistical population.[51]

The inadequacy of these responses has been fully discussed elsewhere.[52] We wish here to stress their costs, especially in relation to the first (more productive) strand in *The Voice of the Past*. As we will argue in more detail later, these responses serve inexorably to reproduce the very social divisions which oral history is supposed to transform. They systematically privilege the historian and researcher as bearer of the scientific canon. This can be best seen, perhaps, in the way 'scientific' require-ments must necessarily impose on the forms of the 'human contact' of the interview itself. The historian must needs approach 'respondents' with a set of standardized questions. A project of the scale of *The Edwardians* requires an hierarchical division of labour *among the researchers themselves*. The historian employs a team of interviewers to perform a particular and relatively programmed research process under his or her direction. Methodology is then largely concerned with 'interview technique': with the means by which people can be persuaded to give you the information which you require of them. The contradictions cannot but be carried through to the moment of interviewing itself:

The problem is to introduce sufficient standardisation without breaking the interview relationship through inhibiting self expression. . . . Encouraging the informant to free expression but gradually introducing a standard set of questions . . . protects the interview relationship but makes the material less strictly comparable.[53]

These are all too familiar problems within the 'parent' discipline from which the techniques are drawn. In sociology, however, this kind of confidence in a positivist methodology has long been undermined.

A second major cost of the empiricist defence of oral history is to render cultural determinations and effects quite marginal. This has two separate and related aspects. Empiricist canons tend to render invisible the 'culture' of the historians themselves. The belief in a model of neutral factual validation underestimates the practical influence of the researcher's own values, theories and preoccupations. Readings of sources, while perhaps not infinite and certainly not arbitrary, are none the less various and competing. Contrary to Paul Thompson's implicit epistemology, major shifts in interpretation or new directions in historiography are more likely to arise from changes in political or theoretical preoccupations induced by contemporary social events than from the discovery of new historical sources. If confirmation is needed here we have only to cite the origins of the new social history of the 1950s and 1960s whose specific political and theoretical genesis has been described by Bill Schwarz. The Communist Party Historians' Group induced a revolution in historiography (without the benefit of oral history). New historical questions inspired the search for new sources. In fact, Paul Thompson's history does rest upon specifically *theoretical* premises which inform, for example, the conceptions of 'society' and of 'social change' that organize the *use* of oral witness in *The Edwardians*. The difficulty of the empiricist stress on 'method' and on 'source' has always been to *disguise* the theoretical premises of accounts.

But empiricist procedures also disguise the culturally-constructed character of 'the sources' themselves. If we treat historical sources only as bearers of 'fact', we will tend, like Paul Thompson, to be interested mainly in certain orders of facticity, concerning past action and behaviour. We will tend to be less concerned with the historically and socially constructed values which are the very medium of this 'information'. At its most banal, historical practice simply ignores this cultural framing of 'fact' – all the symbolic and linguistic features through which human meaning is conveyed. Historians do sometimes treat sources as though they were a transparent medium. In the more critical professional mode frameworks of meaning are treated only negatively: they are a problem, a bias, a distortion. Critical procedure attempts to strip them away revealing the verifiable 'fact' inside. Actually, it is very doubtful if empiricism even describes this process accurately, let alone tells us what it should be. Since all historical interrogation operates, however flexibly, within its own frameworks of meaning, the reading of sources is better described as a process of *the competition of theories*. Our own explanations are judged not against the pre-given facticity of the source (except in the vulgar sense of its material existence) but against the human constructions of meaning that are found there. In the end, the fact–value distinction is itself difficult to sustain since facts only signify, only have human meaning, within explanatory frames.

The problematic of 'bias' or 'distortion' is particularly destructive of any historiography, like the discussion of 'popular memory', that wishes to give due weight to cultural determinations. Following Luisa Passerini, we would add that it is also peculiarly destructive of any open, sensitive and full use of oral history witness.

We cannot afford to lose sight of the peculiar specificity of oral material, and we have to develop conceptual approaches – and indeed insist upon that type of analysis – that can succeed in drawing out their full implications. Above all, we should not ignore that the raw material of oral history consists not just in factual statements, but is pre-eminently a representation and expression of culture, and therefore includes not only literal narrations but also the dimensions of memory, ideology and sub-conscious desires.[54]

From the point of view of the study of popular memory or of cultural phenomena generally, empiricist methods (whether the 'administered questionnaire' or the empiricist interrogation of the source) are of very little value. We might say, indeed, that *the study of popular memory can begin only where empiricist and positivist norms break down.*[55] The alternative and stronger responses to Koss-like criticisms of oral history are, then, as follows: yes, indeed, memory and its narratives *are* cultural constructions in much the way that your histories are. To illuminate both, and especially to help popular memory to a consciousness of itself, requires an understanding of specifically cultural processes and particularly of the making and remaking of memory, on both an individual and a social level. In this way your 'problem' becomes our 'resource', your insuperable difficulty our agendum, your closure our starting-point.

Alternative readings: for structure and culture

The critique of empiricism is familiar enough. There is, however, one persistent problem in breaking with this framework. The fear is that once the cultural character of accounts ('secondary' or 'primary') is admitted, there is no recourse from a relativism in which all accounts are equally socially determined, equally 'valid' and equally subject to political pragmatism. This is to vacate the ground of a serious intellectual project, certainly of a social science.

A concern with 'scientistic' criteria of validity sits well with the monopolization of certain forms of knowledge. None the less, the problem is a serious and general one. It is necessarily posed whenever knowledge is seen as a strategic political resource. In such situations the truth content of any account, and its competitive advantage over rival accounts, matter very much.

There are, however, epistemological alternatives to empiricist codes that recognize the importance of the cultural without falling into a subjectivism. Some of them have been discussed by Greg McLennan in this book under the general rubric of 'realism'.[56] These options start from the position that there is indeed an objective social world which has changed, historically, in ways that are potentially knowable, but does not reveal its secrets by simple observation or the testing of hypotheses. Conscious human activity is the main constituent of this social world even where it unconsciously reproduces existing structures and processes. The subjective dimensions of human action are as much 'social facts' as externally observed behaviour. They possess their own forms, their own dependence on non-cultural processes and their own determinacy on social outcomes. Our theories are both socially determined products and active interventions in the social world.

They are never neutrally 'scientific' or 'objective' in some socially external sense. They are, however, more or less adequate as guides to practice because they conform, more or less, to actual social processes and historical change. If this description could apply to a range of theoretical and epistemological positions, it is especially characteristic of those forms of historical materialism that take cultural and ideological processes seriously while holding to a broadly materialist frame.

Although the argument against empiricism seems abstract, it does have important implications for the way we understand what is going on in oral-historical and autobiographical accounts. It suggests, in fact, two different but mutually dependent ways of reading which we might call the 'structural' and the 'cultural'. A structural reading (which resembles in important respects the historian's 'factual' reading of a 'source') is interested in the conditions which the author of an account has appropriated subjectively – the conditions, structures, processes that have formed, sometimes consciously, sometimes not, this particular lived experience. Such a reading is based on realist premises in that it assumes that what is signified in such accounts has some real existence outside the text and is not wholly constituted in the writing itself. It departs from an empiricism, however, to the extent that the relation between events or process on the one side and the account on the other is rendered thoroughly problematical and subject to its own transformations. This allows us to see that in the search for validity in the face of professional criticism oral history practitioners have greatly underestimated the complexity of their own 'sources'. Oral or autobiographical accounts are both richer and less strictly 'reliable' than has been suggested.

The process of 'reading through' an account to its 'factual' substratum is an extremely complicated business. It depends on at least two further conditions: the presence of sources of relevant knowledge other than the account itself and, as important, the presence of some explicit and productive theory of social relations and of forms of consciousness. The first allows us to bring to view determinations that lie outside the range of vision of a given account; the second allows us an understanding of the relation between social being and the forms in which authors become conscious of their social condition and history. In this respect we agree very strongly with Jerry White in his recent exchange with Ken Worpole and Stephen Yeo. He argues for a more critical, more explanatory and more socialist local history, suggesting that this may involve confronting the way in which people understand their own oppressions.[57] For White popular autobiography is a *raw material* for the development of socialist understandings (a raw material in Marx's classic sense – already produced under given conditions, not a simple 'given'). It needs, however, a further labour. For Worpole and especially for Yeo the very act of working-class writing and expressivity is a slow, necessarily accumulative step along the road to a 'long revolution'.

The difficulty with this argument is that it uncritically assumes that working-class experience will, in the end, produce socialist or proto-socialist forms of understanding.[58] Though this differs from the more formal empiricisms so far discussed, it shares with them a lack of curiosity about specifically cultural determinations, especially those which are of an ideological kind because they hide contradictions, reproduce limitations of understanding, and divert or stultify political energies.

Part of the problem is that White *seems* to be arguing a deeply unpopular case. This is because, in these debates, *secondary* analysis, second thoughts, further research, the struggle for deeper and more explanatory accounts are always associated with the intervention of middle-class commentators, if not professional historians or sociologists. In this way two different but related questions are confused: the need for more adequate knowledge, both in political and explanatory terms and, on the other hand, the existing forms of the social division of intellectual labour. To advocate, therefore, a more analytical approach is to side with the theoretical arrogance of the intellectuals. Historical or community 'activists', in reaction to this threat of cultural domination, take a protective or even a possessive stance on behalf of what they see as really indigenous or authentic popular understandings. This circle (which we have seen repeated many times) actually reproduces the existing relations of power and knowledge. It separates theory (with its tendency to idealism) from the realistic grasp of circumstances (with its tendencies to fatalism and parochialism). It evades or forecloses the one encounter that is of vital political significance and inevitable explosiveness: between a theoretical middle-class left politics and the structures, cultures and problems of everyday working-class life. In fact there is no *necessary* connection between a more analytical or explanatory local history and a middle-class cultural domination. The aim should be to *generalize* the skills of secondary analysis and ancillary research, not to hold them at bay in deference to a more accessible wisdom.

Cultural readings

A cultural reading would focus on the ways in which the account makes sense of a structured experience or life history. This perspective rests on two main premises. The first is that all accounts, whether in answer to the researcher's questions or more autonomously produced, are highly constructed texts or performances. Certainly the model of (more or less adequate) recall or of the tapping of memories is completely inadequate here. It is plain, reading such accounts, that they are the product of thought, artifice, verbal and literary skills, always involving authorship in this sense, having (like all 'sources') an active presence in the world. These skills are not necessarily literary in form; they are very commonly verbal, bearing the signs of transcription from lively conversations and story-telling.[59] So information about the past comes completely with evaluations, explanations and theories which often constitute a principal value of the account and are intrinsic to its representations of reality. Hence the feeling not uncommonly experienced in reading secondary interpretations of first accounts: we wish the bloody historian would go away and let us listen to the account itself! It seems more interesting, more nuanced, more complex and actually more explanatory than its secondary appropriation allows. It is here that we understand the force of the Worpole/Yeo argument and the frequent feeling of revelation to the middle-class listener. Much of this (and the exaggerated inversions which it sometimes produces) comes from the force of dominant ideologies which daily imply that working people have very imperfect understandings – just as it was once argued they had 'no culture'.

The second premise of a cultural reading is, however, that the cultural features of accounts are not simply the product of individual authorship; they draw on general cultural repertoires, features of language and codes of expression which help to determine what may be said, how and to what effect. In charting such repertoires, we might start, for example, from the repeated observation of the centrality of story-telling to working-class accounts of social reality. More or less extended narratives about past events, often of an intimate and always of a personal kind, are certainly one elementary form of popular memory and the commonest way in which past and present are compared and evaluated. These stories are made to carry great significance and may be deliberately told (in the face of probings) in place of more generalized conclusions. Stories come also with intricate variations of form: on the one side tightly sewn up and 'closed', punctuated with a moral at the end, a particular, confident male form; on the other, more open narratives, completed rather by a laugh, often in self-depreciation, dealing with some embarrassing or difficult past happening; then again stories of a largely apochryphal status, more in the form of the proverb, often encapsulating some element of collective memory.[60] A developed cultural reading would have to understand such forms and something of their provenance and of their effects (which we would not suppose to be inherently 'biased' or 'ideological').

It would be in the *relation* of these two readings – the structural and the cultural – that the most important understandings might be reached. Very often this will be a matter of convergence or the confirmation of existing theories. From a marxist-feminist perspective for instance, we would expect to find that life histories accord a special place to those events that are critical for the social existence of a worker or a woman/housewife/mother. And indeed autobiographical accounts do give an important organizing role to salient experiences of this kind: the first entry into labour in the shape of stories about 'my first job', the entry into the employer's household as a critical moment in domestic service, the comparison among women of 'my own' childhood and the way 'I wish to bring my own children up', the moments of courtship and marriage and of major life transitions in general. In these cases 'salient experience' is, in Edward Thompson's phrase, genuinely 'a junction concept':[61] it highlights the historial and social position of the author; it is a structural hinge or condition around which, in historical reality, a life has so far been lived. But it also organizes accounts culturally, appearing there with a particular force and emphasis, as something around which many significant stories are told.

This pattern of convergence is, however, by no means invariable and the two readings may actually be productive of surprises that force the modification or extension of understandings. On the one hand, for example, obvious structural or historical features (known from other sources or predicted theoretically) may not show up at all in accounts. On the other hand there may be surprising and initially inexplicable preoccupations. Most interesting here are Passerini's findings

on the memories of working-class militants in Turin during the struggles of the
fascist period:

Oral sources refuse to answer certain kinds of questions; seemingly loquacious, they
finally prove to be reticent and enigmatic, and like the sphinx they force us to
reformulate problems and challenge our current habits of thought. . . . Indeed,
I received what to my ears were either irrelevant or inconsistent answers.
'Irrelevant' answers were mainly of two sorts; silences and jokes.[62]

Silences were two kinds. Sometimes whole life stories were told 'without any
reference to fascism, except for casual ones'. Sometimes, especially among the
politically conscious, there was simply 'a striking chronological gap' between
Mussolini's rise to power and the Second World War. Later on, in second, more
probing interviews, similar patterns were repeated. Passerini concludes that in an
important sense the period between 1922–5 and 1941–3 has been erased from
memory: 'this self-censorship is evidence of a scar, a violent annihilation of many
years in human lives, a profound wound in daily experience'.[63]

Historically or structurally significant events or processes do not necessarily
show up, then, in retrospective reconstructions. Our two readings, put together,
will often refer us to cases of these kinds: to silences, suppressions, amnesias and
taboos. These cases, in turn, force us to 'think again' about structural significance,
modifying secondary theories. These surprises may, however, happen in a
different way: a particular story or episode may carry more significance for its
author than its structural or historical salience may, at first sight, warrant. There
are several possibilities here. We may be experiencing a specifically cultural or
subjective process by which stories about one domain of social life stand in for
other experiences that are too problematic, difficult, embarrassing or traumatic
to be spoken of in any other way. Sexual themes seem often to be handled in this
way, either as vehicles for especially condensed meanings, or as an emotional charge
that electrifies, so to speak, the telling of a tale about something else. What is
interesting about this kind of surprise is that it indexes experiences and conditions
that are not adequately understood within our own dominant frame of reference.[64]
Certain rather limited and mechanical forms of marxism or socialism, for instance,
but also many kinds of social-structural sociology, have been notoriously incapable
of handling the dimensions of subjectivity in general and of gender and sexuality
in particular. These dimensions are often present even in accounts where formal
closure has not occurred. In cases such as these, where explanatory theories remain
open and flexible, a really dialectical relation of a socialist feminist kind may be
established between first accounts and a more explanatory secondary discussion of
them.

In conclusion of this part of the essay it is worth reasserting two key themes.
First, the process of working up first thoughts about our social existence and our
history and our own ways of understanding the world is part of the central dynamic
of 'making socialists'. This is not a process by which, whatever our class and gender

position, we simply express or confirm our *existing* view of the world. This holds both for 'common sense' and for 'theory'. Since everyone possesses a social consciousness and is, in that sense, 'a philosopher', there is no *necessary* feature of this situation that privileges the 'intellectual' (in its usual narrow meaning). The problem is that intellectual skills and functions *are* subject to a social division in our society: there *are* processes of cultural dispossession and monopoly. The characteristic result is to rob theory of the elements of practical realism, especially in relation to the social conditions of the great majority of people, but also to withhold from common sense the skills and perspectives that might enable it to become more wide-ranging and critical. To fight to preserve the authenticity of common sense against both dominant discourses and radical intellectual alternatives is, in this situation, a kind of conservatism. The solution must lie in the establishment of *connections* between socialist and feminist theory and popular movements which work at and attempt to transform the intellectual divisions of labour in new, more democratic educational forms, forms of learning, that is, for *all* those involved. We will look later in this article at attempts to achieve such transformations in the broad areas of popular historical production.

The second point recapitulates the argument about empiricism, realism and an understanding of the cultural character of accounts. Commitment to a more culturally sensitive understanding, behind which lies the belief in the political significance of the cultural, is *not* incompatible with a realist concern for historical and structural conditions. On the contrary these two forms of understanding are complementary. A concern with symbolic and cultural forms is *part of* historical and contemporary analysis, not just a problem of historical 'bias' in source material. As Roland Barthes, a key figure for the development of the critical analysis of cultural forms, has put it:

Less terrorised by the spectre of formalism, historical criticism might have been less sterile; it would have understood that the specific study of forms does not in any way contradict the necessary principles of totality and History. On the contrary: the more a system is specifically defined in its forms, the more amenable it is to historical criticism. To parody a well-known saying, I shall say that a little formalism turns one away from History, but that a lot brings one back to it.[65]

Historical process and autobiographical form

Oral history and popular autobiography are forms which systematically individualize; yet an historically-informed political knowledge requires a much broader sense of social context. How can autobiographical materials be the source of, or contribute to, a more structural account of past and present? Like the problem of the empiricist use of sources, the difficulty can be found in a representative form in Paul Thompson's work, where it appears, however, as a technical or methodological dilemma to do with the way of presenting oral-historical material.

Thompson suggests three different ways of presenting oral-historical accounts: 'the single life-story narrative', especially important for informants with 'a rich memory'; the collection of life histories, grouped, perhaps, around common themes, perhaps the better way of presenting most 'typical life-history material'; 'cross-analysis' in which oral material is used as a 'quarry from which to construct an argument'.[66] The first two of these, which may be grouped together as effectively one mode, preserve most of the original material intact. The second mode is governed by the logic of the historian's own argument, and involves a briefer, less contextualized, more promiscuous use of quotation.

On the whole Thompson prefers the second mode of analysis since 'argument and cross-analysis are clearly essential for any systematic development of history'. The notion that oral history material 'speaks for itself' is 'blind empiricism'.[67] Yet he is distinctly uneasy about this preference. He has qualms on two main grounds. First, he realizes that the use of materials as a 'quarry' and a form of analysis that gives primacy to the historian's own explanations is incompatible with part of his political aim: giving 'history back to the people in their own words'. Second, he doubts whether 'analysis' uses the oral material to the full advantage. There is something there that excites him – a quality frequently identified as 'richness' – which is often absent from other types of source.

One of the deepest lessons of oral history is the uniqueness, as well as representativeness, of every life-story. There are some so rare and vivid that they demand recording, whatever the plan.[68]

The oral evidence can be evaluated, counted, compared and cited along with the other material . . . But in some ways it is a different kind of experience. As you write, you are aware of the people with whom you talked; you hesitate to give meanings to their words which they would wish to reject.[69]

In *The Edwardians* Thompson uses a combination of the two methods of life history and cross-analysis. More correctly, perhaps, the two methods coexist, rather unhappily, in different parts of the same text. Part I of *The Edwardians* employs cross-analysis to 'establish the most important dimensions of social change in the early twentieth century'.[70] In Part III Thompson analyses 'the main reasons for social change'.[71] But in Part II he marshals 'twelve accounts of childhood in real families' 'to give a place, within this evaluation of general social change, to the contribution and experience of ordinary individuals'.[72]

Those parts of *The Edwardians* that are based on cross-analysis none the less use direct quotation a great deal. Passages are selected for quotation according to their contribution to the argument and this necessarily involves removing them from their original context and re-presenting them with a new meaning. It is worth taking one example of Thompson's characteristic method here: the announcement of some general theme (derived from his working through of oral and other sources) followed by a quotation from oral sources, in illustration.

Nevertheless there were many teenagers who frequently had to accept being disciplined by informal violence from adults: from the police, from employers, from schoolteachers, from parents, sometimes in bewildering succession. One Essex youth worked before starting school as the kitchen boy at a farm, cleaning boots among his tasks. The farmer's son would give him a cigarette if he told him when the farmer had his best boots cleaned, for 'he knew he'd gone to London, you see, on business, which enabled him to have the day off going on the spree'. The unfortunate kitchen boy one morning 'was smoking in the woodshed, chopping sticks, when the farmer caught me and picked up a twig and gave me – not a thrashing because I just bolted, but he caught me three times. . . . [I came home, crying, to father, who said] "What did he hit you for?" I said, "Because I was smoking" . . . so he gave me a clip with his hand . . . a backhander right across me cheek. And off I went to school crying. By that time, you see, it had gone ten . . . and that's where the headmaster was strict . . . so we got one on each hand, then, the cane on each hand'.

Farmers were perhaps the employers most likely to strike a boy whom they employed.[73]

There are two main points to make about this passage. First, we are given no contextual information about 'the youth', nor do we discover what significance he attributed to his story, or why it remained in his memory. There is no commentary on the *way* in which the story was told: in cold print, it has a faintly humorous structure and tone, rather like the typical chapter of physical accidents in silent film comedy; but was such a pattern of punishment regarded as 'normal' in that period? Did the three punishments rank as equally legitimate? Attention to the specificity of this anecdote (and further questions about it) could elicit important indications of the interrelation between the three spheres of power – family, school and work – and the three kinds of authority – employer's, father's and schoolteacher's – to which the young man was subjected. But Thompson offers no analysis either of the content of this quotation nor of its cultural forms, passing on immediately to his next generalization.

So, second, the quotation adds very little to the overall argument. As evidence it has *already* contributed to the 'factuality' of the preceding statement, in its form as an imprecise average (*'many* teenagers *frequently* had to accept'). It now functions only as an illustration. As such, we might ask, what is its value? Surely it has been included because it is an interesting story in itself: it injects 'life', 'richness' into the otherwise conventional account. In this way, argument and quotation are used to support each other, but at the expense of locking away the meanings of the quotation itself and the further structural relations that lie behind it.

What of the second form of the use of oral history material in *The Edwardians*? Here the life histories (or rather the succession of answers to the interviewer's questions)[74] are presented in 'the untidy reality upon which, though too many scholastics would wish it forgotten, both theoretical sociology and historical myth rest'.[75] They are presented not as integral to the analysis of social change or social structure but as a kind of unanalysable extra. Thompson speaks of the life histories as indeed 'an antidote to the simplifications with which I have had to outline the dimensions of social structure'.[76] Despite being produced under very definite conditions, the accounts are treated as a rather precious resource. In the end, there is nothing for it but simply to present them 'raw', to allow them to 'speak for themselves'.

These problems of method index many of the weaknesses of orthodox oral history, including some we have already discussed. That sense of richness betrays the failure to deal with cultural forms, with memory as an active restructuring process, with the forms of intersubjective transaction that produced the 'evidence' in the first place, and with the large question of the relation between the historically produced subjectivity of this particular 'witness', then and now. The richness remains elusive because it cannot become a specific object of knowledge within Thompson's *own* epistemological and theoretical framework. Similarly there is a kind of guilty pull between the desire to present popular memory directly (with its own unacknowledged interpretative framing) and the desire not to abandon the overarching interpretative responsibility of 'the historian'. What especially concerns us here, however, is the failure to secure a really organic and internal relation between large historical categories like 'social change' and 'social structure' and the individual stories and interviews. What is missing in Thompson's method, or more correctly in his theory, is some way of bridging the large-scale social processes which are the usual objects of historical accounts and the small-scale 'private' narratives which are the very stuff of personal memories.

The individual and social relations

We need to ask what it is about autobiographies or life histories that makes them not merely 'rich', but significant and 'representative' in some stronger and more definite sense. Part of the answer has already been given: once read in a non-empiricist way, these forms may make available elements of lived culture and of subjectivity not easily reached otherwise. But we need to go further than this along lines indicated by our insistence on 'structural' readings. Such accounts are representative and significant for a larger account not because they express a general abstract humanity, or a particular unique subjectivity, but because they are the product of *social individuals*. Their authors speak out of particular positions in the complex of social relations characteristic of particular societies at particular historical times. These accounts appropriate and make a sense of salient features of social relations within which their authors have been implicated and within which they have acted and struggled. Oral historians, like contemporary ethnographers, require a theory of these social relations – of structure in that sense – to see the representative elements of individual life histories as *part of* a more general history: a history, for example, of the formation or recomposition of a class, or of a break or reinforcement in the patriarchal relations between men and women. They require, moreover, some parallel understanding of the same or similar relations of force in contemporary society, the society in which a collective memory of these processes

is, from particular social standpoints, to be formed. Without some such understanding, we can only judge of the 'representativeness' of accounts according to
some passive, descriptive or quantitative criteria (so many working-class 'witnesses';
so many women) or fall back on unexamined quasi-literary criteria, similar to those
used in the evaluation of 'great' literature.

This is one of the reasons why a meeting point between debates in marxist
theory and the practice of oral history is so important. Marxism has always contained within it both a stress upon human individuality as a socially produced
phenomenon *and* a recognition that our constitution within social relations is an
active process of which we may become conscious and over which we may engage
in struggles of a collective kind. Particular marxisms, it is true, have stressed one
or other side of Marx's double vision, but marxist debate today is beginning to
recover both sides of these insights. This is not the place for a long theoretical
detour, but we would point to the debate between 'structuralist' currents in
contemporary marxism (Althusser's stress for example on the determinacy of
social relations) and the broadly 'humanist' stress on agency and struggle (Edward
Thompson's *Poverty of Theory* or Victor Seidler's critique of Althusser in the
collection *One-Dimensional Marxism*).[77] More synthesizing enterprises are to be
found in Perry Anderson's discussion of 'agency' in *Arguments within English
Marxism* and, very importantly for our themes, Raymond Williams's successive
treatments of the problem of society, the social individual and fictional and
autobiographical ways of writing from his earliest work to *Politics and Letters*.[78]
In the contemporary debate about 'realism', the work of Bhaskar and Wal
Suchting's translation and reading of Marx's *Theses on Feuerbach* are especially
important.[79] But much of what we take from these debates is most fully expressed
in Gramsci's attempt to redefine the old philosophical question 'What is Man?'
in the light of a marxist understanding of social relations.

In his notes on the study of philosophy,[80] Gramsci argues against the tendency
of Catholic social theory to locate the sources of evil in 'the individual man
himself'. This is to treat human beings as essentially 'spiritual', as uniquely individual, and also as already 'defined and limited', not capable, that is, of further
development. As Gramsci says, such a view of human beings is not limited to a
religious framework: it has been characteristic, perhaps, of 'all hitherto existing
philosophies'. It certainly remains an important mainstream philosophical legacy
fifty years after Gramsci was writing. It remains common, for example, in both
historical and literary studies: in the portrayal of leading national politicians
or great writers as uniquely, individually, creative persons. There is more than a
hint of this perspective in the notion of individual oral witness as irreducible and
'unique'.

It is on this point, Gramsci argues, that 'it is necessary to reform the concept
of man'. Consciousness of one's individuality is important – it is to become very
important in Gramsci's own argument – but it is not the only element to be taken
into account. We have also to consider the relations between human beings and
'the natural world', and their relations to each other. But the relationship between
human beings and nature is not a simple one: it is above all 'active'. Human beings

don't just 'dwell' in the natural world – they are related to it actively by work and technique. Similarly, our relations to each other are not those of adjacent individual persons but involve membership of socially-organized groups, of a more or less complex kind. One might conceive of 'Man' then as 'a series of active relationships'.

Relations of this kind, however, must not be seen as mechanical or deterministic: they involve both human subjectivity and the possibility of change:

Further: these relations are not mechanical. They are active and conscious. They correspond to the greater or lesser degree of understanding that each man has of them. So one could say that each of us changes himself, modifies himself to the extent that he changes and modifies the complex relations of which he is the hub.

Of course, social relations are of different kinds: they have varying degrees of determinacy and are more or less easily changed. Yet to be conscious of them, in the sense of knowing how they might be modified, is already to modify them. This is even the case with relations that are found to be 'necessary' (for example the necessity to earn a living from nature) which take on a new light when viewed in this way. All this suggests, indeed, a change in the way we define 'philosophy'. Knowledge really *is* power:

In this sense the real philosopher is, and cannot be other than, the politician, the active man who modifies the environment, understanding by environment the *ensemble* of relations which each of us enters to take part in.

Similarly, the old philosophical project of 'know yourself' takes on a new light, both as a project for all (everyone as a 'philosopher') and as a more than contemplative practice:

If one's individuality is the *ensemble* of these relations, to create one's personality means to modify the *ensemble* of these relations.

But this form of understanding, which remains static, is not enough. We have to understand 'Man' not just as a social and natural being, but as an historical one too:

It is not enough to know the *ensemble* of relations as they exist at any given time as a given system. They must be known genetically, in the movement of their formation. For each individual is the synthesis not only of existing relations, but of the history of these relations. He is a precis of all the past.

It is because it allows us to grasp 'history' in this sense that the approach to 'Man' through social relations is greatly to be preferred:

That 'human nature' is the 'complex of social relations' is the most satisfactory answer, because it includes the idea of becoming (man 'becomes', he changes continuously with the changing of social relations) and because it denies 'man in general'.

Indeed, if it is useful to talk about 'man in general' at all, we must refer the inquiry to history – ' "human nature" cannot be located in any particular man but in the entire history of the human species'.[81]

Gramsci's discussion of 'What is Man?' recovers and restates arguments found in the origins of marxism, especially in the tussles between Feuerbachian humanism and the emerging perspectives of historical materialism. It recapitulates and develops, especially, *The Theses on Feuerbach*. It could be criticized on several grounds: the failure to develop a thesis about the 'natural' character of human beings (the way they do not only *work on nature* but are also *a part of it*);[82] the incompleteness of a theory of individual subjectivity. But the most important criticism, for today, is Gramsci's neglect of social relations other than those of class, and in particular his neglect of the historical construction of gender relations, a neglect indexed by his acceptance of the philosophical figure of 'Man' to indicate the whole human race.

In fact, modern feminism has made peculiarly important contributions here, filling out, developing, and critiquing existing marxist conceptions. The contribution has been especially important in the context of our own argument because it has centrally concerned the relation between individual experience and social relations.

Feminist theory has worked from the practical implications of women's politics, especially from the forms of 'the consciousness-raising' group.[83] The experiences of individual women, often 'publicly' spoken about for the first time, and in the form of individual witness, were seen as evidence for a general social condition. Women's sense of oppression was not the product of individual problems or personal inadequacies: it sprang from systematic causes, a general social condition shared by women as a whole. This general social condition, even where given the same name – 'patriarchy' – was subsequently defined in many different ways, sometimes as existing, rather weakly, in archaic or residual attitudes. In stronger versions of the theory of patriarchy, greatly to be preferred in our view, the stress is upon patriarchal *social relations*, a particular organization of relationships between men and women in the process of which gender differences are also produced and defined. Relations of gender, in their historically specific forms, have resembled relations of class in that they have conferred radically unequal chances for the development and satisfaction of human needs. They have, therefore, necessarily involved struggle, wherever women have become conscious of the forms of male control and the unequal exchanges involved in most gender-based transactions – from romantic love and the marriage contract to the production and bringing up of fresh human beings.

Feminism insists, then, that 'the ensemble of social relations' be thought of as still more complex. Moreover, because of the personal character of women's oppressions in the forms in which they are first experienced, many of the major feminist texts have been quite unlike the main productions of marxist theory. They have taken the form of stories and novels and autobiographical writing, forms of writing that have also managed to capture, however, a sense of representative experience, true for women in a particular historical phase.

Vera Brittain's *Testament of Youth* seems to us to be a superb example of this kind.[84] It centres upon the experience of Vera herself, yet it tells us more than most works of 'history' about the experiences of the First World War more generally, and even about the determinations upon events. If such an assessment were agreed, it would be worth considering what it is that makes this book so successful.

Our own answers relate back to the more general arguments about individuals and social relations. Part of the strength of *Testament of Youth* lies in its author's location within key sets of social relations, especially, in this case, relations of gender. This is 'lived' in her own personal relationships, especially with her brother, her lover and their mutual male friends in the years before the War. The War impacts on these relationships in a way that is not merely representative of the position of women at this time, but has a kind of super-representative character. Vera's own life is massively, crushingly over-determined by the European holocaust; she loses a much-loved brother, the man whom she hopes to marry, and her other male friends. Her own active response to the threat and reality of this is to become involved in the War herself, as directly as she possibly can. So she becomes a nurse in the battlefields of Europe, and further experiences the contrast between the idealistic hopes of young men going to the War and the physical and mental effects of their mutilation. This in turn removes her both from the certainties of her own middle-class family and from the naivety of most of her later fellow-students at Oxford. In a very important sense, Vera personifies the woman's experience of the First World War, something that she herself began to realize as she wrote *Testament of Youth* over twenty years after the War had ended. She wanted to show what the whole period meant to 'the men and women of my generation'. She wanted 'to write history in terms of personal life'. After various experimentations with form, including a novel and the reproduction of her war diary, she opted for autobiography:

There was only one possible course left – to tell my own fairly typical story as truthfully as I could against the larger background, and take the risk of offending all those who believe that a personal story should be kept private, however great its public significance and however wide its general application. In no other fashion, it seemed, could I carry out my endeavour to put the life of an ordinary individual into its niche in contemporary history, and thus illustrate the influence of world-wide events and movements upon the personal destinies of men and women.[85]

We cannot explain the force of *Testament of Youth*, however, simply in terms of 'structure' and a strategic personal location in social relations in their particular historical form. Vera also developed a particularly heightened consciousness of herself, her intimate relationships and of a wider catastrophic context. Moreover this was a developed and critical consciousness, unrelentingly suspicious of easy explanations, comforting resolutions and surface appearances. It expressed itself typically in a kind of measured irony, turned especially against patriotic and religious dogmas, and, in effect, the whole tissue of pre-war nationalistic pieties. It was also a political consciousness: feminist and pacifist in its active orientations. In many ways, then, *Testament of Youth* is one powerful model for the kind of practice we have been discussing in this essay – a socialist and feminist popular memory.

The mature properties of 'emotion remembered in tranquillity' have not been my object, which, at least in part, is to challenge that too easy, too comfortable relapse into forgetfulness which is responsible for history's most grievous repetitions.[86]

It is important to add that our own advocacy has nothing in common with some other arguments in favour of autobiographies of 'representative individuals'. It has nothing in common, for example, with elitist versions of this argument that ascribe an importance in principle to a biography when it concerns a personage of great formal power or influence. An interesting case to set beside Vera Brittain's account of the First World War is Sir Winston Churchill's extended autobiographical account of the Second World War.[87] Here, a sense of personal significance and 'historic role' is asserted in almost megalomaniac proportions, but the accounts that follow, though certainly personally revealing, are rarely self-consciously so, and remain locked up within an upper-class military and high-political culture and a highly mythical Conservative version of national character and history.[88] 'Representative-ness' in our sense, is *more* likely to be found in popular autobiographical forms where dominant social relations are viewed from the typical subject position: that of daily oppressions and of the struggle against them. Representativeness, moreover, is a feature of social positions that are understood to be *shared* and *collective*: the main feature of much autobiographical writing is to *distinguish* the author from the people and the determinations that surround him. Such accounts belong not to the construction of 'popular memory', but to the reproduc-tion and dissemination of 'dominant memory', of which the Churchillian myth is indeed a salient and persistent modern feature.

Our argument does have implications, however, for a practice of popular memory within which oral history or popular autobiography will have a central place. There are, perhaps, two main implications: that the choice of subject (individual, or community, or historical period) will matter very much; and that our method must give maximum opportunities for self-conscious political reflection upon first accounts.

It does matter what subjects are chosen or what subjects choose themselves. And And once they have emerged, such subjects have to be understood critically in relation to their representativeness. Some subjects will have a massive general salience; all remain important 'in themselves' but may speak less directly to widespread social experiences. They may be severely limited, indeed, by the social *milieu* from which they arise. Brittain's *Testament*, for example, is, in important ways, bounded by the middle-class character of her own social position, and her subsequent profession as writer and agitator. But accounts may be community-bounded too, locked up in the specificities of a particular area, where, for example, class relations take a particular, perhaps more archaic, form. In the same way, certain communities may have a peculiar significance, representing new social forms, new transformations, the sudden destruction of a whole way of life and the emergence of a new. It is important not to press this argument too far, too mechanically. In particular we must not assume that we have a perfect knowledge of what is typical before the accounts themselves emerge. But relevant issues *are* raised: why, for instance, are most 'community-based' studies focused on areas with a traditional industrial infrastructure – mining valleys or villages, or older working-class urban neighbourhoods? Why not the newer housing estates, or the inter-war or post-war settlements, many like the steel-town Corby, now suffering equally dramatic transformations? Again, the assumption that history anyway is about the past encourages complicity with a certain conservative nostalgia. The ideal cases may well be those not with the greatest or longest continuities but those with the most dramatic contemporary transformations.

The implications for method follow from the recognition that social location is no guarantee of politically useful knowledge. If our arguments about 'consciousness' are exact, the method needs to maximize opportunities for second thoughts, for further analysis of primary results and first impressions, for retheorizing and 'making strange' familiar appearances. Some of us rebel against this, because the ugly figure of the 'historian' (or 'sociologist') once more intrudes, telling us what our explanations *should* be, fitting *our* 'facts' to *his* theories, presenting our experience back to us, sometimes in unrecognizable forms. But secondary analysis *need* not take this form, or be constrained within the existing social divisions of intellectual labour. It *could* be a more internal process: a working up of first accounts by authors themselves, in the light of further research and thinking. Again we need to detach the *general* question (the necessity of study for overcoming ideological ways of thinking) from the particular social and educational forms in which this problem currently appears. Our point is that it is not enough that the production of first accounts be respected in the sense of being left untouched. Really to 'respect' them is to take them as the basis for larger understandings, for the progressive deepening of knowledge and for active political involvement.

Presents and pasts

In this section we want to draw out some implications of the view that the proper object of history is not the past but the past–present relationship. So obvious a point would not be worth stressing had not historians striven so strenuously to deny it. Our argument, here, parallels the case against empiricism: just as history-writing is necessarily a theoretical and political activity, so it is also a practice in and for the present. Theory, politics and contemporaneity are basic conditions of the practice, present even when denied. To treat organizing assumptions and political implications as 'bias' or as 'ideology' (in the everyday sense) is to expect professional integrity or technical methodology to transform the very conditions of knowing.

Again oral history is an especially useful ground on which to think through these problems. In accounts of oral-historical methodology, the past–present relation appears mainly as a problem – the unreliability of memory. There is a model of memory implicitly at work here and it is a particularly passive one. Memory is the sedimented form of past events, leaving traces that may be unearthed by appropriate questioning. It is a completed process, representative of the past which is itself dead and gone and therefore stable and objective. Once laid down in this way, memories may certainly cease to be available, but this, too, is a mainly technical problem. In *The Voice of the Past*, for example, Paul Thompson has recourse to the laboratory experiments of social psychologists and to knowledge about the biochemistry of the brain in old age. His strategy, again a conservative one, is to cite psychologists' findings as evidence for the relative reliability and constancy of memory over longer periods of time.[89]

The most conspicuous absence in such accounts is the present conjuncture in which oral witness is actually recorded. The present is absent both as a source of determinations on and meanings of the stories that are told and as the location of current responsibilities and needs. Thompson does have a short discussion of the problem of 'retrospective bias', the perils of which he tends, however, to minimize.[90] Yet there remains a point to Koss's objection that the 'Edwardians' are 'Elizabethans' too. Their stories are necessarily influenced by present events and by the restructuring of what it is possible to think and say. Oral history testimonies do not form a simple record, more or less accurate, of past events; they are complex cultural products. They involve interrelations, whose nature is not at all understood, between private memories and public representations, between past experiences and present situations. Figure 3, though not intended as a developed alternative to the notion of memory as record, indicates something of this complexity.

Imagine yourself my oral history witness. The tape recorder has been turned off and since you are co-operative to a fault (and because I am writing this and can make you do anything I want) we start to consider the fuller history that lies behind what you have been saying. We are seated in the right-hand room on the first floor of Figure 3 (which has, you see, particularly strong walls so that you couldn't get out anyway). I insist you start by considering your present social position and experiences, which I am sure have influenced your story. You are, besides, an avid reader of the *Daily Mail* and a supporter of Mrs Thatcher; you have been sure, for some time, that the country has suffered a moral decline. I insist we take that into account too. 'But', you say, 'all that can't change the reality of what happened to me then.' 'That's true', I reply, 'but it will frame, shape, evoke or even obliterate your memory of it. Anyway, your reality was a

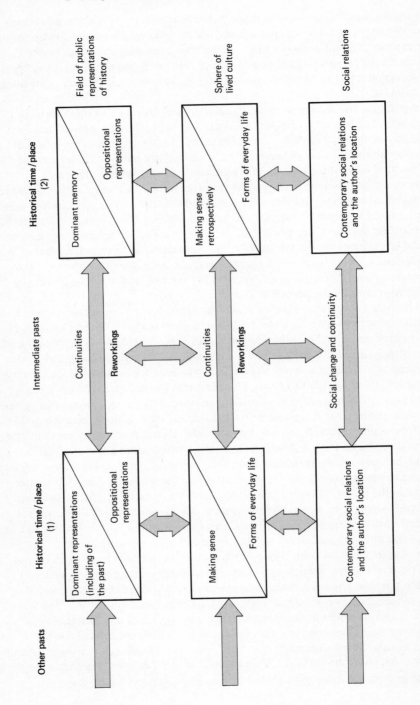

Figure 3 *Popular memory as social process*

complicated thing in itself. It too was part material relation, part cultural form. And since then you have had many experiences, many dramatic changes of heart, even engaged in guilty self-criticism. Some things you would rather forget and have in fact forgotten. Other things now acquire an importance which they didn't have before. (I noted how your moment of adolescent socialism, for example, was rather skated over.)' 'I see what you mean', you say, apparently capitulating, 'but haven't you forgotten the most important thing of all? It was *your* questions to which I was replying; my answers are also produced by *your* power.'

Oral history testimony, in other words, is profoundly influenced by discourses and experiences in the present. That is the standpoint from which oral accounts (and formal histories) are constructed. Memory is therefore itself a profoundly complicated construction and a very active process. In memory past events, in their own complexity, are worked and reworked. Of course, there are also continuities and people do relive *certain* past events imaginarily, often with a peculiar vividness. This may be especially the case for those (e.g. the elderly) who have been forced into a marginal position in the economic, cultural and social life of a society, and, fearful of absolute oblivion, have little to lose but their memories. But, in addition, as a further set of mediations, the intervention of the historian or sociologist is of crucial significance, as a catalyst for a whole process of structured remembrance.

There is, besides, something, absolutely problematic, politically, in treating oral history witnesses as 'sources'. It is to treat them as a form of walking, talking documentation, the person as archive. Is there a flat contradiction here between oral history as professional research and oral history as politics? We think there is, insisting, however, that we should not equate 'professional' with 'intellectual', still less with explanatory or analytic as such. But the approach of a professional historian to a person-source does involve an entirely different relationship than that which ought to characterize political-intellectual encounters. The historian's attitude must needs be preservative, rather like a museum curator's. The impulse is 'to get this on tape'. The attitude of mind is non-interventionist (unavailingly however). The rich mental material must not be disturbed too much: the point is to record it. Political engagements, by contrast, where they are not self-seeking, narrowly partisan or actually manipulative, must needs involve an active mutual incitement to *rethink* experiences and understandings, to struggle to see the world differently, to go beyond existing social relations, to see that, under other arrangements, personal problems might become collective solutions. Such an active 'educative' process will necessarily affect memory, even in its private forms. Older constructions may be preserved, but they will be overlaid by newer thinking. Sometimes we will wish to disavow whole passages in our own past both in terms of how we have acted and how we have understood our actions. The past is understood, in this practical framework, not as a given 'thing' which we must preserve, but as a force constantly resonating in the present, producing new layers of sound and meaning.

There are two practical implications of this argument, the one broad, the other more specific. Our argument about past and present points to the *unity* of history and politics, to historical work as an *aspect* of politics. If this seems paradoxical, even 'dangerous', it is often because we conceive of 'politics' too narrowly, as dealing only with 'great public issues' in ways familiarized in existing political routines. God forbid that history should be linked to 'politics' only in that sense! Yet in a larger political project – that of debating and struggling over the whole social future – 'memory' is a vital resource, helping us to understand the nature, historicity and changeability of current conditions.

More specifically, socialists and feminists need to develop a politics of later life. It is clear that the contribution of older people to a socialist and feminist popular memory *involves* such a political strategy. Our existing understandings are insignificant here, not least because 'age' seems yet another kind of relation to be compared with class, gender or race. But such a politics should certainly start from a proper analysis of the experience of older people today – the specific forms of oppression and of cultural marginality – and from the assumption, very different from official or conventional wisdoms, that their memories, sometimes actively rethought, may contribute to a politics of today in which they are, themselves, active participants.

Some forms of popular memory

Ideally, at this point in the argument, it would be useful to take some examples of popular memories and try to see the various processes we have tried to describe actually at work there. Aside from reservations about doing this outside a more situated political project, it would really require a larger separate study. We do, however, want to look more briefly at some of the *typical* forms in which memories are expressed in published oral-historical accounts and in popular autobiography. We will be trying to generalize over a wide range of material here, at the risk of large simplifications.

We have already noted some of the recurrent features of these accounts: the different forms of artifice that have gone to make them, from literary to verbal skills; the omnipresence of the story-telling form; the necessary constitutive influence of the past–present relation as the basic retrospective condition. In addition it seems important to stress the intensely 'personal' character of most of the accounts we have read and their distance, therefore, from the common forms of public historiography, most academic history, and especially from histories of a 'structural' or non-narrative kind.

By 'personal' in this context we mean two rather different things. First, and most generally, we refer to the 'humanism' of the texts, using this term quite descriptively, and neither pejoratively nor in a simple, morally-affirmative way. What marxism or an explanatory social history will wish to treat as social relations or as social classes, these accounts tend to treat as persons. If this is a fetishism (and the term may not be appropriate) it is a fetishism of people and not of things. These worlds are not only 'dense', 'concrete' and specific but also very heavily 'peopled'. Social relations are understood through the qualities of persons who inhabit them. Structural determinations appear as relationships between people. This 'humanism' runs through the commonest form of story-telling, in which real or imaginary events are re-created in the form of conversations between particular people: 'My father said to him . . . . He said to my father . . . .', a form, incidentally, which crosses national and class cultures and is certainly not limited to working-class culture in Britain. It informs, more generally, the 'theatre' of relived memory with its dramatis personae of 'strong characters', vivid feelings and minutely described episodes. One striking instance is the centrality accorded to persons in retrospective accounts of work experience, as in the collection *Working Lives*. These tend to centre on the personalities of employers (slave-driving, posh and distant, or 'reasonable') and on the qualities of forepersons or workmates. The character of persons is seen as making an immense difference to working experience, the difference between a good job and a bad. As Betty Ferry puts it in *Working Lives*:

This man was a tonic to anyone that was feeling a bit down in the dumps. He was always the same. If more men like him were employed in factories what a pleasure it would be to go to work! He gave a lot of pleasure to us all. People that worked with him could never forget him.[91]

Similarly, waged employment, especially the very first job, is almost always remembered, in part, through the personality of the employer or the employer's agent, often through a short, pungent pen-portrait. In *Working Lives* these range from the Pickwickian:

So again the next day we found ourselves in the office of the head of the firm. Mr Thomas Muddiman was an important but kindly and pleasant looking little man, dressed in the conventional morning dress of that period with a gold watch chain and gold rimmed glasses, topped by a shining bald head.[92]

To the villainous:

Then there was Charlie Griffiths, which is now a big firm. In those days there was just Charlie Griffiths and his two sons, Bert and Sid. I could have spat in Sid's eye more than once. He was a slave driver.[93]

The ubiquity of such portrayals in the Hackney accounts may have much to do with the small scale of industry in the area in the period of many of the memories of volume 1, but the stress on character, personality and the capacities and abilities of individuals does seem to be a key feature of the whole genre, and indeed, of the lived culture from which it arises.

The second feature of the personal character of the texts is the way in which the past–present relation is handled through the intimacies of personal relationships and especially through the comparisons of generations. We might take *Dutiful Daughters* as an example here, because it is especially rich in 'historical' references and because it may give particular insights into a specifically feminine view of the past. On the whole there is very little that is recognizable in these accounts as a 'public history' though we certainly glimpse the personal implications of larger changes. If we worked with a very conventional view of 'the historical' it is doubtful if we would recognize these accounts as 'historical' at all. Only occasionally do 'great' public events intrude on a more personal story. The major exception here is the Second World War, almost always experienced as a major reorganization of everyday life. Even the War, however, most often serves as a sort of historical marker for more intimate events, a reminder of what 'we' were doing when this or that happened. We have a strong sense that the history of monarchy, undoubtedly a popular history in many of its forms, acts more generally in this way, as the bearer of a more general chronology, in relation to which private stories may be placed. The following passage from Peggy Wood's account in *Dutiful Daughters* condenses much of what we are saying here:

I was telling the children the other night, and the telly was on, they had this thing about 1945 and when the War ended, and David [her husband] was sneering at all the crowds coming round the palace and waving to the King and Queen and little princesses, and I said, 'Don't you sneer, one of those people's me.' Jonathan [her son] looked at me in amazement, and I said, 'Yes, what else could you do?' The pubs were dry, and we just wandered round the streets, and the lights were still out. It took weeks for them to be all fixed up again. But the black-outs were torn down so the lights shone into the streets for the first time. Terrific.[94]

A lot of the basic conditions and forms of popular memory come out of this short extract: the centrality of generation ('telling the children') as a fundamental impulse to remember; the precipitating role of the public media entering right into domestic relations; the struggle to assert the validity of memories against adult scepticism and youthful incredulity; the use of royal occasions (in an unroyalist family) as a marker for 'experience'; the struggle to *connect* public events and private experiences which are actually obverse sides of the same processes ('one of those people's me'); and, again, the story form, the narrative of personal experience. In the same way, in other parts of *Dutiful Daughters*, a sense of past and present is constructed through accounts of personal life transitions – childhood, puberty, school, courtship, marriage, children – or through generational comparisons. One common form of this, related, perhaps, to the feminist context of the project, is the gauging of change in the lot of women through comparisons between 'my' childhood and the childhood wished for my own children. Often, in the most painful parts of accounts, the comparison rests on a really strong hostility to mothers and a determination that such relationships will never be repeated again: 'And I often used to say how I was treated I would never treat mine'.[95] But such comparisons may be the basis for much larger historical constructions which embrace an understanding of the intensity of the problems faced by an older generation of women, and some appraisal of real, if limited improvements especially in matters to do with sexuality.[96]

This very short account does not begin to exhaust the forms and conditions of popular memory. It would be interesting, for example, to examine the capacity of *things*, especially *old* things with personal associations, to embody conceptions and emotions about the past.[97] It would be interesting to compare this with the role of historical things in a culture of the museum. But we have said enough, perhaps, to pose some further questions. How do the dominant historical constructions acquire a purchase within these more lived senses of the past? How and to what extent are the forms of popular memory rendered ideological? How are they made to conform, for example, to a thoroughgoing political Conservatism?

These questions are complex and can scarcely be resolved without a close account of particular historical ideologies. We can approach some of this complexity, however, if we return to the vexed question of 'humanism'.

If we recall the full weight of Gramsci's 'philosophy' of social relations and our own discussion of the social individual, it is clear that not all humanism can be disposed of as ideological or as socially conservative. Social relations *are* produced, reproduced or changed in and through the activity of concrete social individuals. To think otherwise implies that social relations lie behind or outside practical activity, 'determining' it externally. To centre on the roles and characters of individuals is not in itself to hide or disguise social relations or larger structured causes. These must be seen to work precisely through human action and subjectivity. Moreover the notion of humanism as ideology disguises the importance of the attempted *humanization* of social relationships as a way of resisting their force or rendering them meaningful. You appropriate my labour but I insist on treating your person, shiny pate and all, as an object of amusement or fun.
In some of the accounts in *Working Lives* this theme of humanization through personal humour is made completely explicit and is, as Paul Willis has argued, a quite persistent and general feature of shop-floor culture. As Betty Ferry puts it, talking about a particularly scrupulous manager:

Mr Howarth was a very stern looking man, rather tall and very businesslike. He came from Liverpool and sounded just like my favourite comedian, Al Read . . . . I could never take Mr Howarth seriously when he got annoyed or angry with anyone, because he always sounded so funny. He was most entertaining for me. Sometimes I had to run to the toilet out of the way in case he caught me laughing, especially if he was telling someone off, which he did quite often.[98]

It is only after we have grasped these features – the 'realism' of a humanism and the role of humanization in resistance – that we must, in the end, return to the question of costs and to the elements of truth in the Althusserian critique of a 'theoretical humanism', humanism, that is, in a systematically *explanatory* form. For what if the personal capacities of individuals (as unique representatives of 'humanity') becomes our main explanatory principle, such that we blame ourselves and others, all the time, for the things that go wrong in our lives? Such frameworks, which undoubtedly have a pervasive common-sense existence, are easily assimilated into a thoroughgoing conservative individualism with its characteristic heroes and heroines ('those who work hard') and its characteristic scapegoats and villains. The objective tendency of such ways of thinking is to hold us within existing social arrangements and to increase the depth of inequalities. In these particular respects, then, a thoroughgoing humanism may inhibit deeper and more activist under-standings of everyday life such as produce, for instance, collective struggles against difficulties. But there is no warrant here for thinking of humanist figures of expression and understanding as ideological through and through, in all their manifestations.

We suggest, still more tentatively, that historical ideologies work most power-fully in relation to general conceptions of social improvement or decline. This is a crucial point of intersection between popular memory and public political discourse: it is an aspect of the construction of a national-popular will. It also unites conceptions of the past, analyses of the present crisis, and hopes and possi-bilities for the future. It is part of everyday historical consciousness: as people reflect upon their own experience, they make evaluations of this kind, by no means limited to a simple nostalgia or a one-sided progressivism. In Britain today, however, such evaluations are almost always framed by a sense of national decline, connected to the question 'what's wrong with this country?'. As Stuart Hall and others have argued, in studies especially of education and 'law and order', it is the New Right that has presented the most powerful and wide-ranging answers to this question, making an historical sense of the experience of crisis,[99] connecting with a larger Conservative historiography in which 'we' are again an embattled people, prepared for (very unequal) sacrifices.

There is, so far, little to set against this. The main themes of a liberal and social-democratic historiography – of real popular progress through 'economic growth' and 'social reform' – are revealed as idealist constructions, rebuked by the realist elements in common sense. In particular the notion that late capitalist develop-ment is necessarily associated with the progressive extension of welfare provisions of all kinds now looks entirely implausible. On the other hand, the historical rhetoric of the Left seems to be dominated by the negative, static backward-looking image of the 1930s, a form of popular history with no orientation towards a future different from the Thatcherite or social-democratic utopias. Among men and women who can recall a more synthetic socialism in the past, there is a widespread sense of loss that recognizes how politics have been narrowed and professionalized since the 1940s, that idealism has been lost in an everyday pragmatism, and that there has been a profound liberalization of the Labour Party. As Annie Davidson puts it in *Dutiful Daughters*, speaking from her own socialist formation in the Glasgow of the 1920s:

What I call myself is an 'idealist socialist', and it's laughed at nowadays because the world has become so complicated. Idealism is not very popular nowadays because there are so many practical things that have to be decided where your ideals have to be pushed aside to some extent in order to get a result now. But I feel that a long-term result must be the real goal of socialism, and in the end the best rather than trying to do something as a short-term measure. If the short-term measure becomes permanent then it's no use, because the short-term measure is the wrong measure to me. That's not very well-expressed but that's what I have a feeling about.[100]

Perhaps what is elusive here is the need for a historically-informed view of a socialist future. Annie's sense of loss points to the absence, in contemporary socialism, of a popular historiography that links past, present and future. It is only within such a framework that the long-term and short-term issues can be properly worked out. It is interesting that the socialists (and especially the Communists) of her youth were often possessed of such a vision, informed also by a marxist historical science. It is interesting to find, for example, that Annie herself read the historical novels of Eugene Sue, getting from them a comprehensive sense of proletarian history linked to a 'family saga'.[101] Bill Schwarz and Raphael Samuel have noted how a long-durational marxist history, back often to 'primitive communism', allowed socialists and marxists to place their own struggles with a much larger (indeed often grandiose) historical framework.[102] The problem, of course, is not to simply recover this older marxist historical anthropology. A popular memory that is socialist, feminist and anti-racist will have to start from what already exists in relation to some popular constituencies, particularly in feminist and black history. It will have to rethink a history of the white, male working class too. But the need for an active, popular and politicized sense of the past has never been clearer.

On the social relations of research

We have stressed throughout that epistemological and theoretical problems rest, in the end, upon certain social conditions, especially the position of authors of different kinds in the social relations of intellectual production. We have been especially concerned with the role of 'the historian' as a professional monopolist, or would-be monopolist of historical knowledge production. How can these forms of monopoly (and the professional ideologies which they tend to reproduce) be broken down?

There is already a range of qualitatively different practices in this area. They seem to us to conform, more or less, to three main types of organization. There are, first, the large, heavily funded 'projects' in oral history, sometimes, as in the USA, with official backing too.[103] The key features of such projects tend to accent social divisions and, indeed, multiply them: not only divisions between the subjects and objects of research, but also among the researchers themselves – between those who write, think and theoretically frame projects and those who mainly administer them. These divisions have reached such a stage in the USA that it is now possible to design a research project and then hire a commercial firm to conduct the fieldwork. It seems to us, even where conducted under politically radical auspices and with the help of marxist or feminist theorizations, such projects are problematic in their very forms, though this may not be sufficient reason for abandoning them. They certainly, in their actual working as practices, tend to reinforce existing relations of knowledge and power. They may exercise a kind of symbolic violence by which people's memories are taken from them and used to further an academic or official career with no proportionate return to the originating constituency.

In Britain, however, such large-scale projects have been unusual. Much more commonly oral history and similar practices have been linked to the contradictory social position of the researchers themselves. The most obvious instance is the salience of oral history and 'people's history' in adult working-class education, as in the projects based on Ruskin College.[104] It is in adult education (especially in the residential colleges) that the contradictions between working-class origins and loyalties and the academic and middle-class character of knowledge and of knowledge-production are experienced most sharply. One common form of this is the pull between 'going back to the community' and 'going to university', the main form in which an intensive continuation of intellectual activities presents itself. Whether or not the academic choice is eventually made, projects in 'people's history' may serve as a way of affirming a continuing class or local loyalty. At the same time the actual relation to a community of origin is being subtly changed by the acquisition of new languages, knowledges and, sometimes, habits of life. We suggest, but cannot demonstrate, that the main impetus for people's and oral history derives from this or similar situations.[105] In this respect social-historical studies conform to a broader social pattern, common in sociology and in cultural studies too: the importance of the experience of class mobility (especially through formal education) in precipitating political questions and intellectual work around class-cultural differences and relations.[106]

Despite the intimacy of the subject and object of research, in these cases, the division of labour remains. Academic careers can be made out of personal memories or communities of origin too! As in the previous case, this does not necessarily negate the intellectual *results* of the research, but it does raise the further question: for whom, then, to guide whose practice, is this knowledge intended? Much depends, here, upon the extent to which such knowledge returns to its originating constituency, and no doubt this sometimes happens. More commonly the reading constituencies are similar to those for this book: not the popular constituencies themselves but those particular social groupings to which the author now belongs, the more academic or intellectual elements in the professional middle class, especially the more radicalized sections. We might add that the conditions of life and, especially, the terms of access to this group, are currently undergoing a major restructuring.[107]

It is in this context that some individuals and groups within the radical intellectual constituency have sought to develop the forms of community-based writing and publication which we have already discussed. One aim here has been to challenge, even to recompose, the social relations of intellectual production, distribution, and readership. Working-class authors, as individuals or collectives, have been encouraged to develop popular ways of writing history, autobiography, or fiction, for a primarily working-class audience and often a local distribution. The community-based movements very accurately identify the social divisions of intellectual production as a crucial area of struggle. We cannot conceive of an adequate politics of popular memory that did not involve, as one moment, the production and circulation of first accounts with a direct popular authorship. Even so, such projects are surrounded by difficulties, the product of the unreconstructed context in which they necessarily operate. We want to end by stressing two of these, the latter to be further developed in the last essay in this book.

One major difficulty is that divisions of labour and relations of power, challenged and modified in one place, promptly reappear in another. We democratize authorship so that the oral history 'witness' now writes as popular autobiographer. We may organize such productions collectively, as at Centreprise. But social divisions, abolished in the shape of the historian and 'the source', may reappear as, for example, differences of skill and cultural power within an organizing group. In educational or quasi-educational contexts, in the WEA or extramural class, they may be reworked as a problem of pedagogy, as a teacher–taught relation. As anyone with experience of 'collective work' knows, small-scale organization does not abolish powers and inequalities of initiative, direction or definition (though it may make their negative sides easier to identify and struggle over). In all this, however, there is a danger that social divisions (now removed 'elsewhere') are resolved by an *imaginary identification*: middle-class initiator with working-class group, teacher with class, activist with 'community'. In such cases the danger is that the exercise of cultural power (which remains) becomes quite unconscious or, in its effects, merely recycles what is known in the community already.

Such contradictions aren't going to be solved by arguments. But we think it is productive to restate the problem less in terms of *social identity* than in terms of *standpoint* and *connection*. Organic intellectual work is not, in other words, only or primarily a question of who you are; it is more a question of whose problems you set out to study and resolve. The decisive question is the standpoint of projects and the connections they require. Social identity may help or hinder here, though not always in predictable ways. More important is the source of the agenda in the everyday life of subordinated classes and social groups and the production of knowledge which is useful from that standpoint. This applies as much to 'critical' academics as to political activists. It is the connection between popular experiences and a developed intellectual function that is the essential thing. The key problems then become how to organize such a connection politically, how to generalize skills of secondary analysis and how to connect this popular education to other daily struggles.

The second main difficulty concerns the relation between popular historical writing and the field of public representations of history. From the standpoint of the community activist, who may value authentic popular expression above all else, the pervasiveness of a dominant memory may not be visible. Yet the dominant historical constructions will necessarily be a presence in the first sketches of a people's history. For the ruling ideas are not just those of the dominant social group – those they live their own lives by, those they seek to generalize. They are ideas also with particular tendencies, 'bourgeois' not necessarily in origin, but in their conformity to dominant social relationships. Since we all live in a capitalist, patriarchal and racist social order, such ideas may be spoken by anyone. There are limits, then, to the pursuit of authenticity, of really popular expression. Struggle at this level – the production and working up of alternatives – has to take account of the dominant discourses and *their* means of production. It is to these public histories and their general forms that Chapter 7 is addressed.

7 'Charms of residence': the public and the past

Michael Bommes and Patrick Wright

This chapter was prompted by two sets of questions. The first concerns the ways in which subordinated social groups and communities can develop and maintain a sense of their own history. How does this consciousness arise? What is the extent and form of its autonomy? How, and for what political purposes, can it be mobilized? The second set of questions has to do with the dominant and publicly instituted representations of the past. How is a particular version of the past produced, privileged, installed and maintained as a public and national 'consensus'? How, above all, does this process bear upon the subordinated historical consciousness indicated in the first set of questions?

We explore these issues in three parts. In the first we consider recent debates in France about popular memory and culture, and ask how certain social relations have come to be categorized and instituted as 'public' and others as 'private'. This distinction is crucial for understanding the social definition of the past, because it determines what forms of historical consciousness can be raised to a 'public' significance. Our discussion of public and private draws on an analysis developed in West Germany. While this analysis is inevitably rather dense and difficult, we have found it to be of real use in our attempt to understand the public status of 'the past' in Britain.

The second part describes and analyses what we take to be the dominant public representations of the past. 'National Heritage' indicates a whole battery of discourses and images which are not only limited to state agencies. Thus we discuss the parliamentary debates on the National Heritage Act (1980) and also the work and development of the preservation lobby. Since capitalist business can also play a part in the construction of the past, we analyse, as an example, the Shell advertising programme of the last sixty years, looking in particular at its characteristic images of 'the British countryside'.

In the third and concluding part, we briefly raise the question of how these dominant representations of the past and the nation shape, and constrain, oppositional practices. We believe this has immediate importance for situating the work of those endeavours which seek to recover a community's sense of its past.

This chapter is closely connected to the previous one, which approached popular memory through an argument about oral history. Here we approach similar questions from a somewhat different perspective. We focus on 'public' forms rather than on private or privatized memories. The justification for this will, we hope, already

'THE PAST SOON BECOMES A CONSTRUCTION OF THE IMAGINATION OF THE FUTURE'

written in large stencilled red letters (and apparently with financial assistance from the Greater London Arts Association) on the hoardings surrounding a 200,000 square foot office development on the site of the Covent Garden Community Garden, 1981 be clear from the previous chapter: there can be no adequate oppositional practice without knowledge of the power of the dominant constructions against which it must work.

Popular history and the public sphere

Foucault and popular memory

In the mid-1970s Michel Foucault raised the question of 'popular memory' in France. His immediate concern was with film, but the following passage from an interview with *Cahiers du Cinéma* (1947) makes it clear that wider issues were also involved:

There's a real fight going on. Over what? Over what we can roughly describe as *popular memory*. It is an actual fact that people – I'm talking about those who are barred from writing, from producing their books themselves, from drawing up their own historical accounts – that these people nevertheless do have a way of recording history, of remembering it, of keeping it fresh and using it. This popular history was, to a certain extent, even more alive, more clearly formulated in the 19th century, where, for instance, there was a whole tradition of struggles which were transmitted orally, or in writing or songs etc.[1]

There was considerable debate at the time, but none of Foucault's more recent work has made extensive use of the notion 'popular memory'. Indeed, despite passing remarks such as 'And popular memory will reproduce in rumour the austere discipline of the law',[2] Foucault's later books suggest an abandoning of this notion on account of a twofold problem. To think in terms of 'popular memory' is to risk treating 'the popular' as if it were wholly unified, fully achieved and therefore capable of sustaining a memory wholly apart from the dominant constructions of the past. It is also to risk isolating these dominant constructions from any 'popular' response which may be made to them. Questions of acquiescence, deference and resistance cannot be dealt with adequately if the construcions in question are considered apart from 'popular memory' – as if they were entirely programmatic and defined only in the motions with which they are laid on from above. As Foucault has said of some eighteenth-century pamphlets and other publicity about crime:

Perhaps we should see this literature of crime, which proliferated around a few exemplary figures, neither as a spontaneous form of 'popular expression', nor as a concerted programme of propaganda and moralisation from above.[3]

Foucault leaves no doubt that while it is actively subordinated, 'popular memory' does not exist outside the realm of discourse. In asserting that 'popular memory' has a discursive materiality, and that it exists *in* its relations to the dominant discourses and not apart from them or by itself, Foucault puts two ghosts to rest. He indicates the inadequacy of purely psychologistic accounts of memory, and he leaves little room for the historian (and especially the oral historian) conceived as 'tapper' of a distinct popular record and account. Memory has a texture which is both social and historic: it exists in the world rather than in people's heads, finding its basis in conversations, cultural forms, personal relations, the structure and appearance of places and, most fundamentally for this argument, in relation to ideologies which work to establish a consensus view of both the past and the forms of personal experience which are significant and memorable.

Discontinued it may be, but Foucault's discussion of 'popular memory' raises important questions: how is it that some articulations of history come to be instituted as dominant and others subordinated, and how are these relations of dominance and subordination actually lived? We take these questions to be of crucial significance, but we do not see a way of answering them in terms only of discourse. Foucault himself has never really defined 'popular memory' except by isolating the obviously discursive and textual elements of popular culture and practice. As he has established, discourses are specific and powerfully determining, but his earlier work, like much of that of his Anglo-American followers, has been inattentive to the conditions of production of discourse, and this has encouraged a kind of poetics of the archive which treats discourses as if they were written on the wind. In nineteenth-century France, for example, 'popular memory' of crime may indeed have borne the stamp of the conventions of broadsheet and ballad, but one is still left with some stark questions. Are not these conventions rooted in political and institutional domination? Is every aspect of social reality 'discursive', and if so what do we gain from saying so? As for resistance, is it simply the bipolar opposite of power? Is resistance only the refractory agency which is necessary if power is to stage and display itself at all?

Some of these questions have been approached and worked through in Paris by the collective responsible for a journal called *Les Révoltes Logiques* (Cahiers du Centre de Recherches sur les Idéologies de la Révolte). The earlier issues of *Les Révoltes Logiques* (the first of which appeared in 1975) structure historical research around the question of a popular and oppositional practice and memory which tends to be thought of as 'other' – as detached and distinct from that against which it is aligned. This led to accusations of 'workerism' which have been aimed most noticeably at Jacques Rancière since his noisy defection from the school of Althusser.[4] A recent editorial in *Les Révoltes Logiques* acknowledges, however, the *naïveté* of the position informing earlier issues: 'We have learned that there is no popular memory to be retrieved in its virginity.'[5]

One of the most usefully provoking aspects of this work associated with *Les Révoltes Logiques* is its concern to understand the reduction of history and the occultation of actual forms of resistance which can follow what Rancière has described as 'the grafting of the Marxist discourse onto the voice of working class protestation'.[6] In this operation, it is asserted, a theoretical unity is attributed to practices which are actually never fully accomplished or unified. This attributed unity is that of a class subject and consciousness defined idealistically in relation to the development of the productive forces, and as Rancière has claimed it makes scant allowance for the elements of archaism, spontaneity and utopianism involved in the historical actuality of working-class culture and resistance. In recent issues of *Les Révoltes Logiques* it has been suggested that in May 1968 the militant bearers of this inadequate conception of 'the popular' left the university only to come up against a working class which was not prepared to join them on the streets. This failure certainly indicated the importance of reworking and developing the terms of socialist analysis and activism, but historically it was also political disenchantment that followed, a political disenchantment which has since led to the ideological capture of sections of the intellectual Left. As a result, it is suggested, the oppositional discourse can be found working in the interests of the status quo. 'Soft socialism' is in order now – a new form of relief from below – and the working class is being theoretically reconstituted by its advocates. It is no longer a political attention which these intellectuals direct towards the working class. The discourse has been readjusted, filtered through nostalgia certainly, but also through ethnology and a kind of cultural sociology, and it now identifies the working class in terms of life-style, the popular ethos, craft-skills etc. To use Rancière's ironic words, in this readjustment the class struggle is dropped so that the class of the struggle may be preserved: 'workers today, those are the people who like their meat in sauce and their clothes to be without fashion'.[7] As the political stress of history is buried under the weight of all this ethnological detail, a new ideological discipline is consecrated a discipline which Philippe Hoyau has named 'Ethno-history'.[8]

We will come back to some of these points in the third part of this chapter. *Les Révoltes Logiques* has made a valuable critique of cultural sociology, and the preservational emphasis which it has been describing is also very important. At this stage; however, we are more concerned with Rancière's rather sombre conclusion about a form of working-class discourse which 'never functions so well as when it is cast in the logic of others, or to their profit'.[9] This question is familiar in the slightly different terms of the British debate about culture: can popular and/or oppositional culture exist except within measures of control? The link between the two debates is this: discursive and cultural forms must be approached through a wider analysis of dominance and subordination, in other words, of hegemony. This involves considering the institutional deployment of discursive and cultural forms. Such an analysis is essential even though the forms which we are approaching in this article – those which establish the dominance of one version of the past over others – frequently function in a state of relative unachievement and disorder.

Hegemony and the public sphere

The analysis of hegemony addresses the problem that while capitalist social formations are always determined by class contradiction they are not always riven by open class conflict. In the development of marxist theory this has led to a more complex concept of class domination, conceived now as a unity of dictatorship and leadership through which the ruling class alliance is not only able to control the means of force – in the end the basis of domination – but also gains political, intellectual and moral leadership. The ruling class alliance must be able to create a collective will by articulating the interests of the dominated classes in hegemonic terms. While there is a risk of being too instrumentalist in this analysis, it is important to recognize that the process of articulation works by mechanisms of transformation, inclusion and exclusion. Some interests and experiences of the subordinated classes and groups are transformed and included within ideological contexts determined by the dominant classes and/or values, while others are excluded, suppressed and socially devalued.[10] Because our argument is concerned with the ways in which 'the past' is written into present social reality we are particularly interested in a hegemonic organizational practice which in the Western capitalist countries has developed out of 'the main reality' of bourgeois society, i.e. market relations. We refer to the categorization of social relations as public or private, a categorization which has developed in relation to, and against, the absolutist state and which has played a major role in securing the domination of the bourgeois classes during the history of capitalist societies. It is with the *public* institution of the past that this chapter is concerned.

The word 'public' is customarily applied to a welter of different objects, ideas and practices: the public house, publication, the public event and image, public buildings, the public interest etc. Against this, the main events of social life are customarily understood to be private: the family, but also through the legal definition of work, the experience of production itself.[11] Far from being random, this differentiation of the public from the private is historically specific. In the next few pages we attempt to outline some of the problems implicit in understanding the public and private as historically differentiated social spheres. We follow the discussion of the public and private which is to be found in two books: *Strukturwandel der Öffentlichkeit* (*The Structural Change of the Public Sphere*) by Jürgen Habermas (1962) and *Öffentlichkeit und Erfahrung* (*The Public Sphere and Experience*) by Oskar Negt and Alexander Kluge (1972).[12]

West German concern with the problems of the public sphere – the context of these theorizations – is to be understood in terms of what Paul Connerton has described as 'the belated and consequently disturbed' consolidation of the German nation-state.[13] German history is heavily characterized by the problem of unity. The nation-state was formed under Bismarck in 1871, and until 1914 German society was still marked by the absolutism of the Prussian state. The Weimar Republic brought a short interlude of parliamentary democracy which was shattered by the rise of fascism. It was consequently only in 1949 with the establishment of the West German state that the second period of parliamentary democracy began. More recently, the findings of the Russell Tribunal (1978–9) indicate the extent to which the West German public sphere continues to be characterized by what amounts to an undemocratic national tradition.[14] It is in relation to this tradition that Habermas approaches the question of the public sphere, and his book is largely concerned with historical developments in Britain and France, countries in which parliamentary democracy is far more firmly established. The work by Habermas and Negt and Kluge on the problems of the public sphere is most valuable for us because it suggests a way in which discursive forms can be analysed not just textually, but in the institutional practices which are their historical relation to power. The public sphere recuperates and domesticates social problems, taking up their content and granting them public status but organizing them, nevertheless, according to the logic of dominance.

In *The Structural Change of the Public Sphere* Habermas traces the emergence of what he calls the Traditional Bourgeois Public, and then goes on to discuss the transformations undergone by this public sphere up until the 1950s. The Traditional Bourgeois Public comes into existence with the bourgeoisie and replaces a feudal practice of power in which authority is identified with the person holding it. Crucial to the formation of this public sphere was the development of a national economy and continuous state activity (change from personal to more generally objectified relations of dominance, the development of a non-personalist public authority and a standing army etc.). In Habermas's words,

the nobility became the organs of public authority, parliament and the legal institutions; while those occupied in the trades and professions, insofar as they had already established urban corporations and territorial organisations, developed into a sphere of bourgeois society which would stand apart from the state as an area of genuine autonomy.[15]

This is a twofold process. On the one hand 'private' individuals are now *negatively* defined as those who are affected by the measures of public authority; but there is also the *positive* meaning of privatization, a meaning which is related to the development of the capitalist economy. As opposed to the feudal economy, the relations of which it destroys, the capitalist economy is based on *individual*, and therefore private, behaviour. Economic behaviour becomes the centre of existence, and is defined as private activity. This *private* activity is, however, dependent upon *public* conditions in the sense that it has to direct its activities towards commodity exchange which develops under the shelter of the bourgeois public sphere. The economic conditions of commodity exchange lie beyond the boundaries of private enterprises: they are of general and therefore of public interest to the individuals operating as private on the economic level. The bourgeois public sphere thus develops as the means by which these individuals start to criticize and control the measures of the state. Public authority (e.g. the government) and the public sphere (e.g. parliament) become distinct from one another: the public sphere becomes an arena in which private individuals seek to subordinate public authority to their own interests.

After describing the rise of the Traditional Bourgeois Public – a process which includes the development of cultural forms such as the novel – Habermas discusses its transformation in response to the growth of the labour movement and its demands for participation. This transformation is seen as a dialectical process in which the public and private spheres interpenetrate.

Negt and Kluge are more concerned with what they call the Transformed Bourgeois Public. In their book, they have given a systematic characterization of the
bourgeois public sphere as it exists today, stressing the extent to which the public
sphere remains a bourgeois form and organizes the experience of the dominant
classes at the same time as it *dis*organizes and negates the mode of experience of
the working classes. The purpose of Negt and Kluge's study is to trace within this
process of domination those potential elements of a working-class mode of organization. Their interest is in oppositional public forms: in the possibility of what they
term the 'proletarian public'.

As Negt and Kluge argue, the bourgeois public sphere is no longer limited to its
traditional form, having been through considerable transformations, but it continues, nevertheless, to function as a front of legitimation. Despite this, the public
sphere is no longer all of a piece (if it ever was), and it has no substantial unity.
We find instead an accumulation of public forms which are abstractly related to
one another: television, the press, the educational apparatus, political parties,
parliament, the army, church, law, monopoly corporations etc. If we compare this
catalogue with the Traditional Bourgeois Public described by Habermas, then
it becomes evident that more recent social developments have involved an increasing colonization of public forms by capital. For the purposes of our discussion of
'National Heritage' it is also important to note that while all the single public forms
or sites appear as parts of a unified public sphere no such unified sphere actually
exists, except as an *impression* of unity differently constructed by (and often
in the particular interests of) the single forms in question. Despite this, however,
in ordinary usage we tend to refer to the public sphere as if it were still unified
in the traditional way. This, according to Negt and Kluge, demonstrates an important difference: that existing between what is produced at the different public
sites (e.g. consent, the destruction of other forms of organization etc.), and the way
in which these productions are appropriated in everyday life (as expressions of a
collective will, democracy, participation etc.).[16] This leads us to another meaning
of the public sphere: besides its single sites, the public exists as a shared social
horizon for the members of a society. This again possesses different aspects: the
social horizon functions to construct a front of legitimation (the collective will)
but at the same time it controls perception by defining socially relevant events,
practices and relations.[17]

If we now look at the private as it stands in relation to the developing public
sphere we find the two to be in close mutual dependence: capital is only private
in so far as social wealth is publicly accessible – a person can only behave as a
private individual because of the public existence of the market. However the way
in which private and public are experienced by the individual in everyday life
obscures their relation; indeed, Negt and Kluge suggest that this obscurity forms the
basis of the bourgeois ideology of the 'individual'. The *production* of social
relations (including 'individuality') goes on beyond the range of the Transformed
Bourgeois Public, and from within this public sphere the really meaningful decisions
have therefore always already been taken.[18] To put this a different way, the

relations of capital and state are pregiven conditions of existence for the Transformed Bourgeois Public, a sphere which consequently only deals with experience in a technical and distributive sense: it reproduces existing divisions between public and private, between politics and production, between 'public' language and the social efficacy of experience, between high culture and the experience of the mass of people. In reproducing these divisions, the Transformed Bourgeois Public hinders the organization of subordinated groups. As the public sphere has no unique substance of its own, the Transformed Bourgeois Public is always an accumulation of practices and appearances which have different respective properties and origins. As a combination of traditional and new forms the Transformed Bourgeois Public can be schematized as follows:[19]

(i)   Public forms which have developed directly around capitalist production – the organizational structure of industry; the monumental spaciousness of bank and insurance headquarters; city centres and industrial areas; the social means of consumption such as housing, streets, transport etc. The overwhelming objectivity of these particular relations produces a distinct ideological effect of its own.
(ii) The consciousness industries, as well as the relations of consumption and advertising, which superimpose and connect with the relations in (i).
(iii) The public operations of corporations, social institutions such as political parties, the traditional state apparatuses such as parliament, the military and legal establishments etc., work with the different public forms in (i) and (ii), and also tend to superimpose themselves on these.

Oppositional public forms

The most important operation of the Transformed Bourgeois Public can be described in terms of inclusion and exclusion. Existing social relations which are difficult to legitimate become part of a *produced non-public*, while other relations which are also difficult to legitimate are transformed and restructured until they appear as a justified general or 'national' public interest. It is in this way that the Transformed Bourgeois Public excludes oppositional proletarian practices. When these practices are included it is only at the expense of their transformation. The dialectic of inclusion and exclusion obstructs autonomous organization: some aspects of working-class experience are reconstructed and absorbed, while others, though not obliterated, are disqualified from the constructed field of public relevance. The disqualified part does not lose its value as social experience, but it is excluded from the bourgeois system of communication. In this system it becomes incomprehensible; it is privatized.

The Structural Change of the Public Sphere is concerned with the development and transformation of the Traditional Bourgeois Public. In his Preface, however, Habermas also mentions a 'plebeian version of the public which is, as it were, repressed in the historical process', but he never develops this as a potentially oppositional and different form of public organization. Against this Negt and Kluge insist that the 'historically repressed plebeian version of the public' is not just a different version of the bourgeois public, but rather a completely different way of organizing experience. For this reason they use the phrase 'proletarian public' to indicate the different direction of their work. The idea of a 'proletarian public' is useful in several respects, but we cannot discuss its possible uses without also mentioning some reservations. We prefer to talk about oppositional public forms in the plural since groups other than classes are dominated under the Transformed Bourgeois Public and organize their experience against this public sphere in different ways. It is clear, for example, that while women are affected by the mechanisms of inclusion and exclusion characteristic of the bourgeois public sphere their subordination is not the same as that of the male working class, and also that under particular circumstances simply to gain access to bourgeois public forms can mark a success for women.[20] Our second reservation derives from our view that the meaning of the concept 'proletarian public' is not always clearly defined in Negt and Kluge's book and that it has too speculative a cast. Negt and Kluge argue that oppositional forms are always *related* to the dominant bourgeois public sphere, but it is necessary to specify the concrete forms of this relation more closely. One way in which this can be done is by drawing on studies of working-class culture which have been produced in this country.[21]

Negt and Kluge argue that the elements of a 'proletarian public' have to be reconstructed out of moments of historical rupture: they cite crises, war, revolution, counter-revolution, strikes and factory occupations as moments in which the potential form of a 'proletarian public' can be traced. Bearing in mind British studies of working-class culture we add to this the suggestion that everyday struggles in the factory or work-place – over the use of streets, even over the form of the pub – are a permanent negotiation between the subordinated and dominant classes over forms of social organization, public propriety, political participation etc. The struggle over working-class forms of public life occurs at a variety of levels. Negt and Kluge argue, for example, that if a worker tries to participate in the Transformed Bourgeois Public and actually manages to win elections or take political initiatives he faces a dilemma. In order to use the bourgeois public the worker must accept that sphere's construction of him as yet another 'private' interest seeking 'expression'. In other words, the bourgeois public sphere is only available for private use, and the collective interests of the working class are therefore reconstructed before they can appear within it. Working-class interests do not, indeed cannot, appear in a qualitatively different public form. The production of social relations is, as we have already said, precisely *not* the object of the bourgeois public sphere. Either the worker enters the bourgeois public sphere in the acknowledged political ways and is separated from his collective means of production, or he doesn't enter the bourgeois public at all. In either case his experiences are blocked from the publicly acknowledged social horizon of relevant relations. In Negt and Kluge, this point remains excessively abstract. A much more particular description of the same process of subordination to public meaning can be found in Armstrong, Goodman and Hyman's book *Ideology and Shop-floor Industrial Relations*:

There is a public, as well as a private, dimension to legitimisation which is more important when, as is very often the case in industrial relations, questions of legitimation are actually contested. Suppose, for example, that a worker objects to a new management rule but can find no publicly acceptable legitimising principle to justify his objection. However personally aggrieved he may feel, there is then no way of mobilising his colleagues' support on the issue. It is even possible for such feeling to be shared, for a group of workers to feel individually ill-used, but, unless there is some means of transforming their private grievances into a public issue they will not be able to mobilise effectively. Although the impulse to mobilise may originate in a private sense of legitimisation, the effectiveness of mobilisation depends on linking the issue to what is publicly acknowledged as legitimate.[22]

The problem is hugely increased by the extent to which what is publicly acknowledged as legitimate is already heavily determined by the structure of the bourgeois public. Legitimation is structurally weighted from the start.

Another example of how oppositional public forms exist in relation to the dominant public sphere can be found in Phil Cohen's work on street culture. In his article 'Subcultural conflict and the working class community', for example, Phil Cohen describes the redevelopment of a working-class community after the Second World War. He argues that the relative stability of this community was underpinned by three main social factors: extended kinship structures, the ecological structure of the working-class neighbourhood, and the structure of the local economy. Cohen maintains that

the street forms a kind of 'communal space', a mediation between the *totally private* space of the family, with its intimate involvements, and the *totally public* space, e.g. parks, thoroughfares, etc., where people relate to each other as strangers, and with indifference. The street, then . . . maintains an intricate social balance between rights and obligations, distance and relation in the community.[23]

What Cohen describes as a 'mediation' between the totally private and the totally public is indeed a different public form. Later in the article, he describes the consequences of the destruction and reconstruction of the street: the destruction of the street as a collective space of mutual support changed the family itself, imposing the form of the nuclear family. Thus the 'totally private' space was itself changed; it had previously taken a different form of privacy from the bourgeois one.

So the bourgeois definitions of private and public propriety enter into the construction of cities, forming the immediacy of public space. In a more recent article Cohen discusses struggles over the street and public propriety in Islington from the middle of the last century. He describes conflicts between the police and the working class over the social definition and use of space, and how a new balance of forces is struck.

. . . a system of informal, tacitly negotiated and particularistic definitions of public order were evolved which *accommodated* certain working class usages of social space and time, and *outlawed* others . . . if you were a legal subject caught following a less than pedestrian line of desire, or a class subject caught out of your legal place, you were not only out of (statutory public) order, but had broken a moral code of respectable public behaviour.[24]

Cohen shows how this order is negotiated between working class and police: certain spaces of a different order are sanctioned, whilst others are declared inaccessible for use in a specifically working-class mode. As the novelist John Hawkes once wrote, 'it's a day's work to stop cars, take strangers by the elbow, and see public places closed on time'.[25]

National Heritage: calling the Imaginary Briton

On account of the past nothing has happened.

Jack Spicer[26]

Will we go to England again, she says, to sit in the cathedrals.

Guy Davenport[27]

It seems characteristic of contemporary Britain that the occasional academic historian can still be heard lamenting the dwindling of historical consciousness among the public while at the same time the strident pageantry of National Heritage announces, in no uncertain terms, that our streets are 'brimful of history'.[28] In this part we attempt to outline a critique not simply of cathedrals, but of the diverse combination which is exhibited as National Heritage. National Heritage is a public articulation or staging of the past, and apart from being of immense extent, variety and ubiquity it is also closely connected to the impulses of contemporary conservatism. We begin with a general discussion which identifies some of the basic characteristics of National Heritage and indicates the historically-based approach of the sections which follow.

The arrival of history

Initial attention to the ways in which a sense of tradition is produced and re-produced within the public sphere is liable to yield a delirious impression. National Heritage is being invoked all over the place: through the press, television, political speeches, cultural policy, the exhibition of old photographs,[29] advertising etc. It is as if a strange and obliterating glaciation is being drawn across the entire surface of social life, as if history is being frozen over, arrested and in this sense 'stopped'. National Heritage appears to involve nothing less than the abolition of all contradiction in the name of a national culture: the installation of a spectacular display in which 'the past' enters everyday life, closing time down to the perpetual 'extension' of an immobilized but resonantly 'historical' national present. Under the current regime history seems finally to have arrived and the past to have achieved a new social location. It is no longer 'behind' the present on the long road to forever; instead it spreads itself out as, to quote the title of a book recently produced by the Reader's Digest Association, *The Past All Around Us*. History is suddenly concrete and coalesced with the monumental geography of nationalism. As it culminates in itself, history appears not as necessity, struggle or transformation but as 'our' National Heritage, and it draws 'us' into a veritable Age of Dead Statues as it does so.[30]

National Heritage projects a unity which tends to override social and political contradiction. It may not be practised as a controlled and unified political strategy, but diverse articulations of past and nationhood are nevertheless at work. They function as lures which oppose their brilliance to the more tawdry and divided experience of contemporary Britain, offering the serene and apparently natural unity of a 'national' subjectivity to those who identify with them. A formulation can usefully be borrowed from Tony Wilden in order provisionally to name this national subjectivity the 'Imaginary Briton'.[31]

Two relatively distinct stages can be identified in the formation of the 'Imaginary Briton'. The first is the historical process by which representations of the national past arise. The second is the more variable and evasive process whereby people consent or acquiesce to these representations. (Any adequate analysis must be attentive to both stages.) At the first stage it is possible to contest laundered and dehistoricized (i.e. naturalized) representations of the past by working up a really historical understanding of them. Where do they come from and what are their institutional supports? To what social and historical processes do they owe their definition, and what social values do they reproduce? What is their status within the public sphere? What is needed at the second stage is some understanding of the complex constraints leading people in very different situations to make a comforting and gratifyingly 'national' sense of what, in the present socio-economic climate, is likely to be an increasingly insecure experience.[32]

The unity of this 'national' subjectivity may not be 'real', but then neither is the unity of the 'nation' to which the 'Imaginary Briton' subscribes. As Le Guyader has suggested is the case in France, the unity of the 'nation' tends to be projected as an ideological and poetic equivalent to the more prosaic and functional unity of the modern state.[33] Similarly, the subjective unity of the 'Imaginary Briton' stands as an equivalent to the unity of the good citizen: defined according to normative measures from outside, immobilised, perhaps even slightly stupefied, but superficially 'steeped in history' nevertheless.

In this second part of our chapter we seek to demonstrate how National Heritage works to create its own constituency of support. This constituency plays its part in the reproduction of existing social relations. As we have suggested in our discussion of hegemony, the modern state strives to create a single collective will and identity in the face of social differences. Under the sign of National Heritage this equilibrium is sublimated, restaged and reproduced, not as an historical balance of forces but as a utopian tribal pact. It becomes a national essence which can be invoked – as it is endlessly, for example, in a recent Green Paper on *Trade Union*

Immunities – as 'the community as a whole'.[34] This is a community of those good citizens who are fit and able to participate in the 'informed public debate' which the Green Paper seeks to inaugurate. But in terms of social reproduction it is also a utopian community of 'Imaginary Britons' bearing both an undivided heritage and what the same Green Paper vaunts as a 'national interest' in common.

The reproduction of social relations in contemporary Britain is only indirectly related to individual acts of initiative and leadership, but it is achieved in part by the public valorization of past incidences of leadership, of the greater acts of kings, the occasional queen, generals and admirals, of ancestry and filiation. In this valorization history is framed up as National Heritage and drawn into the ideological and political arena. National Heritage is politically active, but if we are to describe this political activity we must first make some remarks about what it is not. National Heritage is not directly controlled by one class or party, nor is its relation to the state one of simple emanation or reflection (it is not just a state-controlled kink in the mirror). While National Heritage has indeed provided one of the grounds on which the Thatcher government attempts to rest its case, it is not solely attributable to Tory party conservatism. Nor can it be identified in any simple way with the slightly phobic puritanism of Mary Whitehouse, who opens her autobiography (aptly titled *Who Does She Think She Is?*) by hallucinating the genetic mainline which raises the Whitehouse germ-plasm up from that humble but honourable 'yeoman family' in the sixteenth century to the tarnished moral atmosphere of present times.[35] We should also say that it is not *necessarily* valuable to condemn National Heritage as a distortion, and to oppose it abstractly with a supposedly true account of history. Our point here is that National Heritage is not history at all, and that it needs to be analysed in its character as a publicly instituted structuring of consciousness. As such National Heritage can be as significantly indifferent to truth as to falsity. The contestation of definitions imposed as National Heritage involves a much wider social practice than history-writing customarily occupies.

This said, however, one only has to think of the specific 'heritages' which have been mobilized in opposition to the dominant 'national' one – local heritage, women's heritage, working-class heritage, black heritage – to realize two things. First, that the expression of oppositional demand is likely to involve struggle over the right to, meaning and public status of existing traditions. Second, that National Heritage, as a publicly instituted structuring of consciousness, functions by excluding traditions which it cannot incorporate. It is in relation to this second point that the notion of the 'Imaginary Briton' seems most useful. Of course there are numerous reasons for denying the fully accomplished existence of a unified 'national' subjectivity, but there is, nevertheless, a publicly instituted tendency towards homogeneity and conformity, and this does work within formative boundaries which exclude certain social processes. Constituted as it is by those articulations of past and nationhood which underlie it, the 'Imaginary Briton' has no explicit connection with class. It is apparently genderless, and it has no regional location. That these are not simple absences, mere omissions, can be seen by considering the question of race. While the 'Imaginary Briton' appears to bear no more trace of race than of class, gender or region, it is actually sufficiently dependent on suppositions of ancestral continuity to be not only white but also actively exclusive of what it helps constitute as 'Others'.

The racism latent in National Heritage and the 'Imaginary Briton' can be approached through Sartre's excellent but neglected essay *Anti-Semite and Jew*. As we will be referring back to this essay it is worth quoting at some length.

In a bourgeois society it is the constant movement of people, the collective currents, the styles, the customs, all these things, that in effect create values. The value of poems, of furniture, of houses, of landscapes derive in large part from the spontaneous condensations that fall on these objects like a light dew; they are strictly national and result from the normal functioning of a traditionalist and historical society. To be a Frenchman is not merely to have been born in France, to vote and pay taxes; it is above all to have the use and sense of these values. And when a man shares in their creation, he is in some degree reassured about himself; he has a justification for existence through a sort of adhesion to the whole of society. To know how to appreciate a piece of Louis Seize furniture, the delicacy of a saying by Chamfort, a landscape of the Ile de France, a painting by Claude Lorrain, is to affirm and to feel that one belongs to French society; it is to renew a tacit social contract with all members of that society. At one stroke the vague contingency of our existence vanishes and gives way to the necessity of an existence by right. Every Frenchman who is moved by reading Villon or by looking at the Palace of Versailles becomes a public functionary and the subject of imprescriptible rights.

Now a Jew is a man who is refused access to these values on principle. . . . He can indeed acquire all the goods he wants, lands and castles if he has the where-withal; but at the very moment when he becomes a legal proprietor the property undergoes a subtle change in meaning and value.

Only a Frenchman, the son of a Frenchman, son or grandson of a peasant, is capable of possessing it really. To own a hut in a village, it is not enough to have bought it with hard cash. One must know all the neighbours, their parents and grandparents, the surrounding farms, the beeches and oaks of the forest; one must know how to work, fish, hunt; one must have made notches in the trees in child-hood and have found them enlarged in ripe old age. You may be sure that the Jew does not fulfil these conditions. For that matter, perhaps the Frenchman doesn't either, but he is granted a certain indulgence. There is a French way and a Jewish way of confusing oats and wheat.[36]

Although Sartre's analysis is specific to anti-Semitism in wartime France, it can inform a discussion of National Heritage in contemporary Britain. Sartre describes anti-Semitism as 'the expression of a primitive society that, though secret and diffused, remains latent in the legal collectivity.' A comparable neo-tribalism is kept in place by the articulations of National Heritage. And alongside all the evocation and mystification surrounding it, this neo-tribalism comes down to ground in the produced collective will. Indeed, as was recognized in the early phase of the Thatcher government, at times of crisis appeal to this hegemonic single aim and interest, defined as it is against 'Others', becomes a major source of social stability. In this context it is worth quoting a remark made by Norman St John-Stevas, prime mover of the National Heritage Act (1980), and a man who may well have reconsidered his position since: 'The public have recognized that Margaret Thatcher has shown herself, in just over a year in office, to be a national leader as well as a party leader.'[37]

There are two points to be made about the *diversity* of National Heritage, and both of them indicate limits beyond which the notion of the 'Imaginary Briton' ceases to be very useful. The first of these concerns the diversity of meaning which can be derived from, or attributed to, the articulations of past and nationhood which form the repertoire of National Heritage. The meaning of National Heritage is not univocally determined by the representations which support it, and analysis needs to accommodate the extent to which these representations can be appropriated differently in various circumstances. For example, while Enoch Powell has cited the English countryside along with a number of Great Authors as his formative influences, it is also possible to be racist without having any feeling at all for the English countryside (or, for that matter, to be devoted to the countryside without being racist). The same point can be made in relation to the recent Royal Wedding, and similar 'splendid occasions' which support festivities and forms of celebration. The enjoyment of these events cannot be simply identified with conservative ideologies of monarchy, family and nation.

Our second point concerns the repertoire itself, rather than its appropriation. This repertoire is characterized by a tension between articulations working at the 'national' and 'local' levels. If we examine this tension the 'Imaginary Briton' appears to explode into so many fragments that even the most expanded notion of hegemony seems unlikely to draw them back together again. But the fragments are active too: they operate at a level apart from that of the 'nation', having specific and *local* resonances; and their hegemonic function persists to the extent that they bury political contradiction under a celebratory display of local diversity. To put this in descriptive terms which we will develop shortly, the *macro-heritage* – framed as it is by the large and overriding unity of the 'nation' – coexists with a more molecular diversity of locally based *micro-heritages* which are at work in local scene rather than capital city; in sayings, ballads and dialects rather than in great literary works and the mother tongue; in classically undistinctive but still irreplaceable 'artisans' dwellings' rather than stately piles of 'national' significance; in collective craft and production skills rather than the greater acts or discoveries of heroes and leaders; in curious and particular factory buildings rather than 'nationally' significant battlefields and prison cells.

Both the 'national' and the 'local' are thus caught up in what Jacques Rancière has described as the grand collects of patrimony. At the *macro* level, heritage is inscribed within a framework which distinguishes what it stages as 'national' from everyday life. At the *micro* level, that of locality and community, heritage appears to have been spilling over during the last fifteen years or so, breaking with its publicly fielded 'national' location and merging more closely with the everyday. In the third part of this chapter we try to account for the increasing penetration of everyday life by National Heritage. Before this can be done, however, it is necessary to establish and understand the historical nature of the representations on which the *macro* or 'national' institution of heritage rests.

Preservation and the state

'The story of the Castle is as fascinating as a romance,' wrote Sarah A. Tooley in 1902.[38] Although this may sound like a comment on Franz Kafka, the next sentence returns us to the labyrinthine register of National Heritage: 'Each stone breathes memories of the poetry, tradition and legendary lore of the country'. Seventy years later, Raphael Samuel's Foreword to Jerry White's book *Rothschild Buildings* declares: 'Historians have long since recognized that in the city every stone can tell a story, just as in the countryside there is a history in every hedge'.[39] What is involved in this sense of the past as a concrete presence, and to what extent does it imply assumptions which may be held in common by historians different enough to make explicit political denunciations of one another's work? We cannot fully address these questions here, but the concretization of history which is so central to National Heritage over the same seventy years has considerable relevance.

There is nothing especially modern about the conception which establishes heritage as that legacy of knowledge and culture which is necessary if the continuity of civilization is to be secured. More specifically modern is a concrete emphasis rather like that to be found in the two passages just quoted. Over the last two hundred years there has been a progressive reorientation which has concretized heritage, identifying it with property rather than with knowledge and culture, with paintings and cultural artefacts, and through these, as Williams has shown, with actual landscapes and views themselves.[40] This developing social materiality of National Heritage must be understood in terms of the historic transformation of the public sphere: a transformation which has involved the hegemonic generalization and re-presentation of the bourgeois public sphere as 'national'. Just as the Transformed Bourgeois Public Sphere has no unique substance of its own there is no singular discourse of National Heritage. We are concerned instead with a dispersed configuration of images, emphases, ways of seeing, discursive forms (historiographic, legal, educational, literary etc.); in short a widely varied matrix which is not unified through any intrinsic common property so much as it is inclined *towards* unity through the activities of the different public sites within which it is inscribed. This matrix of National Heritage calls for a fuller historical analysis than we can supply in this article, but some key processes can be described all the same. After discussing the National Heritage Act (1980), we go on to characterize the development of the preservation lobby in relation to the state. We also consider how the development of National Heritage has been influenced by public forms of the kind that Negt and Kluge distinguish from the traditional and see emerging directly from the activities of capital. Taking Shell's advertising as an example we will look at the way in which 'national' images have been publicly shaped and reproduced directly around the developments of capital and market.

The National Heritage Act (1980) was prompted in part by the case of Mentmore, a stately home which lost its treasures and ended up being bought for the purpose of transcendental meditation while a Labour government appeared to fiddle and a Conservative lobby complained about Rome burning. National Heritage had a pungent ideological presence throughout the Thatcher election campaign, and the National Heritage Bill was introduced into the House of Commons with considerable patriotic clamour. At the second reading St John-Stevas, prime mover of the Bill, announced that this Act alone would justify his career, claiming that the Government would be remembered for this legislation long after its other achievements were forgotten.[41] The speech is worth quoting, parkland metaphors and all, for it gives an immediate impression of the evocative and imprecise rhetoric which, in its very vagueness, is central to the definition of National Heritage:

What has for so many years been a dream of visionaries and enthusiasts is about to become a reality. It is a measure of the importance that the Government attach to the preservation of our heritage that, despite all the pressures for the reduction of public expenditure which the government are quite rightly exerting, they have found room for the extra investment needed in this area. It is not an extravagant beginning, but it is not a derisory one either. 'Tall oaks from little acorns grow.' I believe that in future the branches of this fund will spread over the heritage ever more widely, protecting it from the economic storms and changes that make it especially vulnerable.[42]

The arboreal metaphor is peculiar to St John-Stevas, but a comparable language seems to have risen from all sides of the house. A Labour member spoke of other honourable members who have 'taken up cudgels' for the heritage, and Patrick Cormack, a Conservative MP and author of *Heritage in Danger*, announced that 'It is vital for the preservation of our heritage that it should never become a political football.'

Like most of the preservation legislation which had preceded it, the National Heritage Act (1980) has two main co-ordinates: it is concerned with the maintenance of that range of property which it defines as 'the heritage', but it also seeks to secure public access: to ensure that 'the heritage' is available for cultural consumption, and also that it is *displayed* as such. The National Heritage Act (1980) is a threefold measure: it eases the means whereby property can be transferred to the State in lieu of capital transfer tax and estate duty; in order to facilitate exhibition it provides indemnity to museums which might otherwise be unable to afford the cost of insuring objects loaned to other exhibitors; and it establishes the National Heritage Memorial Fund.

The National Heritage Memorial Fund was grafted onto the remains of the National Land Fund, a fund which was established under the guidance of Hugh Dalton in 1946 with £50 million, and which was intended to stand as a memorial to the Britons killed in the Second World War. That august lover of the English countryside Enoch Powell supervised the reduction of the National Land Fund to £10 m in 1957, and the National Heritage Memorial Fund took over the £16.6 m which remained in 1980. £5.5 m will, at least according to the Act, be added to the fund each year, but for all the ideological noise, and as St John-Stevas knew, this is not a vast sum of money. The National Heritage Memorial Fund, however, is a redesignation of more than just money; it also takes over the memorial function of the National Land Fund. In the era of the 'Imaginary Briton' those actual Britons who died in the Second World War lose their particularity completely, and we are left with a fund which stands (in the words of the Act) as 'a memorial for those who have died for the UK'. When? Where? How? And on which side? This is a memorial which gestures only towards itself.

The National Heritage Memorial Fund is administered by a group of independent trustees led by a chairman appointed by the Prime Minister. Judging from the parliamentary debates, these trustees were to be drawn from the heartlands of establishment ideology. There are to be amateurs, or, as St John-Stevas put it to the Commons, 'a group of what I call cultured generalists, reflecting the whole British heritage rather than experts in particular fields'.[43] Or, as Lord Mowbray and Stourton was to tell the Lords, 'the trustees are people of great common-sense in the world of art'.[44] The trustees, rather than the law, are to be responsible for formulating 'a working definition' of the national heritage. Like other working definitions, this one has never been explicitly formulated and one is left wondering what cultured generalism and common sense in the world of art amount to. There are clues, however, and one is to be found in the affiliations of the Chairman, Lord Charteris of Amisfield, who was appointed on 16 April 1980. The kind of understanding Lord Charteris is liable to bring into play is indicated by the fact that he is also the Provost of Eton College. Other interesting views have emerged from that quarter. During the strike which closed *The Times*, Michael McCrum, then headmaster of Eton, wrote to *The Guardian* contesting the view that public schools should not have charity status. McCrum described the use made of foundation funds, saying that 34 per cent is spent on scholarships, religious services, and 'other charitable activities'. He then went on to remark that:

Most of the rest was spent on the upkeep of the foundation buildings and grounds, only parts of which are used by those whose parents pay full fees, the oppidans. The college chapel and ancient buildings are part of the national heritage and were visited during the year by more than 60,000 tourists.[45]

The establishment, then, is not only shored up by charity status, but held above all criticism by the gaze of 60,000 tourists. If the gaze itself is not always charitable it is certainly by now a public institution.

As it has been phrased in the debates which surrounded the National Heritage Act, the national 'past' – 'our' common heritage – seems to be identifiable as the historicized image of the establishment. If this constitutes no stunning revelation nor will the fact that the Great Tradition of bourgeois culture was frequently invoked in the same debates: it is class culture, not simply class interests, which is being generalized as 'national'. There is certainly a defence and mystification of property relations at work in the National Heritage Act, but strategically this is not necessarily something which should be attacked head on – and not just because dispossessing a few well-heeled 'guardians' of 'our' heritage would be hopelessly inadequate as a social and political goal. Instead, and as a preliminary measure, it seems more useful to ask what it is that makes National Heritage so powerful as *ideology*. It is this power which stands in the way of head-on criticism, and which also prevented any concerted challenge being made against the National Heritage Act while it was still being debated, either for its involvement with a particular distribution of wealth or for its assumptions about the nature of history. At present there seems to be no public position from which criticism can be sustained: indeed it sometimes seems as if questioning National Heritage were akin to turning a flamethrower onto a Rembrandt canvas. The rebuttals are well known, if only because they hold government office at the moment: 'These are just the politics of resentment'; 'You are advocating nothing more than a uniform equality of deprivation – everyone herded together in some East European style housing project'; 'Either you leave things as they are or you move us all one step closer to the Gulag'; 'This is just vandalism. Why shouldn't people enjoy their past?'; etc.

In a climate such as this it is not always productive to contest dominant ideologies by opposing them in terms of a partisan and separatist truth. Any engagement must be *with* the ideologies in question, and it is for this reason that it is crucial to understand the ideologies and images which provide much of the motivation for the National Heritage Act. To what historical process do they owe their definition? One of the main agencies of this definition has been the preservation lobby, which has been working to extend the range of public intervention in the preservation of monuments, beauty spots and buildings of historic interest ever since its formation in the latter half of the nineteenth century. Patrick Cormack finds the significant history beginning in 1854 when John Ruskin submitted a proposal to the Society of Antiquaries suggesting that an Association be established to maintain an inventory of 'buildings of interest' threatened by demolition or the wrong kind of restoration.[46] The 1860s saw legislation to protect wildlife from the ravages of the fashion for plumage – a fashion which had numerous bourgeois women sporting half a seagull on their hats (and many others protesting) – but the first parliamentary manoeuvre on the preservation of monuments came a decade or so later when the Liberal MP Sir John Lubbock drew up his National Monuments Preservation Bill. Influenced by Ruskin's earlier initiative, this proposed the establishment of a National Monuments Commission along with a schedule of those monuments which the Commission would protect. This bill was rejected on its second reading in 1875 as were Bullock's next two attempts to get preservation legislation enacted in 1878 and 1879. The opposition to preservation may have been enhanced by Tory anti-aestheticism, but repeatedly it came down to one fundamental objection: the enactment of any of Lubbock's bills would introduce into 'the law of the land' a principle which elevated public interests above private property rights. This transformation of the public sphere was resisted heavily, and the resistance was expressed clearly by the Tory, Francis Hervey, who asked:

are the absurd relics of our barbarian predecessors, who found time hanging heavily on their hands, and set about piling up great barrows and rings of stones, to be preserved at the cost of infringement to property rights?[47]

In 1882, with Gladstone in power, a bill prepared by Lubbock was enacted as the Ancient Monuments Protection Act. It was a weak affair which established a schedule of some twenty-one monuments which the 'nation' might take into guardianship or purchase. The 1882 Act was strengthened in 1900, but even then it was not sufficient to resolve the conflict between growing pressure for public intervention in matters of preservation and the private property rights which were so heavily represented in both Houses of Parliament. The Act provided no compulsion and it didn't apply at all to inhabited monuments. While Parliament hesitated at the brink of infringing property rights the extra-parliamentary preservation lobby continued to expand its activities. It was in the institutionalization of this lobby that a working solution to the conflict between public interest and private property was eventually negotiated. This can be seen at work in the early history of the National Trust.

The National Trust was formed in 1895, but the impetus for its formation lies in the 1880s with the experience of an organization called the Commons Preservation Society which had campaigned successfully over Hampstead Heath and Epping Forest. Because the Commons Preservation Society did not have corporate status it was legally barred from acquiring land and could consequently not purchase common rights. In 1884 Robert Hunter, solicitor with the CPS, proposed that a body be created which was incorporated under the Joint Stock Companies Act, and therefore able to buy and hold land and buildings 'for the benefit of the nation'. As Hunter said, 'the central idea is that of a Land Company formed . . . with a view to the protection of the public interests in the open spaces of the country'. Hunter was supported by Octavia Hill who suggested that the name be National Trust rather than Company so that the benevolent side of the operation would be stressed. The third founding figure was Hardwick Rawnsley, a friend of Ruskin's who was a priest in Keswick. Rawnsley had been active with the Lake District Defence Society, an organization which had been rallying the ghosts of Coleridge and Wordsworth in order to oppose the construction of railways and the closure of traditional rights of way in the Lake District. The Lake District Defence Society was caught in the same impasse as the Commons Preservation Society: it might try to 'save' threatened beauty spots with money raised by public subscription, but there existed no body which could hold land for the benefit of the nation. In 1894 the constitution of the National Trust was drafted and a meeting resolved:

that it is desirable to provide means whereby landowners and others may be enabled to dedicate to the nation places of historic interest or natural beauty, and to this purpose it is expedient to form a corporate body, capable of holding land, and representative of national institutions and interests.[48]

In 1895 the Association was registered as 'The National Trust for Places of Historic Interest and Natural Beauty': it was registered under the Companies Act, but because the Trust was not profit making it was not obliged to include 'Limited' in its title.

Especially during the first twenty years of its existence, the National Trust worked as a campaigning pressure group. This brought it into explicit conflict with government on several occasions. Nevertheless, in its concern with what it has defined and reproduced as at once the 'public' and the 'national' interest the Trust has also had a ground in common with government. At the institutional level, the Trust has been effective by working in close relation to both government and capital. Within two years of its formation it was advising County Councils on the listing of historic buildings, and in the same early years it was attempting to unite and organize preservation groups. In 1900, for example, archaeological societies and field groups were brought into affiliation. This organization of the preservation lobby was double-edged: it brought about a more concerted and effective lobby at the same time as it produced a more corporate and therefore, under certain circumstances, a more *manageable* one. In 1907 an Act of Parliament gave the National Trust the right to hold land 'inalienably' – i.e. it was protected so that no one could acquire Trust property without permission from Parliament. Legally instituted in this novel way under the Companies Act, the National Trust seems to have provided the state with a way out of the conflict between public interest and private property. The two are now negotiated, if not wholly reconciled, but at a displaced level: as a registered company the National Trust holds property *privately*, and yet it does so in what it defines as the national and public interest. Indeed this national public interest occupies a position analogous to that of the shareholder in an ordinary limited company. We do not take a completely negative view of the National Trust, but the inalienability of the Trust's property can be seen, and is certainly often staged, as a vindication of property relations: a spectacular enlistment of the historically defined categories 'natural beauty' and 'historic interest' which demonstrates how private property *is* in the national public interest.

With preservation established as a national public concern *within* the relations of private property, the tone of Conservative thought on the matter appears to change. Hervey's pompous complaints about relics and barbarians gives way to an almost opposite assertion. This can be heard in the words of the Tory Lord Curzon, who spoke against his party's previous opposition to preservation law in the debates which surrounded the extension of the Ancient Monuments Protection Act which became law in 1913:

This is a country in which the idea of property has always been more sedulously cherished than in any other, but when you see that to get that Bill through Parliament it had to be denuded of its important features, and only after many years was it passed in an almost innocuous form into law, one feels almost ashamed of the reputation of one's countrymen.[49]

How is one to account for this shift in emphasis? While it may not be wholly determined, the shift does accompany a change in the role of the bourgeoisie. In the mid nineteenth century the bourgeoisie, as bearer of capital, was transforming the whole fabric of society. By the end of the nineteenth century, and more acutely as the twentieth developed, the dominance of the bourgeoisie was less secure. Economic crisis, change in the state of imperialism, the rise of working-class organizations and war all threatened its position. A growing concern with the *preservation* of capitalist social relations develops in this context. The preservation of social relations and the attempt to preserve monuments and landscapes are obviously not identical processes. However, these two forms of preservation appear to have developed in close relation to one another throughout the twentieth century. The bourgeois emphasis on preservation is concerned to perpetuate the social relations which are basic to capitalism, and the remarks which we will be making about Patrick Cormack's book *Heritage in Danger* indicate the extent to which it can still affect this preservation, by constructing the social relations in question into the vocabulary and image-repertoire of National Heritage. There is no easy solution found here, though, and the relation between capitalist property interests and the preservation of heritage sites has remained fraught throughout this century. The problem has been that capitalist property relations can only be preserved if they are reproduced through new accumulative cycles. Preservation of these relations therefore necessitates the constant transformation of social relations in accordance with the needs of capital. It entails widespread change and actual demolition and this brings it into conflict with the preservation lobby.[50] This conflict, which we have described only schematically, certainly needs more specific historical analysis if its actual forms are to become clear. We suggest, however, that it still underlies the publicly constructed serenity of National Heritage.

The preservation lobby is not class-determined in a direct or mechanical way, and it never lies simply in the pocket of the state. The struggle over public access to land and rights of way continued with real intensity through the 1920s and 1930s, and in organizations like the Ramblers Association it had a strong working-class base. The preservation movement continues to involve resistance to the inroads of capital into urban space, and it does oppose the destruction of traditional towns and landscapes for purposes of speculation or development. However, in the early twentieth century there seems to have developed an increasingly stable and safe means of negotiating the emergent conflict between preservation and property. Crucial to this is the organization of the preservation lobby in close relation to Parliament.

The growing complex of extra-parliamentary pressure and amenity groups concerned with preservation, and the activities of this complex in relation to the various apparatuses of the state have contributed largely to the repertoire of National Heritage. We can identify this contribution initially by indicating the conjunction of 'historic interest' and 'natural beauty' which is to be found in the full name of the National Trust. Obviously this conjunction does not originate with the National Trust,[51] and one place where it exists before 1895 is in the academic Fine Art tradition. The National Trust may work to preserve, but it is also an organization through which class-specific academic culture has been generalized and more widely disseminated. It should be remembered that John Ruskin figures in the background, that there are links between the early National Trust and the remains of the Pre-Raphaelite Brotherhood, and that in 1900 three out of four Vice Presidents of the National Trust were members of the Royal Academy. The preservation lobby has been active in bringing this coalescence of 'historic interest' and 'natural beauty' into prominence in national public life. Both categories were historically constituted to start with, and their coalescence has produced a merger in which a conventional realism is used to naturalize a bourgeois interpretation of history and society. This coalescence is basic to the repertoire of National Heritage, and it continues to play an important part in generalizing bourgeois into 'national' culture. The heritage lobby often speaks of the country house as the 'soul' of Britain. Certainly the country house is the most classical instance of the coalescence in question: it combines its own 'historic interest' with the 'natural beauty' of what are actually heavily landscaped and aestheticized surroundings: the 'soul' of a nation or just the perfect naturalization of a dominant view of the nation, or both?

'Reinstating the land'

We moderns are in love with the background. Our art is a landscape art. The ancient landscape painter could not, or would not, trust the background to tell its own tale.

Jane Harrison (1913)[52]

The view of the landscape, of the trees, of the sky – these are the charms of residence.

Stephen Graham (1927)[53]

The urbanism which destroys cities recomposes a pseudo-countryside which loses the natural relations of the ancient countryside.

Guy Debord (1967)[54]

You can't drive along the A4 in Wiltshire and ignore history.

Sandra Carpenter (1980)[55]

Negt and Kluge claim that the Transformed Bourgeois Public consists not only of transformed traditional public forms, but also of public forms which are produced and reproduced directly around the activities of capital. If we turn to the advertising produced by Shell from the early 1920s it becomes apparent that the preservation lobby is linked into this process, and that it is not only effective in relation to

Parliament and other state institutions. A typical advertisement which Shell placed in the trade magazines in October 1973 carried the heading 'Do you know any other petrol company which encourages motorists to walk?':

Last year once again, thousands of people got out of their cars and starting walking.
  Along cliff-tops, through deep rich woodlands and down by the seashore.
  They were following Shell–National Trust Nature Trails.
  A trail followed by thousands of motorists before them.
  For Shell and the countryside are old friends.
  No other company since the invention of the motor car can claim to have done so much to help open up the countryside to the ordinary motorist.
  Or to have helped preserve it for future generations of motorists to enjoy.
  Whether tramping the nature trails, reading about it in the Shell Guide, or listening to it on Shellsound guides, the Shell name is constantly in front of them.
  For the Shell name is one of the most continuous and rewarding of promotions in the history of advertising.
  It helps Shell sell more petrol than any other petrol company in the UK.
  And it's ours the moment you become a Shell dealer.
  Along with 73 years of goodwill, advertising and promotional activity second to none.
  You'll have to walk a long way to do better than that.

Shell   *The name every other petrol company would like to have.*[56]

Nature and preservation are evidently good for business, both as a direct induce-ment to consumption (on the brink of the energy crisis) and also in the more general terms of public relations. But above all it is the stylized sense of paradox which is indicative of Shell's recent advertising strategy. It is aimed at the general public now, at the driver rather than the garage owner or tenant. One such advertisement appeared in the *Guardian* on 13 September 1979. Most of the page was occupied by a spell-binding colour photograph the quality and effect of which can usefully be described in the terms of Walter Benjamin and Jakov Lind. In 'The work of art in the age of mechanical reproduction' Benjamin discusses a photo-graphic naturalism which is both profoundly technical and at the same time apparently free of all technical mediation. He then commented that 'the equipment-free aspect of reality here has become the height of artifice; the sight of immediate reality has become an orchid in the land of technology'.[57] This says quite a lot about the image which burst into a certain area of public consciousness from that Thursday's *Guardian*. As for Jakov Lind, on the opening page of his novel *Landscape in Concrete*, he writes that 'a landscape without faces is like air nobody breathes. A landscape in itself is nothing'.[58]

  This photograph makes an immediate impact; indeed, it is designed to leap off the page. Stunningly 'natural', the image shows a river meandering across the page and into the distance: green grass, trees and hedges in the foreground, and a climbing landscape of fields and foothills in the distance. There is no sign of humanity, except that of course this is a singularly worked form of 'nature'. We are

This, believe it or not, is how Shell goes recruiting its marine ecologists.

Every few weeks, a Shell scientist visits beautiful Dornoch Firth, cradled in the heather-blue hills of northern Scotland, to hand-pick 100 sturdy mussels.

They're part of a unique environmental study taking place in the depths around Shell's North Sea oil platforms, where they sit sampling seawater and helping Shell ecologists monitor any signs of pollution from our massive oil-production effort.

The fact is that our oil-platforms and rigs aren't isolated specks lost in grey ocean wastes.

The Brent Field is a self-contained oiltown where, on a clear day, you can see more than 20 huge structures ranging from giant production platforms like Brent Charlie to drilling rigs that crouch like enormous spiders on the horizon.

Operating the field involves the discharge into the sea of large quantities of water pumped up with the crude from oil reservoirs deep below the seabed.

And although all waste water is filtered and cleaned far more thoroughly than government safety limits require, tiny traces of impurity inevitably remain.

Hence our experts, the mussels. They have the blotting paper-like ability to extract and accumulate the minutest quantities of chemical impurities and hydrocarbons from seawater.

By examining the body-chemistry of Dornoch mussels before and after a spell in the Brent Field, we can detect and check any pollution threat long before it's had time to become a problem.

It's an early warning system designed to protect the entire ocean food-chain: plankton and algae, bright feathery sea-anemones, brown shrimp, jellyfish, whiting, cod, grey seal and even whales.

Britain needs North Sea oil. But we must guard against any unwanted consequences of that need. Which, in a nut- (or rather a mussel-) shell, is what our splendid Dornoch Shellfish are doing.

You can be sure Shell's playing its part

Wouldn't you protest if Shell ran a pipeline through this beautiful countryside?

They already have!

Tom Allen,
Shell Horticulturist

"When Shell proposed a pipeline from the North East coast of Anglesey to Stanlow refinery, seventy eight miles away in industrial Cheshire, people were worried.

The line would run through part of the Snowdonia National Park and have to pass under rivers Conwy, Elwy, Clwyd and Dee.

What scars would remain?

It is five years since the line was laid, and as I fly along the route today, even I can see no sign of it.

On the ground, the course of the pipe can be followed by a series of small unobtrusive markers. Apart from these, there is nothing to tell you that the top of a pipeline runs one metre beneath your feet.

The sheer invisibility of the line surprises visitors but not me. I was responsible for re-instating the land and well know what unprecedented lengths we went to. Every foot of the way was photographed before digging started, and the vegetation restored the way the record showed it ... even to the exact varieties of grass.

Sometimes, I agreed deviations in the line to avoid disturbing rare trees. In addition, a team of archaeologists preceded pipeline contractors to make sure that the route would avoid cromlechs, barrows, earthworks and other historical sites.

We are proud of the result, and it shows the way for other conservation projects."

You can be sure of Shell

in Snowdonia National Park, and the sky is a deep dark yellow: a thundering effect, a sense of strangeness and menace, but also a photographic cultivation of the wild. As for the point of view and the perspectives which it introduces into the image, it too is strangely unaccountable: slightly higher than might be expected of the tourist's regulated glance from the driver's window, and yet lower than the customary aerial photography. Nature is strange, an 'other', a place to go, a goal for the city-dweller. The somewhat unreal position that consumerism sets up for the tourist is embodied in this image. Dislocated and caught in a constructed sense of the 'natural' view, the reader of the *Guardian* can only answer 'Yes' to the slogan which appears beneath the image: 'Wouldn't you protest if Shell ran a pipeline through this beautiful countryside?' But, as the text goes on to say, 'They already have'. Beside a comforting mugshot of an expert, of the distinctly 'rural' looking Shell horticulturist, comes the authoritative elaboration:

When Shell proposed a pipeline from the North East coast of Anglesey to Stanlow refinery, seventy eight miles away in industrial Cheshire, people were worried.

The line would run through part of the Snowdonia National Park and have to pass under the rivers Conwy, Elwy, Clwyd and Dee.

What scars would remain?

It is five years since the line was laid, and as I fly along the route today, even I can see no sign of it.

On the ground, the course of the pipe can be followed by a series of small unobtrusive markers. Apart from these there is nothing to tell you that the top of a pipeline runs one metre beneath your feet.

The sheer invisibility of the line surprises visitors but not me. I was responsible for reinstating the land and well know what unprecedented lengths we went to. Every foot of the way was photographed before digging started, and the vegetation restored the way the record showed it . . . even to the exact varieties of grass.

Sometimes, I agreed deviations in the line to avoid disturbing rare trees. In addition, a team of archaeologists preceded pipeline contractors to make sure that the route would avoid cromlechs, barrows, earthworks and other historical sites.

We are proud of the result, and it shows the way for other conservation projects.

Finally, there appears the slogan which has been kept in public consciousness since at least the 1930s: 'You can be sure of Shell'.

On 15 October 1980 another full page advertisement in the *Guardian* extended the contemporary theme of the suburban fox: a fox in the foreground and scrub grass leading up to an oil refinery silhouetted against a reddish and slightly smoky sky. 'A Shell refinery alive with wildlife' reads the slogan, and then comes the reassuring narration from the horse's mouth; this time it is one of Shell's 'Environmental Technicians' who begins by saying:

An oil refinery is not the first place you'd look for herons, or a marsh harrier, or a kingfisher, or a fox. Yet, strange as it may seem, the open spaces in and around Shell's Stanlow refinery literally abound with wildlife.

More recently, one of the *Observer* colour supplements in December 1980 contained a Shell advertisement in which the photograph presents a modernized yeoman, a rather stalwart agricultural worker standing behind some harvesting machinery. The fields lead back to a sky which is blackish-green, and the slogan breaks in as follows: 'To you, it's a barley field. To us, it's a battlefield'. Turning back to the *Guardian*, on 12 August 1981 a full page advertisement announced that 'This, believe it or not, is how Shell goes recruiting its marine ecologists'. The photograph shows an outdoor type scrabbling around under another freaky sky (blackish-red). He is 'recruiting' mussels with a sack from among green kelp on the shores of what the text announces as 'beautiful Dornoch Firth'. The mussels are to be installed around North Sea oil rigs (which 'crouch like enormous spiders on the horizon') and monitored for signs of pollution.

The same insistence permeates these four advertisements: that those two constructed neutralities 'nature' and 'technology' walk hand in hand through this progressive, if slightly bizarre, modern world. It is not only that, as in the advertisement addressed to garage owners, 'nature' and conservation are good for business. More significantly, 'nature' provides the final layer of insulation around the pipeline: the wilds are literally wrapped around the oil company's operations. It is certainly remarkable that Shell, a company whose entire operation has been premised upon that vast transformation of relations to the environment which accompanies the development of the automobile, can not only present itself as the guardian of 'nature' and 'historical sites', but can also secure the assistance of the preservation lobby for the sake of this presentation.

With the exception of a period around the Second World War when the government took over petrol distribution and advertising was consequently suspended, Shell has been producing advertisements which work with the themes of 'nature' and 'history' since before the First World War. The constraints have obviously changed – in recent years, for example, it has not been possible openly to promote profligate consumption of petrol – but the advertisements produced over the last sixty years show a remarkable consistency. The recent advertisements which have just been described draw and elaborate on a well-established repertoire which extends far beyond the well-publicized slogan 'You can be sure of Shell'. The ruralism going alongside a celebration of technology, the perspectives of the images, the almost parental claim to care for both 'nature' and 'history', the reassuring text with its mixture of comfort, expertise and good common sense, the cultivatedly pedagogical relation between text and image: these and other characteristics of the advertisements can be traced through the developments of five decades.

Through the early part of the twentieth century Shell was operating in sharp competition with other oil companies, and more than in other areas of industrial production this competition was heavily concentrated on the control of markets. Shell's early growth was partly due to its access to Russian oil and its ability to subsidize one market by playing it off against another. The fundamental question within the British market, however, seems to have been different. How does a company strive to control a market when there is no visible difference between its merchandise and that of rival companies? There is surely now no difference between petrol from Esso, BP and Shell, for example, and even before refining procedures were standardized it is unlikely that the differences were very recognizable. From the twenties onwards – and alongside a whole series of 'secret ingredients' and measures to control outlets – Shell appears to have found a strategy to deal with this problem through advertising. This advertising redefined the countryside in terms of tourism and leisure, and in doing so at a time when so much of the target population was dissociated from traditional relations to the land, it represented the countryside in strikingly abstract terms. The countryside is equated with cyclical time, with colour and the seasons, and as such it is repossessed in bright advertising images and a marketing approach which differentiates 'Summer Shell' from 'Winter Shell'. In the more homogenized space of commodity circulation, distance is no longer experienced in any traditional sense: indeed, Shell restages it as 'the measured mile' with which the motorist causes the countryside to pass in review, as so many miles per gallon.[59] The countryside is a goal now, a place of strange allure, a utopian zone which in its 'historical' capacity still holds residues of a former world: traces of an Albion in which time is still cyclical but to which the motorist can still make his progressive way. History, progress, the time of travel all lead to a timeless *Gestalt* of earth with 'nation', and the consumerist 'visit' is sublimated in advertising which makes oblique references to an earlier and less predictable kind of travel which, after Debord, can be called the 'journey'. The tourist is the questing hero, motorized and on wheels.

It would be wrong to assert a total continuity of development in Shell's advertising, but there are noteworthy developments nevertheless. In the late 1930s, for example, the car tends to be removed, taken out of the ruralist image (the growing tension between motoring and preservation seems to encourage this). Over the same period of time the road, which has always been carefully positioned in relation to landscape, becomes evident as a principle of perspective. In numerous advertisements it provides the continuity between foreground and viewed distance, and in many of the advertisements its passage through landscape is likened to that of a river: as if, as indeed is the case in one sense, the countryside takes its shape around the passage of the motor car. In a series produced in the early sixties and called 'Explore the Roads of Britain with Shell' the road itself becomes prehistoric, natural and immemorial: the series is concerned with ancient roads such as the Fosse Way or the Roman Steps in Merionethshire, and although the perspectives are identical to those of earlier images, the roads are now green or of natural stone. The tarmac has gone and the road has become a primordial pathway, 'natural' and 'historic' combined. Nothing is left but a primitive and 'timeless' pact with the earth. Given the links between earth and nation that an image such as this invokes, the pact seems very similar to that mentioned in the passage quoted earlier from Sartre's *Anti-Semite and Jew*.

It is as an agency in the reproduction of hegemonic cultural values and ideas that Shell is of interest to this discussion. There are two aspects of this process of reproduction which are especially worth identifying more closely. The first

Explore the roads of Britain with Shell

painted by David Gentleman

BERKSHIRE RIDGEWAY and ICKNIELD WAY

The Berkshire Ridgeway is one of the most ancient of roads—a 'green road' nowadays—a downland loop, over the dry chalk heights of Berkshire and North Wiltshire, of the longer Icknield Way, which runs up from Salisbury Plain past Stonehenge and over the Chilterns towards the Wash. When the Icknield Way was dry, it probably went on to Lincolnshire and eastern Yorkshire. How old are Ridgeway and Icknield Way? 4,000, or perhaps nearer 5,000 years: they were used in times before history by pedlars who brought down axes and adzes and knives from the neolithic flint mines at Grime's Graves in Norfolk, where the miners worked with picks of red-deer horn (1) and ornaments of whitby jet from Yorkshire.

In this section (easily reached from B 4507, between Wantage and Swindon), the Ridgeway passes Wayland Smith's Cave (2), in the left-hand clump of trees, a neolithic tomb of sarsen stones about as old as the road itself. A thousand and more years ago, our English ancestors gave this tomb its name, believing it had been the workshop in which the legendary smith Wieland made his magic swords and armour. Down below are the Vale of White Horse, and (out of sight) the Uffington White Horse (3) itself, cut into the chalky slope. To the right are the ditch and bank of Uffington Castle. Horse and Castle are much younger than the road or the 'smithy'. The strange horse was cut on the hillside not long before the Romans came, perhaps because a white horse was the emblem of the British tribe hereabouts.

The complete series of the Shell guides to the Roads of Britain will be published in book form by Ebury Press in May 1964, and may be ordered from any bookseller at 21/6 net.

YOU CAN BE SURE OF [Shell] *The key to the Countryside*

Explore the roads of Britain with Shell

painted by David Gentleman

THE ROMAN STEPS

The Roman Steps in Merionethshire, North Wales (reached from Llanbedr, up the valley of the Artro, and then past the very beautiful little lake of Cwm Bychan), are not Roman, but probably mediaeval—the best surviving example in Wales of 'horse steps' up a pass. Whatever their exact date, these great, richly massed slabs of stone form a causeway or paved way—in Welsh a *sarn*—lifting a trail for packhorses (4) over the Rhinogs, via the pass or gap called Bwlch Tyddiad (Rhinog Fawr rises above the Steps and then the pass to 1,361 ft.). This trail—through wet country of valley and crag, wild rose and foxglove and mountain ash (5), heather and bilberry, curlew (6) and sandpiper (7)—seems to have started at Harlech Castle (8), which guarded a small port in the 14th century. Beyond the Roman Steps and the Rhinogs, it apparently crossed the moorland (astride the modern A 487 between Dolgelley and Ffestiniog) to Bala, where several other early roads intersected.

Many of the ancient packhorse trails of Britain were paved, in the same way over soft or difficult ground. In North Wales, there are remains of several other paved lengths of this kind—for instance, in the Nant Francon Pass, below Telford's Holyhead Road (A 5); and at Fedw-Deg, south of Betws-y-Coed, above the road to Dolwyddelan (A 496).

The complete series of the Shell guides to the Roads of Britain will be published in book form by Ebury Press in May 1964, and may be ordered from any bookseller at 21/6 net.

YOU CAN BE SURE OF [Shell] *The key to the Countryside*

concerns the involvement of the preservation lobby in Shell's advertising, and the second has to do with Shell's use of existing 'Culture' to lend its advertising campaign substance, resonance and credibility.

Shell and the preservation lobby

Shell's involvement with the preservation lobby is some sixty years old. In 1929 an advert was formulated under the title 'Shell and the Countryside'. The text read as follows:

Shell began removing its advertisement signs from the countryside as long ago as 1923. In 1927 they also asked their garage owners to remove Shell enamel plates from their premises. Many thousand such plates were, in consequence, abolished, and the work is still in progress. Shell's ways are different.

This piece of publicity, directly related to the start of 'lorry bills' (fairly large posters which were exhibited from the sides of Shell's delivery lorries), led into a concerted advertising campaign in the early 1930s. The campaign moved in two related directions, the first of which involved publishing facsimiles of letters sent to Shell by organizations such as the Royal Society of Arts and the Scapa Society for Prevention of Disfigurement in Town and Country. These letters acknowledge Shell's endeavours to protect the countryside from disfiguring advertisements, and were published under the sign of Shell in periodicals like the *Tatler* and the *Royal Society of Arts Journal*. The second direction is taken through rather more generally distributed adverts featuring photographs of beauty spots and the following text: 'The proprietors of Shell do not advertise their petrol in places like this'. In the 1950s and 1960s Shell's involvement with the preservation lobby takes on a far more emphatic pedagogical aspect, involving any number of calendars and nature guides which were taken up largely in schools. The images in these advertisements tend to follow an identifiable form: they show a collection of bits and pieces – feathers, cones, berries and suchlike – fragments of 'nature' which are singled out for pedagogical identification. These items are gathered together for the purposes of a nomenclature which forms the substance of the text, and they are displayed in the foreground of the image. A long view stretches out behind them to a landscape in the distance. The emphasis throughout is that one 'knows' nature in order to be better able to appreciate and care for it. In these later advertisements it is knowledge and education – the act of naming – rather than the car and the road which bridges the distance between near and far.

Shell and the cultural connection

Shell has made extensive use of established cultural values in developing its advertising repertoire. In terms of 'Art' this is evident in the still-famous series of 'lorry bills' which were produced throughout the 1920s and 1930s. These 'lorry bills' always featured paintings, and while some of the earlier images certainly do work in terms of a conventional realism it is much more significant that the series also make continuous appeal to what begins to look like a conventional *un*realism.

Considering these images one is not, for example, dealing only with an art which seeks to efface itself, to bury all trace of its production in the view which it sets up as 'natural' and 'real'. The commissioned paintings which were reproduced as 'lorry bills' also tend to stress their character as paintings. One result of this is to lend the reproducible aura and authenticity of 'art' to those sites of 'natural' and/or 'historic' interest to which the advertisements encourage the motorist to drive. But there is something else at work here too, and it can be described as the identification of heritage sites and the countryside, not with any constructed sense of 'reality' so much as with *style*. 'Lorry bills' were produced in the thirties by artists such as McKnight Kauffer, Duncan Grant, Barnett Freedman, Paul Nash, Graham Sutherland and Ben Nicholson. Many of these later lorry bills, and especially those of the American expatriate McKnight Kauffer, tended to situate an assertively modernist style in the historically transforming disjunction between the urban motorist/viewer and the countryside. They use a modernist style to link the unfamiliarity with which the countryside appears to the city-dweller with the 'strangeness' of what, for all its oddity, is actually accepted as proper to 'modern art'. The evocation may still be nostalgic and pseudo-pastoral in many cases, but like motoring it is also stridently modern. The countryside is thus caught up in a tensed movement between a traditionalist display of 'nature' and a stylized celebration of the machine. It is caught up in a commotion which asserts both the cyclical time of the seasons, of the eternal return of 'nature', and also the irreversible historical time of progress, the time which has brought us the motor car. This commotion has become fairly basic to the image-repertoire of National Heritage – in the most familiar form progressive time is embodied as the road and the cyclical order of time is presented as scenery, the pastoral landscape through which the road sweeps. The same confluence of different orders of time facilitates another development which is at work in Shell's images during the 1920s: in this development the horse is lifted out of the rustic traditional field, transformed into a futuristic and metallic image, and then returned to the countryside as the horse-power which gets the driver out of the city.

But it is not just a developing battery of images which Shell has used to weld ideas of countryside, the visit and national history to the brand name. These connections are also attempted through an identification of a recognizable vocabulary and text. In the early 1920s Shell's advertising is not particularly articulate, its utterance being limited mostly to short and rather flat slogans. However, by the 1950s a language had been developed: a language full of cultural assumption, irony (even self-mockery), and display. In the early 1960s, for example, there appeared advertisements announcing that 'here you can relive legend and history on the spot', or, in the same scene-of-the-great-event vein, 'Glen Trool: where Bruce fled his own bloodhound'. But there is also a more evocative gibberish of authenticity, represented by the ridiculous text which accompanies a washed-out painting of Lower Lough Erne: 'Wrapped in morning mists of centuries, monks still hide'. A little bit of 'history', some 'beauty', a touch of 'artistic' and 'literary' style: these are among the basic elements of Shell's constructed national archaism

1920 (unsigned)

1925 (unsigned)

1931 (E. McKnight Kauffer)

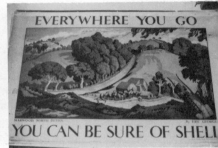

1932 (Eric George)

1932 (Paul Nash)

1934 (Denis Constanduras)

Six 'lorry bills' from the 1920s and 1930s

which is both spectacular and approachable by road.

It is worth outlining some of the more evident stages in the development of this vocabulary with its pseudo-literary edge. In the late 1920s a series of 'historical' cameos appeared in the *Listener*. These featured quite lengthy dialogues which were written in supposedly archaic language and mixed 'historical' figures (e.g. Pepys and Nell Gwynne) in discussion about places held abstractly in common (e.g. Whitehall). The dialogues always stacked time and space up on the well-publicized platform of Shell. In the thirties there were at least three noteworthy developments. The first is an extensive series of advertisements which made a stylized and 'witty' use of limerick structures to link places with the name of Shell: 'Stonehenge Wilts but Shell goes on forever'; 'Lover's Leap but Shell gets there first'; 'Stow on the Wold but Shell on the Road'; etc. In the 1930s Shell also introduced its 'Valentines' campaign. Shell 'Valentines' consisted of 'poetic' twitterings which were printed in the centre of closely drawn ruralist friezes:

Stop fair motorist divine
Here I am
   Your Valentine

Third, towards the end of the 1930s Shell started to publish its Country Guides. The first of an immensely influential series which still occupies a central place in the heritage canon, these were written, as the company announced, by authors 'who are generally poets or artists with a bump of topography'. Reminiscent, perhaps, of those 'cultured generalists' who were to be the trustees of the National Heritage Memorial Fund.

In sum, Shell draws on the established practice of Literature in much the same way as it draws on Art. Soft poets of a class-specific and stylized country lyricism (an upper-class equivalent of straw-chewing?) like John Betjeman and Geoffrey Grigson, were used extensively in the 1950s, for example. The significance of this cultural connection becomes evident if one considers the shifting audience to which Shell's advertising is addressed. It is evident, for example, that the earliest advertisements mentioned in this discussion – those from the early 1920s – derive from a time when motoring was available to a small and wealthy social fraction. It is the culture of this fraction which influences the formation of Shell's advertising repertoire: its vocabulary, its images and also what develops increasingly explicitly as a pedagogical relation between image and text. This cultural influence is a process of regulation, and it works in two ways. First, it is directly at work in the formation of Shell's early images in the 1920s. Second, developing bourgeois culture is influential in that it provides the milieu, indeed the 'public', from which later copywriters and artists were to be drawn, and in terms of which potential advertisements were judged before general dissemination. An example of this latter kind of cultural regulation is clearly described in Vernon Nye's unpublished 'Recollections of Shell and BP advertising'. Nye, who worked in Shell's Publicity Department during the thirties, describes how new advertisements were first published in pre-booked space on the 'Imperial and Foreign' page of *The Times*. In this way what Nye calls 'Management and Top People' would see the advertisement, and their reaction brought to bear on the decision whether the advertisement in question would be distributed more generally.

As the automobile became available to a wider public, Shell's advertising was directed towards a wider audience. By the 1960s and 1970s the automobile is within the reach of members of all social classes. At this point the advertisements go general, or rather 'national', in their appeal. They are now addressed to everyone: the citizen as motorist. In this shift of address, the repertoire certainly goes through some changes, but the overall effect is, nevertheless, the generalization as 'national' of those cultural values which, in origin and function, are specific to developed bourgeois culture. For a consideration of hegemony, then, Shell is significant as an apparatus of cultural reproduction. This process of reproduction can be seen very clearly in Shell's early entrance into television advertising with a series called 'Discover Britain'. As Vernon Nye recalls, 'the first advertisements were really an extension into television of the kind of advertising Shell had found so successful in the press and on posters':

The method chosen was to invite John Betjeman to select places worth visiting and talk about them. To do this effectively required the use of three minutes of time, whereas the limit allowed by the regulations was only two minutes. However, the agents Colman, Prentis and Varley, were able to persuade the authorities to allow three minutes. Research conducted by the London Press Exchange after commercial television had been operating for a time showed that the Shell commercials helped to make TV acceptable to the public who felt that if television advertising was to be like this then it did not mind at all.

Rented culture not only pleases 'the public', it also takes part in the continuous process of regulating the public as a specific social sphere.[60]

'The historic past'

With Mills and Boon you can discover romance in exotic faraway places, the historic past, and even in a busy hospital.[61]

The foregoing discussion of the National Trust and of Shell's advertising should have indicated the extent to which hegemony has been maintained through a public regulation of images and ideas about history, beauty and the 'nation'. If we return now to consider the rhetoric which has surrounded the National Heritage Act (1980) we will see that it interlocks with the various emphases of a constructed public sense of history. The first thing to consider is the fundamental vagueness which characterizes many 'definitions' of the National Heritage. As has been mentioned, the National Heritage Act delegates the question of definition to trustees who have since gone on to say:

We decided that it was unanswerable; we could no more define the national heritage than we could define, say, beauty or art . . . . So we decided to let the national heritage define itself. We awaited requests for assistance from those who believed they had a part of the national heritage worth saving.[62]

A 'working definition' if ever there was one . . . . Where the trustees of the National Heritage Memorial Fund deflected the difficulty of definition into the pragmatics of the Fund's administration, many pundits and enthusiasts tend to escape into a language of vague and evocative gesture. The result is a sub-lyricism well represented by the following passage from Patrick Cormack's book *Heritage in Danger*:

When I am asked to define our heritage I do not think in dictionary terms, but instead reflect on certain sights and sounds. I think of a morning mist on the Tweed at Dryburgh where the magic of Turner and the romance of Scott both come fleetingly to life; of a celebration of the Eucharist in a quiet Norfolk Church with the medieval glass filtering the colours, and the early noise of the harvesting coming through the open door; or of standing at any time before the Wilton Diptych. Each scene recalls aspects of an indivisible heritage, and is part of the fabric and expression of our civilisation.[63]

At first glance this passage seems to be clear only as an example of what Hermann Glaser once described in a different context as 'the deadening of thought through mythicizing vagueness.'[64] In a way that also recalls Sartre's remarks about anti-Semitism in wartime France, it proposes 'our heritage' as a sacrament encountered only in exquisite and fleeting experiences which lie beyond words precisely to the extent that they go without saying for initiates, for members of the 'nation'. Cormack rests his case on what is self-evident to the 'Imaginary Briton', part of a national common-sense and experience, of established public ideologies about history and belonging.

But the vagueness of the passage from Cormack indicates more than this. It also suggests that National Heritage does not just consist of *meanings* which are ideologically and publicly instituted. The experience and advocacy of heritage is not merely a matter of accurate conformity to public semantics. The historical texture of National Heritage as a way of thinking is also very closely connected to proto-narrative *structures* which can be articulated in different ways, which can be over-determined and pressed into service by various meanings, and which are capable of organizing and making sense of many different experiences.[65] Hence the various experiences which Cormack ascribes to National Heritage. Hence also the numerous early twentieth-century 'country' books which are now being republished on the contemporary vehicle of 'heritage'.[66] In this section of our chapter we will attempt to trace out some of the figures and structures which are active in the organization of National Heritage.

'The historical' as an abstract system of equivalences
At the ideological level of the nation, 'heritage' involves the extraction of history –

of the idea of historical significance, process and potential – from everyday life and its restaging and display in particular coded sites, images and events. In this process history is abstracted as 'the historical', and it becomes the object of a similarly transformed and generalized social attention. This process of abstraction is evident at one level in an advertisement which the Sun Alliance Insurance Group issued in 1980. As the text of this advertisement announced, 'Better bring your insurance problems to us. People have since 1710.' A similar presentation of history as the time of a certain kind of national test informs the memorable chorus line of Rober Altman's film about American populism, *Nashville*: 'We must be doing something right to last two hundred years'.

That this abstracted sense of history stands as more than just the proof of the pudding can be seen in the advertisement issued in the same year for *The Times Atlas of Western History* ('The book that puts history on the map'). The image of this advertisement combined four devastatingly 'historical' faces, including those o Gandhi, Elizabeth I and Hitler. In this image history is reproduced as a gloss, as the light touch of a dab hand, an impression which can be caught in a glance. This moonshine impression of history actually submerges the differences between the four figures and leaves only a multiple invocation of the same sense of 'the historical'. In this sense it is reminiscent of the 'memorial' function of the National Heritage Memorial Fund. Abstracted and redeployed, history is purged of difference; it has become a unifying spectacle, the settling of all disputes. In this respect the heritage relation appears to work analogously to exchange value. It brings all its different sites into a system of equivalence, and within this system the sites have meaning not in relation to everyday life but overwhelmingly in relation to one another. This system of equivalence provides the rationale for the combinatior of 'historical' portraits in the advertisement just described. A comparable system o equivalence provides the basis for the consumption of National Heritage in tourism equivalence is integral both to the guided tour within museum and gallery and also to the tour which takes place out on the road where the English, Welsh and Scottish Tourist Boards have recently been promoting 'Norman Heritage Trails' leading from one 'historical' site to the next:

This booklet contains nine trails which can be followed in whole or part, and which will help you to follow the 'Conqueror' on his triumphant route from Hastings to London: to visit the countryside where half-legendary guerrillas such as 'Edric the Wild' and 'Hereward the Wake' held out against William's soldiers: to see the great Abbeys of the Northcountry and the castles of the Welsh border and to seek out gems of Norman architecture throughout the land.

Take the road from the Tower and discover what Britain's Norman Heritage has to offer.[67]

'The historical' as timelessness

As it is taken up into these systems of equivalence and becomes 'historical', history also becomes 'timeless'.[68] This paradoxical sense of timelessness is in part a measu of endurance, of having 'come through' the trials of centuries. However, it also reflects the immobility which descends on the present when history is stylized and worn self-consciously over the social body. In order to become spectacular – something which one can stand outside and then reconnect within regular acts of appreciation – history must be completed and fully accomplished. As a process which is fully accomplished, history, with all its promise of future change and development, is closed down and confined entirely to what can be exhibited as 'the historic past'.

History as entropy: a process of ageing

If endurance is some sort of measure of achievement, value and quality, this is because historical time is now experienced as movement into degeneration, ignorance and disorder. The future apparently holds little in store but further decline, and therefore one can only hope for stalling measures improvised by necessarily conservative governments. As that embittered stager of ideology Wyndham Lewis wrote after the Second World War in *Rotting Hill*, Britain is now little better than a rabbit warren on top of a burned-out coalmine.[69] In this vision, human dignity is residual only, sustained by a continuously publicized nostalgia for 'roots' in an imperial and 'pre-industrial' past, and for the childhood which is increasingly caught up in these public constructions. In Flann O'Brien's words, 'I do not think the like of it will ever be there again'.[70]

The experience of history as entropy gathers momentum in the sharpening of the British crisis. National Heritage is the backward and predominantly hindering glance which is taken from the edge of the abyss, and it accompanies a sense that the future is foreclosed. With organic history in the last stages of degeneration we enter more than just a commemorative age of dead statues. Under the entropic view of history, supported as it is by High Cultural paradigms, 'the past' is revalued and reconstructed as an irreplaceable heritage – a trust which is bestowed upon the present and must be serviced and passed on to posterity. In this process the land or country house owner is transformed from owner to 'custodian'. He emerges as the 'steward' who does 'us' and the future a favour by living in the draughty corridors of baronial splendour. One can hear some of the key accents in the Duke of Edinburgh's stupefying Introduction to the Department of the Environment's booklet *What is Our Heritage?*:

The great achievement of European Architectural Heritage Year has been to draw attention to the shortcomings of our generation as curators of the European Architectural collection.[71]

The status quo becomes objective reality in a new sense. All Western Europe is now a museum, and those citizens who are not 'curators' of 'the collection' shouldn't worry that they have been left out, for they are still subjects of this new archaism. Their position is to look, to pay taxes, to visit, to care, to pay at the door (even when entering cathedrals these days), to 'appreciate' and to be educated in the process. In this context it is worth recalling that one of the objectives of the National Heritage Act is to increase the exhibition of 'the heritage'.

National Heritage makes numerous connections with what was initially an aristocratic and high-bourgeois sense of history as decline. As the *Spectator*'s view of Patrick Cormack's book *Heritage in Danger* announced, 'Physical decay, rather than politics, is Mr Cormack's main theme'.[72] Comparably, during the second reading of the National Heritage Bill, W. Benyon, Tory MP for Buckingham, made a curious statement which seems to have been intended to get preservation funds directed more towards property owners than towards the conservation of landscapes and wildlife. He defined national heritage as *that which moulders*.

Heritage and danger
Given an entropic view of history, it is axiomatic that 'heritage' is in danger. It is danger that defines 'the heritage' in the first place, and the struggle to 'save' it can only be a losing battle. The 'stewards' struggle valiantly on behalf of their trust, but a barbarian indifference is all around. It is against this indifference that the urgent tone of the parliamentary conservationist tends to direct itself: 'legislation designed to preserve the best of the past has often come too late' etc. As for the country house, because it is in danger owners are 'stewards' as we have said, but there is a manically fraudulent development on this theme which brings in the issue of inheritance:

The problems of the country house are not only fiscal, but physical. The owner has to do more and more physical work for himself, with the result that a large country house is no place for elderly people: hence the need to be able to hand on to the next generation – and the next generation will need just as much income, and probably more, than at present.[73]

Amazing passages such as this leave no doubt that National Heritage is not just a regulated and public accumulation of images and ideas. Like Debord's spectacle, National Heritage is a social relation mediated through images and publicly instituted ideas. It is this social relation which is in danger.

Objectified history: the landscape as palimpsest and the country house as hero
The idea of the palimpsest, a parchment which has borne more than one layer of inscription, has often been used to idealize the historical character of the British countryside. In this understanding, history is a series of inscriptions each of which half-cancels its predecessors. The partial erasure of earlier inscriptions is the devastation wrought by the degenerate later stages of an entropic history. In the midst of this landscape stands the country house, and Patrick Cormack presents it as a hero which has survived the ravages of time and now stands on its hill not only as a record of its own endurance, but also as an exhibition of the period treasures and touches of style which it has gathered on its way:

Rockingham is in many respects typical. The house has withstood the changes of fashion and the ravages of war, and now stands on its hill in Northamptonshire, a pleasing blend of medieval, Tudor and post Civil War architecture. It suffered considerably in that war and was altered fairly extensively in the 19th century. It is not a vast house, not in the same league as Chatsworth, Castle Howard, Blenheim or the great ducal palaces, but to enter between its twin round towers, to walk through its hall or along its long gallery, or to survey the shires from its tower, is to absorb a vast panorama of English history. And its changes in structure and internal design reflect the changing tastes of generations of owners who have sought to make it more comfortable for themselves and their families. Its furnishings are fascinating but homely, its portraits and country pictures interesting, in some cases lovely, but in no case of outstanding national importance. Yet no-one could argue that England would not be the poorer if the Reynolds or the Marshalls or the lovely Zoffany in the long gallery, or the intriguing portrait of Elizabeth I in the great hall were lost to the nation. Every year 30,000 people or more enjoy its sense of timelessness.[74]

History has withdrawn into the aesthetic.

National geography and Gestalt: *'the past' as an existent*
Considering the merger of history and landscape which lies at the heart of what is publicly fetishized as a national geography, it is consistent that 'the past' should be treated as if it were a simple existent. This emphasis takes two forms: 'the past' is there both to be dug up and also to be visited.

The first of these two objectifications of history derives from antiquarianism and archaeology. In this construction it is as if one only had to kick a stone in Ironbridge Gorge to uncover early industrial society. What might start as an (industrial) archaeological emphasis opens up a perspective in which 'the past' is defined entirely as bits and pieces which can be recovered, commodified and circulated in exchange and display. This emphasis on tangible remains tends to decontextualize the very objects through which it stages 'the past'. After all, it is difficult to 'recover' social relations – to auction them off or fit them inside glass cases. Industrial archaeologists and museum staff may well appreciate this as a problem of exhibition (as the Education Officer at Ironbridge Gorge asked us: 'skills, techniques and machines yes, but how does one exhibit social history?'), but this rendering of 'the past' as buried and recoverable bric-à-brac or treasure is not confined to the museum. For example, with the advent of the cheap metal detector 'the past' has become the quarry of a bizarre field sport. The resulting protest is to be heard in the voice of 'Stop Taking Our Past', an organization sounding as peculiar as the right-wing pressure group 'Land Usage Decayed', which was founded in March 1980 'to prevent Britain's archaeological heritage being wiped out':

We are appalled by the thought that one of the biggest threats to our heritage now comes not from the building of motorways, not from the building of new towns, but from hundreds and thousands of people with metal detectors.[75]

This passage is more than just the record of an existing problem (the updated barrow thief who leaves gaping holes in the verdant surface of historical sites). The hyperbole also ushers us into the theatre of middle-class images of the working class. The passage works on the transforming theme of the great un-washed, taking it far beyond even the later image of the urban proletariat spilling back onto the land in charabancs to leave litter and broken fences to mark the incomprehension of days of leisure.[76] The barbarians have now enlisted techno-logy in their search for 'the past', and if something isn't done soon they will surely dig it all up.

This quasi-archaeological sense of 'the past' as recoverable and talismanic bits and pieces is linked with a supposition which lies at the heart of contemporary tourism: that 'the past' is really there to be visited. Many television presentations of history have contributed to this rendering of 'the past' as an existent. One might, for example, recall the BBC's reconstituted 'Iron Age Village' which, as so much publicity and journalism announced, was not just in 'the past' but also hidden away 'somewhere' in the south of England between 1978 and 1980. Generally speaking, much television history is premised upon a valuation of *the scene* of past events: through the medium of television the viewer can 'visit' the past. It is worth considering what happens when the connection is actually made, when the past and present are brought together in the achieved National Heritage relation. To quote a narration by George Melly from a BBC2 programme entitled 'Shakespeare in Perspective':

The city traffic may roar past outside . . . but here for a moment the real estate agent from Dallas, the insurance clerk from south-east London may enjoy an hour or two in a simpler more gay world.[77]

It is this sense of transformation which needs to be understood, and one needn't worry unduly that it applies equally to Texan and Londoner (there is a whole industry of genealogists giving white American and post-Commonwealth tourists access to the National Heritage via 'roots'). A National Heritage site must be suffi-ciently of this world to be accessible by car and/or camera, but it must also provide access to that other 'simpler' world when the tourist/viewer finally gets there. This publicly instituted transformation which moves between the real and the imaginary is central to the operation of National Heritage. National Heritage has its sites, but like amulets to believers these sites exist only to provide that momentary experience of utopian gratification when the grey torpor of everyday life in contemporary Britain lifts and the simpler pre-political, and usually pre-industrial measures of Albion stand revealed to the initiate's glance. This publicly instituted lapse into neo-tribalism can be understood in terms of Sartre's descrip-tion of the primitive community of anti-Semitism. As can be seen from the following letter which was sent to the *Birmingham Evening Mail* by an expatriate now resident in Africa, the pleasure of this ideology involves the pseudo-poetry of a 'national' and implicitly racist *Gestalt*:

I received a copy of the *Evening Mail*'s Our England special today. A curse on you.

I had just (after 12 months) convinced myself that I was well rid of the rotten weather, football hooligans, unions, dirt, inflation, traffic, double standards of politicians – and suddenly it's back to square one. The grimy façade is lifted, and the real England comes flooding back.

Long winter walks through the Wyre Forest ending at the George at Bewdley, chestnuts roasted on an open log fire and swilled down with a pint of mild, house hunting round Ludlow for the mythical half-timbered home, the joy of finding one at a price I could afford and trips to auctions to furnish it for £60. . . .

Summer evenings at the Royal Shakespeare, scents wafting across the river. . . . The sounds and scenes of England.

Thanks for helping me regain a sense of perspective.[78]

National Heritage is visitable, but it also provides access to another world. Hence not only the British Tourist Authorities' slogan 'Go away to Britain', but also a slogan from the Irish Tourist Board: 'Take a small step sideways and find yourself in another world.' British Rail hasn't missed out on this theme either. In 1980 BR advertised a special train of 'historical' carriages under the slogan 'In the high speed world of today it's nice to have a quick look back'. With some of the Inter-City trains now moving at 120 m.p.h., it doesn't seem entirely facetious to suggest that this 'quick look back' is increasingly just a glance out of the window. For isn't the very look of rural Britain now publicly identified with 'the historical' itself? Isn't that the eighteenth century which can be seen flying past outside the window? Or has agribusiness won the field and landed us in the prairies?

National Heritage: leisure and utopia

What is the significance of this division of social life into two distinct worlds threaded together by tourism and cultural consumption? Familiar polarities are clearly basic to the public status of National Heritage: freedom as opposed to necessity, leisure as opposed to work, country and traditional town as opposed to modern urban development, hope as opposed to despair of everyday stoicism, the imagination as opposed to objective activity, organic history as opposed to the bureaucracy and administration of the modern industrial state. But there is more to be said than this mapping of contraries necessarily indicates. We have already mentioned the utopian gratification which is afforded by National Heritage, and at this point it is worth considering this gratification in relation to the *explicit* utopianism which is also characteristic of National Heritage. National Heritage borrows many of the trappings of the English utopia (of Arthurian legend, of Blake and Samuel Palmer, of Morris and Pre-Raphaelitism), but it stages utopia not as a vision of possibilities which reside in the real – nor even as a prophetic perspective on the real – but as a dichotomous realm existing alongside the everyday. Like the utopianism from which it draws, National Heritage involves positive energies which certainly can't be written off as ideology. It engages hopes, dissatisfactions, senses

of tradition and freedom, but it tends to do so in a way that diverts these potentially disruptive energies into the separate and regulated space of leisure. Leisure is
not merely the realm of acquirable beauty and health (the holiday sun-tan etc.); it
is also the removed and anodyne realm in which gratification is offered for dissatisfaction developed in relation to work, contemporary urbanism etc.[79] Increasingly,
it is through the realm of leisure that 'the past' is encountered, and the encounter
itself involves a second displacement which positions National Heritage, along with
all that it engages, 'behind' the present. In this way, what much utopianism has
alluded to or postulated as the challenge of history – something that needs to be
brought about – ends up behind us already accomplished and ready for exhibition
as 'the past'.

The link between National Heritage and leisure has been brought about largely
through the development of tourism. The character and public status of National
Heritage has therefore been formed in relation to the systems of communication
which provide the basis for tourism. Edward Jesse, one of nineteenth-century
England's more prominent ruralists, knew this as early as 1847 when his *Favourite
Haunts and Rural Studies* was published:

In these days of rapid travelling by railroads, it has often struck me that many of
those interesting spots to which the traveller was formerly enticed by the convenience of coaches passing near them, and the comfort to be found in small country
inns, will now seldom be visited. All the world seems to be hurrying from one point
to a far distant one, intent only on transacting some business, or in paying visits to
friends or relations. Objects and places of interest are consequently but little sought
after, except they happen to be near the terminus of a railroad, or in the neighbourhood of the place at which the traveller is sojourning. The steady, well-ordered
coach, which used to deposit me at a country inn, where I found a cheerful fire,
great civility and cleanliness, with good fare and a smiling welcome, is at present
seldom to be met with.[80]

This passage suggests an infrastructural influence which, even if it doesn't simply
account for the emergence of the nation, certainly tells a lot about the development
of tourism. The development of tourism and the emphasis which it places on
particular sites has followed along the same lines of communication as the circulation of commodities. As Debord has written, capitalist production has unified and
redefined space, and the totalization of the market has broken through regional
barriers as well as destroying the autonomy and quality of places. Consumerist
tourism operates along the same lines of communication as commodity exchange,
but it recodes their use in terms of leisure. In this development, history has been
drawn up into the system of equivalence in which it is exhibited as sites for national
inheritance and possession. But while its sites have meaning and value specifically
in relation to one another, National Heritage tends also to recoil on the space
between its sites, declaring it void of interest and barren of historical potential,
a kind of twilight zone in which nothing has ever happened and in which nothing
will ever happen. While this denigrated space is indeed the space of everyday life,
it would be too simple to conclude that under National Heritage all historical

potential has been drained from it and concentrated at scheduled sites for controlled consumption.[81] This tendency certainly does exist, but there are other
considerations which complicate its existence. We take up these considerations
in the concluding part of our chapter.

Community history and struggles over tradition

This is the picture, full of contrasts and confusion, in which new social contradictions are inextricably linked with boy scout attitudes, where you get a rejection of
new forms of oppression at the same time as a hankering after the 'good old days',
where revolutionary action is juxtaposed with a defence of the social contract of
neighbourliness.

Manuel Castells on urban protest[82]

National Heritage may appear to stand above, and in opposition to, everyday life.
But in the form of *micro-heritage* it can actually enter this mundane world by
'historicizing' the familiar, the diverse and the local at the level of the community.
Over the same period which has witnessed the extension of National Heritage, the
movement for community-based history has also developed, attempting to construct an oppositional historical consciousness on the terrain claimed by National
Heritage. This has produced an important field of contestation in which the local
community is decisive. But conceptions of the community itself, of its traditions
and inheritances, frame and define the boundaries of these struggles.

The public status of 'community'

Micro-heritage has evolved as a result of historical development indexed by
changing understandings of the idea of 'community'.[83] There has been a striking
shift in the meaning of 'community' from the late 1950s to the 1970s. In the earlier
phase, the emergence of 'community studies' within sociology was a moment of
lasting importance. Community studies were closely associated with a critique of
the embourgeoisement thesis and the widespread assumption that working-class
people were becoming incorporated into the middle-class culture of an increasingly
'affluent' society. This critique belonged, however, to a tradition of social reform
which privileged the state as an agent of reform. Post-war community studies
formed part of a wide spectrum of social analysis which asserted that, despite
ideologies of affluence, considerable inequalities continued to exist and that the
state should be the instrument of their amelioration. While recognizing the value of
cultural relations generated in traditional communities, the logic of 1950s
community studies was premised on the ultimate beneficence of the mixed
economy. The understanding of community which became prevalent in the mid
1970s stands in contrast to this earlier reformism. The characteristic approach
today is to place a greater emphasis on the preservation of the cultural autonomy
of the community. This approach is cast within a framework of community
activism rather than institutional reform.

The social developments which underlay this conceptual shift can briefly be sketched. The period following the Second World War was one of massive social restructuring, in education and social services, housing, transport and communication. Transformations in the lived relations of the working class were often directly connected to the recomposition of capital and the reorganization of the apparatuses of the state. The concentration and centralization of capital, the move to the production of consumer durables on a mass basis, the generalization of production line technology and alterations in the actual composition of labour power all combined to have a fundamental impact on local communities. The mobility of capital encouraged the mobility and interchangeability of labour. This directly impinged on locally bounded patterns of cultural reproduction, particularly through the agency of state intervention. Occupational traditions lodged within specific regional sectors of working-class culture were disrupted and dispersed. Divisions between social production and the family were deepened by state planning and by the separation of industrial from residential zones. Social relations within localities have been changed by the concentration of distributive capital (the supermarket, for example, which introduces a new form of social reproduction). In recreation as well as in production and consumption, the effects on communities have been similar. For instance, the pub as a place of recreation, or the culture of the street, have sometimes changed within a matter of years out of all recognition. Capitalization of working-class recreation imposed by the acceleration of the leisure industry has been integral to the process of the restructuring of the community.

This is not to suggest that older cultural forms and resistances of the working-class community have all been obliterated in the process. They were certainly dislocated, sometimes quite brutally, but the outcome was complex, involving both survivals and modifications. But what most interests us is the relation between this vast upheaval in social relations, and the accompanying representations of the community's 'past' and tradition.

The restructuring of the community, especially when carried out by direct or indirect state regulation, contributed to the heightening politicization of social relations within the locality. By politicization, we mean the process of defining issues as legitimate and integrated into formal political procedures, made 'public', or brought within politics in this (limited) sense. By social relations, in this context, we refer to the characteristic forms of 'social' provision: the expansion of education, rehousing, social services and employment policy. One feature of the dominant politics of the post-war settlement was a stress on provision of this kind, as opposed to more direct transformation of class relations. The model of this strategy was Anthony Crosland's 'social politics', in which economically related struggles were reduced to 'growth'.

In the 1970s, by contrast, political stress has been placed on the force of 'necessary' economic relations shielded by a more coercive state, under the banner of freedom. This is the characteristic monetarist combination. This new mode of regulating the community – an apparent *de*politicization – is clearly to be seen in a more traditionalist discourse about key institutions of social control, pre-eminently the family and the law.

The modern conservative attempt to reactivate such traditions is not unproblematic, given the continuing erosion of older social forms.[84] Yet those who would challenge conservative definitions of the community face a parallel dilemma. Social upheaval may generate no more than nostalgia for 'older ways' which no longer exist, and socialist attempts to develop local awareness of history must seriously consider the extension of National Heritage, as a recuperable form of the organic community, into representations of local traditions.

Struggles over tradition

The starting point for socialist community-based history projects is the effort to reclaim and draw upon the cultural experience of local people. As both Jerry White and Ken Worpole have argued, a crucial element in the effort to develop new cultural forms must be the reappropriation of traditions.[85] However, there is some danger that this reappropriation of local traditions may become an end in itself. Unless clearly linked with a more broadly conceived oppositional practice, community history can reproduce those representations of the community's past already present and active in the public sphere.

The idea of creating new traditions is something of a contradiction in terms, and at this point there is a possible convergence between conservative traditionalism and community-based history projects.[86] Both dominant and subordinate classes and groups call upon tradition for their different cultural identities and political purposes, and this fact provides the ground for contestation over the meaning and inheritance of traditions: a contestation in which different modes of public organization struggle and compete. The balance of forces is weighted from the start in favour of the dominant representations, for a sense of tradition constructed solely in terms of locality can be appropriated independently of any critical perspective on the larger framework of capitalist social relations. In Jerry White's words the experience of locality alone can produce merely superficial historical consciousness;[87] and it is precisely the determinations at work in the expanded repertoire of National Heritage which can intersect with community histories at this very point, supplying the broader social and cultural context.

The expansion of National Heritage in Britain is comparable with the situation Philippe Hoyau has described in France. In a discussion of France's (or, more accurately, Giscard d'Estaing's) 'Heritage Year', Hoyau quotes the remark made by the Minister of Culture:

The notion of heritage is enlarging; Heritage is no longer the coldness of stone, the glass separating us from objects in museums; it is also the village laundry-house, the little rural church, local speech and song, family photos, know-how and skills.[88]

In accounting for this shift of emphasis, Hoyau explains that Heritage is no longer organized by an academic or aesthetic model. Now it is organized around

> three major models: *the family* (rituals and habits, diets and modes of domestic production), *conviviality* (community life, festivals, production etc.), and *the country* (languages and argots, architecture, representations, techniques, cultural identities, ecology etc.).[89]

As Hoyau comments, 'the circulation of models with such a wide adherence as these authorizes the emergence of a "cultural" consensus around stable values which, we are told, modernity has failed to install'. The reorientation which directs the heritage relation towards locality and the everyday life of 'ordinary' people provides the occasion for 'a reinvestment of politics and a relaunching of adherence in the local and the regional'. In a context such as this there is certainly a risk that attempts to develop community-based consciousness of tradition will enter the public sphere only to be recuperated as examples of the 'people's' humble contribution to the heritage of the nation.

Clearly, this is a two-sided contest, and the threat of recuperation can't be considered in isolation from the challenge which community history can deliver. We can exemplify this contest as it bears on two aspects of the community-based history movement's activities. The first is the autobiographical mode which is prevalent in the writing produced by the worker-writer movement, community centres such as Centreprise in Hackney, and which also characterizes oral history such as Raphael Samuel's book of Arthur Harding's memories, *East End Underworld*. Books such as *Working Lives* and *East End Underworld* stress the problematic and contradictory nature of individual experience.[90] Indeed, a reading of these books suggests that autobiography plays an important part in oppositional publication because it enables people to convey their personal experience as a constellation of still unresolved disputes and tensions. Thus there is no justification for treating this use of the autobiographical mode as if it inherently conformed with an ideology of individualism. However, it is important also to acknowledge that the prominence of individualism within the public sphere opens the ways for a recuperative reading of this autobiographical material – a reading in which the past is individualized, in which collective forms of experience are played down, and in which memory is historicized anecdotally in terms of individual recollection. To this extent texts such as *Working Lives* and *East End Underworld* might be read against the grain of their initial and motivating impulse. The people speaking or writing might be appropriated as quaint characters who disclose 'the past' as lines of experience etched into their extraordinary faces. No doubt these are just urban straw-chewers according to one publicly instituted view; but there is another approach which sees these autobiographical subjects as canny entrepreneurs who have manipulated their way through the impossibly hard times of bleak decades; vindicating a reactionary notion of 'humanity' and, for that matter, also of the individual 'career' in the process.[91]

The second point of contestation concerns the burying of political contradiction under a celebration of local difference and cultural diversity. This problem can be identified with reference to a passage from Raphael Samuel's Foreword to Jerry White's *Rothschild Buildings*, which we quoted earlier:

historians have long since recognized that in the city every stone tells a story, just as in the country there is a history in every hedge. What Jerry White has shown is that every street – if historians were able imaginatively to reconstitute it – could be the subject of a book.

As such a book, *Rothschild Buildings* is impressive in its attempt to balance a recovery of local detail with a discussion of the wider social and political processes defining it. In this sense, the book exemplifies the strengths of the History Workshop movement. There is, nevertheless, a risk that the study of forms of conviviality and local experience will come adrift, imaginatively reconstituting such a diversity of stones, hedges, tenement buildings with their faces and railings, that the political stresses of history will be lost to what is ready and waiting in the public sphere: the serene and fascinating variety of an expanding National Heritage, with its plurality of histories – all of them indiscriminately 'ours'.

Emily Davison's death at the Derby (4 June 1913)

Emmeline Pankhurst by Georgina Brackenbury (1927)

8 'The public face of feminism': early twentieth-century writings on women's suffrage

Tricia Davis, Martin Durham, Catherine Hall, Mary Langan and David Sutton

Writing of the experiences and aspirations of the First World War women's movement, Olive Schreiner's comments raise questions for the modern reader:

You will look back at us with astonishment! You will wonder at passionate struggles that accomplished so little; at the, to you, obvious paths to attain our ends which we did not take; at the intolerable evils before which it will seem to you we sat down passive; at the great truths staring us in the face, which we failed to see; at the truths we grasped at, but could never quite get our fingers round.[1]

Her book, she explained, was only the 'remnants' of a larger effort destroyed by fire in the Boer War. Nevertheless what remains from the flames of British imperialism are a series of historical sketches which illuminate the origins of women's consciousness of their oppression in the concept of 'parasitism'. By 'parasitism', Schreiner meant the increasing removal of women in contemporary society from the labour functions performed in primitive societies and the resulting sense of being superfluous to the needs of society, and a drain on its resources. Schreiner used the concept to signify the appearance of a consciousness which was elemental and not theorized.[2]

Possibly not one woman in ten, or even one woman in twenty thousand among those taking part in this struggle, could draw up a clear and succinct account of the causes which have led to the disco-ordination in woman's present position.

However the level of consciousness had become sufficient to represent a common interest.

It is this abiding consciousness of an end to be attained, reaching beyond her personal life and individual interests, which constitutes the religious element of the women's movement of our day and binds with the common bond of an impersonal enthusiasm into one solid body the women of whatsoever race, class, and nation who are struggling after the readjustment of women to life.[3]

Schreiner's comments highlight some of the themes we wish to address in this chapter. Like the other chapters in this part of the book, it focuses upon the relationship between past and present, framed, in this case, by the concerns of a modern feminist politics. But rather than discuss the general features of a 'popular memory' or look at dominant historical representations in the present, we want to consider, more intimately, a particular past–present relation – that between the suffragette struggles of the pre-First World War period and the modern Women's Movement. As a subsidiary theme, largely because of absences in even a feminist history, we wish to approach these issues through our own reading of suffragette autobiographies. As we shall suggest later, this choice of form is as important as that of period, since autobiographical modes of writing have played a particularly important part in the development of feminist consciousness, both today and in previous periods. They also provide an interesting way of posing questions central for feminism and significant for the earlier chapters in this part: the relation between the 'public' and the 'private'. This question takes on a particular significance within the context of women's experience and feminist politics, since assignment to the private sphere and exclusion from the public have been key features of women's oppression. If not 'with astonishment', therefore, how should we view 'the passionate struggles' of Olive Schreiner's generation of women?

Feminist history, feminist politics

The development of interest in women's history and feminist history – an off-shoot of the Women's Liberation Movement – has resulted in major new studies of women's work, the changing character of the sexual division of labour, the social construction of motherhood and the development of state policy on women and the family. However with certain exceptions (notably the work of Rowbotham, Liddington and Norris) the history of feminism has not been a primary object of study for the new generation of feminist historians. There are various possible explanations for this. First, the contemporary movement developed after a period of relative quiescence during the 1950s and the early 1960s, which encouraged the feminists of the late 1960s and early 1970s to see themselves as a new breed. Modern feminists felt they had little in common with an earlier generation whose work had focused on the entry of women into the public sphere. A second reason is linked to the changing emphasis of the feminist struggle. The struggles of the early twentieth century were centred on the vote; in the past decade the emphasis has shifted from the question of formal equality with men to a recognition of the inadequacy of the analysis of women's oppression which remained at the institutional level, insisting instead on tackling the personal and informal dimensions of a thoroughly patriarchal society. The slogan 'the personal is political' sums up this new approach which asserts the importance of the personal as well as the public and institutional levels of society. To take one example: important as it was to establish equal educational opportunities for girls and boys, this could not in itself ensure that girls and boys would in effect be equal. Educational inequality rests on more than formal access to qualifications. The discovery of this new dimension – of personal power relations – led to an assumption that our kind of feminism had little to do with what had gone before. Furthermore, one of the critical questions for the contemporary Women's Movement has been how to develop a new analysis of women's oppression which can incorporate insights into the political nature of the personal and yet can also grasp the importance of more traditional concerns as well. This emphasis has meant that a great deal of energy has been put into analysing the position of women, both in our own and other societies, in an attempt to tackle the theoretical questions about the relation between class and gender and how this relates to the vexed issue of patriarchy. More attention has been focused on how societies work and how women's oppression is reproduced than on the forms of struggle which women have adopted. This is related to the influence of Althusserian Marxism in the Women's Liberation Movement, though this is not always a debt that is recognized.

But things are beginning to change: the history of feminism itself is now emerging. Even the journal *Social History*, which in several years of production has not shown any interest in feminist history, has at last published an article which recognizes new work on feminism, although in a grudging and unsympathetic manner.[4] There are good political reasons for this shift. The early optimism of the Women's Liberation Movement has proved to be unfounded. The belief that we could change the world and the early limited, though important, successes have given way to a much more long-term view of the nature of the struggle. Gains which were won in the 1970s are being removed in the 1980s, encouraging the Women's Movement to take a more historical view of the conditions under which successes and failures take place. This is not to underestimate the success which the movement has had in terms of putting the 'woman question' back on the agenda, but it is clearly going to be a long struggle. The resulting sense of historical relativism encourages a return to the movements of the past and a reconsideration of the conditions in which they arose, and the circumstances which led to their defeats and victories.

A contemporary feminist rereading of feminist history is bound to raise different kinds of questions from those which would have been raised at the time. We need to understand previous varieties of feminism both in their own terms and in terms of the new insights which we can bring. This is not to claim any moral or political superiority over earlier generations. It is simply to recognize the historical specificity of kinds of analysis, or particular institutional forms and to learn what we can from them. Our interest in this article has been focused on the nature of feminist consciousness in the period of the most acute struggle over suffrage. We have approached this issue through autobiographical and biographical writing. Inevitably the fact that we have taken up the question of feminist consciousness reflects our own political history. One effect of the political break represented by 1968 was to highlight the question of consciousness: we had to break with an economic perspective and assert the need for confronting personally our own racism or sexism. The political movements of the last ten years have thus devoted far more attention to the construction of ideologies and the ways in which they are received and understood than had previously been the case. Attention to consciousness has been institutionalized in the Women's Liberation Movement through the practice of consciousness raising. Consciousness raising is a deliberate attempt to understand daily forms of oppression. It aims to move from a stress on individual inadequacy as the source of an inability to cope with particular forms of oppression to a consciousness which recognizes these forms as a part of the systematic subordination of women. Women's oppression is experienced personally; that experience has to be translated into an understanding of its political character, which inevitably means that it cannot be dealt with individually.

This relates to our second major concern – the division between public and private. The break which contemporary feminists have made with traditional notions of the realm of the personal and the realm of the political has challenged this long-accepted division. Personal life and domestic life have been put on the political agenda. As a result they are open to political analysis and discussion in a way which has not been acceptable previously. This scrutiny of our own lives, and recognition of tensions and contradictions which have long remained hidden, leads us to ask new questions about earlier feminists. How did they deal with those tensions in their lives, how did they reconcile their demands for political equality with their knowledge of the sexual division of labour in the home? What did equality mean without the easy availability of birth control? Were these kinds of questions simply ignored, or merely not brought out into the open? If they were, how were they then managed? The conventional wisdom of the nineteenth century was that public life was for men only and that the home and family defined women's world. What happened once women demanded full entry into the public sphere? What effect did this have on their private lives and those of the men with whom they were associated?

'My own story'

We have tried to tackle these questions through a study of a number of key personal texts – the autobiographies, biographies and memoirs of a number of different kinds of early twentieth-century feminists, all of whom had some kind of relation to the suffrage struggle.[5] The Pankhursts are heavily represented in these personal texts with Mrs Emmeline Pankhurst, the mother of Christabel and Sylvia and the founder with Christabel of the Women's Social and Political Union (WSPU), leading the field. While Emmeline and Christabel changed political direction in the course of the suffrage struggle, Sylvia remained true to her socialist principles. All three were charismatic figures who played leading roles in suffrage politics. Emmeline and Frederick Pethick-Lawrence were for many years part of the inner leadership of the WSPU but finally were asked to leave after a serious political disagreement with Mrs Pankhurst and Christabel. Another faithful lieutenant was Annie Kenney, who came from a working-class background, and was taken in by the Pankhursts and lived with the family for many years. Teresa Billington-Greig, another WSPU supporter, described by Annie Kenney as a woman accustomed to use 'a sledgehammer of logic and cold reason',[6] was one of the founder members of the breakaway Women's Freedom League. Mary Richardson was another WSPU activist, active in London. Hertha Ayrton was a well-known scientist and WSPU supporter. Hannah Mitchell was, for a time, a member of the WSPU, having matured politically in the Independent Labour Party. Her parents worked a farm in Derbyshire. When she left home she became a servant and later a seamstress. Margaret Bondfield came from a Wesleyan background, worked in a shop for many years and later became a Labour minister. Her friend Mary Macarthur came from a more well-to-do background and became involved in trade union activities through her father's firm. She worked full time for the Women's Trade Union League. Vera Brittain – a later generation than the rest of our grouping – became politicized through her fight for education and her experience in the First World War; she was a lifelong feminist and pacifist, working particularly for the League of Nations and the Peace Pledge Union.

The main suffrage organizations were the National Union of Women's Suffrage Societies, led by Mrs Fawcett, and the WSPU, formed in 1903. As the struggle gained momentum in the 1900s other groupings emerged. Of these the most important were the militant Women's Freedom League and another split from the WSPU, Sylvia Pankhurst's organization of working women in the East End – the East London Federation.

Through a close reading of these texts we have attempted to get nearer to understanding the nature of feminist consciousness and the various forms of feminism in the early twentieth century. Schreiner's sense of 'a common bond of impersonal enthusiasm' uniting the different traditions of socialist feminism, radical liberal individualism and sexual antagonism (the focus on men as the enemy) indicates a central element in the consciousness of women involved in the suffrage struggle. Much of the history of women's campaign for the vote focuses on the intricacies of parliamentary negotiations and the regional studies of particular groups of militants. But important questions about the meaning of the struggle for the women concerned remain unanswered. One of the most striking features of the early-twentieth-century women's movement was that although its members shared common assumptions about the political subordination of women, they were very much divided over aims and objectives. These political differences might be more clearly understood if placed in the context of individual lives. For example, how did particular women manage the 'common bond of impersonal enthusiasm'? What did that feminist unity and those crucial years devoted to 'The Cause' mean to them? How did they reconcile their political activities with their personal lives?

Experience and consciousness cannot be taken as unproblematic categories. Consciousness can only make sense when read against contemporary ideological representations. A reading of this kind of personal material, however, gives us interesting insights into those representations which were available. A history of the consciousness and experiences of women in the suffrage movement would need to be placed within an account of the available discourses on women, the family and politics, together with the more easily available political, social and economic histories of the period. In directing attention back to autobiographies and biographies we are not suggesting that this can give us anything more than a fragment of the whole story. But it is a fragment which has received little attention.

Recent academic work on suffrage is not centrally preoccupied with the effects of social, ideological and political forces on women. Autobiographies – with their primary concern for 'personal stories' – clearly stand at the opposite extreme. The use of this form provides particularly important tools for the feminist historian. Writing about the self and the private sphere has always been seen as a legitimate area for women. It has not only been acceptable for them to write, but also to read. One of the most interesting aspects of the personal writings of the suffrage movement is that, unlike the personal writing of the novel or the diary there is very little evidence of private life: domesticity, the home and personal relationships are not what it is all about. The emphasis is much more on the public sphere and there is an insistence on the part of the authors of their right to be seen as individual political subjects, just like men. They are asserting the right of women to be political, not to have to write about their families and their feelings, but rather about their campaigns and alliances, their successes and failures. There is an interesting distinction to be made here between these early feminist works, and contemporary feminist writing with its emphasis on the essentially inter-related areas of public and private. Modern forms of women's writing reflect this development. The absences, however, in the earlier writing give us important clues about the different forms of feminism.

We have used various criteria in our choice of texts. First, we have used the familiar accounts of the views of the leadership of the various women's groups (thus the Pankhurst volumes or Teresa Billington-Greig). At a time when the public representation and articulation of the demands of women's groups were so important leaders clearly played a particularly important part in the movement. Second, we have consulted the personal writing, including letters and personal diaries, of women who were involved in the movement. Third, we have used texts from different kinds of feminists – socialist feminists, liberal feminists and labour women. We have been careful not to be bound by middle-class writing – thus the inclusion of the works of Annie Kenney and Hannah Mitchell. The nineteenth-century women suffragists were almost wholly from middle-class backgrounds, but it would be reductive to assign formative political traditions such as radicalism, which fed into late-nineteenth-century socialist feminism, a strict and necessary class belonging. While it *is* important to recognize the re-emergence, at the end of the nineteenth century, of a conscious, 'working-class politics', the crisis in hegemony which engendered its rise also produced fluidity of ideological, political and social ideas which cannot be situated simply in class origins. Two examples are of particular relevance here: the place of the 'sexual politics' tradition and the role of Liberalism in its party-political sense, and of liberalism in its philosophical sense.

Kinds of feminism

The 'sexual politics' tradition took its most coherent form over the struggle in the late nineteenth century to repeal the Contagious Diseases Acts, condemning the outrageous sexist 'double standard' which those Acts embodied. Mrs Fawcett, who became secretary of the new National Union of Women's Suffrage societies in 1897, consciously attempted to keep the suffrage struggle aloof from a campaign which, because of its subject, might impair or tar the suffrage claims in the public mind. None the less if Mrs Fawcett embodied the 'perfect Victorian lady' it was to the 'sexual politics' tradition that Christabel and Emmeline Pankhurst looked when they broke from their radical and socialist backgrounds. Their assertions about a deep-seated 'sex antagonism' between women and men, which took its most polemical form in Christabel's *The Great Scourge*,[7] is just one example of the attention the historian must give to the transformations of the pre-existing traditions within which women were making their political case. The aggressively militant route to women's suffrage which the WSPU increasingly tended to favour was divisive for the 'women's movement' as a whole. (The most celebrated split took place between Sylvia and her mother and sister; also important was the resignation of the women who formed the Women's Freedom League.) But if the militants' class origin, their organizational form, their political action and their 'ideologies' have been seen by some socialist feminists as fragmenting the struggle, it is undeniable that militancy signified a *confluence* of ideas – a high-pitched ensemble of resentment and frustration. The frustration and impotence which women experienced in the face of a male-dominated political system was first expressed through heckling and the unfurling of 'Votes for Women' banners at political meetings. It escalated through angry scuffles with outraged Liberal Party supporters to more serious confrontations with the burly arm of the law. Terms of imprisonment led to forced feeding as a result of the government's refusal to allow suffrage supporters the status of political prisoners. Fury at the cruelty and humiliation imposed on women led to a shift in the tactics of the WSPU, towards violent attacks on property.

The liberal feminist tradition was crucial in the suffrage struggle even though liberal feminists often took their distance from militancy. The pro-liberal historians are quick to point out that the liberal women and the constitutionalists rejected the militant and the violent methods of the suffragettes. This is largely true, but liberal historiography often also denies the sisterly generosity which Mrs Fawcett, long-time leader of the constitutionalists, paid to the militants. However the limits of liberal feminism are clearly recognizable to socialist feminists. For a more radical feminism, its 'humanism' may underrate questions of sexual difference. Nevertheless its influence upon other traditions is undeniable. As Stacey and Price have noted in their recent article, liberal individualism had a highly pertinent purchase for women pre-suffrage. 'What the feminist movement did when it made a bid for the vote was to demand that women be treated as *persons*, as *individuals*, that the newly developing notions of individualism must be applied to them as well as to all adult men' (our emphasis).[8] This humanist tradition, the demand to be treated as a human being and as a person, had enormous resonance through liberalism and beyond. In particular it influenced Labour women like Margaret Bondfield and Mary Macarthur. The tradition is perhaps best represented by Ray Strachey's important book *The Cause*.[9]

A third available tendency was that of socialist feminism and labourism which clearly influenced the positions of some women on suffrage. The distance between socialist women and bourgeois feminists was well established. Eleanor Marx felt it was impossible to work with middle-class feminists, and such views were widespread among socialist women in Western Europe. The position was most clear in Germany where the Social Democrats fully accepted the importance of women organizing, but linked that organization to the established demands of the socialist movement. Despite the many differences between Clara Zetkin and Margaret Bondfield they saw eye to eye on this point. Both assumed that the class struggle must be the primary struggle and that, in order to win, women must struggle with men. The activities of bourgeois feminists were seen as a deviation from this central conflict. As is well known Sylvia Pankhurst tried very hard to find some way of reconciling her feminism with her socialism, continuing to put women first while also engaging in the common struggle.

The autobiographies and biographies we have used draw on these three traditions. It can be argued that the position of leadership which many of these particular women occupied make them rather special and unrepresentative. Several of them clearly thought of themselves as extraordinary women with special gifts and great influence. But the structure of the women's movement at that time meant that the leadership was very important. Leaders were interested in being both representative and special – it was precisely this combination which gave them their legitimacy.

One important reason for the study of these texts is that a consideration of the forms of feminist consciousness helps to extend the range of existing accounts of the suffrage movement. The surface message of these texts is that feminism is about the public sphere. They are indeed public texts, some written virtually as manifestos and others as celebrations of women who had made it in the previously closed world of male politics. The dominant historiographical tradition on women's suffrage takes this focus on the 'public face of feminism' as unproblematic and simply assumes that this is all there is to it. The major exception to this is Dangerfield's *The Strange Death of Liberal England* which tries to come to grips with the new forces unleashed by feminism, but ends up speculating about lesbianism and 'long-neglected masculinity'.[10] The new liberal historians, who have been enjoying a revival in recent years, see the failure of successive Liberal governments to concede female suffrage as something of an embarrassment. The Liberal Party's catch-phrase was 'Retrenchment and Reform' and the women's suffrage movement expected that franchise reform would be forthcoming from the party that boasted political reform and freedom from its platform. The same historians who consider that the Liberal Party was becoming capable of representing the working class set about analysing the tortuous political response to the campaign for women's suffrage. In their accounts Pugh, Morgan and Harrison emphasize that in their eyes a simple equation of suffragette militancy with the eventual securing of the vote is not acceptable. In terms of 'electoral politics' Pugh is the most technically proficient in analysing the shifting allegiances of politicians on the issue of women's suffrage.[11] Morgan usefully puts together evidence from politicians' manuscript and printed sources to demonstrate the complexities of decision-making from the politicians' point of view.[12] Nor is Harrison one to privilege the suffragettes. His account revolves around the assumption that the parliamentary politicians had to satisfy a number of different 'publics' – the suffragette public being only one. He takes Mrs Fawcett to task for reducing the obstacles to women's suffrage to the sole factor of Asquith's intransigence.[13] These texts complicate the Dangerfield thesis and they will be established historiographical reading. They raise a number of questions about just how far the campaign for women's suffrage did cause the furore which Dangerfield suggested, and to what extent the militant campaign reached beyond London. They also question the role of the constitutionalist societies in different regions, and their relationship to the Labour Party.

The mainstream 'new liberal' historians, although they have been careful to distinguish the specifically philosophical nature of liberalism from its Liberal Party form, have asked few questions about its importance for the Women's Movement. Harrison, Pugh and Morgan have read and utilized women's writing. However they tend to take as their field of study the 'public' domain of politics and therefore give only small attention (if any) to the private space of home, family and sexual relations. Feminist writers, by contrast, are increasingly beginning to realize that liberal individualism, with its stress upon personal independence *and* its claim for public recognition, was of considerable importance in framing the early Women's Movement.

When analysed from a feminist perspective, the women's writing selected for this article reveals gaps, absences and tensions which are an inevitable result of the limited definition of feminism prevalent in the suffrage movement. There is a kind of repressed feminist consciousness at work in the texts which prevents the full exploration of a whole range of issues, and yet which cannot be completely silenced. This shadowy presence is particularly marked in this period because of the effects of militancy. The struggle for the vote had been a part of feminist politics since the advent of the organized Women's Movement in the mid nineteenth century. But the methods used in the 1900s marked a decisive break with established respectable feminist practice. The aim was the same but the tactics used were decisively different. For middle-class women the shift into militancy could not be achieved without enormous cost. They were challenging established notions of female propriety, respectability and femininity while repudiating attempts to vilify them as viragos. The suffocating weight of tradition, and particularly the ideology of separate masculine and feminine spheres, based on the assumption of biological difference, cannot be overemphasized.[14] As the struggle intensified and the stakes became higher, married women gradually disappeared from active participation. This alienation from social mores was not only a middle-class experience. Hannah Mitchell suffered a breakdown in mid campaign, and her shift into 'religious belief' corresponded with the route that several active feminists took. To our knowledge there is no work which has sought to explain that consciousness of an 'alternative world' (almost religious in its intensity) that appears to have gripped active feminists in this period. We do not want to follow Cominos[15] in seeing Annie Besant's experience as a form of sublimation of a repressed womanhood – a form of expression that men in late Victorian society did not require. We do think however that there are interesting parallels with what Yeo[16] has called the 'religion of socialism'. While noting that some forms of feminism took connotations of an explicitly Conservative and feverish anti-Bolshevism, we should be careful to avoid condemning theosophical and spiritual experiences as reactionary. Perhaps the retreat into other-worldliness was the product of a consciousness which, out of joint with a society in transition, sought an active solace elsewhere.

These tensions within feminism could not be broken as long as feminism kept up its public face. The conflict between feminists' commitment to specific reforms for women and their need to remain respectable was greatly intensified by the adoption of militancy in the early 1900s. No break could be made with the dominant existing tradition until the demand for the vote had been won; only then could the limited nature of that victory be understood. Similarly, until women had won some greater measure of economic independence it was not possible to challenge the institution of marriage on any scale. Public feminism had to sit uncomfortably astride the unexploded time bomb of marriage and childcare. Meanwhile those unresolved contradictions silently ticked away.

Being a feminist: the personal and the political

At a German women's meeting in 1908, Annie Kenney spoke about the differences in the treatment of men and women that she had experienced as a young factory worker. These differences, she pointed out, occurred not only in the factory but also in the home. When work was over, it was the mother who hurried home to collect the children, prepare the tea and do the cleaning and sewing. For the huband, however, the day's work was over. 'I used to ask myself why this was so. Why was the mother the drudge of the family and not the father's companion and equal?'[17] However, such insights do not appear in her memoirs where it would seem that she, like Mary Richardson, came to an involvement in the suffrage struggle through the emotional and political appeal of one of the movement's public meetings.[18]

Almost all the feminist autobiographies and biographies trace the formation of a feminist outlook from an early awareness of female oppression and the need to struggle against it. For example, Emmeline Pankhurst recalled that although she came from a good and comfortable home, 'while still a young child, I began instinctively to feel that there was something lacking even in my own home, some false conception of family relationships, some incomplete ideal'. This unease crystallized for her around the fact that her brothers' education was taken more seriously than her own, while she was encouraged to make the house attractive for them. 'It was never suggested to them as a duty that they make the home attractive for me. Why not? Nobody seemed to know.' Later the mystery was solved when her father, thinking her asleep, remarked, 'What a pity she wasn't born a lad', making it clear to her that 'men considered themselves superior to women and that women apparently acquiesced in that belief'.[19]

Sylvia Pankhurst gave a similar account of Emmeline's youthful experience. According to Sylvia, when Emmeline's sister tried to sell some of her paintings, their father was disturbed in case 'it would lead to rumours that he was short of money and thus adversely affect his business'. Whilst their brothers were being prepared for business, the girls were expected to stay at home, dusting the drawing-room and arranging flowers. Their mother, anxious for her tall, handsome sons, whom she feared might marry imprudently, urged her impatient daughters to 'make the home attractive' for their brothers. Her injunction 'You should bring your brother's slippers' raised the retort that if she were in favour of ' "women's rights" she did not show it in the home'.[20]

In quite a different class setting Hannah Mitchell had a very similar experience. She recalled that 'her first reaction to feminism' was at eight years old when she was forced, as a weekly task, to darn all the stockings for the family while her brothers read or played dominoes. Sometimes the boys helped with domestic jobs like rug-making. 'But for them this was voluntary work, for the girls it was compulsory, and the fact that the boys could read if they wished filled my cup of bitterness to the brim.' In the account of her childhood Hannah pointed to the anger she felt at the endless domestic labour that her mother forced on her. Although she ran away from home at the age of fourteen, the harsh experience undoubtedly stayed with her. When she went into service she refused to perform the most personally degrading function of waiting on table. Nor would she wear the cap for she 'absolutely refused to don the muslin badge of servitude'. On resigning her servant's post, the employer demanded a month's spring cleaning as notice. Hannah left without wages rather than submit.[21]

Given the radical tradition from which many of these women emerged, this recounting of a sense of experienced injustice is hardly surprising. A personal awareness of social inequality is still an important route into socialist activism. It certainly was in the late nineteenth and early twentieth century, when conversion to socialism meant for many the attempt to build a new way of life as well as a commitment to a more formal set of demands. Most of our authors considered their feminist politics as part of a wider political tradition, as well as an expression of their personal experience. Many of them came from politically active families which encouraged these women to identify themselves as potential political beings; this was the case with Hertha Ayrton, or both generations of the Pankhursts. As Sylvia wrote, 'Bred into us was a sense of destiny, a duty to be servants to the common weal'.[22] Identification with a radical in the family past was recalled to explain a tendency towards politics and rebellion. Emmeline Pankhurst identified as an important source of a rebellious spirit her paternal grandfather, who was nearly killed in the Peterloo massacre, and her grandmother, an early member of the Anti-Corn Law League. Hannah Mitchell thought she inherited 'a streak in my own blood' from her Chartist grandfather.[23]

What is interesting is that an open and critical consciousness of oppression and differential treatment of men and women does not, on the whole, shape the later parts of the texts. Sometimes there is a specific rejection of the political significance of the personal. Emmeline Pethick-Lawrence, for example, in *My Part in a Changing World* gave a frank account of her first love affair and formative relationship with the settlement pioneer, Mark Guy Pears. However, in the account of her life after marriage, although her husband is mentioned with fondness, the details of domestic life were seen as irrelevant. 'Our intimate personal relationship, growing deeper every year, does not belong to the story told in this book.'[24] Similarly, Mrs Pankhurst described the significance of her early life to her politics but rarely talked of her marriage. Her autobiography demonstrates her diffidence in this respect, omitting any reference to the courtship between herself and Richard Pankhurst. She merely recorded that her marital status changed. Emmeline refuted the myth that the suffragettes were embittered women. 'My home life and relations have been as nearly ideal as possible in this imperfect world.'[25] However any further reference to her husband was connected only to their political life, in which she played a secondary role. Even his death Emmeline treated as something she responded to by becoming Registrar for Births and Deaths, rather than an event she grieved over.

In part this rejection of the significance of the personal can be understood as an outcome of the middle-class position of many of the leading feminists. For them domestic labour was not an inevitable concomitant of marriage. The availability of servants, who could maintain the household and look after children even if the mistress were imprisoned for her suffragette struggles, protected most of the active suffragettes from some of the consequences of militancy.

Significantly, it is working-class Hannah Mitchell's autobiography that contains the most sustained account of feminism as a personal experience at a day to day level. Mitchell's bitterness about the fact that domestic labour drained her time and energy is evident throughout her book. 'Sewing, cooking, washing, starching and baking bread, pies and cakes left no time for reading or study and I found myself caught in a sort of domestic treadmill.'[26] In describing her relationship with her husband and son she was more discreet. However, there are clues. She talked of being suspicious of marriage; the traditional married life lived by her siblings held no attraction for her. At the time of her own marriage she was impressed by the socialist idea of marriage as comradeship, though she quickly grew sceptical. 'Perhaps if I had understood my own nature as I came to do later, I should not have married for I soon realised that married life, as men understand it, called for a degree of self-abnegation which was impossible for me. I needed solitude, time for study and the opportunity for a wider life.' She highlighted the sexism of socialist men who, like other men, expected to be waited on with cake, jam and bread. 'Most of us who were married found that "Votes for Women" was of less interest to our husbands than their dinner.'[27]

But even for Hannah Mitchell there was no possibility of a total reformulation of the connection between the personal and the political, given the nature of suffrage politics. She handled the tension by defining herself as different from other women. She saw her antagonism to housework as a personal quirk rather than integrating it into an analysis of women's oppression. Thus although she defined domestic labour as oppressive to women generally, at the same time she thought many women were more 'naturally' inclined to it than herself. She therefore welcomed the help with housework provided by women neighbours and eventually employed a neighbour who was 'one of those happily constituted women who enjoy cooking, which I never did'.[28] When her son married a woman who was not politically active she was pleased, but doubtful about the compatibility between femininity and active politics.

The women who fought the suffrage battle were made of sterner stuff than the average stay at home women. So I was glad to think some gentler influence than mine would now be able to help my son to recover from the depression of the war years. The younger women, even if they were as keen on self-expression as we were did not have to fight so hard for it, and so escaped the hardening process we went through, and we had at least taught our sons that women had the right to political equality.[29]

The feminism of the suffragettes embodied no conscious attempt to rework the connections between the personal and political or the public and the private. However, by bringing together questions asked by modern feminists about these relations with an awareness of the historical specificity of the period, we can understand better the different forms of early feminist consciousness. We can also see the way in which this consciousness was shaped and obscured by the public face of the feminism at the time.

Autobiographies

From the perspective of contemporary feminism it is possible to characterize both the content and the form of Christabel Pankhurst's account of the suffrage struggle, in Unshackled, as evidence of her preoccupation with the public simply at the expense of the private. For Christabel, it seems, feminism was totally subsumed within suffrage. Although unspecified improvements in women's domestic lives were seen as necessary, these improvements could only be achieved through legislation and legislation required that women (or at least some women) had the vote. She quoted, with apparent approval, a speech made by Mrs Pankhurst when charged with inciting people to rush the House of Commons. 'This is the only way in which women can get the right of deciding how the taxes to which they contribute should be spent and how the laws they have to obey should be made.'[30] In Christabel's writing there was no analysis of women's oppression which went beyond their exclusion from the formal democratic processes, no enemy to be overcome greater than the Liberal Government and no sense in which the granting of the vote in 1918 was anything other than a total victory.

> The fifty years' story with its militant last chapter had a happy ending. . . . Later the first woman, Lady Astor, was elected to the House of Commons. Many others have been elected since then and their numbers will grow. The presence of women in the House of Commons signalizes the great change that has taken place in the position of women.[31]

If feminism was contained within the suffrage movement, suffrage was contained within parliamentary politics. However unconventional the militant suffragettes appeared when contrasted with their peaceful, constitutional suffragist sisters, the aims of militancy were not to challenge parliamentary structures but to open them up to women. After her first attempt to disrupt a meeting by raising the cry of 'Votes for Women', Christabel reflected upon her weakness in not going further. She resolved that 'next time such a meeting was held, a mark should be made that could not disappear. Thus militancy had its origin in purpose'.[32] Similarly, the creation of an autonomous women's movement was developed as a tactic in a parliamentary battle. 'Mother and I', wrote Christabel,

> arrived at the conclusion that who would be politically free herself must strike the first blow and women could do no better than pay the independent Labour Movement the compliment of imitation by starting an independent women's movement. 'Women', said Mother on a memorable occasion, 'we must have an independent women's movement. Come to my house tomorrow and we will arrange it.'[33]

There is a clear link between this view of suffrage and feminism and the form of autobiography. Just as suffrage was the focus of feminist politics, and could only be worked out in a parliamentary arena, so history, for Christabel, was about parliament, politics and great men and women. Individual women were transformed into heroines, 'links in a long strong chain that reached from the earliest efforts to victory'.[34] Heroine-in-Chief was Mrs Pankhurst. Even unnamed women 'consecrated themselves to a great cause in which self was lost', just as Annie Kenney in *Memories of a Militant* was content to describe herself as Christabel's 'blotting paper'.[35] The dynamic of *Unshackled*'s narrative, therefore, lies not in 'how we won the vote' – Pethick-Lawrence's editorial addition to the title – but in terms of the achievement of a movement, and in the movement's role as a force within the public arena. Anything which detracted from this view of the WSPU as moving unceasingly and unerringly forward, or which might draw attention to the conflicts between personalities, was summarily dismissed.

Christabel's feminism operated at the public level. It is important to note, however, that public and private are shifting categories. Any simple application is liable to miss the context, the use of historically specific languages, and the modes of personal expression. Christabel's stress on the impersonal nature of the movement can be understood not as sublimation or avoidance of the personal but as an assertion of seriousness and commitment, a chafing, in fact, against one aspect of the separate sphere, the trivialization and marginalization of women's concerns. Equally, the language of sacrifice and service within which this belief was couched was one of the few means available to women without access to politics as a career to express a depth of personal commitment.

A third theme within *Unshackled* is the contradictory stress on femininity in all areas of the suffragettes' lives other than their militant, and definitely un-feminine, politics. 'Suffragettes', Christabel wrote, 'were not lunatics and viragos but just ordinary women who had made up their minds to get political fairplay; Mother, especially, made many converts, even before she had begun her speech, simply by her appearance and manner which were so completely different from all expectations.'[36] In fact conventionally expressed femininity, as far as Christabel was concerned, was official WSPU policy. Writing about the young local organizers, she commented, 'To parry any charges of "unwomanliness", "extreme views" and so forth, conformity to convention in all but militancy was the rule.'[37] This con-ventionality was evident in the descriptions that Christabel and the more radical Sylvia gave of the circumstances of their mother's betrothal and marriage. As we have seen, Emmeline herself was diffident in this area. According to Christabel,

Mother was no revolutionary in her views of marriage. She wished to try no new experiments. On the wedding eve, as they parted in happy anticipation of the morrow, it was to hear him tell her again how unendingly he loved her and should ever love her. He seemed to her so wise and wonderful in comparison with her own youth and smaller knowledge. 'Are you sure you will always love me and want me for ever?' she said. 'Wouldn't you have liked to try first how we should get on?' It is easy to imagine how tenderly he smiled, how completely he satisfied her wish to hear him say, yet once again, all that the morrow's marriage meant and always would mean to him.[38]

Sylvia by contrast claimed that Emmeline, influenced by radical ideas about the inequality of marriage, had suggested to her fiancé that they should live together without the formalities of a legal ceremony. He was moved by this proposal, but declined, disturbed that such an unorthodox arrangement would cause her a great deal of trouble.[39]

Modern feminism, with its challenge to conventional ideas about femininity, finds no obvious antecedents in Christabel's concern for 'respectability', while it has some affinities to Sylvia's radicalism. However, what is historically interesting about these claims to conventional femininity is that it was felt necessary to make them and to juxtapose them to militancy. Within this framework, such claims represent a rebuff to the anti-suffrage accusations of unwomanliness, and signal an attempt to explore the new relationship between feminism and femininity which militancy had highlighted.

The language of religion was another mode of personal expression open to women in this period. Stephen Yeo, in his account of socialism in Britain in the

1880s and 1890s, has defended the socialism of the various groups and individuals who used the language of religion to convey their message. 'It is tempting to dismiss socialists who spoke a moral language of evangelical exhortation as not-quite-socialists, as fuzzy, peculiarly British, soft, unrevolutionary socialists who could not quite moult religious feathers.'[40] Equally Yeo has defended the socialists against the charge of opportunism, of using the intense and personal language of religion to sugar some bitter socialist pill. The religious language of socialism had genuine strengths, not only in the sense that it expressed a unity between material and cultural demands, but also in the sense that it emerged from and conveyed a prefigurative experience of socialism.

It is in these terms that we can best understand Emmeline Pethick-Lawrence's account of the suffrage movement in *My Part in a Changing World*. In spite of her failure to develop some aspects of her socialism within the WSPU, Emmeline clearly remained within the socialist current and this is reflected in her writing. Influenced by the works of Whitman, Morris and Carpenter, as well as by the non-conformist mysticism of her father, she joined the ILP. Here she found the labour movement deeply influenced by Christian socialism, and for Emmeline this evangelical approach was carried into the Women's Movement. 'There was something of a religious fervour in the way we embraced these ideas,'[41] wrote Emmeline. Similarly she described the suffrage movement as 'a spiritual struggle', 'a mission', 'a crusade' 'a religion' and saw it as being motivated by a spiritual force. In the Preface to her book she described an experience she had while sitting on top of a London bus

I realised how few we were and how insignificant! I looked at the crowds thronging the street. I thought of the millions of people in London and the millions more throughout the country who cared nothing about the Idea which meant so much to us. Suddenly I realised they counted as nothing against us, because to us had been committed the power of the Creative Thought, the 'Word' that could not return to the spiritual realm, void. The conviction that took possession of me then never left me again. I realised that Creative Thought had descended from the spiritual realm down into the human mind, had possessed the reason and the emotions and had passed finally into the blood and had thus become a power in the physical world.[42]

She spoke of her own life as a pilgrimage and understood the experience of other women in similar terms. She also related these ideas to the suffrage movement as a whole in a way that confronted the conventional divisions between the public and the private.

But though the movement meant much to the public life of the country, to us who were personally involved it was fraught with deeper issues. It meant to women the discovery of their own identity, that source within of purpose, power and will, the real person that often remains throughout a lifetime hidden under the mask of appearance. It also meant to women the discovery of the wealth of spiritual sympathy, loyalty and affection that could be formed in intercourse and friendship and companionship with one another. Gone was the age old sense of inferiority, gone the intolerable weight of helplessness in the face of material oppression, gone the necessity of conforming to conventional standards of behaviour, gone all fears of Mrs Grundy. And taking the place of the old inhibitions was the release of powers that we had never dreamed of. While working for the idea of political liberty we were individually achieving liberty of a far more real and vital nature. ... It was our education in that living identification of the self with the corporate whole which means an intensification and expansion of consciousness.[43]

There are echoes here of 'the intensity of aspiration' which Yeo has described as characteristic of the socialism of this period. It is a constant theme throughout the book, expressed in phrases like 'a quickening of the intelligence and wit', 'a quickening of the whole emotional life', 'a heightening of the values of life for all of us . . . an inward sense of marching in step to music'.

The split between the public and the private is, of course, a social construction. There are institutions which cannot simply be fitted into either category. The church, for example, is in one sense a public institution, but it also enters people's private worlds. Similarly, many working-class women who are supposed to occupy the private sphere of home and family have always occupied the public sphere of paid employment. Nevertheless, in the nineteenth century the division between the public and the private came to be one of the central organizing principles of society. The suffrage movement was restricted by given definitions of the boundaries between the public and the private, and the suffragettes thought within those categories. As they saw it, women were struggling to enter the public world fully. The limitations of conceptualizing the world in this way could not be fully realized until that entry had been achieved.[44] Within this context, the public face of feminism had primacy. Nevertheless, being a feminist, especially a militant feminist, had a personal meaning too, which found various forms of expression even in the most public writings of the suffragettes.

Sex antagonism: the problem of men

Since there was no self-conscious examination of the personal as a political category, the problems with men as a sex, and relationships in marriage, could only be alluded to. This unresolved tension is visible in the politics, and played some part in the relative decline of feminism once the vote had been won. As Constance Rover has written:

A sort of impasse developed: to ignore conventional public morality was to invite and attract censure in a way which harmed efforts to obtain education, wider opportunities for employment, yet not to attack 'the enemy' was to perpetuate a situation where women were valued (or undervalued) for little other than their functions as wives and mothers.[45]

It is also visible in some of the texts. In *My Own Story*, for example, Emmeline

Pankhurst characterized the suffrage struggle as 'a women's war', with men as the enemy. She saw this 'masculine hostility' to women's suffrage as an extension of the double standard in sex morals. 'Why is it', she asked,

that men's blood-shedding militancy is applauded and women's symbolic militancy is punished with a prison cell and the forcible feeding horror? It means simply this, that men's double standard of sex morals, whereby the victims of their lust are counted as outcasts while the men themselves escape all censure really applies to morals in all departments of life. Men make the moral code and they expect women to accept it. They have decided that it is entirely right for men to fight for their liberties and their rights, but that it is not right and proper for women to fight for theirs.[46]

This was never developed in the practical politics of the WSPU or in Mrs Pankhurst's consciousness precisely because of the containment of suffrage and feminism within the public arena of parliamentary politics. The contradictions are all too apparent. On an American tour, for example, Mrs Pankhurst visited a suffrage state and commented on the 'Respect, courtesy and chivalry' shown to women.[47] On another occasion, when threatened by a group of men after a suffrage meeting, she reflected on how weak and pathetic they appeared and called out to them, 'Are none of you *men*?'[48]

Furthermore there arose the problem of how to deal with those men who were sympathetic to the Women's Movement. On at least one occasion this led to obvious difficulties of logic. When on trial with Emmeline and Fred Pethick-Lawrence she proclaimed, 'It is not a movement of misguided people. It is a very serious movement. Women, I submit, like our members, and women, I venture to say, like the two women, and like the men who are in the dock today, are not people to undertake a thing like this lightly.'[49]

Nevertheless, subdued and contradictory though this 'sex antagonism' was, it does indicate that some strands of suffrage struggle – especially under the pressure of militancy – strayed outside the boundaries of the constitutional, and located women's oppression in wider terms than their formal exclusion from public life. If this is so it suggests that historians who base their analysis of the WSPU *solely* on its parliamentary efficacy miss at least some of the point. They ignore that it was also a consciousness-raising experience of a particularly dramatic kind. For if militancy meant a flouting of some conventions of femininity, as it clearly did, it also precipitated as a response some very 'ungentlemanly' behaviour.

Class and sex: great hopes

Given the social background of many suffragettes, a preoccupation with the relationship between class and sex is hardly surprising. Great stress was laid on women of different classes working 'shoulder to shoulder'. At the same time, there was an awareness that no form of socialist politics answered the needs of women

Writing of her early failure, as a socialist, to see the significance of feminism, Mrs Pethick-Lawrence noted:

I was convinced that all injustice and wrong would come to an end if a system of socialism could supplant the old capitalist regime. I had not yet awakened to the fact that a system of socialism planned by the male half only of humanity would not touch on some of the worst evils that were engendered by a politically and socially suppressed womanhood.[50]

Hannah Mitchell, whose ties to socialism were much stronger than the majority of suffragettes, expressed similar sentiments to those of Mrs Pethick-Lawrence, but in a more combative spirit. Whilst recognizing the importance of socialism, she nevertheless challenged the idea that any easy alliance could be made with feminism. 'I still felt women must work out their own salvation. "God helps those who help themselves", I thought, and stuck to my feminist guns.'[51]

The assertion of a common cause helped to contain this tension within suffrage campaigns.[52] The suffrage struggle and the dangers of militancy encouraged an emotional sense of sisterhood. Hannah Mitchell, for example, saw the feminist movement as having significantly eroded class distinction between women. Equally from within the Women's Freedom League Billington-Greig, who of all the suffragettes was the most perceptive of the need for a broad struggle, came to support militancy on the grounds that militants got support from working-class women. She cherished 'great hopes of a union of women of all classes to serve the common cause'.[53] Even Sylvia, who always worked within a class perspective, was *not* dismissive of the middle-class militants.

However, the links were always fragile. In its initial phase the WSPU was interested in attracting working-class support. When Annie Kenney went to London it was assumed she would organize in the East End. The increasing stress on sexual solidarity, however, gradually turned into an emphasis on the key role of middle-class women. Christabel, who was not one to mince her words, wrote:

It was the right and duty of women more fortunately placed to do their share, and the larger share, in the fight for the vote. Besides . . . it was evident . . . that the House of Commons . . . was more impressed by demonstrations of the feminine bourgeoisie than of the feminine proletariat. My democratic principles and instinct made me want a movement based on no class distinctions and including not mainly the working class but women of all classes.[54]

The growing emphasis on the key leadership roles of middle-class women was by no means coincidental. In part it reflected a wider tradition. Labour Party women like Mary Macarthur and Margaret Bondfield believed in the importance of middle-class women teaching working-class women the necessary skills for political struggle.[55] In part this too followed from the logic of suffrage politics, with its emphasis on limited legislative objectives and its adoption of parliamentary tactics.

This was a very serious weakness. Because of their failure to make firm an alliance between working-class and middle-class women the suffragettes could never represent an organized base of sufficient power.

Another generation

None of the tendencies within the suffrage movement made any total break with nineteenth-century feminism, either in an analysis of women's oppression or, consequently, in forms of organization. Sylvia Pankhurst's work in the East End broke new ground for feminism, but can best be understood from within a socialist politics and tradition. The primary focus of the suffrage movement was on women' exclusion from the public sphere. The relationships between men and women, the connections and disconnections between class and gender, and the boundaries between the personal and public political world, although all posed as questions, remained marginal.

At the same time militancy pushed to the limits both the theory and the practice of feminism and dramatically affected feminist consciousness. This of course in no way denies the validity of those arguments which are critical of the extremism of militancy and its focus. In particular we have to take seriously Mrs Pethick-Lawrence's belief that after 1912 the militants alienated popular support. This impression is confirmed by Mary Richardson's account of the public hostility at the funeral of Emily Wilding Davison, the suffragette 'martyr'.[56] However, militancy, by challenging ideas about propriety and respectability, not only altered the public character of feminism, it also intensified existing contradictions. The campaign against the Contagious Diseases Acts contained the conflict between conventional notions of feminism and conventional notions of femininity. Militancy brought these contradictions to a head in a way that other campaigns had not. As Frederick Pethick-Lawrence wrote of the arrest of Emmeline, 'It was a great shock to me; for things which happen to other people assume an entirely different aspect when they come right home to one's own family circle'.[57] This challenge to convention was reinforced by the level of commitment required by a sustained militant campaign. As Winifred Holtby later wrote,

The suffrage movement had enfranchised women, and from more than their lack of citizenship. It had disproved those theories about their own nature which were – and still sometimes are – among their gravest handicaps. This was the great value of militancy. It broke down hitherto intangible tabus. It was no longer after 1905 possible perpetually to convince an intelligent girl that women care nothing for political issues, since women had been ready to jeopardise their lives for them, and – worse ordeal – to make themselves ridiculous. It was no longer possible to convince her that women were incapable of political acumen, since their leaders had shown powers of strategy and action unsurpassed in struggles for reform. Women had accepted discipline, displayed capacity of organisation, courage and tenacity. The very recklessness and extremism of militancy had shaken old certainties. An emotional earthquake had shattered the intangible yet suffocating prison of decorum. The standard of values which rated women's persons, positions, interests and preoccupations as affairs of minor national importance had been challenged.[58]

Winning the vote, for all its limitations, did change women's relationship to the public world of politics. One result was that feminist concerns changed; it became possible, and indeed necessary, to think through the relationship between the public and private. The vote gave new weight to the question of why, if women were formally equal, things did not change in their favour? It made it possible to rethink the nature of women's oppression. What constituted the oppression of women if not their exclusion from the public sphere? It put the informal and personal dimensions of patriarchy on the feminist agenda.

This change, of course, could not take place overnight. Nor did it simply supersede an equal-rights feminism, with its emphasis on gaining formal equality for women. There were plenty of other aspects of the law in which women remained unequal and these were taken up by organizations like the Six Point Group. In Vera Brittain's writing and career we can see a self-consciousness about movement and change, and indications that she saw herself as part of a new, post-suffrage generation. In *Testament of Experience* she described her interest in her husband's dead mother who had joined the suffrage movement despite the disapproval of her husband. 'In some ways I thought I was fulfilling in another generation my dead mother-in-law's aspirations for women.'[59]

Vera Brittain's writing indicated a new awareness that there were problems faced by women which legislative change could not touch, although the solutions she offered tended to be individualistic and moralistic. She was particularly concerned in *Testament of Friendship* to show the effects of family demands on Winifred Holtby's health and career, quoting from Mrs Gaskell's life of Charlotte Brontë. 'A woman cannot get away from her family even in its absence. She may abandon it; it may abandon her; but she is bound to it by intangible, indestructible bonds.'[60] The conflict between the new public world of careers and politics and her own personal life was certainly lived by Vera Brittain herself as a real struggle. This was especially so during the early and difficult days of her marriage when America proved as bad for her career as it was good for her husband's. In fact it was this problem of how to combine public and private which she saw as the central question for feminism. In *Testament of Youth* she quoted a letter she had written to George Catlin before their marriage:

'For me' I told G., 'the feminist problem ranks with your economic problem. Just as you want to discover how a man can maintain a decent standard of culture on a small income so I want too to solve the problem of how a married woman, without being inordinately rich, can have children and yet maintain her intellectual and spiritual independence as well as having . . . time for the pursuit of her own career. . . . The need to solve it is so urgent that it is raised to the level of those cases where it is expedient that one man – and more than one man – should die for the people.'[61]

Several key feminist concerns are raised in this passage. The feminism of the early 1900s had been built on the demand for the vote. Vera Brittain, however, was concerned to combine marriage and family with a career which would provide economic independence and an active intellectual life of her own. She knew, as did Virginia Woolf, that it was hard to maintain an independent intellectual life while economically dependent. Women needed a room of their own, a space to live their own lives. Vera Brittain was a privileged middle-class woman and was able to resolve the contradictions between her professional life and the demands of her children by employing other people to look after them. Her daughter Shirley Williams observed in a fascinating interview on the republication of *Testament of Youth* that such a choice was not open to her in the post-war era. By the 1960s it was assumed that married women could combine maternity with their professional lives, but no mother could afford to be seen to be putting her career first. Contemporary feminism has in part been built upon the contradictions generated by conflicting demands on women as mothers and workers. Early-twentieth-century feminism was structured around the demand for the vote; it focused on the public world of politics, the centrality of Parliament and of government. But feminists could not stop at that point in their personal lives even if they played the game publicly. They puzzled away behind the scenes and between public events at the less-established concerns – the question of domestic relations, of marriage and of sexuality – even if their main focus was on the public world. Personal life as a political matter could not be overlooked even if there was no organizational and, indeed, little theoretical framework to deal with its political meaning. Personal politics appeared as a central concern for feminists once the limitations of equal-rights feminism and liberal individualism had been clearly demonstrated. Feminism, in both its public and private aspects, lived to fight another day . . . .

Notes and references

Chapter 1 Radical liberalism, Fabianism and social history

1   R. Samuel, 'British marxist historians I', *New Left Review*, no. 120, p. 37.
2   This chapter is intended as complementary to Richard Johnson's more wide-ranging 'Culture and the historians', in J. Clarke, C. Critcher and R. Johnson (eds.), *Working Class Culture* (Hutchinson, 1979); for the emergence of 'economic history' in this period see N. B. Harte (ed.), *The Study of Economic History* (Frank Cass, 1971).
3   P. F. Clarke, *Liberals and Social Democrats* (Cambridge University Press, 1978), pp. 1-4.
4   R. Williams, *Problems in Materialism and Culture, Selected Essays* (Verso, 1980), pp. 148-69.
5   R. Johnson, 'Educating the educators: "experts" and the state 1833-9', in A. P. Donajgrodski (ed.), *Social Control in 19th Century Britain* (Croom Helm, 1977), p. 91.
6   Alan Lee's *The Origins of the Popular Press 1855-1914* (Croom Helm, 1976), examines these fears and finds them unduly pessimistic.
7   K. Burgess, *The Challenge of Labour* (Croom Helm, 1980).
8   For the intellectual hinterland of the Rainbow Circle, B. Porter, *Critics of Empire: British Radical Attitudes to Colonisation in Africa, 1891-1914* (Macmillan, 1968), ch. 6.
9   B. Gilbert, *The Evolution of National Insurance in Great Britain* (Michael Sharp, 1966), p. 452.
10 H. V. Emy, *Liberals, Radicals and Social Politics, 1892-1914* (Cambridge University Press, 1973), p. 105.
11 R. H. Tawney, 'J. L. Hammond', in *Proceedings of the British Academy*, vol. XLVI (1960), p. 268.
12 The assumption that T. H. Green had a large influence on the development of collectivism is no longer held so strongly as before.
13 G. Lansbury, *My Life* (Constable, 1928), p. 105.
14 The computations and differences over imperialism and social reform are well dealt with in a series of essays, B. Semmel, *Imperialism and Social Reform: English Social-Imperial Thought, 1895-1914* (Allen and Unwin, 1960).
15 'Fabianism and the Empire I', *The Speaker* (6 October 1900), p. 82.
16 Clarke, *Liberals*, p. 82.
17 H. Pelling, *Popular Politics and Society in Late Victorian Britain* (Macmillan,

1968), p. 9.

18   Clarke, *Liberals*, pp. 101–2.

19   Clarke, *Liberals*, p. 104.

20   L. Masterman, *Charles Masterman: a Biography* (Nicholson and Watson, 1939), p. 384; Clarke, *Liberals*, pp. 158–9.

21   Clarke, *Liberals*, p. 103.

22   M. A. Hamilton, *Remembering my Good Friends* (Jonathan Cape, 1944), p. 83.

23   J. Winter, *Socialism and the Challenge of War: Ideas and Politics in Britain, 1912–18* (Routledge and Kegan Paul, 1974), p. 5.

24   J. M. Winter and D. M. Joslin (eds.), *R. H. Tawney's Commonplace Book* (Cambridge University Press, 1972), pp. 5 and 9.

25   B. Drake and M. Cole (eds.), B .Webb, *Our Partnership* (Longmans and Green, 1948), p. 25.

26   E. J. Hobsbawm, 'The Fabians reconsidered', in *Labouring Men. Studies in the History of Labour* (Weidenfeld and Nicolson, 1974), pp. 250–72. Clarke himself takes up the comparison in a shorter essay but omits it from his larger text, 'The progressive movement in England', in *Transactions of the Royal Historical Society*, 5th Series, no. 24 (1974), p. 175.

27   Quoted in E. Halévy, *The Rule of Democracy, 1905–1914* (Ernest Benn, 1932), p. 279.

28   'The significance of the budget', *The Nation* (20 April 1907).

29   M. Freeden, *The New Liberalism: An Ideology of Social Reform* (Clarendon Press, 1978), p. 151.

30   K. Marx, *The Eighteenth Brumaire of Louis Bonaparte* (Progress, 1972), p. 43.

31   ibid., pp. 40–1.

32   H. C. G. Matthew, R. I. McKibbin and J. H. Kay, 'The franchise factor in the rise of the Labour Party', *English Historical Review*, vol. 16 (1976), pp. 743–4.

33   L. T. Hobhouse, *Democracy and Reaction*, 2nd ed. (Fisher and Unwin, 1909), p. 69.

34   ibid., p. 71.

35   C. F. G. Masterman, *The Condition of England, 1909* (Methuen, 1968), pp. 3–4.

36   ibid., pp. 64–5.

37   ibid., p. 67.

38   P. Hollis, *The Pauper Press: A Study in Working-Class Radicalism of the 1830s* (Oxford University Press, 1970), pp. 203–19. The old analysis made a critique of taxation but considered the employing class as productive.

39   C. F. G. Masterman, 'Politics in transition', *Nineteenth Century and After*, vol. CCCLXXI (1908), pp. 9 and 12.

40   Marx, *Eighteenth Brumaire*, p. 44.

41   Hobson's and Hobhouse's writing can be seen as a shared project. The most

useful texts other than Clarke's are Freeden, *New Liberalism*, and S. Collini, *Liberalism and Sociology: L. T. Hobhouse and Political Argument in England, 1880-1914* (Cambridge University Press, 1979).

42   For a general discussion of the tendency for these intellectuals to reject marxist economics, see Kirk Willis, 'The introduction and critical reception of marxist thought in Britain, 1850-1900', *The Historical Journal*, vol. 20, no. 2 (1977), pp. 219-59.

43   J. A. Hobson, *The Crisis of Liberalism: New Issues of Democracy* (1909) (ed. P. F. Clarke; Macmillan, 1974), p. 81.

44   ibid., p. 77.

45   J. A. Hobson, *The Industrial System: An Inquiry into Earned and Unearned Income* (Longmans, 1909), p. ix.

46   ibid., p. 220.

47   See, for instance, R. Douglas, 'God gave the land to the people', in A. J. A. Morris (ed.), *Edwardian Radicalism, 1900-14* (Routledge and Kegan Paul, 1974).

48   For different varieties of land reformers and taxation, see H. V. Emy, 'The Land Campaign: Lloyd George as a social reformer', in A. J. P. Taylor (ed.), *Lloyd George: 12 essays* (Hamish Hamilton, 1971).

49   Hobson, *The Industrial System*, p. 219.

50   *The Nation* (30 June 1908).

51   Matthew, McKibbin, Kay, 'The franchise factor', pp. 723-53.

52   R. McKibbin, *The Evolution of the Labour Party, 1910-24* (Oxford University Press, 1974), p. 97.

53   For a similar thesis, see T. Nairn, *The Break-up of Britain* (New Left Books, 1977), p. 49.

54   Stuart Macintyre, *A Proletarian Science: Marxism in Britain, 1917-33* (Cambridge University Press, 1980), ch. 2.

55   Gilbert Murray, 'John Hammond', *Dictionary of National Biography* (1941-50), p. 351.

56   J. Hammond, *Gladstone and the Irish Nation* (Longmans, 1938), p. 706.

57   J. and B. Hammond, *James Stansfeld: A Victorian Champion of Sex Equality* (Longmans, 1932), pp. 160-2.

58   Clarke, *Liberals*, pp. 154-5.

59   Clarke, *Liberals*, p. 162; Asa Briggs, *Social Thought and Social Action: Seebohm, A Study of the Work of Rowntree* (Longmans, 1961), pp. 64-9; Emy, *Liberals, Radicals*, p. 66.

60   J. and B. Hammond, *The Village Labourer* (Longmans, 1911), pp. 10 and 59.

61   ibid., p. 73.

62   ibid., p. 213.

63   Johnson, 'Culture and the historians', pp. 46-8.

64   *The Village Labourer* (1960 ed.), pp. 136-40.

65   J. and B. Hammond, *The Town Labourer* (Longmans, 1917), p. vii.

66   ibid., p. 21.

67   ibid., p. 64.
68   ibid., p. 65.
69   ibid., p. 287.
70   ibid., p. 288-9.
71   *The Skilled Labourer* (Longmans, 1920), p. 12.
72   R. Williams, *Culture and Society 1780–1950* (Penguin, 1971). The absence of the Hammonds from this book and also Williams's *The Country and the City* (Paladin, 1975), is surprising.
73   *The Skilled Labourer* (Longmans, 1920), pp. 377-9.
74   Clarke, *Liberals*, p. 194 (my emphasis).
75   Credit and thanks are due to Janet Batsleer and Rebecca O'Rourke for guidance in this section.
76   *James Stansfeld*, p. 165.
77   C. Dyhouse, 'The role of women: from self-sacrifice to self-awareness', in J. Lerner (ed.), *The Victorians* (London, 1978).
78   P. Stubbs, *Women and Fiction: Feminism and the Novel, 1880–1920* (Harvester, 1979), p. xv.
79   O. Schreiner, *Woman and Labour* (Fisher and Unwin, 1911), p. 24.
80   E. Wilson, *Women and the Welfare State* (Tavistock, 1977), p. 24.
81   See for instance E. J. Hobsbawm, 'Man and woman in socialist iconography', *History Workshop Journal*, no. 6 (1978), pp. 129-31.
82   T. McBride, 'As the twig is bent: the Victorian nanny', in A. S. Wohl (ed.), *The Victorian Family. Structure and Stresses* (Croom Helm, 1978).
83   Florence Low, 'The educational ladder and the girl', *Nineteenth Century and After*, vol. 62 (1907), p. 396.
84   See J. Mackenzie, *A Victorian Courtship: The Story of Beatrice Potter and Sidney Webb* (Weidenfeld and Nicolson, 1979).
85   B. Harrison, *Separate Spheres: The Opposition to Women's Suffrage* (Croom Helm, 1976), p. 204.
86   A radical liberal model would not be dissimilar though Clarke, *Liberals*, p. 5, does make a useful distinction between Fabianism as 'mechanical reformism' and radical liberalism as 'moral reformism'. Perhaps some of the Fabian women had a less mechanical interpretation of consciousness than their male counterparts.
87   S. Webb, 'Socialism true and false', *Fabian Tract*, no. 51 (1894), p. 51.
88   S. Webb, 'Twentieth century politics: a policy of national efficiency', *Fabian Tract*, no. 108, p. 7.
89   A good case in point was women's part in the campaign for the 1909 Trade Boards Act. John Rickard, 'The anti-sweating movement in Britain and Victoria; the politics of Empire and social reform', *Historical Studies*, no. 73, vol. 18 (1979).
90   B. L. Hutchins and A. Harrison, *A History of Factory Legislation* (P. J. King, 1911), p. 184.
91   M. Pember Reeves, *Round About a Pound a Week* (1913) (Virago, 1975),

p. xvi.
92 C. Black (ed.), *Married Women's Work* (G. Bell and Sons, 1915), p. 1 and 5.
93 'The economic foundations of the Women's Movement', *Fabian Tract*, no. 175 (1914), p. 8.
94 ibid., pp. 14–15.
95 A. Clark, *Working Life of Women in the Seventeenth Century* (1919) (Frank Cass and Co., 1968), p. 1.
96 ibid., p. 5.
97 ibid., pp. 6–7.
98 ibid., p. 13.
99 R. Hamilton's *The Liberation of Women: A Study of Patriarchy and Capitalism* (Allen and Unwin, 1978), compares Alice Clark's work with marxist approaches to the seventeenth century.
100 Clark, *Working Life of Women*, p. 308.
101 B. Webb, *The Wages of Men and Women: Should They Be Equal?* (Fabian Society, 1919), p. 72.
102 J. Lewis, 'In search of real equality: women between the wars', in F. Glover-smith (ed.), *Class, Culture and Social Change* (Harvester, 1980), p. 216.
103 For example Hilary Land, 'Women: supporters or supported', in D. Barker and S. Allen (eds.), *Sexual Divisions and Society: Process and Change* (Tavistock, 1976); M. Barrett and M. McIntosh, 'The family wage: some problems for socialists and feminists', *Capital and Class*, no. 11 (1980).
104 J. Hammond, 'The terror in action', *The Nation and Athenaeum* (supplement), 30 April 1921, p. 186.
105 Tawney, 'J. L. Hammond', p. 272.
106 B. Simon, *Education and the Labour Movement* (Lawrence and Wishart, 1975), p. 257.
107 A. Freeman, *An Introduction to the Study of Social Problems* (WEA, 1914), p. 3.
108 P. Yorke, *Ruskin College, 1899–1909* (Ruskin Students' Labour History Pamphlet, no. 1, 1973); W. Craik, *The Central Labour College* (Lawrence and Wishart, 1964); A. Phillips and T. Putnam, 'Education for emancipation: the movement for independent working class education', *Capital and Class*, no. 10 (1980).
109 J. and B. Hammond, *The Bleak Age* (Longmans, 1934), pp. vii and ix.
110 Macintyre, *A Proletarian Science*, p. 70.
111 Geo. Guest, *An Introduction to English Rural History* (WEA, 1920), pp. 3 and 6.
112 *Times Literary Supplement* (19 July 1917), p. 339.
113 *Times Literary Supplement* (4 January 1912), p. 3.
114 *Times Literary Supplement* (10 December 1925), pp. 141–2.
115 For a useful history of the optimist/pessimist debate, B. Inglis, *Poverty and the Industrial Revolution* (Panther, 1972), Foreword.
116 J. L. Hammond, 'The Industrial Revolution and discontent', *Economic*

History Review, vol. 2 (1929-30), p. 219.

117   J. and B. Hammond, *The Bleak Age*, p. 4.
118   J. Clapham, *The Economic History of Great Britain*, vol. 1 (Cambridge University Press, 1930), p. viii.
119   B. Inglis, *Poverty*, pp. 19ff.
120   F. A. Hayek (ed.), *Capitalism and the Historians* (Routledge and Kegan Paul, 1954).
121   *The Long Debate on Poverty* (Institute of Economic Affairs, 1974), p. xvi.
122   E. P. Thompson, *The Making of the English Working Class* (Penguin, 1968), p. 213.
123   ibid., pp. 629, 637 and 647.
124   Samuel, 'British marxist historians', p. 37.
125   For the 'moral economy', *The Village Labourer*, pp. 96-8 refers to the 1795 'revolt of the housewives', price fixing, and 'spontaneous leagues of consumers'. E. P. Thompson, 'The moral economy of the English crowd', *Past and Present*, no. 50 (1971); for time and work formulations, *The Town Labourer*, ch. 2, 'The new discipline'.
126   E. J. Hobsbawm and G. Rudé, *Captain Swing* (Penguin, 1973), p. xx.
127   ibid., pp. xxi-xxii.
128   P. Anderson, *Arguments within English Marxism* (Verso, 1980), pp. 31 and 39.
129   M. Dobb, *Studies in the Development of Capitalism* (Routledge and Kegan Paul, 1946), p. 265.

Chapter 2   'The people' in history: the Communist Party Historians' Group, 1946-56

1   E. J. Hobsbawm, 'The Communist Party Historians' Group', in M. Cornforth (ed.), *Rebels and Their Causes* (Lawrence and Wishart, 1978), p. 25.
2   In a paper delivered at Ruskin History Workshop 13 (1980). And see Stuart Macintyre, *A Proletarian Science: British Marxism, 1917-33* (Cambridge University Press, 1980) for the contraction of the tradition of socialist autodidacts in the 1920s.
3   R. Williams, 'The Bloomsbury fraction', in *Problems in Materialism and Culture* (New Left Books, 1980), p. 159.
4   For the 'essays in honour', see: E. J. Hobsbawm, 'Maurice Dobb', in C. H. Feinstein (ed.), *Socialism, Capitalism and Growth* (Cambridge University Press, 1967); R. Hilton, 'Christopher Hill, some reminiscences', in D. Pennington and K. Thomas (eds.), *Puritans and Revolutionaries* (Oxford University Press, 1978); R. Miliband, 'John Saville', in D. Martin and D. Rubenstein (eds.), *Ideology and the Labour Movement* (Croom Helm, 1978); M. Cornforth, 'Leslie Morton', in *Rebels and Their Causes*. For the interviews, see 'Interview with E. P. Thompson', *Radical History Review*, vol. 3, no. 4 (1976); and 'Interview with E. J. Hobsbawm', *Radical History Review*,

no. 19 (1978–79). In addition to Hobsbawm's account of the Group, see Daphne May, 'The work of the Historians' Groups', *Communist Review* (May 1949); and Raphael Samuel, 'British marxist historians I', *New Left Review*, no. 120 (1980).

5   'The Communist Historians', p. 22.
6   ibid., p. 23.
7   This isolation as a Communist lecturer clearly made him conspicuous. The recent batches of 'treason' literature all have chapters devoted to the 'Communist Cambridge' of the thirties, and there are usually a scatter of references to a more or less conspiratorial Dobb. One cites him (in 1932) proposing a motion that 'This house sees more hope in Moscow than Detroit'. His opponent was Kitson Clark.
8   Demolition jobs on Dobb can be found in B. Hindess and P. Hirst, *Pre-Capitalist Modes of Production* (Routledge and Kegan Paul, 1975); and Simon Clarke, 'Socialist humanism and the critique of economism', *History Workshop Journal*, no. 8 (1979). We have argued against the former in R. Johnson, G. McLennan and B. Schwarz, 'Three approaches to marxist history, *CCCS Occasional Paper*, no. 50 (1978); and the latter in 'The case of Dobb', *History Workshop Journal*, no. 11 (1981).
9   However Lucio Colletti follows Dobb's theoretical investigations: see his Introduction to K. Marx, *Early Writings* (Penguin, 1975), and *From Rousseau to Lenin* (New Left Books, 1972).
10   'Marxism and social science', *Modern Quarterly*, vol. 3, no. 1 (1947–48), p. 9.
11   *Political Economy and Capitalism* (Routledge, 1937), p. 4.
12   ibid., p. 32.
13   ibid., pp. 131–2.
14   ibid., p. 8.
15   ibid., p. 4.
16   *Studies in the Development of Capitalism* (Routledge and Kegan Paul, 1963), pp. 1 and 12.
17   ibid., pp. 27 and 32.
18   Clarke, 'Critique of economism'. It would appear that Dobb, Hill and Hilton were very close intellectually for a period in the 1940s. Both Hill and Hilton were acknowledged in the *Studies*, both reviewed it enthusiastically (Hilton twice), Hill calling it 'the most profound and thought-provoking work on English history that has yet been written by a Marxist', *Modern Quarterly*, vol. 2, no. 3 (1947), p. 272; and both intervened to defend Dobb's position in *Science and Society*. They all worked together, editorially, on *Past and Present*.
19   Our assessment of Dobb's contribution in this respect can be found in Johnson *et al.*, *Three Approaches to Marxist History*. See also the splendid essay by Robert Brenner, 'Dobb on the transition from feudalism to capitalism', *Cambridge Journal of Economics*, vol. 2, no. 2 (1978). More recently see the

important reformulations by Michael Ignatieff and Hans Medick in R. Samuel (ed.), *People's History and Socialist Theory* (Routledge and Kegan Paul, 1981). The original material has been collected in R. Hilton (ed.), *The Transition from Feudalism to Capitalism* (New Left Books, 1976).

20   'A comment', in Hilton, *From Feudalism to Capitalism*, p. 119.

21   Alongside Dobb, Kosminsky – in providing a marxist account of feudal England – was a critical figure in influencing a more substantial marxist historiography in Britain; his articles went back to the 1920s, but see especially the English translation of *Studies in the Agrarian History of England* (Blackwell, 1956), edited by Hilton where, in turn, Kosminsky pays tribute to Dobb, Hill and Hilton.

22   See *Labour Monthly* October 1940 to February 1941. Kiernan sided with Küczynski, and Douglas Garman and Dona Torr with Hill. 'State and revolution in Tudor and Stuart England', *Communist Review* (July 1948) – in which it was recognized that with Dobb's *Studies* the issues had been 'raised to a higher theoretical level', p. 208.

23   Minutes 22 March 1953. This refers to the Minutes of the Committee of the Historians' Group, which are now in the possession of John Attfield and the present CP History Group. Apart from some fragments in the Marx Memorial Library (in the *Our History* box) whatever else exists for the period is scattered far and wide. I'm extremely grateful to John Attfield and the History Group of the Communist Party for letting me look at these Minutes; and to John Attfield for help and information.

24   *Studies*, p. 32.

25   Brenner, 'Dobb on the transition'.

26   This appeared as a major factor in Trevor-Roper's rejection of the Dobbian reading. Hugh Trevor-Roper, 'The general crisis of the 17th century', in T. Aston (ed.), *The Crisis in Europe: 1560–1660* (Routledge and Kegan Paul, 1965), pp. 65–6.

27   See Hill's 1955 'Introduction' to *The English Revolution* (Lawrence and Wishart, 1972). Of all the British historians it is perhaps Hilton who has remained most committed to the explicitly logical problems introduced by Dobb and – integral to this – committed also to theorizing and locating in history those forms of struggle constituted by the extraction of surplus labour. For an early example, 'Peasant movements in England before 1381', *Economic History Review*, 11, vol. 2, no. 2 (1949).

28   In his Ruskin paper Samuel makes the interesting suggestion that one effect of anglicization was to overcome the treason image associated with Comintern. Such a perspective was not alien to Dobb, who was arguing the point in 1927: 'We surely need a creative school of British Marxism – not a hole-in-the-corner affair, but a live body of critical, creative, first-rate minds who understand the present and are organically part of the active working class movement'. Quoted by Macintyre, *Proletarian Science*, p. 284.

29   'Where are the British historians going?', *Marxist Quarterly*, vol. 2, no. 1

(1955), p. 25. Throughout this period Tawney was under sustained attack, notably from Trevor-Roper and Hexter, for his views on the Tudor gentry.

30   As an example, the fact that Dobb's methodological protocols were produced in his critiques of mainstream economic theories has received little recognition in recent assessments. The strongest testament to the openness of his project in the *Studies* is the running engagement with the British economic historians – Ashley, Clapham, Cunningham, Lipson, Power, Tawney, Unwin, although not, surprisingly, Alice Clark or Ivy Pinchbeck.

31   The Communist Party of Great Britain, *The British Road to Socialism* (1951), p. 14.

32   For an account which adopts a different outlook to my own, Alun Howkins, 'Class against class: the politics of the Communist Party of Great Britain', in F. Gloversmith (ed.), *Class Culture and Social Change: A New View of the 1930s* (Harvester, 1980).

33   *The Italian Road to Socialism* (Journeyman Press, 1977), p. 9.

34   Quoted by Ernesto Laclau, *Politics and Ideology in Marxist Theory* (New Left Books, 1977), pp. 139–40. This passage is taken from the section on 'The ideological struggle against fascism' from Dimitrov's opening Report to the Seventh Congress of the Communist International. It can be found, with his Concluding Speech, in G. Dimitrov, *Selected Works*, vol. 2 (Foreign Language Press, 1972), pp. 7–121.

35   'The crisis of the thirties', in J. Clark *et al.* (eds.), *Culture and Crisis in Britain in the 30s* (Lawrence and Wishart, 1980), p. 25 (my emphasis).

36   I rely here on Gary Werskey's impressive study of the leading Communist scientists, *The Visible College* (Allen Lane, 1978); I also found useful the chapter 'Utopians of science', in Neal Wood, *Communism and the British Intellectuals* (Gollancz, 1959).

37   An instance of this in historiography although written later is Isaac Deutscher's chapter on fascism, 'Reason and unreason', in *The Prophet Outcast: Trotsky 1929–1940* (Oxford University Press, 1963). Deutscher was completely outside the tradition of anglo-marxist historiography, but it is interesting to compare him in exile in England in the 1950s – thinking his marxism in the categories of a pre-positivist eighteenth-century enlightened rationalism – to the English marxists.

38   Dominique Lecourt suggests in *Proletarian Science* (New Left Books, 1977), that in the Soviet Union Lysenkoism was the ideology of such experts – located specifically in a stratum of intellectuals organic to the Party. This could not apply to Britain as such, although parallels do exist in 'Bernalism'. Modern critiques of Bernalism sometimes forget how pressing and urgent, in the eyes of all the left, was the need for planning in inter-war Britain.

39   *Visible College*, ch. 5; and Ruskin History Workshop Collective, 'Worker historians in the 1920s', in Samuel, *People's History*.

40   This is from an article by M. Goldsmith in *The Times Higher Education Supplement* (21 March 1980). It's also a major theme of Bernal's own

Science in History (Watts and Co., 1954); see also the earlier works of
Benjamin Farrington, and slightly later, S. F. Mason.

41   Thompson's superb autobiographical evocation of the 1940s is absolutely
central here, where he defends a democratic conception of the people against
the authoritarian-bureaucratic construction represented by 'Pincher's people'.
This should be read alongside T. J. and E. P. Thompson (eds.), *There Is a
Spirit in Europe: A Memoir of Frank Thompson* (Gollancz, 1947); and Basil
Davidson, *Partisan Picture* (Bedford Books, 1946).

42   E. P. Thompson, *The Poverty of Theory* (Merlin Press, 1978), p. 145.

43   Hilton, 'Christopher Hill'.

44   Most striking is the long-conditioned reflex of hostility to marxist historiography to be found in the *Times Literary Supplement*, especially between
1951 and 1953. One reviewer claimed that 'Marxian historiography is fundamentally opposed to the canons of Western scholarship' which prompted an
editorial declaring it was a 'dereliction of duty' for administrators of the
educational system to retain marxists in teaching posts. For the background,
A. Rothstein, 'Marxism and the *Times Literary Supplement*', *Modern
Quarterly*, vol. 8, no. 2 (1953). In this the *TLS* has been consistent in the
intervening years.

45   Werskey, *Visible College*, p. 262.

46   Andrew Chester, 'Communist strategy from the 1940s to the 1970s', *Marxism
Today* (September 1979), p. 378.

47   This raises the *political* question of the precise forms of Stalinist populism
in the British Communist Party in the specific conjuncture after 1947–8.
I see little evidence of 'Stalinism' *in the historiography* of the 1940s or
early 1950s although at times even with the best – Gordon Childe, Dona Torr,
Christopher Hill, Edward Thompson – a debilitating rhetoric and dogma
broke through. In Scott Meikle's eyes Dobb, Hobsbawm and Hilton are all
revealed through their historiography as unequivocally Stalinist (*Critique*,
nos. 10–11, 1978–9). I find Thompson's assessment more credible:

> Marxist historiography was never in Britain deformed beyond recovery, even
> when failing to make a clear intellectual disengagement from Stalinism. We
> had, after all, the living line of Marx's analysis of British history – in *Capital*,
> in Marx and Engels' correspondence – continually present to us. To work as
> a Marxist historian in Britain means to work within a tradition founded by
> Marx, enriched by independent and complementary insights by William
> Morris, enlarged in recent times in specialist ways by such men and women
> as V. Gordon Childe, Maurice Dobb, Dona Torr and George Thomson, and to
> have colleagues such scholars as Christopher Hill, Rodney Hilton, Eric Hobs-
> bawm, V. G. Kiernan and (with others whom one might mention) the editors
> of this (*Socialist*) *Register*.
>
> *Poverty of Theory*, p. 123.

48   E. P. Thompson, 'Caudwell', *Socialist Register* (1977), p. 273.

49   Perry Anderson, 'Components of the national culture', *New Left Review*, no. 50 (1968).

50   John Saville gives a brief insight in *Marxism Today* (March 1980); also in a talk on the 1930s at Ruskin History Workshop (1975). As for the profession of historian: 'Good heavens, no! I never "took a decision" to become a historian' - (Thompson, 'Interview', p. 12).

51   Republished in Dobb, *On Economic Theory and Socialism* (Routledge and Kegan Paul, 1953). In 1932 Dobb had been admonished by the Party when he had criticized the 'abstract separation of events into "material" and "ideal" ' (Macintyre, *Proletarian Science*, p. 121).

52   Hilton, *From Feudalism to Capitalism*, p. 157.

53   Minutes 12 November 1949.

54   In particular, the brilliant study by George Thomson of *Aeschylus and Athens* (Lawrence and Wishart, 1941), which not only raised questions about transitions in modes of production, but also the social functions of drama, issues of democracy, and fascinating investigations into totemic structures, language and ritual. (It was Thomson who provided the main defence of Caudwell, and for whom Caudwell was the exemplar of the Communist intellectual.) V. Gordon Childe's archaeological analyses distinguished the social world from the natural by way of 'material cultures' - as for example in his enormously popular *What Happened in History* (Penguin, 1942). Francis Klingender's superb *Goya in the Democratic Tradition* (Sidgwick and Jackson, 1948) was completed in 1940. And lastly Hill's 1946 essay on Marvell (republished in *Puritanism and Revolution* (Mercury, 1969)) appears to have been very influential for the historians themselves.

55   For Thompson's views on *Left Review* see his 'Organizing the Left', *Times Literary Supplement* (19 February 1971).

56   Francis Mulhern, 'The marxist aesthetics of Christopher Caudwell', *New Left Review*, no. 85 (1974).

57   When in 1977 there occurred a clumsy, premature lurch to McCarthyism (under the guidance of Professor Julius Gould) it was the *Economist* which quietly insisted upon the intellectual integrity of Hill, Hilton and Hobsbawm.

58   *Scrutiny*, vol. 1, no. 4 (1933), p. 326.

59   'The literary mind', *Scrutiny*, vol. 1, no. 1 (1932), p. 21. This theme received its full treatment in F. R. Leavis and Denys Thompson, *Culture and the Environment* (Chatto and Windus, 1933).

60   Francis Mulhern, *The Moment of Scrutiny* (New Left Books, 1979), p. 63. My interpretation of *Scrutiny* follows Mulhern and Iain Wright, 'F. R. Leavis, the *Scrutiny* Movement and the crisis', in Clark, *Culture and Crisis*.

61   F. R. Leavis, 'Under which king, Bezonian?', *Scrutiny*, vol. 1, no. 3 (1932), pp. 206 and 212.

62   'History and the marxist method', *Scrutiny*, vol. 1, no. 4 (1933), pp. 342-3 and 351. As an aside he added: 'I am not certain that we realise the full context of the words: "the history of the English people", or that we

remember how little the history of England we possess in our minds really corresponds with the fulness of the concept', p. 342.

63   Not only were Leavis and the Communist historians theorizing cultures according to national peculiarities, but so too Eliot. In his *Notes Towards a Definition of Culture* (Faber and Faber, 1948), he drew particularly an Anglicanism which was increasingly in vogue among intellectuals of the period. (In the late 1930s Eliot believed: 'The *great* danger seems to me to be the delusion of the Popular Front', quoted by Arnold Kettle in Clark, *Culture and Crisis*, p. 89.) Eliot's also was an ideology which looked back to the seventeenth century and to the instigation by 'science' of the 'dissociation of sensibility'.

64   'William Morris and the moral issues of today', *The USA Threat to British Culture* (*sic*), special issue of *Arena*, vol. 2, no. 8 (1951), p. 29. Some notion of folk art was contrasted to Americanism. The British contingent involved in building the railway in Yugoslavia after the War were embarrassed by the contemporary paucity of British folk traditions: E. P. Thompson (ed.), *The Railway, an Adventure in Construction* (British-Yugoslav Association, 1948). It was within this context that A. L. Lloyd published numerous articles in Communist journals on English and other folk traditions. For the first intelligent discussion of 'Americanism' in this period, see Dick Hebdige, 'A cartography of taste, 1935–1962', *Block*, no. 4 (1981).

65   'Outside the whale', *Poverty of Theory*, p. 2.

66   R. Williams, *Politics and Letters* (New Left Books, 1979), pp. 68–70 and 75.

67   *Culture and Society* (Penguin, 1971), p. 248. Much later the driving force of Raymond Williams's *The Country and the City* (Paladin, 1975) was the urge to dismantle the 'escalator' perspective on history, integral to *Scrutiny*, of an illusory organic past built on a common culture.

68   E. P. Thompson, 'Review of *The Long Revolution*', *New Left Review*, nos. 9–10 (1961); V. G. Kiernan, 'Review of *Culture and Society*', *New Reasoner*, no. 9 (1959).

69   *Politics and Letters*, vol. 1, no. 1 (1947), p. 42.

70   A. Gramsci, *Selections From the Prison Notebooks* (Lawrence and Wishart, 1971), pp. 132–3.

71   A. L. Rowse, *The Use of History* (Hodder and Stoughton, 1963), p. 153.

72   *The Englishman and His History* (Cambridge University Press, 1944), p. 107. See Hilton's onslaught on Butterfield in *Communist Review* (July 1949).

73   Geoff Roberts, 'How the peace was lost: British Communism 1941–5', (forthcoming) argues that strategic miscalculation in 1945 resulted in the isolation of the CP as an independent political force. An alternative reading weaves in and out of Edward Upward's trilogy, *The Spiral Ascent* (Quarto, 1978).

74   Hobsbawm, 'Where are the British historians going?'; Minutes 17 July 1955.

75   A. L. Morton, 'The writing of marxist history', *Communist Review* (July 1949).

76   'The Communist Historians', p. 29. Between 1948 and 1949 were published: E. Dell and C. Hill (eds.), *The Good Old Cause* (Lawrence and Wishart, 1949); M. Morris (ed.), *From Cobbett to the Chartists* (Lawrence and Wishart, 1948); J. B. Jefferys (ed.), *Labour's Formative Years* (Lawrence and Wishart, 1948); E. J. Hobsbawm (ed.), *Labour's Turning Point* (Lawrence and Wishart, 1948). The first and last of these were republished in a climate when marxists could be rather less defensive. (See also the rather later collection of documents edited by John Saville, *Ernest Jones: Chartist* (Lawrence and Wishart, 1952).) It is interesting to compare this 1940s venture with the similar, more successful enterprise of the 'Teach Yourself History' series. These biographical histories were written under the general editorship of A. L. Rowse who declared they were intended 'to bring the university into the homes of the people'.

77   I argue throughout this chapter that a distinctive feature of the marxist historiography of the period was its stress on anglicization, that this developed out of the anti-fascist strategy of the Popular Front, and that Torr was a key figure in this alignment. This text however was meant as a clear political intervention to demonstrate that the War was an imperialist conflict and not a fight against fascism. It was written during the time of the Nazi-Soviet pact.

78   J. Saville (ed.), *Democracy and the Labour Movement* (Lawrence and Wishart, 1954), p. 8.

79   D. Torr (ed.), *Marxism, Nationalism and War*, vol. 1 (Lawrence and Wishart, 1940), p. 10.

80   D. Torr, 'Productive forces: social relations', *Communist Review* (May 1946); and Torr, ibid., p. 15.

81   Quoted by D. Torr, *Tom Mann and His Times* (Lawrence and Wishart, 1956), p. 269. Cf. C. Hill, *Lenin and the Russian Revolution* (Hodder and Stoughton, 1947).

82   A. L. Morton, 'Socialist humanism', *Communist Review* (October 1953).

83   V. Gordon Childe, *History* (Cobbett Press, 1947), p. 68.

84   C. Hill, 'Marxism and history', *Modern Quarterly*, vol. 3, no. 2 (1948), pp. 59 and 64. Compare this to G. M. Trevelyan, *English Social History* (first published Longman, 1942) who asserted that 'Truth is the criterion of historical study; but its compelling motive is poetic' (Penguin, 1976), p. 12; and to Butterfield, *The Englishman and His History*, who argued that history 'resembles poetry rather than geometry', p. 138.

85   P. Anderson, 'Socialism and pseudo-empiricism', *New Left Review*, no. 35 (1965).

86   All quotes from the version published in *Democracy and the Labour Movement*. For a mind-boggling attempt at an alternative reading A. P. Thornton can be sampled: 'For the strength of the "Norman Yoke", as the Plantagenets, Jack Cade, Levellers, Diggers and Tom Paine had understood, lay not in its oppressive force, but in the acquiescence of the English people that it was a

useful yoke, under which useful work was done', *The Habit of Authority: Paternalism in British History* (Heinemann, 1966), p. 254.

87   Again, this must not be read as a complete break with past practices. In the very moment of transition to the Popular Front, Joseph Needham was writing: 'Is it not of some value to English socialists tired of hearing Communism defined with foreign-sounding names and doctrines, to know that the Communists of the seventeenth century had names that run like English villages – John Lilburne, William Walwyn, Gerard Winstanley, Robert Lockyer, Giles Calvert, Anthony Sedley? So it will be again, and not for failure', quoted by Samuel, 'British marxist historians', p. 51. Raphael Samuel traces the origins of English populist historiography to J. R. Green's radical liberal *A Short History of the English People*, first published 1877.

88   R. Hilton and H. Fagan, *The English Rising of 1381* (Lawrence and Wishart, 1950), p. 10. The social banditry of Robin Hood was integrated into this tradition on the same grounds.

89   Quoted by Hobsbawm, 'The Communist Historians', p. 43.

90   R. Hilton, *Communism and Liberty* (Lawrence and Wishart, 1950), p. 6.

91   Minutes 29 November 1953.

92   *Our History*, no. 20 (1960).

93   Torr, *Tom Mann*, pp. 102–3.

94   ibid., pp. 98 and 110.

95   ibid., p. 101.

96   ibid., p. 133.

97   The 'continuity' was lived. It can be assumed that as a founder member of the CP Dona Torr must at least have been acquainted with Tom Mann who was active in Party politics until the 1930s (imprisoned at the age of seventy-eight in 1934). He died in 1941.

98   E. P. Thompson, *The Making of the English Working Class* (Penguin, 1968), p. 914.

99   Samuel, 'British marxist historians', pp. 56–91.

100   Minutes 10 April 1948. For some light on the depth of these sentiments it's worth looking at the autobiography of the Communist turned Catholic, Douglas Hyde, *I Believed* (Heinemann, 1950).

101   As in Hill's 1955 'Introduction' to *The English Revolution* in which the Revolution is regarded as progressive 'because it developed the national wealth', p. 5. This point is made by Samuel, 'British marxist historians', p. 84. For Hill's later reformulations, see *The World Turned Upside Down* (Viking, 1973), p. 270.

102   *The English Utopia* (Lawrence and Wishart, 1978), p. 15.

103   ibid., p. 43.

104   ibid., p. 276.

105   *Democracy and the Labour Movement*, p. 270.

106   E. P. Thompson, *William Morris: Romantic to Revolutionary* (Lawrence and Wishart, 1955), p. 745.

107 Minutes 16 March 1952.

108 In the people's cultures of Bulgaria and Yugoslavia, Thompson highlighted the agency of the common people, and their rediscovery of their national and international heritages. While in Bulgaria Thompson interviewed Dimitrov on the role of cultural workers; it also appears that Dimitrov was instrumental in securing information about the fate of Thompson's brother, a British officer fighting with the partisans, murdered by Bulgarian fascists.

109 Thompson, *William Morris*, pp. 47 and 281.

110 ibid., pp. 832, 790 and 805.

111 Perry Anderson notes that the radical temper of Thompson's commitment to an active conception of the people was at odds with the politics of the British CP in the middle of the 1950s; *Arguments Within English Marxism* (New Left Books, 1980), pp. 188–9. This may very well be the case. But the Morris book was appreciatively reviewed by R. Page Arnot in *Marxist Quarterly*, vol. 2, no. 4 (1955).

112 Samuel, 'British marxist historians', p. 74.

113 Laclau, *Politics and Ideology*; G. Nowell Smith in *Screen Education*, no. 22 (1977); and for a lively historical discussion, Paul Ginsborg in J. Davis (ed.), *Gramsci and Italy's Passive Revolution* (Croom Helm, 1979). The project of the History Group was not modelled on an explicitly Gramscian perspective. But it is significant that it was through the Group that Gramsci was first introduced into the English-speaking world. As it appears in the Minutes: 'It was also noted that arrangements were being made for translation of the works of Grammschi (*sic*)', 27 May 1956. This task was in the hands of Louis Marks, a long-serving member of the Group. He wrote a useful introduction to Gramsci (with the stress falling on 'the battle of ideas') in *Marxist Quarterly*, vol. 3, no. 4 (1956) and the translation appeared as *The Modern Prince* (Lawrence and Wishart, 1957). For almost the next decade it was primarily through historical debate, or through the work of historians, that Gramsci arrived at take-off point in the British Isles.

114 G. Thomson, *Marxism and Poetry* (Lawrence and Wishart, 1945), pp. 60 and 62.

115 In 1971 and 1972 BBC radio transmitted an ambitious series of programmes under the general title of *The Long March of Everyman*, subsequently published and edited by Theo Barker, with contributions by Hilton, Hill, Gwyn Williams, Samuel and Kiernan (André Deutsch, 1975). This can be seen as a late, and ironic, culmination of the project inspired by the Communist historians in the 1940s. The title is apt.

116 During the Popular Fronts this dilemma found its sharpest expression in the debates between the German and Central European exiles on the relationship between literary tradition and popular culture, in the controversy between 'realism' and 'expressionism'. See especially the contributions by Bloch, Lukacs and Brecht in E. Bloch *et al.*, *Aesthetics and Politics* (New Left Books, 1977), and Franco Fortini, 'The writers' mandate and the end of

anti-fascism', *Screen*, vol. 15, no. 1 (1974). My argument suggests that the British historians were closer to the 'realist' and traditionalist pole in their conception of popular culture.

117   8 April 1956. This is quoted by Hobsbawm, 'The Communist Historians', p. 41. It was not in the Minutes I saw. Apparently fairly full minutes were circulated to members and I suppose that the reference comes from there.

118   Hobsbawm, 'The Communist Historians'.

119   See especially the second issue (1957) and Raymond Williams's review of Richard Hoggart's *The Uses of Literacy* (Penguin, 1973). A more strikingly modernist approach to popular culture, which begins to break with the emphasis on a popular conjunction of tradition and common values, can be found in S. Hall and P. Whannel, *The Popular Arts* (Hutchinson, 1964). To someone entering the New Left from a different route, the *New Reasoner* was recognized by 'its tendency to lapse into roll-calls of the Marxist great (from William Morris through Tom Mann to Christopher Caudwell)', Peter Sedgwick in D. Widgery (ed.), *The Left in Britain 1956–68* (Penguin, 1976), p. 135.

120   Minutes 2 January 1955.

121   ibid., 16 September 1950.

122   ibid., 20 November 1955.

123   Hobsbawm, 'The Communist Historians', p. 26.

124   John Saville, 'The 20th Congress and the British Communist Party', *Socialist Register* (1976), p. 7.

125   Minutes 25 November 1956.

126   E. P. Thompson, 'Homage to Tom Maguire', in A. Briggs and J. Saville (eds.), *Essays in Labour History* (Macmillan, 1960), p. 314.

127   See Anderson, *Arguments Within English Marxism*, p. 146.

128   Anderson, 'Socialism and pseudo-empiricism'. A later debate on Raymond Williams and 'romantic populism' picked up some of these themes: Terry Eagleton, Anthony Barnett, Edward Thompson in *New Left Review*, nos. 95 and 99 (1976).

129   Anderson, *Arguments Within English Marxism*, p. 157.

130   Hill, 'Marxism and history', p. 64.

131   *Puritanism and Revolution*, p. 31.

132   Thompson, *The Making of the English Working Class*, p. 26.

133   ibid., pp. 85–110. See also Hill, *The Century of Revolution* (Panther, 1978), p. 257.

134   Thompson, *The Making of the English Working Class*, pp. 913–14.

135   B. Hill, 'The emancipation of women and the Women's Movement', *Marxist Quarterly*, vol. 3, no. 1 (1956). In 1953 the Group planned some local research on women's industrial struggles. Interestingly, the topics were more contemporary: Annie Besant and the Match Girls' Strike, the Birmingham rent strikes of the 1930s, the miners' committees after the General Strike. At the Netherwood Conference the seventh (and last) 'absence' noted was

'the economic position of women'. This appears to be the extent of the Group's commitment, in the historiography, to feminism.

136   Geoffrey Best, 'The making of the English working class', *Historical Journal* (1965), p. 278, quoted by Thompson, *The Making*, p. 916; Anderson, *Arguments Within English Marxism*, p. 37.

137   Laclau, *Politics and Ideology*, p. 167. A study directly pertinent to these questions has recently been published: Geroge Rudé, *Ideology and Popular Protest* (Lawrence and Wishart, 1980). In what can be seen as a résumé of his own historical work and, to some extent, of many of the other historians of his generation apprenticed in the Communist Party, Rudé attempts to codify and assess some of the theoretical conclusions in this area. Despite the richness of his own historical investigations over the past two or three decades, and despite also the welcome move from one so well placed to theorize his findings, the result is disappointingly orthodox and mechanical.

138   Thompson, *The Making*, p. 103 and *Poverty of Theory*, p. 54. The history of British imperialism forcefully throws into relief the problem of the production of a democratic national-popular will in the metropolitan countries. This issue needs extensive investigation. As Hugh Cunningham argues, 'in the age of imperialism it was impossible to demarcate a patriotism of the left; the language had passed to the right and those who employed it did so too'; 'The language of patriotism', *History Workshop Journal*, no. 12 (1981), p. 27.

139   Thompson, *Poverty of Theory*, p. 80. First emphasis mine.

140   Richard Johnson, 'Three problematics: elements of a theory of working class culture', in J. Clarke *et al.* (eds.), *Working Class Culture* (Hutchinson, 1979); Stuart Hall, 'Cultural studies: two paradigms', *Media, Culture and Society*, vol. 2, no. 1 (1980); Anderson, *Arguments*.

141   C. Hill, 'R. H. Tawney: an appreciation', *History Today* (December 1980).

142   Samuel, 'People's history' in Samuel, *People's History*, p. xxvii. And for a remarkable recent attempt at rethinking the tradition of the free-born Englishman – building on Thompson's later studies of the law in the eighteenth century – see J. Brewer and J. Styles (eds.), *An Ungovernable People* (Hutchinson, 1980).

143   Hill, 'Marxism and history', p. 64.

144   Rudé, *Ideology and Popular Protest*, p. 11.

145   C. Hill, *Change and Continuity in 17th Century England* (Weidenfeld and Nicolson, 1974), p. 238.

146   T. Bennett, 'Teaching popular culture', *Screen Education*, no. 34 (1980), p. 27; and for the periodization of popular cultures, Stuart Hall, 'Notes on deconstructing "the popular" ', in Samuel, *People's History*.

147   This observation clearly needs strong qualification. Most important to mention is E. J. Hobsbawm's final essay in *Labouring Men* (Weidenfeld and Nicolson, 1964), on 'Labour traditions' which begins by recognizing historical discontinuities and raises many questions which relate to the

national-popular. His own attack on one-dimensional labour history can be found in the *Journal of Social History*, vol. 7 (1974). Also, in the period of drafting this chapter, it looks as if things may be changing in this respect. It may be significant, however, that two of the most culturally sensitive histories of the modern period are still concerned with the actual transition from 'pre-industrial to industrial': Gareth Stedman Jones, *Outcast London* (Penguin, 1979), and Raphael Samuel, *Village Life and Labour* (Routledge and Kegan Paul, 1975).

148   C. Hill, *Intellectual Origins of the English Revolution* (Clarendon Press, 1965), p. 130.

149   C. Hill, *Milton and the English Revolution* (Faber and Faber, 1977), pp. 5 and 477.

150   See the marvellous work of Gwyn Williams which concentrates at its very core on the conjunction of the national-popular and social memories – on the entry of the Welsh nation and the Welsh people 'into history'; especially the recent triology *The Merthyr Rising* (Croom Helm, 1978); *Madoc: The Making of a Myth* (Eyre Methuen, 1979), and *The Search for Beulah Land* (Croom Helm, 1980); and the more methodological, 'Locating a Welsh working class. The frontier years', in David Smith (ed.), *A People and a Proletariat: Essays on the History of Wales 1780–1980* (Pluto Press, 1980). Cf. the journal of Welsh labour history, *Llafur*.

151   Bob Scribner comes to a surprisingly similar conclusion in his essay on the successive reinterpretations of the German Peasant War of 1525: 'Revolutionary heritage', in Samuel, *People's History*.

152   This phrase comes from the self-critical reflections of Tommy Jackson in V. Morton and S. Macintyre, *T. A. Jackson, Our History*, no. 73 (1979), p. 22.

153   Thompson, *The Making*, p. 13; and Hobsbawm, 'Interview', p. 130.

154   Samuel, 'British marxist historians', p. 96. And cf. Jo O'Brien's comment on the importance of feminist history for the women's movement: 'A people without a history is a dispossessed people', quoted by Jill Norris, 'Women's history', *Women and the Labour Movement: North West Labour History Society Bulletin*, no. 7 (1980–1).

155   Hill, *Change and Continuity*, p. 284.

156   Hill, *Intellectual Origins*, p. 198. It is interesting to contrast this appreciation of the seventeenth-century scientific revolution – as providing the conditions for the 'humanization of history' – to the structuralist emphasis on the 'decentring of the human subject'.

157   An eloquent example comes from John Vincent's analysis of mid-Victorian Liberal hegemony which, he argues, was articulated on a principle not derived, as one might expect, from political economy, but from a recollection and reconstruction of the history of seventeenth-century England: *The Formation of the Liberal Party* (Penguin, 1972), pp. 289–90. See also Hobsbawm's essay on 'The social function of the past', *Past and Present*, no. 54

(1972); and his more recent 'History and the future', *New Left Review*, no. 125 (1981).

Chapter 3   E. P. Thompson and the discipline of historical context

NB. There is a substantial bibliography in P. Anderson, *Arguments Within English Marxism* (1980). It is not quite complete ('The crime of anonymity' being the major historical omission) but it is very useful nevertheless. Here, only texts referred to are listed.

1   Perry Anderson, in *Arguments Within English Marxism* (Verso, 1980), p. 1, comes close to arguing that Thompson is the greatest *marxist* historian, and also the greatest socialist *writer*, of recent times. While in my view Thompson certainly is the most influential and outspoken *socialist historian*, both of Anderson's attributions strike me as excessive. Another recent assessment, good in details, is Bryan D. Palmer's *The Making of E. P. Thompson: Marxism, Humanism, and History* (New Hogtown Press, Toronto 1981). However, this defence of Thompson and critique of Anderson is little more than hagiographic, presenting Thompson's career as an 'odyssey as an historian and dissident Communist', p. 36.

2   Anderson's fine set of arguments has had a considerable bearing on the way in which this essay has been developed. Many of his points are not especially original, but a series of important debates is nicely condensed and sometimes definitively treated in Anderson's presentation. This is particularly true of his chapter 'Agency'. However, much of Anderson's book is a confrontation between, first, Althusser's detailed positions and those of 'The poverty of theory', and, secondly, between Anderson's own editorial and political positions and Thompson's 'reformism' (as Anderson regards it). On both these issues, I have relatively little to say. For other recent assessments, see R. Johnson, 'Edward Thompson, Eugene Genovese, and socialist humanist history', *History Workshop Journal*, no. 6 (1978); K. Nield and J. Seed, 'Theoretical poverty or the poverty of theory: British marxist historiography and the Althusserians', *Economy and Society*, vol. 8, no. 4 (1979); P. Q. Hirst, 'The necessity of theory', *Economy and Society*, vol. 8, no. 4 (1979); G. McLennan, 'The historian's craft: unravelling the logic of process', *Literature and History*, vol. 5, no. 2 (1979); R. Q. Gray, 'E. P. Thompson, history, and Communist politics', *Marxist Today* (June 1979); A. Dawley, 'E. P. Thompson and the peculiarities of the Americans', *Radical History Review*, no. 19 (1978); S. Hall, 'In defence of theory', in R. Samuel (ed.), *People's History and Socialist Theory* (Routledge and Kegan Paul, 1981); F. K. Donnelly, 'Ideology and early English working class history: E. P. Thompson and his critics', *Social History*, vol. 1, no. 2 (1976).

3   In E. P. Thompson, *Writing By Candlelight* (Merlin Press, 1980).

4   ibid., p. 201.

5 ibid., p. 205.
6 ibid., p. 232.
7 ibid., p. 213.
8 *Observer* (4 February 1979).
9 In Thompson, *Writing By Candlelight*.
10 ibid., p. 166.
11 ibid., p. 166.
12 'An interview with E. P. Thompson', *Radical History Review*, nos. 3-4 (1976), p. 25.
13 ibid., p. 21.
14 'Commitment in Politics', *Universities and Left Review*, no. 6 (1959).
15 E. P. Thompson, *The Making of the English Working Class* (Penguin, 1968), p. 9.
16 *Midland History* (Spring 1972).
17 ibid., p. 54.
18 ibid., p. 55.
19 Cf. E. P. Thompson, 'Comment' (on common values), *Stand*, vol. 20, no. 2 (1978).
20 Thompson, *The Poverty of Theory and Other Essays* (Merlin Press, 1978), p. 267.
21 ibid., p. 270.
22 ibid., p. 270.
23 Collected in *Poverty* (1978); written 1960.
24 Thompson, 'Socialist humanism: an epistle to the philistines', *New Reasoner*, no. 1 (1957), p. 129.
25 Thompson, *Whigs and Hunters* (Penguin, 1975), p. 262.
26 *Poverty of Theory*, p. 198.
27 ibid., p. 271.
28 Thompson, 'Testing class struggle', *The Times Higher Education Supplement* (8 March 1974).
29 Thompson, 'Caudwell', *Socialist Register* (1977), p. 244.
30 Collected in *Poverty in Theory*.
31 ibid., p. 78.
32 For marxist 'realism', see this book, Chapter 4.
33 *Poverty of Theory*, p. 229.
34 ibid., p. 230.
35 ibid., p. 221.
36 ibid., p. 231.
37 ibid., p. 221.
38 The debate about 'narrative' in *Past and Present* is of interest here, see L. Stone, 'The revival of narrative: reflections on an old new history', *Past and Present*, no. 85 (1979); E. J. Hobsbawm, 'The revival of narrative: some comments', *Past and Present*, no. 86 (1980); P. Abrams, 'History, sociology, historical sociology', *Past and Present*, no. 87 (1980).

39   *Poverty of Theory*, p. 221.

40   ibid., p. 220.

41   ibid., p. 222.

42   ibid., p. 234.

43   ibid., p. 239.

44   ibid., p. 235.

45   ibid., p. 218.

46   'An interview', p. 15.

47   *The Making*, p. 13.

48   G. M. Young, *Victorian England: Portrait of an Age* (Oxford University Press, 1978), p. 18.

49   'An interview', p. 7.

50   In A. Briggs and J. Saville (eds.), *Essays in Labour History*, vol. 1 (Macmillan, 1960).

51   Thompson, *William Morris: Romantic to Revolutionary*, 1st ed. (Lawrence and Wishart, 1955); 2nd ed. (Merlin Press, 1977).

52   'An interview', p. 15.

53   *William Morris*, 1st ed., p. 270.

54   ibid., p. 795.

55   ibid., p. 732.

56   ibid., p. 832.

57   *William Morris*, 2nd ed., p. 721.

58   *The Making*, p. 214.

59   ibid., p. 211.

60   ibid., p. 213.

61   ibid., p. 223.

62   P. Anderson, *Arguments Within English Marxism*, p. 33.

63   G. A. Cohen, *Karl Marx's Theory of History: A Defence* (Oxford University Press, 1978), pp. 73–7; G. McLennan, 'Some problems in marxist historiography', *CCCS Occasional Paper*, no. 45 (University of Birmingham, 1976); R. Johnson, 'Thompson, Genovese, and socialist humanist history'.

64   E. J. Hobsbawm, *The Age of Capital* (Abacus, 1977).

65   *The Making*, p. 7.

66   ibid., p. 733.

67   ibid., p. 752.

68   ibid., p. 753.

69   J. Stevenson, *Popular Disturbances in England 1700–1870* (Longman, 1979), p. 316.

70   *The Making*, p. 630.

71   M. I. Thomis, *The Luddites* (David and Charles, 1970). Hayden White goes so far as to maintain that the literary form of *The Making* shares the 'tropological structure' which White discerns in the works of the great 'speculative' thinkers in the human sciences, but which has almost nothing to do with 'the facts'. H. White, *Tropics of Discourse* (The Johns Hopkins University

Press, 1978), pp. 15-19.

72   Thompson, 'Eighteenth century English society: class struggle without classes?', *Social History*, vol. 3, no. 2 (1978).

73   *Poverty of Theory*, p. 238.

74   N. Poulantzas, *Classes in Contemporary Capitalism* (New Left Books, 1975), *passim*.

75   L. Althusser, *Essays in Self Criticism* (New Left Books, 1976), p. 49.

76   ibid., p. 50.

77   *Whigs and Hunters* (Penguin, 1975).

78   *Poverty of Theory*, p. 234.

79   P. Anderson, *Arguments*, p. 83.

80   ibid., p. 94.

81   ibid., pp. 96-7.

82   ibid., p. 88.

83   Thompson, 'Patrician society, plebeian culture', *Journal of Social History* (Summer 1974), p. 387.

84   'Peculiarities', in *Poverty of Theory*, p. 50.

85   Thompson, 'The moral economy of the English crowd in the eighteenth century', *Past and Present*, no. 50 (1971).

86   D. Hay, 'Property, authority and the criminal law', in D. Hay *et al.*, *Albion's Fatal Tree* (Penguin, 1975).

87   'Eighteenth century English society', p. 148.

88   *Whigs and Hunters*, p. 15.

89   ibid., p. 16.

90   ibid., p. 16.

91   ibid., p. 94.

92   ibid., p. 16.

93   ibid., p. 64.

94   ibid., p. 108.

95   ibid., p. 115.

96   ibid., p. 99.

97   ibid., pp. 63-4, p. 161.

98   ibid., p. 191.

99   ibid., p. 115.

100 ibid., p. 115.

101 'Socialist humanism'.

102 Thompson, 'An open letter to Leszek Kolakowski', collected in *The Poverty of Theory*.

103 Thompson, 'The politics of theory', in R. Samuel (ed.), *People's History and Socialist Theory*, p. 406.

104 R. Johnson, 'Thompson, Genovese, and socialist humanist history', p. 82.

105 P. Anderson, *Arguments*, p. 82.

106 See esp. K. McClelland, 'Some comments on Richard Johnson', *History Workshop Journal*, no. 7 (1979); G. Williams, 'In defence of history', *History*

Workshop Journal, no. 7 (1979); and my own over-polemical response, G. McLennan, 'Richard Johnson and his critics', *History Workshop Journal*, no. 8 (1979).

107 Thompson, 'The long revolution', *New Left Review*, nos. 9, 10, 11 (1961).
108 Thompson, 'Commitment in politics', p. 55.
109 'An interview', p. 18.
110 *Poverty of Theory*, p. 148.
111 ibid., p. 302.
112 Thompson, 'Time, work-discipline and industrial capitalism', *Past and Present* 38 (1967).
113 *Poverty of Theory*, p. 381.
114 Thompson, 'The politics of theory', p. 399; R. Williams, *Marxism and Literature* (Oxford University Press, 1977).
115 *Poverty of Theory*, p. 251.
116 ibid., p. 215.
117 Thompson, 'Revolution', *New Left Review*, no. 3 (1960).
118 'Caudwell', *Socialist Register* (1977).
119 *Poverty of Theory*, p. 396.
120 G. Kitching, 'The preoccupations of Edward Thompson: a view from the stalls', *New Statesman* (14 March 1980).
121 *Poverty of Theory*, p. 380.
122 Thompson, 'Through the smoke of Budapest', *The Reasoner*, no. 3 (1956).
123 'Socialist humanism', p. 182.
124 'Revolution again', *New Left Review*, no. 6 (1960).
125 'Socialism and the intellectuals', *Universities and Left Review*, no. 2 (1957).
126 *Writing by Candlelight*, p. 185.
127 P. Anderson, *Arguments*, p. 180.
128 ibid., p. 179.
129 ibid., p. 191.
130 E. J. Hobsbawm, 'The forward march of labour halted?', *Marxism Today* (September 1978).
131 'The New Left', *The New Reasoner*, no. 9.
132 Raymond Williams has contributed an important argument ('The politics of nuclear disarmament', *New Left Review*, no. 124, 1981) in which he maintains, amongst other things, that the refusal of nuclear weapons has to be connected with a positive, constructive, socialist alternative perspective. It is thus important to retain the slogan 'socialism or barbarism' in spite of the difficult questions it throws back at us. Thompson's main views on disarmament are set out in 'Notes on exterminism; the last stage of civilisation', *New Left Review*, no. 121 (1980).
133 H. White, *Metahistory* (University of Baltimore Press, 1973).
134 'Eighteenth century English society'.
135 In D. Hay *et al.*, *Albion's Fatal Tree*.
136 *The Making*, ch. 1.

137   'The crime of anonymity', p. 306.
138   *Poverty of Theory*, p. i.
139   ibid., p. 331.
140   ibid., p. 317.
141   'Outside the whale', *Poverty*, p. 32.
142   'Open letter', *Poverty*, pp. 109, 120, 124, 186–8.
143   ibid., p. 109.
144   In *Writing by Candlelight*.
145   *Poverty*, p. 242–3.
146   ibid., p. 342.
147   ibid., p. 281.
148   ibid., p. ii.
149   'Open letter', *Poverty*, p. 109.
150   Thompson, *Protest and Survive*, 1st ed., CND Pamphlet (1980).
151   *Whigs and Hunters*, p. 260.
152   ibid., p. 266.
153   *Poverty*, p. 384.
154   *Writing by Candlelight*, p. 122.
155   ibid., p. 166.
156   ibid., p. 129.
157   ibid., p. 131.
158   ibid., p. 130.
159   ibid., p. 131.
160   ibid., p. 131.

Chapter 4   Philosophy and history: some issues in recent marxist theory

1   R. Hilton (ed.), *The Transition from Feudalism to Capitalism* (New Left Books, 1974), p. 69.
2   *History Workshop Journal*, nos. 6–9.
3   Lenin had no doubt that philosophical argument was of great political importance; cf. *Materialism and Empirio-criticism* (Progress, 1970).
4   For a fuller presentation of this point, see G. McLennan, 'The historian's craft: unravelling the logic of process', *Literature and History*, vol. 5, no. 4 (1979), and chapter 3 of this book.
5   Cf. T. Benton, 'Natural science and cultural struggle: Engels and philosophy and the natural sciences', in J. Mepham and D.-H. Ruben (eds.), *Issues in Marxist Philosophy*: vol. 2, *Materialism* (Harvester, 1979); M. Fisk, 'Dialectic and ontology' in J. Mepham and D.-H. Ruben, *Issues in Marxist Philosophy*: vol. 1, *Dialectics and Method* (Harvester, 1979); M. Fisk, 'Materialism and dialectic', *Critique*, no. 12 (1980).
6   G. A. Cohen, *Karl Marx's Theory of History: A Defence* (Oxford University Press, 1978).
7   ibid., p. 165.

8   G. A. Cohen, 'The labour theory of value and the concept of exploitation', *Philosophy and Public Affairs*, vol. 8, no. 4 (1979). The principal argument within marxist economic theory which rejects value-theory is contained in I. Steedman, *Marx After Sraffa* (New Left Books, 1977).

9   Appreciative but critical assessments of Cohen are J. Elster, 'Cohen on Marx's theory of history', *Political Studies*, vol. XXVIII, no. 1 (1980); A. Levine and E. O. Wright, 'Rationality and class struggle', *New Left Review*, no. 123 (1980); L. Pompa, 'Defending Marx's theory of history', *Inquiry*, no. 23 (1981); G. McLennan, *Marxism and the Methodologies of History*, ch. 3 (Verso, 1981).

10 L. Kolakowski, *Main Currents of Marxism*: vol. 1, *The Founders*; vol. 2, *The Golden Age*; vol. 3, *The Breakdown* (Oxford University Press, 1978). Kolakowski, once an orthodox marxist philosopher in Poland, has progressively distanced himself from marxism. He now works in All Souls, Oxford.

11 *Main Currents*, vol. 3, p. 524.

12 B. Hindess and P. Q. Hirst, *Mode of Production and Social Formation* (Macmillan, 1977); A. Cutler *et al.*, *Marx's Capital and Capitalism Today*, 2 volumes (Routledge and Kegan Paul, 1978).

13 Hindess and Hirst, *Mode of Production*, p. 8.

14 P. Q. Hirst, *On Law and Ideology* (Macmillan, 1979).

15 S. Gaukroger, *Explanatory Structures* (Harvester, 1978), p. 57.

16 Hirst, *On Law and Ideology*, p. 19.

17 ibid., p. 21.

18 G. Lukacs, *History and Class Consciousness* (Merlin, 1971), p. 1.

19 These familiar phrases come from K. Marx, *Capital*, vol. 1 (Pelican, 1976), p. 102; Marx and Engels, *Selected Correspondence* (Lawrence and Wishart, 1936), p. 473; V. I. Lenin, 'What the friends of the people are', in *Collected Works*, vol. 1 (Progress, 1972), p. 184.

20 Lukacs, *History and Class Consciousness*, p. 15.

21 See note 106 to chapter 3 of this book.

22 Karl Korsch, 1886–1961. An important marxist theorist and independent communist from the 1920s to 1950s. Former member of the KPD, Korsch came to reject marxism as a theoretical perspective.

23 Yet Korsch is a complex figure: he had no time for empiricism, and defended the role of intellectual and philosophical struggle against reductionism. See especially his *Marxism and Philosophy* (New Left Books, 1970), and *Karl Marx* (Chapman and Hall, 1938).

24 D. Sayer, *Marx's Method* (Harvester, 1979).

25 P. Corrigan, H. Ramsay, D. Sayer, *For Mao: Essays in Historical Materialism* (Macmillan, 1979).

26 Cohen, *Karl Marx's Theory of History*; W. Shaw, *Marx's Theory of History* (Hutchinson, 1978).

27 For example, F. Engels, *Dialectics of Nature* (Progress, 1934), and *Anti-Duhring* (Foreign Languages Press, 1976); N. Bukharin, *Historical Materialism* (Russell and Russell, 1965); G. Plekhanov, *Fundamental Problems of*

Marxism (Lawrence and Wishart, 1976); J. V. Stalin, 'Dialectical and historical materialism', in *Essential Writings* (Croom Helm, 1973).

28   For example, E. Bloch, *On Karl Marx* (Herder and Herder, 1968); H. Lefebvre *Dialectical Materialism* (Cape, 1968).

29   In *For Mao*, P. Corrigan *et al.* argue, to my mind unconvincingly, that Mao's marxism provides the answer to Stalinist pragmatism and philosophical obscurantism. Cf. Mao Tse Tung, 'On contradiction', *Selected Works* (Foreign Languages Press, Peking, 1971).

30   L. Althusser, *For Marx* (Penguin, 1969); *Reading Capital* (with E. Balibar) (New Left Books, 1974); *Essays in Self-Criticism* (New Left Books, 1976). G. Della Volpe, *Logic as a Positive Science* (New Left Books, 1980). L. Colletti, *Marxism and Hegel* (New Left Books, 1973); and 'Marxism and the dialectic', *New Left Review*, no. 93 (1975).

31   E. P. Thompson, *The Poverty of Theory and Other Essays* (Merlin, 1978); D. Sayer, 'Science as critique: Marx versus Althusser', in J. Mepham and D.-H. Ruben (eds.), *Issues in Marxist Philosophy*; vol 3, *Epistemology, Science Ideology*; R. Edgley, 'Marx's revolutionary science', in *Issues*, vol. 3, and 'Dialectic: the contradictions of Colletti', *Critique*, no. 7 (1977). Good earlier criticisms appeared in N. Geras, 'Althusserian marxism', *New Left Review*, no. 71 (1972), and S. Timpanaro, *On Materialism* (New Left Books, 1975). A later and considerably weaker set of views hostile to Althusserianism is contained in S. Clarke *et al.*, *One-Dimensional Marxism* (Allison and Busby, 1980).

32   However, one common complaint is not, in my view, decisive; namely the charge that Althusser must conceive of science and philosophy as having no social determinants. The development of science and philosophy can be socially and historically explained, but there remain questions about their truth or validity which require separate treatment. The same would not be true of what Althusser thinks of as 'ideology'.

33   P. Anderson names some of these in his *Arguments Within English Marxism* (Verso, 1980), but his list could be extended.

34   Balibar (*Reading Capital*, Part 3), having defined a mode in terms of the correspondence between forces and relations of production, attempts, illogically, to argue for a transitional mode based on the absence of such correspondence.

35   For a more general assessment of Thompson's work, see Chapter 3 of this book.

36   B. Hindess, *The Use of Official Statistics in Sociology* (Macmillan, 1973).

37   E. Mandel, *Late Capitalism* (New Left Books, 1976).

38   A. Hussain, 'Crises and tendencies of capitalism', *Economy and Society*, vol. 6, no. 4 (1977).

39   B. Fine and L. Harris, *Re-reading Capital* (Macmillan, 1979).

40   R. Bhaskar, *A Realist Theory of Science* (Harvester, 1978) and *The Possibility of Naturalism* (Harvester, 1979).

41   D.-H. Ruben, *Marxism and Materialism* (Harvester, 1979).
42   R. Keat and J. Urry, *Social Theory as Science* (Routledge and Kegan Paul, 1976).
43   T. Benton, *The Philosophical Foundations of the Three Sociologies* (Routledge and Kegan Paul, 1977).
44   For example, H. Putnam, *Meaning and the Moral Sciences* (Routledge and Kegan Paul, 1978). Fisk, 'Materialism and the dialectic', p. 102.
45   By 'correspondence' I mean the general belief that the real world is progressively penetrated by successful science. The narrower notion that the criterion by which to judge true statements is their 'correspondence to reality' is arguably another issue. Both Ruben and Bhaskar have expressed their dissatisfaction with it.

Chapter 5   Reading for the best Marx: history-writing and historical abstraction

1   See Chapter 4 and, for a more extended statement of these themes, Gregor McLennan, *Marxism and the Methodologies of History* (Verso, 1981).
2   Ted Benton, *Philosophical Foundations of the Three Sociologies* (Routledge and Kegan Paul, 1977), p. 155.
3   See Chapter 3.
4   Perry Anderson, *Arguments Within English Marxism* (Verso, 1980), p. 15.
5   I have already noted that I now regret some elements of the 'authoritative' use of Marx in Richard Johnson, 'Edward Thompson, Eugene Genovese, and socialist humanist history', *History Workshop Journal*, no. 6 (1978), not, however, the main tendencies of this argument.
6   See Chapter 4. See also the parallel argument in John Mepham, 'From the *Grundrisse* to *Capital*: the making of Marx's method' in John Mepham and D.-H. Ruben (eds.), *Issues in Marxist Philosophy*: vol. 1, *Dialectics and Method* (Harvester, 1979).
7   For an interesting discussion of these questions see Kate Soper, in John Mepham and Ruben (eds.), *Issues in Marxist Philosophy*; vol. 2, *Materialism* (Harvester, 1979).
8   See especially McLennan, *Marxism and the Methodologies of History*; McLennan, 'The historian's craft: unravelling the logic of process', *Literature and History*, vol. 5, no. 2 (1979); unpublished papers by McLennan, Bill Schwarz, Andrew Green, Andrew Lowe. I am especially grateful to McLennan, Schwarz and Dave Sutton for comments on this chapter.
9   Karl Marx, *Grundrisse: Foundations of the Critique of Political Economy*, ed. and trans. Martin Nicolaus (Penguin, 1973).
10   The fate of the 1857 Introduction is mentioned by Marx in his Preface to *A Contribution to the Critique of Political Economy* (Lawrence and Wishart, 1971), p. 19.
11   Nicolaus, Translator's Preface, *Grundrisse*, esp. p. 25.
12   This is the main emphasis both in Nicolaus's Introduction and in the classic

commentary – Roman Rosdolsky, *The Making of Marx's Capital* (Pluto, 1980).

13   Marx, *Contribution to the Critique*, Preface, pp. 19–22.

14   Karl Marx and Frederick Engels, *The German Ideology: Part I with selections from Parts II and III*, ed. and intro. C. J. Arthur (Lawrence and Wishart, 1970).

15   For answers to critics, and much else of value, see especially the Prefaces and Postfaces to *Capital*, vol. 1 (intro. Ernest Mandel, trans. Ben Fowkes; Penguin, 1976), pp. 89–120.

16   Karl Marx, 'Notes on Adolph Wagner', in Terrell Carver (ed. and trans.), *Karl Marx: Texts on Method* (Basil Blackwell, 1975).

17   Karl Marx and Frederick Engels, *Selected Correspondence* (Progress, 1975).

18   See especially the essays in Karl Marx, *Surveys from Exile*, ed. and intro. Fernbach (Penguin, 1973) and in *Marx and Engels on Britain* (Foreign Languages Publishing House, 1962).

19   *Capital*, vol. 1, p. 102.

20   For a concise view of the della Volpean reading, which is very close to that pursued in this essay, see 'For a material methodology of economics and of the moral disciplines in general' in Galvano della Volpe, *Rousseau and Marx and Other Writings*, trans. John Fraser (Lawrence and Wishart, 1978), pp. 161–203.

21   Engels to Marx, 19 November 1844, *Letters*, p. 21.

22   Marx to Kugelmann, 6 March 1868, ibid., p. 188.

23   Marx to Engels, 24 August 1867, ibid., pp. 180–1.

24   Marx to Danielson, 10 April 1879, ibid., p. 296.

25   Marx to Annenkov, 28 December 1846, ibid., p. 31.

26   Marx to Engels, 9 August 1862, ibid., p. 126.

27   Marx to Engels, 24 August 1867, ibid., p. 181.

28   For an interesting discussion of Marx on 'testing' see Derek Sayer, *Marx's Method: Ideology, Science and Critique in 'Capital'* (Harvester, 1979), pp. 135–41. Though I differ on a number of points, especially in a stress on abstraction, I have found Sayer's among the most valuable of recent commentaries.

29   Karl Marx, *Economic and Philosophical Manuscripts of 1844*, ed. and intro. Dirk J. Struik (Lawrence and Wishart, 1973).

30   'I am of course no longer a Hegelian, but I still have a great feeling of piety and devotion towards the colossal old chap.' (*Letters*, p. 162).

31   In stressing the necessarily 'philosophical' character of the critique of philosophy I very much follow McLennan; see Chapter 4.

32   See *Economic and Philosophical Manuscripts*, especially Preface, p. 63.

33   Louis Althusser, 'On the young Marx', in *For Marx* (Penguin, 1969).

34   Thompson, *The Poverty of Theory*, pp. 249–61.

35   It is in this quite limited sense that Marx is a 'structuralist': hence the (also limited) force of the Althusserian reading.

36 Jindrich Zelený, *The Logic of Marx* (Blackwell, 1980), p. 9. Along with the work of della Volpe and of Sayer, I have found Zalený's commentaries particularly valuable.

37 Stuart Hall, 'A "reading" of Marx's 1857 Introduction to the *Grundrisse*', *CCCS Stencilled Paper*, no. 1.

38 *Capital*, vol. I, Preface to first edition, pp. 89–90.

39 *Logic of Marx*, p. 51.

40 Marx to Annenkov, 28 December 1848, *Letters*, p. 48.

41 *Capital*, vol. I, chs. 1–3.

42 ibid., Preface to first edition, p. 90.

43 Marx to Engels, 27 June 1867, *Letters*, p. 179.

44 Marx to Lange, 29 March 1865, *Letters*, p. 161.

45 *Grundrisse*, Introduction, p. 105.

46 ibid., p. 106.

47 For example, Marx to Annenkov, 28 December 1846, *Letters*, p. 37, para 1.

48 This is a huge and much-contested topic. Some of the issues are discussed in essays in Mepham and Ruben (eds.), *Issues in Marxist Philosophy:* vol. 1, *Dialectics and Method* (Harvester, 1979).

49 The attempt to drive a wedge between Hegel and the 'later' Marx is a distinct weakness of Althusserian interpretations and leads to some real travesties of 'readings' of the Marx texts themselves. I have drawn considerably on Zelený on this point.

50 *Capital*, vol. I, Postface to the second edition, p. 103.

51 Marx to Engels, 1 February 1958, *Letters*, p. 94.

52 Marx to Kugelmann, 27 June 1870, ibid., p. 225.

53 See especially Chapter 6.

54 Maurice Dobb, *Studies in the Development of Capitalism* (Routledge and Kegan Paul, 1946); Marc Bloch, *Feudal Society*, 2 vols. (Routledge and Kegan Paul, 1965); Fernand Braudel, *The Mediterranean and the Mediterranean World in the Reign of Philip II*, 2 vols. (Collins, 1975); E. P. Thompson, *The Making of the English Working Class* (Penguin, 1968); Ronald Fraser, *Blood of Spain* (Allen Lane, 1979); Emmanuel Le Roy Ladurie, *Montaillou* (Penguin, 1980).

55 *Grundrisse*, p. 249.

56 ibid.

57 For the play on 'sacred' and 'profane' see Marx to Annenkov, 28 December 1846, *Letters*, pp. 31–4.

58 Marx to Schweitzer, 24 January 1865, *Letters*, pp. 144–5.

59 Marx to Annenkov, 28 December 1846, ibid., p. 33.

60 On population see *Grundrisse*, Introduction, pp. 100–1. 'Thus, if I were to begin with the population, this would be a chaotic conception of the whole.'

61 ibid., pp. 83–5 (my emphasis).

62 ibid., p. 888.

63   ibid.
64   ibid.
65   *Grundrisse*, Introduction, p. 89.
66   ibid., p. 90.
67   Marx to Engels, 2 April 1858, *Letters*, p. 98.
68   *Grundrisse*, p. 888.
69   ibid., pp. 886–7.
70   *Capital*, vol. I, p. 333.
71   *The German Ideology*, pp. 59–60.
72   ibid., p. 80.
73   ibid.
74   ibid.
75   ibid. and cf. passages quoted above from the letter to Annenkov on Proudhon
76   *Letters*, p. 37.
77   ibid.
78   *Grundrisse*, Introduction, p. 85.
79   ibid., pp. 852–3.
80   Cf. Sayer, *Marx's Method*, pp. 77 for an interesting discussion of this.
81   *Capital*, vol. I, p. 283.
82   Especially the notions 'alienation' and 'objectification'.
83   *Grundrisse*, Introduction, p. 85.
84   ibid.
85   ibid., p. 86.
86   ibid., p. 87.
87   *Grundrisse*, pp. 256–9.
88   ibid., p. 257.
89   ibid., p. 258.
90   ibid.
91   *Grundrisse*, pp. 264 ff.
92   ibid., p. 265.
93   ibid.
94   ibid., pp. 249–50 (Marx's emphasis).
95   See, for example, Simon Clarke *et al.*, *One-Dimensional Marxism: Althusser and the Politics of Culture* (Allison and Busby, 1980).
96   This is, by now, a well-known feature of structuralist views of 'the social formation' and of some theorists of 'social reproduction'.
97   As in, for example, working-class experiences of schooling.
98   Marx to Kugelmann, 11 July 1868, *Letters*, pp. 196–7.
99   For a startlingly modern treatment of money as the sign or symbol of value see *Grundrisse*, pp. 143–5.
100   *Letters*, p. 34.
101   *Capital*, vol. I, Postface to the second edition, p. 102.
102   *Grundrisse*, Introduction, pp. 101 ff.
103   ibid., p. 101.

104   ibid. It is quite unclear, in this translation, what is meant by 'mental'.
105   ibid., pp. 101–2.
106   *Notes on Adolph Wagner*, p. 191.
107   Marx to Engels, 25 March 1868, *Letters*, p. 190.
108   *German Ideology*, esp. pp. 51–2.
109   *Letters*, p. 39; *Notes, passim*, e.g. p. 190.
110   *German Ideology*, p. 51.
111   Engels to Marx, 16 June 1867, *Letters*, p. 175.
112   *Grundrisse*, Introduction, p. 105.
113   *German Ideology*, p. 60.
114   *Capital*, vol. I, Postface to second edition, p. 95.
115   Marx to Engels, 2 April 1858, *Letters*, pp. 98 and 99.
116   *Grundrisse*, pp. 449 ff.
117   ibid., pp. 449–50.
118   *Grundrisse*, Introduction, pp. 103–5.
119   ibid., p. 104.
120   ibid., p. 120.
121   ibid., p. 105.
122   Marx to Kugelmann, 11 July 1868, *Letters*, p. 197.
123   Hall, 'A reading'.
124   *Grundrisse*, Introduction, p. 106.
125   Marx to Editorial Board of the *Otechestvenniye Zapiski*, November 1877, *Letters*, p. 294.
126   Marx to Meyer, 30 April 1867, *Letters*, p. 174.
127   Marx to Weydemeyer, 1 February 1859, *Letters*, p. 174.
128   *Grundrisse*, Introduction, pp. 101–2.
129   I use the translation in Wal Suchting, 'Marx's *Theses on Feuerbach*', in Mepham and Ruben, *Issues in Marxist Philosophy*, vol. II, pp. 5–26. For the second thesis see p. 11.
130   ibid., p. 24.
131   For a fuller discussion, in the light of Gramsci's clarifications, see Chapter 6. 'The ensemble of social relations' is a phrase taken from the sixth Thesis.
132   Marx to Meyer, 30 April 1867, *Letters*, p. 173.
133   *Surveys from Exile*, p. 170.
134   The phrase 'arid steppes' is Althusser's.
135   Most of them with the status of aphorisms, e.g. on the peasantry and 'consciousness' (p. 239), on the force of historical traditions (pp. 146 ff.).
136   For example, *German Ideology*, pp. 68 ff.
137   *Capital*, vol. I, p. 283.
138   ibid., pp. 283–4.
139   ibid., pp. 290–1.
140   ibid., p. 291.
141   ibid.
142   ibid., Preface to first edition, p. 92.

143   ibid., p. 372.
144   ibid., p. 373.
145   ibid., p. 342.
146   ibid., p. 343.
147   ibid., p. 375, note 72.
148   Frederick Engels, 'Karl Marx, a contribution to the critique of political economy', in Marx and Engels, *Selected Works*, 2 vols. (Foreign Languages Publishing House, 1962), vol. I, p. 373.
149   *Capital*, vol. I, p. 325.
150   As Thompson tends to do in *The Poverty of Theory*.
151   That is, pp. 307-44.
152   *Capital*, vol. I, p. 315.
153   ibid., e.g. pp. 336-8, note 11.
154   ibid., p. 343, note 6.
155   Remember Marx's use of 'the odour of sanctity' in the case of Mr Glass-Capital.
156   *Capital*, vol. I, pp. 344 ff.
157   ibid., p. 345.
158   ibid., pp. 345 ff.
159   ibid., p. 375.
160   ibid., p. 377.
161   ibid., pp. 389-416.
162   ibid., pp. 439-639; ibid., pp. 877-926.
163   I hope Bill Schwarz will be publishing more of his important work in this area soon.
164   For example, *Capital*, vol. I, p. 397.
165   ibid., pp. 382-9.
166   ibid., p. 390. This is not one of Marx's most startlingly concrete portrayals.
167   ibid., pp. 412-13.
168   ibid., p. 416.
169   Especially *The Class Struggles in France: 1848 to 1850, The Eighteenth Brumaire of Louis Bonaparte*, the articles on Britain and, later, *The Civil War in France*, Marx's account of the Paris Commune. For a more complete assessment see McLennan, *Marxism and the Methodologies of History* to which, in general in this section, I am indebted. The most important essays are published in *Surveys from Exile*.
170   There are a number of interesting and useful commentaries on *The Eighteenth Brumaire*, none comprehensive, perhaps, on the subject of its importance for a method of history-writing. See especially McLennan, *Marxism and the Methodologies of History*; Stuart Hall, 'The "political" and the "economic" in Marx's theory of classes' in Alan Hunt (ed.), *Class and Class Structure* (Lawrence and Wishart, 1977); Gwyn Williams, 'France 1848-1851', Open University, Course A 321, Units 5-8 (1976).
171   *Surveys from Exile*, p. 152.

172 See David Fernbach, introduction to *Surveys from Exile* and Hall and Williams, cited in note 170.
173 *Surveys from Exile*, pp. 172 ff.
174 ibid., p. 224.
175 ibid., pp. 152-3, 175-7, 177-81.
176 ibid., pp. 238-45.
177 ibid., p. 157.
178 ibid., p. 147.
179 ibid.
180 ibid., p. 150.
181 ibid., p. 236 (my emphasis).
182 ibid., pp. 236-7.
183 The most conspicuous example is *Capital*, vol. I, ch. 32.

Chapter 6   Popular memory: theory, politics, method

1   Compare the editorials in *History Workshop Journal*, no. 1 (1976) and *Social History*, vol. 1, no. 1 (1976).
2   Ken Worpole, 'A ghostly pavement: the political implications of local working-class history', in Raphael Samuel (ed.), *People's History and Socialist Theory* (Routledge and Kegan Paul, 1981), p. 23.
3   Jean Chesneaux, *Pasts and Futures or What is History For?* (Thames and Hudson, 1978), especially pp. 1 and 11.
4   Quoted p. 95.
5   We draw here on the work of Rita Pakleppa and Hans Poser who were members of the Popular Memory Group in 1979-80. Their presentations on representations of the Second World War in Britain and West Germany enlivened and informed the work of the group. We hope their study will eventually be available in English.
6   E. P. Thompson, *Writing by Candlelight* (Merlin, 1980), pp. 130-1.
7   One provocative exception was B. Hindess and P. Q. Hirst, *Pre-Capitalist Modes of Production* (Routledge and Kegan Paul, 1975).
8   Cf. pp. 94-5.
9   For example, Michael Foot's speech to the Liverpool mass demonstration against unemployment, subsequently used in a Labour Party Political Broadcast on 5 December 1980.
10 This is one of the ways – by connecting up the instances of struggle – that Edward Thompson uses history politically. See especially the title essay in *Writing by Candlelight* and Greg McLennan's assessment in Chapter 3.
11 We may expect something of a boom of historical work on the 1940s, for example, partly because of the release of archives. But this comes long after popular memory, the media and the politicians have invested deeply in the period which looms increasingly large in political discourse.

12   This applies especially to attempts to apply theorizations derived from other national cases which 'forget' their specific origin: e.g. applications of Gramsci's 'hegemony'; the discussion of socialism and nationalism in Ernesto Laclau, *Politics and Ideology in Marxist Theory* (New Left Books, 1977).

13   CCCS Popular Memory Group is currently working on various present-day memories of the 1940s.

14   For an example of popular Conservative historiography of a proto-racist character see the works of Sir Arthur Bryant, e.g. *English Sage* (Collins and Eyre and Spottiswoode, 1940).

15   See especially, C. A. R. Crosland, *The Future of Socialism* (Jonathan Cape, 1962).

16   See Chapter 1.

17   See especially Chris Cook and John Stephenson, *The Slump: Society and Politics during the Depression* (Jonathan Cape, 1977), but as can be seen in the citations of this book economic historians have been developing a parallel argument for some time now.

18   Perry Anderson, 'Components of the national culture', in A. Cockburn and R. Blackburn (eds.), *Student Power* (Penguin, 1969).

19   Quintin Hoare and Geoffrey Nowell-Smith (eds. and trans.), *Selections from the Prison Notebooks of Antonio Gramsci* (Lawrence and Wishart, 1971), *passim* but especially pp. 324–5.

20   See especially the debate between Ken Worpole, Jerry White and Stephen Yeo in Samuel, *People's History*, pp. 22–48.

21   The FWWCP was founded in 1976 and 'links some twenty or more working class writers' workshops and local publishing initiatives around the country'. For a useful account of the history of History Workshop see Raphael Samuel, 'History Workshop, 1966-80' in Samuel, *People's History*, pp. 410–17.

22   For the first results: Paul Thompson, *The Edwardians* (Weidenfeld and Nicolson, 1975).

23   Paul Thompson, *The Voice of the Past: Oral History* (Oxford University Press, 1978).

24   *Oral History: The Journal of the Oral History Society* (first published 1971).

25   Nor do we want to imply that Paul Thompson's work is peculiarly 'flawed' in any way. We are interested in it as typical of oral history in its more professional historical connection. We are grateful to Paul Thompson himself for correspondence and discussions which have helped to clarify points of agreement and disagreement.

26   Luisa Passerini, 'Work ideology and consensus under Italian fascism', *History Workshop Journal*, no. 8 (1979), pp. 82–108; Luisa Passerini, 'On the use and abuse of oral history' (mimeo translated from L. Passerini (ed.), *Storia Orale: Vita Quotidiana e Cultura Materiale delli Classe Subalterne* (Rosenberg and Sellier, 1978.) We are grateful to the author for sending us a copy of this paper. See also her position paper given at History Workshop, 13: 'Oral history and people's culture' (mimeo, Nov.–Dec. 1979).

27 Passerini, 'Italian fascism', p. 83.
28 Passerini, 'Use and abuse', pp. 7-8.
29 Ronald Fraser, *Blood of Spain: The Experience of Civil War 1936-39* (Allen Lane, 1979). See also Ronald Fraser, *Work: Twenty Personal Accounts*, 2 volumes (Penguin, 1967).
30 We are grateful to Bill Schwarz for sharing his responses to this book.
31 'A people's autobiography of Hackney', *Working Lives*, 2 vols. (Hackney WEA and Centreprise, n.d.). For Centreprise more generally see Ken Worpole, *Local Publishing and Local Culture: An Account of the Centreprise Publishing Project 1972-77* (Centreprise, 1977), and *Centreprise Report* (December 1978).
32 Keith Armstrong and Huw Beynon (eds.), *Hello, Are You Working? Memories of the Thirties in the North East of England* (Strong Words, 1977); Strong Words Collective, *But the World Goes on the Same: Changing Times in Durham Pit Villages* (Strong Words, 1979). We are grateful to Rebecca O'Rourke for introducing us to the work of this collective.
33 ibid., p. 7.
34 For example, the use of autobiographical material in J. Liddington and J. Norris, *One Hand Tied Behind Us* (Virago, 1978).
35 Jean McCrindle and Sheila Rowbotham (eds.), *Dutiful Daughters* (Penguin, 1979).
36 Jeremy Seabrook, *What Went Wrong? Working People and the Ideals of the Labour Movement* (Gollancz, 1978).
37 Michel Foucault, 'Interview', in *Edinburgh '77 Magazine* (originally published in French in *Cahiers du Cinéma* (1974)). See also *Radical Philosophy*, no. 16 (1975).
38 Philippe Hoyau, 'Heritage year or the society of conservation', *Les Révoltes Logiques* (Paris), no. 12 (1980), pp. 70-7. See also the report on *Cahiers du Forum - Histoire* in *Les Révoltes Logiques*, no. 11 (1979-80), p. 104, a group with similar interests and aims to our own. These French debates are further discussed on pp. 255-7.
39 Hence the debate in Britain on radical filmic practices and historical drama. See, for example, Colin MacCabe, 'Memory, phantasy, identity: *Days of Hope* and the politics of the past', *Edinburgh '77 Magazine*; Keith Tribe, 'History and the production of memories', *Screen*, vol. xvii, no. 4 (1977-8); Colin McArthur, *Television and History* (British Film Institute, 1978).
40 G. R. Elton, *The Practice of History* (Sydney University Press and Methuen), pp. 52-3.
41 *The Practice of History* is in large part a response to E. H. Carr, *What is History?* (Penguin, 1961).
42 Thompson, *Voice of the Past*, p. x.
43 ibid., p. 17.
44 Chesneaux, *Pasts and Futures*, esp. ch. 2.
45 Thompson, *Voice*, p. 5.

46   ibid., p. 8.
47   ibid., p. 11.
48   ibid., p. 226.
49   Stephen Koss, 'Review of *The Edwardians*', *The Times Literary Supplement*, 5 December 1975.
50   Thompson, *Voice*, pp. 91-8.
51   ibid., pp. 100-37.
52   Graham Dawson, 'Oral history: a critique of *Voice of the Past*', *CCCS Stencilled Paper* (forthcoming).
53   Thompson, *Voice*, pp. 91-8.
54   ibid., pp. 100-37.
55   This holds, perhaps, for cultural studies more generally. It is interesting, for example, that early critiques of the media and especially of news and current affairs programmes were heavily influenced by a dual critique of empiricism – in Roland Barthes's early semiological writing and in the phenomenological sociologies of Schutz and Cicourel. See, for example, Stuart Hall, 'The structured communication of events', *CCCS Stencilled Paper*, no. 5.
56   See Chapter 4 and Gregor McLennan, *Marxism and the Methodologies of History* (Verso, 1981).
57   Jerry White, 'Beyond autobiography' in Samuel, *People's History*, especially p. 47. For examples of White's own practice see 'Campbell Bunk: a lumpen community in London between the wars', *History Workshop Journal*, no. 8 (1979); *Rothschild Buildings: Life in an East End Tenement Block 1887-1920* (Routledge and Kegan Paul, 1980).
58   As Yeo puts it, 'Yes, Jerry, the assumption underpinning nearly all of this work *is* that for working people to speak for themselves, about their own history, is somehow a political act in itself.' (Stephen Yeo, 'The politics of community publications' in Samuel, *People's History*, p. 46.) For the idea of a 'long revolution' by this route see Worpole's 'A ghostly pavement', ibid., pp. 31-2. For a full critique of this view of 'experience' see Perry Anderson, *Arguments Within English Marxism* (Verso, 1980), pp. 25-39.
59   Compare, for example, the autobiography of Emily Bishop (clearly a writer) and that of John Welsh (clearly a talker) in *Working Lives*, vol. i, pp. 8-12 and pp. 31-50.
60   *Working Lives* is full of stories of the first two kinds. For the confident 'male' form (with a notably class-conscious moral) see John Welsh's story about the death of his brother (p. 38); for examples of the more 'open' kind see Betty Ferry's story about 'Bill' (pp. 11-12) and Lil Smith's memories of bath night (pp. 62-3). For examples of the proverbial form of collective historical memory see Dave Douglas, ' "Worms of the Earth": the miner's own story', in Samuel, *People's History*, pp. 61-7.
61   'For experience' as a 'junction concept' see E. P. Thompson, 'The politics of theory', ibid., pp. 405-7.

62 Passerini, 'Italian fascism', p. 91.
63 ibid., p. 92.
64 For the idea of 'surprise' more generally in qualitative research see Paul Willis, 'Notes on method', in Hall *et al.* (eds.), *Culture, Media, Language* (Hutchinson, 1981), pp. 90-1.
65 Roland Barthes, *Mythologies* (Paladin, 1972), p. 112.
66 Thompson, *Voice*, pp. 204-5.
67 ibid., pp. 219-20.
68 ibid., p. 129.
69 ibid., p. 209.
70 Thompson, *Edwardians*, p. 3.
71 ibid., p. 3.
72 ibid., p. 4.
73 ibid., p. 66.
74 It is important to note that the life histories used in *The Edwardians* are compilations from answers to questions from interviewers and not, or only in a limited sense, autobiographies. The basic materials for all the accounts are the simple 'factual' responses. The life histories arise from stringing together these answers in a narrative form. Often the questions (see *Voice of the Past*, pp. 243-52) can be reconstructed under the narrative.
75 Thompson, *Edwardians*, p. 4. Evidently 'tidied up' a little, however.
76 ibid., p. 4.
77 Louis Althusser, *Essays in Self-Criticism* (New Left Books, 1976), esp. pp. 201-4; E. P. Thompson, *The Poverty of Theory and Other Essays* (Merlin 1978; Victor Seidler, 'Trusting ourselves: marxism, human needs and sexual politics', in Simon Clarke *et al.*, *One-Dimensional Marxism: Althusser and the Politics of Culture* (Allison and Busby, 1980), pp. 103-56.
78 Anderson, *Arguments*, especially ch. 2; Raymond Williams, 'Individuals and society' in *The Long Revolution* (Penguin, 1965); Williams, *Politics and Letters* (New Left Books, 1979), pp. 271-302.
79 Wal Suchting, 'Marx's theses on Feuerbach', in John Mepham and D.-H. Ruben (eds.), *Issues in Marxist Philosophy*, vol. ii, pp. 5-34; Roy Bhaskar, 'On the possibility of social scientific knowledge and the limits of naturalism', in Mepham and Ruben, *Issues*, vol. iii, pp. 107-39.
80 For what follows see 'What is Man?', *Prison Notebooks*, pp. 351-7.
81 ibid., p. 356.
82 Gramsci is clearly aware of the issues but, in the commonest marxist move, takes 'biological' conceptions of human nature as the main antagonist. On these important issues see Kate Soper, 'Marxism, materialism and biology' in Mepham and Ruben (eds.), *Issues*, vol. ii, pp. 61-100.
83 We do not wish to imply that feminist thinking is homogeneous and what follows represents our own appropriations. For recent statements of some of the key issues see Michèle Barrett, *Women's Oppression Today* (Verso, 1981), the debates in *Feminist Review* on the work of Christine Delphy and

over the concept of 'patriarchy' and the exchanges between Sally Alexander, Barbara Taylor and Sheila Rowbotham in Samuel, *People's History*.

84   Vera Brittain, *Testament of Youth* (Fontana with Virago, 1979). We are grateful to Rebecca O'Rourke for drawing attention to the significance of this example and for discussions on the book and TV programme.

85   ibid., p. 12.

86   ibid.

87   Winston S. Churchill, *The Second World War*, 6 vols. (Cassell, 1948-54).

88   Something of the character of what follows is caught in Churchill's Preface to vol. I (e.g. 'I am perhaps the only man who has passed through both the supreme cataclysms of recorded history in high executive office', ibid., vol. 1, p. vii.)

89   Thompson, *Voice*, pp. 100-4.

90   ibid., pp. 129-37.

91   Betty Ferry, in *Working Lives*, vol. i, p. 125.

92   Emily Bishop, ibid., p. 10.

93   John Welch, ibid., p. 39.

94   Peggy Wood, *Dutiful Daughters*, p. 174.

95   Janet Daly, ibid., p. 19.

96   Editor's introduction, ibid., pp. 4-5.

97   For an interesting example see Maggie Fuller on 'Nowadays' where a whole historical evaluation is woven around 'things' (ibid., pp. 135-6).

98   Betty Ferry, *Working Lives*, vol. i, p. 117.

99   Stuart Hall *et al.*, *Policing the Crisis* (Macmillan, 1978); Stuart Hall, 'Thatcherism – a new stage', *Marxism Today* (February 1980), pp. 26-8; CCCS Education Group, *Unpopular Education: Schooling and Social Democracy since 1944* (Hutchinson, 1981).

100   Annie Davison, *Dutiful Daughters*, pp. 65-6.

101   ibid., pp. 61-2.

102   Raphael Samuel, 'British marxist historians, 1880-1980, part i', *New Left Review*, no. 120 (1980), pp. 23, 34-7, 85-91; Schwarz, Chapter 2 of this volume.

103   For oral history in the USA see Passerini, 'On the use and abuse of oral history' (cited above, note 26).

104   For example, the contributions from Ruskin ex-students in Raphael Samuel (ed.), *Miners, Quarrymen and Saltworkers* (Routledge and Kegan Paul, 1977), and *Village Life and Labour* (Routledge and Kegan Paul, 1976).

105   These thoughts are based in part on discussions with students at Coleg Harlech and are stimulated by a paper given by students there (at a day school with members of CCCS) on the contradictions of their situation.

106   We have in mind, especially, Richard Hoggart and Raymond Williams but lots more examples could be given.

107   Especially through the decimation of the Social Science Research Council, the cuts in higher and further education, the disappearance of new posts at

colleges, polytechnics and universities and the rising fees for postgraduate study. All this contrasts sharply with the expectations and possibilities of the 1960s and early 1970s.

Chapter 7 'Charms of residence': the public and the past

1   Interview with Michel Foucault, *Edinburgh '77 Magazine*, pp. 21-2.
2   Michel Foucault, *Discipline and Punish* (Vintage Books, 1979), p. 113.
3   ibid., p. 67.
4   See Jacques Rancière's *La Leçon d'Althusser* (Gallimard, 1974).
5   *Les Révoltes Logiques*, no. 13 (1980), p. 2.
6   Jacques Rancière, 'Le prolétaire et son double ou le philosophe inconnu', *Les Révoltes Logiques*, no. 13, pp. 4-5. Rancière's recent book, *La Nuit des Prolétaires* (Fayard, 1981) asserts the political and historical inadequacy of a reductive marxism which, in its understanding of the working class, 'reconstructs the world around a centre which its occupants care only to escape', i.e. production itself.
7   Jacques Rancière, 'L'usine nostalgique', *Les Révoltes Logiques*, no. 13, pp. 90, 92.
8   Philippe Hoyau, 'L'année du patrimoine ou la société de conservation', *Les Révoltes Logiques,* no. 12 (1980), p. 74.
9   Jacques Rancière, 'Le prolétaire et son double ou le philosophe inconnu', *Les Révoltes Logiques*, no. 13, p. 6.
10 For a fuller discussion of hegemony see: Chantal Mouffe, 'Hegemony and ideology in Gramsci' in *Gramsci and Marxist Theory* (Routledge and Kegan Paul, 1979); S. Hall, B. Lumley and G. McLennan, 'Politics and ideology: Gramsci', in CCCS, *On Ideology* (Hutchinson, 1978).
11 The contract of employment is individual and private. Collective interests are therefore subordinated to it. See, for example, Jeremy McMullen, *Rights at Work* (Pluto, 1979).
12 Jürgen Habermas, *Strukturwandel der Öffentlichkeit* (Neuwied/Berlin, 1962); Oskar Negt and Alexander Kluge, *Öffentlichkeit und Erfahrung: Zur Organisationsanalyse von bürgerlicher und proletarischer Öffentlichkeit* (Frankfurt am Main, 1972). An extract from Negt and Kluge's book is translated in A. Mattelart and S. Siegelaub (eds.), *Communication and Class Struggle*, vol. 2, *Liberation, Socialism* (International General, 1982).
13 Paul Connerton, *The Tragedy of Enlightenment* (Cambridge University Press, 1980), p. 137.
14 Internationales Russell Tribunal, *Zur Situation der Menschenrechte in der Bundesrepublik Deutschland*, Bände 1-4 (Berlin, 1978-9).
15 Jürgen Habermas, 'The public sphere: an encyclopedia article (1964)', *New German Critique*, no. 3 (1974), p. 51.
16 For this point German-speaking readers might want to see U. Maas, 'Sprachpolitik. Grundbegriffe der politischen sprachwissenschast', *Sprache und*

Herrschaft, no. 6 (1980). A clarification of the difference between the production and appropriation of experience can be found in U. Maas, *Kann man Sprache lehren* (Frankfurt, 1976).

17   See especially Negt and Kluge, *Öffentlichkeit*, pp. 17–44.

18   See also the second chapter of *Capital*, vol. I, where Marx argues similarly about the exchange process.

19   See Negt and Kluge, *Öffentlichkeit*, pp. 35–6, footnote 2.

20   It should be recognized that Kluge has since followed up some of these problems. See for example *Gelegenheitsarbeit einer Sklavin* (*The Occasional Work of a Female Slave*) which is both a film and a book (Frankfurt am Main, 1975)

21   See in particular: L. Taylor and P. Walton, 'Industrial sabotage: motives and meanings', in S. Cohen (ed.), *Images of Deviance* (Penguin, 1971); P. Willis, *Learning to Labour* (Saxon House, 1977); P. Willis, 'Shop-floor culture, masculinity and the age form' in J. Clarke *et al.*, (eds.), *Working Class Culture* (CCCS/Hutchinson, 1979); D. Hebdige, 'Subcultural conflict and criminal performance in Fulham' (University of Birmingham, *CCCS Stencilled Paper*, 1972).

22   P. J. Armstrong, J. F. B. Goodman and J. D. Hyman, *Ideology and Shop-Floor Industrial Relations* (Croom Helm, 1980), p. 37.

23   P. Cohen, 'Subcultural conflict and working class community', *Working Papers in Cultural Studies*, no. 2 (1972), pp. 11–12 (our emphasis).

24   P. Cohen, 'Policing the working class city', National Deviancy Conference/ Conference of Socialist Economists, *Capitalism and the Rule of Law* (Hutchinson, 1979), p. 131.

25   John Hawkes, *The Beetle Leg* (New Directions, 1951), p. 9.

26   Jack Spicer, *The Collected Books of Jack Spicer* (Black Sparrow Press, 1975), p. 179.

27   Guy Davenport, *Da Vinci's Bicycle* (Johns Hopkins University Press, 1979), p. 8.

28   The phrase 'brimful of history' was used in a Canadian tourist brochure to describe the streets of British towns (1978).

29   Susan Sontag has made some useful comments on the ways in which photographs are being used as historical evidence and appeal: 'Photographs, which turn the past into a consumable object, are a short cut. . . . We now make history out of our detritus', *On Photography* (Delta, 1978), p. 68. See especially her comments on Michael Lesy's *Wisconsin Death Trip* (Pantheon, 1973), which are to be found in *On Photography*, pp. 72–5. Sontag reveals a questionable disdain for oral-historical material, but she raises several important points in these few pages.

30   We take the phrase 'Age of dead statues' from Ariel Dorfman and Armand Mattelart who use it as the title of a highly relevant chapter in *How to Read Donald Duck: Imperialist Ideology in the Disney Comic* (International General, 1975).

31   See Tony Wilden, *The Imaginary Canadian* (Pulp Press, 1980).

32 We are dealing here with what Goran Therborn has described abstractly as 'the mechanics of subjection'. See his *The Ideology of Power and the Power of Ideology* (Verso, 1980).

33 See Alain Le Guyader, *Contributions à la critique de l'idéologie nationale,* vol. 1 (Union Générale d'Éditions, 1978).

34 *Trade Union Immunities* (HMSO, 1981).

35 Mary Whitehouse, *Who Does She Think She Is?* (New English Library, 1971), p. 12.

36 Jean-Paul Sartre, *Anti-Semite and Jew* (Schocken Books, 1948), pp. 80-3.

37 Quoted in *The Times*, 5 July 1980.

38 Sarah A. Tooley, *Royal Palaces and their Memories* (Hutchinson, 1902), p. 9.

39 Raphael Samuel, Foreword to Jerry White, *Rothschild Buildings* (Routledge and Kegan Paul, 1980), p. x.

40 See Raymond Williams, *The Country and the City* (Paladin, 1975).

41 *Hansard* (Commons), vol. 975, no. 79, col. 55.

42 ibid., col. 69.

43 *Hansard* (Commons), vol. 95, no. 79, col. 60.

44 *Hansard* (Lords), vol. 405, no. 89, col. 1572.

45 *Guardian*, 23 August 1979.

46 See Patrick Cormack, *Heritage in Danger* (Quartet, 1978). The information used in this description of the preservation lobby is derived from Cormack's book, David Elliston Allen's *The Naturalist in Britain* (Penguin, 1978), and Robin Fedden's 'official' history of the National Trust, *The Continuing Purpose* (Longmans, 1968). A more rigorous discussion and advocacy of the preservation movement has recently appeared in D. Lowenthal and M. Binney (eds.), *Our Past Before Us: Why Do We Save It?* (Temple Smith, 1981).

47 Cormack, *Heritage in Danger*, p. 17.

48 Fedden, *The Continuing Purpose*, p. 6.

49 Cormack, *Heritage in Danger*, p. 20.

50 A contemporary example: while the National Heritage Act (1980) was going through Parliament with due patriotic clamour, Francis Pym, Leader of the House of Commons, was striving to get permission to demolish his scheduled family mansion (reasons of expense . . .).

51 See especially Williams, *The Country and the City*.

52 Jane Harrison, *Ancient Art and Ritual* (Home University Library, 1913).

53 Stephen Graham, *The Gentle Art of Tramping* (Ernest Benn, 1927), p. 82. Graham's curious and romantic account of 'tramping' (the book is evidently influenced by Whitman) went through numerous editions in the late twenties and early thirties.

54 Guy Debord, *Society of the Spectacle* (Red and Black, 1970), paragraph 177.

55 Sandra Carpenter in *Observer*, 30 July 1980.

56 There is no way of referencing this Shell material specifically or item by

item. Except where otherwise mentioned, all the material quoted or described was examined in the British Petroleum archive at Britannic House, London.

57   Walter Benjamin, 'The work of art in the age of mechanical reproduction', *Illuminations* (Fontana, 1973), p. 235.

58   Jakov Lind, *Landscape in Concrete* (Methuen, 1966), p. 9.

59   See Debord, *The Society of the Spectacle*.

60   Colin Macarthur's *Televison and History* (British Film Institute, 1978) is a useful introduction to the question of television presentations of history. Shell's entrance into television with an already established advertising repertoire suggests two points which tend to be overlooked by existing analyses. First, if the materiality of National Heritage consists in part of historically constituted images and ways of seeing, then the analysis of its reproduction through television cannot be confined to those programmes, whether drama or documentary, which announce themselves as 'historical'. Second, it is clearly important not to let an idealist overexaggeration of the 'specificity' of the medium impede analysis of the media career of images which are to an extent formed up elsewhere.

61   This is the text from an advertisement seen on the London Underground, 1981.

62   National Heritage Memorial Fund, *Annual Report 1980/81* (HMSO, 1981), p. 2. Probably the most 'unpredictable' grant which the fund has made in this year amounts to £62,000 and goes to the British Film Institute for the reprocessing of archive film stock. The fund is also pressing for tax reforms, on the belief that 'heritage property can only be made secure through the tax system' (p. 6). The trustees are as follows: The Baroness Airey of Abingdon; the Most Hon. Marquess of Anglesey; Sir Robert Cook; Professor F. G. T. Holliday; Clive Jenkins, Esq.; Charles Kinahan, Esq.; Maurice Lindsay, Esq.; Professor B. R. Morris; Sir Rex Richards; John Smith, Esq.

63   Cormack, *Heritage in Danger*, p. 14.

64   Hermann Glaser, *The Cultural Roots of National Socialism* (Croom Helm, 1978), p. 61.

65   These proto-narrative structures are certainly similar to what Raymond Williams calls 'structures of feeling' (see *The Country and the City*, and also *Marxism and Literature*, Oxford University Press, 1977, pp. 128–34). Our more immediate debt, however, is to Fredric Jameson, whose books *Fables of Aggression: Wyndham Lewis, the Modernist as Fascist* (University of California Press, 1979) and *The Political Unconscious; Narrative as a Socially Symbolic Act* (Methuen, 1981) have been of direct assistance to us in two related ways. First, Jameson has extended Althusser's definition of ideology as 'a "representation" of the imaginary relationship of individuals to their real conditions of existence'. Jameson is concerned to show that as such a 'representation' ideology must 'always be necessarily narrative in its structure'. It is here that Jameson takes up J.-F. Lyotard's dreadful sounding formulation of the 'libidinal apparatus', a narrative structure which has a semi

autonomous social and historical existence. As Jameson writes (*Wyndham Lewis*, pp. 10–11):

The theory of the libidinal apparatus marks an advance over psychologizing approaches in the way in which it endows a private fantasy-structure with a quasi-material inertness, with all the resistance of an object which can lead a life of its own and has its own inner logic and specific dynamics. Such a view then allows us to understand its various uses and investments as a process of appropriation, as a structure which, produced by the accidents of a certain history, can be alienated and pressed into the service of a quite different one, reinvested with new and unexpected content, and adapted to unsuspected ideological functions which return upon the older psychic material or re- or overdetermine it in its turn as a kind of retroactive effect (Freud's Nachtraglichkeit). On such a view, then, the libidinal apparatus becomes an independent structure of which one can write a history.

Jameson's book on Wyndham Lewis is highly successful as an analysis of the persistence and transformation of such structures within a literary writing. The second point of information for us has been Jameson's insistence on the utopian gratification afforded by ideology. The utopian character of this gratification is not necessarily *explicit* as it tends to be in the case of National Heritage (which, as we will be arguing, borrows the trappings of English utopianism and buries them far behind us in 'the past'). For this discussion in Jameson, see *The Political Unconscious* (especially the Conclusion called 'The dialectic of utopia and ideology').

66 See for example Macdonald Futura's 'Heritage Series' (1981). The series includes W. H. Hudson, *Nature in Downland*, Richard Jefferies, *The Toilers of the Field*, Walter Johnson, *Gilbert White*, and T. H. White, *England Have my Bones*. Wildwood House have a comparable series in which, for example, Edward Thomas's ruralist books have been reissued. This growth in Heritage publication is often, in fact, a matter of *re*-publication, drawing together for a developing readership books which are actually quite diverse.

67 From *Discover Norman Britain*, a pamphlet produced by the English Tourist Board in co-operation with the Welsh Tourist Board and the Scottish Tourist Board (1979).

68 Raymond Williams has some interesting things to say about such 'timelessness' in a discussion of Thomas Hardy. See his *The English Novel from Dickens to Lawrence* (Paladin, 1974), p. 89.

69 Wyndham Lewis, *Rotting Hill* (Methuen, 1951).

70 This phrase occurs as a motif throughout *The Poor Mouth* (Picador, 1975).

71 See *What is Our Heritage?* (United Kingdom Achievements for European Architectural Heritage Year 1975) (HMSO, 1975).

72 Quoted on the front page of Cormack, *Heritage in Danger*.

73 ibid., pp. 51–2.

74 ibid., p. 53.

75   Reported in the *Guardian*, 13 March 1980.
76   An interesting example of this latter way of thinking is to be found in Mary Butts, *Warning to Hikers* (Wishart, 1932).
77   A similar sense of transformation was at work in Esmond Knight's programme 'The Archer's Tale' (BBC 2, 30 October 1980). Two actors strolled the pastures of agribusiness and a narrator mustered the strengths of the mother tongue to transform this green scene into another one: 'And suddenly the whole scene is transformed into a seething mass of horse and steel and swirling colour.'
78   *The Birmingham Evening Mail*, 6 May 1980.
79   The dialectical marxism of Karel Kosik is helpful on this division of social life. See in particular the following passage from his *Dialectics of the Concrete* (Reidel Publishing Company, 1976), p. 125:

Freedom does not disclose itself to man as an autonomous realm, *independent* of labour and existing beyond the boundaries of necessity. Rather, it grows out of labour which is its necessary prerequisite. Human doing is not split into two autonomous realms, mutually independent and indifferent, one of which would incarnate freedom and the other constitute the arena of necessity . . . . The objective doing of man that transforms nature and imprints into its meaning is a *unified* process which, though performed out of necessity and under pressure of extraneous purposiveness, also realizes the prerequisites of freedom and free creation. The splitting of this unified process into two *seemingly* independent realms does not follow from the 'nature of the matter' but is historically a transient state. As long as consciousness is a captive of this split, it will not behold its *historical* character and will *juxtapose* labour and freedom, objective activity and imagination, technology and poetry as two independent ways of satiating the human drive.

80   Edward Jesse, *Favourite Haunts and Rural Studies* (John Murray, 1847), p. 212.
81   See Debord, *The Society of the Spectacle*. This paragraph of our article is much indebted to Debord's section on 'The organisation of territory'. Interesting and at times rather extravagant arguments against thinking of the nation as a unity produced by the circulation of commodities have been made by Nicos Poulantzas. See his chapter on 'The nation' in *State, Power, Socialism* (New Left Books, 1978).
82   Manuel Castells, 'The class struggle and urban contradictions', in J. Cowley *et al.* (eds.), *Community and Class Struggle* (Stage 1, 1977), p. 41.
83   For the following discussion see The Work Group, 'A critique of "community studies" and its role in social thought', *CCCS Stencilled Occasional Paper*, no. 44 (1976); Eve Brook and Dan Finn, 'Working class images of society and community studies', in CCCS, *On Ideology*; Dan Finn, Neil Grant and Richard Johnson, 'Social democracy, education and the crisis', in CCCS, *On Ideology*; Chas Critcher, 'Sociology, cultural studies and the post-war

working class', in J. Clarke *et al.* (eds.), *Working Class Culture*; CCCS Education Group, *Unpopular Education* (Hutchinson, 1981).

84   For this point see Claus Offe, ' "Unregierbarkeit", Zur Renaissance konservativer Krisentheorien', in J. Habermas (Hrsg.), *Stichworte zur 'Geistigen Situation der Zeit'*, 1. Band (Frankfurt am Main, 1979).

85   See Ken Worpole, 'A ghostly pavement: the political implications of local working-class history', in R. Samuel (ed.), *People's History and Socialist Theory* (Routledge and Kegan Paul, 1981); Ken Worpole, *Local Publishing and Local Culture: An Account of the Work of the Centreprise Publishing Project 1972-1977* (Centreprise, 1977); *Centreprise Report* (December 1978); Jerry White, 'Beyond autobiography', in Samuel (ed.), *People's History*.

86   It is important to recognize that this strategy of traditionalizing is greatly strengthened by the fact that Conservatism has recently proved itself to be the only publicly established national force which is in a position to accommodate popular fears and objections (and therefore to transform them into a right-wing discourse).

87   Jerry White, 'Beyond autobiography', p. 35.

88   Philippe Hoyau, 'L'année du patrimoine ou la société de conservation', *Les Révoltes Logiques*, no. 12 (1980), p. 72.

89   Hoyau, ibid., p. 74.

90   See Raphael Samuel (ed.), *East End Underworld: Chapters in the Life of Arthur Harding* (Routledge and Kegan Paul, 1981); also *Working Lives*, vols. i and ii (Centreprise, 1976 and 1977).

91   Another example of how literary forms are positioned within the public sphere can be read in Williams's study *The Country and the City*. Williams asserts that 'most novels are in some sense knowable communities'. As Williams writes, 'it is part of a traditional method – an underlying stance and approach – that the novelist offers to show people and their relationships in essentially knowable and communicable ways'. Formally, then, the novel has tended to underwrite the bourgeois world-view to which it has lent expression. It tends to construct people as individual and discrete 'characters', reality as self-evident and identical with experience, and experience as directly communicable. In consequence the novel tends to discourage consideration of relations which do not occur face to face or which are not directly communicable (subordinated collective forms of experience, for example). Williams argues that this conventional realism of the novel was inadequate to the transition from an early and more rural experiential base to the opaque 'experience and community' of the nineteenth-century city, and that a writer like Dickens therefore had to turn the novel, taking it to the point of formal change, in order to articulate an experience which was less and less directly communicable. It should come as no surprise, given the active persistence of forms, that in the twentieth century the novel has supported a whole genre of false retrospective but ideologically powerful

stories *about* 'knowable communities': stories which are set in the 'Heart of England', somewhere in 'The Shires' etc., where the 'Imaginary Briton' strolls the green, meditates upon a landscape and communes with his hallucinated essence in sublimated and narcissistic face to face romance.

Chapter 8   'The public face of feminism': early twentieth-century writings on women's suffrage

1   Olive Schreiner, *Woman and Labour* (Fisher and Unwin, 1911), p. 29.
2   Ruth First and Ann Scott, *Olive Schreiner* (André Deutsch, 1980), discuss *Woman and Labour* at length in ch. 4.
3   Schreiner, *Woman and Labour*, pp. 128-9.
4   Richard Evans, 'Women's history: the limits of reclamation. Problems of research', *Social History*, vol. 5, no. 2 (1980), pp. 273-81. This late initiative contrasts with *History Workshop Journal* which demonstrated an editorial interest in feminist history from its first issue.
5   Emmeline Pankhurst, *My Own Story* (Eveleigh Nash, 1914; reprint edition, Virago, 1979); Christabel Pankhurst, *Unshackled* (Hutchinson, 1959); E. Sylvia Pankhurst, *The Suffragette Movement* (Longmans Green, 1931; reprint edition, Virago, 1977); Sylvia Pankhurst, *The Life of Emmeline Pankhurst* (T. Werner Laurie, 1935); Emmeline Pethick-Lawrence, *My Part in a Changing World* (Gollancz, 1938); Annie Kenney, *Memories of a Militant* (Edward Arnold, 1924); Hannah Mitchell, *The Hard Way Up* (Virago, 1977); Mary R. Richardson, *Laugh a Defiance* (Weidenfeld and Nicolson, 1953); Teresa Billington-Greig, *The Militant Suffragette Movement* (Frank Palmer, 1911); Evelyn Sharp, *Hertha Ayrton* (London, n.d.); Margaret Bondfield, *A Life's Work* (Hutchinson, 1949); Mary Agnew Hamilton, *Mary Macarthur* (Leonard Parsons, 1925); Vera Brittain, *Testament of Youth* (Gollancz, 1933; Virago reprint edition, 1978); Vera Brittain, *Testament of Experience* (Gollancz, 1957; Virago reprint edition, 1979).
6   Annie Kenney, *Memories of a Militant*, p. 30.
7   Christabel Pankhurst, *The Great Scourge and How to End It* (London, 1913).
8   Margaret Stacey and Marion Price, 'Women and power', *Feminist Review*, no. 5 (1980), p. 33.
9   Ray Strachey, *The Cause: A Short History of the Women's Movement* (Bell and Sons, 1928; Virago reprint edition, 1978).
10   George Dangerfield, *The Strange Death of Liberal England* (Paladin, 1970), p. 136. Constance Rover, *Love, Morals and the Feminists* (Routledge and Kegan Paul, 1970), p. 145, can find little evidence for lesbianism. Hints and innuendoes such as those made by Piers Brendon in *Eminent Edwardians* (Secker and Warburg, 1979) are speculations. These issues are considered tentatively but more positively in Carroll Smith-Rosenberg, 'The female world of love and ritual: relations between women in nineteenth century America', *Signs*, vol. 1 (1975), pp. 1-29.

11   Martin D. Pugh, 'Politics and the woman's vote 1914–1918', *History*, vol. 59 (1974); Martin Pugh, *Electoral Reform in War and Peace 1906–18* (Routledge and Kegan Paul, 1978).

12   David Morgan, *Suffragists and Liberals: The Politics of Women's Suffrage* (Blackwell, 1975). We found Andrew Rosen, *Rise Up, Women!* (Routledge and Kegan Paul, 1974) very useful in general.

13   Brian Harrison, *Separate Spheres: The Opposition to Women's Suffrage* (Croom Helm), 1978, p. 15. See also ibid., ch. 1.

14   Harrison, *Separate Spheres*, ch. 4, shows how the notion of 'separate spheres' was the centrepiece of the anti-suffragist case. Martin Pugh, *Women's Suffrage in Britain, 1867–1928* (Historial Association Pamphlet, 1980), recognizes how much these ideologies still carried weight after suffrage had been won. See also Lorna Duffin, 'Prisoners of progress: women and evolution', in Sarah Delamount and Lorna Duffin (eds.), *The Nineteenth Century Woman: Her Cultural and Physical World* (Croom Helm, 1978).

15   As is suggested in P. T. Cominos, 'Innocent *femina sensualis* in unconscious conflict', in Martha Vicinus (ed.), *Suffer and Be Still* (Indiana University Press, 1972). For a more positive interpretation of the religion of socialism and feminism in the period see First and Scott, *Olive Schreiner*.

16   Stephen Yeo, 'A new life: the religion of socialism in Britain 1883–1896', *History Workshop Journal*, no. 4 (1977).

17   Sylvia Pankhurst, *The Suffragette* (Gay and Hancock, 1911), p. 22.

18   Kenney, *Memories of a Militant*, pp. 27–8; Richardson, *Laugh a Defiance*, p. 5.

19   E. Pankhurst, *My Own Story*, pp. 5–6.

20   E. S. Pankhurst, *The Life of Emmeline Pankhurst*, pp. 7, 15.

21   Mitchell, *The Hard Way Up*, pp. 43, 68–9.

22   S. Pankhurst, *The Suffragette Movement*, p. 67.

23   Mitchell, *The Hard Way Up*, p. 163.

24   Pethick-Lawrence, *My Part in a Changing World*, p. 124.

25   E. Pankhurst, *My Own Story*, p. 12.

26   Mitchell, *The Hard Way Up*, p. 96.

27   ibid., pp. 88, 149.

28   ibid., p. 204.

29   ibid., pp. 190–1.

30   C. Pankhurst, *Unshackled*, p. 112.

31   ibid., p. 294.

32   ibid., p. 46.

33   ibid., p. 43.

34   ibid., p. 45.

35   Kenney, *Memories of a Militant*, p. 193.

36   C. Pankhurst, *Unshackled*, p. 60.

37   ibid., p. 126.

38   ibid., p. 21.

39   S. Pankhurst, *The Suffragette Movement*, p. 56.
40   S. Yeo, 'A new life', p. 14.
41   E. Pethick-Lawrence, *My Part in a Changing World*, p. 145.
42   ibid., pp. 9–10.
43   ibid., pp. 214–15.
44   'What we know historically, of course, is that women had begun to take a more active part in the public life of the time: it seems that a public discussion of "private" life – at least as it is reflected in the idealising allegory of the period – remained elliptical, even fey.' First and Scott, *Olive Schreiner*, p. 16.
45   Rover, *Love, Morals and Feminists*, p. 5.
46   E. Pankhurst, *My Own Story*, p. 268.
47   ibid., p. 201.
48   ibid., p. 93.
49   ibid., p. 238.
50   E. Pethick-Lawrence, *My Part in a Changing World*, p. 146.
51   Mitchell, *The Hard Way Up*, p. 179.
52   See Jill Liddington and Jill Norris, *One Hand Tied Behind Us* (Virago, 1978).
53   R. S. Neale, 'Working class women and women's suffrage', in his *Class and Ideology in the Nineteenth Century* (Routledge and Kegan Paul, 1972), usefully builds his account around Billington-Greig's analysis. See T. Billington-Greig, *The Militant Suffragette Movement*.
54   C. Pankhurst, *Unshackled*, pp. 6–7.
55   For Macarthur see Hamilton, *Mary Macarthur*; David Mitchell, *Women on the Warpath: The Story of the Women of the First World War* (Cape, 1966). For Bondfield, see Bondfield, *A Life's Work*.
56   E. Pethick-Lawrence, *My Part in a Changing World*, p. 284; M. Richardson, *Laugh a Defiance*, p. 24. For a periodization of militancy and an assessment of whether violent militancy gained the vote, see A. Rosen, *Rise Up, Women!*, Epilogue.
57   Frederick Pethick-Lawrence, *Fate has been Kind* (Hutchinson, 1942), p. 72.
58   Winifred Holtby, *Women and a Changing Civilisation* (Bodley Head, 1934), pp. 52–3.
59   V. Brittain, *Testament of Experience*, p. 124.
60   V. Brittain, *Testament of Friendship* (Macmillan, 1941), p. 10.
61   V. Brittain, *Testament of Youth*, p. 653.

Index